Richard E. Myers Lectures

Presented by University Baptist Church, Charlottesville

REV. DR. MATTHEW A. TENNANT, EDITOR

.

MORE THINGS IN HEAVEN AND EARTH

More Things in Heaven and Earth

SHAKESPEARE, THEOLOGY, AND THE INTERPLAY OF TEXTS

Paul S. Fiddes

UNIVERSITY OF VIRGINIA PRESS
CHARLOTTESVILLE AND LONDON

University of Virginia Press
© 2022 by the Rector and Visitors of the University of Virginia
All rights reserved
Printed in the United States of America on acid-free paper

First published 2022

1 3 5 7 9 8 6 4 2

Library of Congress Cataloging-in-Publication Data

Names: Fiddes, Paul S., author.
Title: More things in heaven and earth : Shakespeare, theology,
and the interplay of texts / Paul S. Fiddes.
Description: Charlottesville : University of Virginia Press, 2021. | Series:
Richard E. Myers lectures | Includes bibliographical references and index.
Identifiers: LCCN 2021023515 (print) | LCCN 2021023516 (ebook) |
ISBN 9780813946528 (hardcover : acid-free paper) | ISBN 9780813946535 (ebook)
Subjects: LCSH: Shakespeare, William, 1564–1616—Religion. | Religion
in literature. | Religion and drama. | Drama—Religious aspects.
Classification: LCC PR3011 .F4326 2021 (print) | LCC PR3011 (ebook) | DDC 822.3/3—dc23
LC record available at https://lccn.loc.gov/2021023515
LC ebook record available at https://lccn.loc.gov/2021023516

Cover art: Stained-glass window panel of William Shakespeare, ca. 1890.
(UK Architectural Heritage, www.uk-heritage.co.uk)

For the benefactor
of the Richard E. Myers Lectures
and for Matthew Tennant,
its "Onlie Begetter"

There are more things in heaven and earth, Horatio,
Than are dreamt of in your philosophy.

—Hamlet

CONTENTS

CONTENTS

PREFACE

THE GENESIS of this book lies in a series of tutorials on Shakespeare's plays which I received in 1966 from my tutor at St Peter's College, Oxford, the renowned poet and playwright Francis Warner. I remain indebted to him for the inspiration and provocation which he offered, and over half a century later it has been a delight to continue discussing the themes of this book with him in his house around the corner from my present college. I had the opportunity for further reflection on the plays through the invitation from the director for the University of North Carolina Summer School in Oxford, James Stewart, to give lectures on Shakespeare from 1973 to 1978. This was followed by lecturing on Shakespeare for many years to the Summer School of Southwestern Baptist Seminary, at the invitation of its director, Malcolm Yarnell. Generally, my thought about the relation between theology and literature (expressed in a number of publications) was enhanced by teaching and supervising for the "literature and theology" track of graduate degrees of the University of Oxford, and I am grateful to the students who readily engaged with me on the course. Yet further development of my thought came from guest lectures on Shakespeare at Ilia State University, Tbilisi, in 2013, which the University subsequently published in a book available only in the Georgian language, called *Shakespeare and Religion* (*Sheqspiri da religia*, 2015). Then came the invitation to give the Richard E. Myers Lectures at University Baptist Church, Charlottesville, Virginia, 20–22 March 2018, and acceptance of my theme "'The Play's the Thing': Shakespeare and Religion"; I am deeply grateful to the church's minister, Matthew Tennant, to the benefactor of the lecture-fund (who wishes to remain anonymous), and to the congregation of the church for its warm welcome to me. The present book is an expansion of those lectures. In writing it, I have been highly appreciative of many conversations with Lynn Robertson, Fellow and Tutor in English Literature at my college, Regent's Park College, Oxford, who has frequently pointed me in the right direction.

I am grateful to my publishers, the University of Virginia Press, and especially to its editors Eric Brandt and Charlie Bailey for all their willing collaboration. I also owe a debt to the anonymous readers of my manuscript for their helpful responses, and no doubt they will recognize where I have incorporated their suggestions silently but with much appreciation.

I would like finally to alert the reader to three general features about the chapters that follow. First, as befits a work on intertextuality, the plays by Shakespeare are not handled in chronological order, but in a way that best suits their intertextual connections. Second, the number of endnotes referring to Naseeb Shaheen's book *Biblical References in Shakespeare's Plays* shows my debt to this magisterial study even where I have disagreed with it. Finally, all quotations from the Bible, except where explicitly noted, are from the Geneva Bible. I have made my own modernization of the spelling of these and also of quotations from other early English translations of the Bible. It seems odd, and unhelpful, to quote Shakespeare—by convention—in editions that use modern spelling, and to leave the text of a major source of his work in sixteenth-century format. The resonances are more apparent when the eye passes easily from the surface of one text to another, and such a movement between texts is the major theme of this study.

MORE THINGS IN HEAVEN AND EARTH

MORE THINGS IN HEAVEN AND EARTH

1

Shakespeare's "More Things" and Religion

"THERE ARE more things in heaven and earth, Horatio, / Than are dreamt of in your philosophy" (*Hamlet*, 1.5.165–66). These words, spoken by Hamlet to his friend Horatio on the battlements of Elsinore, have dropped from the page and the stage into everyday speech. There they have suffered grievous misuse in the cause of religion. Those who quote the lines have often delighted to identify a "you" ("your philosophy") who can be assailed, as Hamlet is supposedly attacking Horatio. The speaker, with an air of superiority—if not a wagging finger—is usually placing a so-called "supernatural" worldview in opposition to a purely rational, naturalistic account of things. The lines have been evoked in aid of a polemical assault on the kind of philosophy that finds meaning only in what can be verified empirically in the world around us. None of this could have been in Shakespeare's mind, not least because Hamlet counts *himself* among those who have the philosophy which is being challenged: "you" here is being used in the indefinite sense, equivalent to "one's,"[1] and while the Folio edition is incorrect textually in reading "our philosophy,"[2] it is surely correct in its meaning. Nor is there any evidence that Horatio is adopting a secular mind-set over a religious one. He and Hamlet have been confronted by a figure that claims to be the ghost of Hamlet's murdered father, and only a little earlier Horatio had appealed to the apparition to speak to him, with the hope of seeking to discover what it might know about salvation—as well as the military destiny of Denmark and location of buried treasure (1.1.129–38).

Hamlet's words should be read in context. He is responding to Horatio's exclamation, "but this is wondrous strange," and has just urged him to give the "strange" a welcome. Hamlet is commending an open mind when faced by what is alien and unfamiliar, and he is warning against getting trapped in *any* particular system of thought or dogma (a "philosophy"), *including* religion.

He goes on immediately to alert Horatio to the fact that he himself is shortly going to appear "strange" in his actions and words, putting "an antic disposition on." Hamlet's behavior is in fact going to reflect his own response to the "strange," since the hesitation for which he has become famous stems from a basic uncertainty about the identity of the ghost: is it "honest," or what it claims to be? It seems that the negative side of taking the strange seriously can be procrastination, and yet there is another, more positive side to embracing the strange and the "other"—a nondogmatic and tolerant outlook on life.

Rather than a dualism which opposes religion to secularity or which constructs two realms of the "natural" and the "supernatural," Hamlet's lines encourage a view of religion which is not constrained by tight doctrinal boundaries. But we should not thereby swing to the opposite extreme of suggesting that the play encourages a dispensing with religion altogether, or at least an evacuation of religion from the sphere of drama in moving toward a secularist "self-fashioning."[3] There is a religious ethos to the "more things" here, supported by two biblical references. First, Hamlet's advice to Horatio about the "strange"—"as a stranger give it welcome"—echoes Hebrews 13:2: "Be not forgetful to lodge strangers: for thereby some have received Angels into their houses unawares."[4] Second, the tag "heaven and earth" has many biblical resonances as a Hebrew expression for the whole of reality, not least in the Lord's Prayer ("as on earth, so in heaven"). It is even more explicitly biblical in Anthony's expansive declaration about his love, which precisely exceeds the narrow political and ethnic limits imposed by Roman society: "Then must thou needs find out new heaven, new earth" (Rev. 21:1, "I saw a new heaven, and a new earth").[5]

In this book I aim to take seriously the implications of Hamlet's appeal to "more things in heaven and earth" in order to explore Shakespeare's own relation to religion in his time, both the institutions of the Christian church and their theology. But this book will differ from many others which have recently taken a similar route, by also reversing the journey of discovery. I am proposing a mutual "dialogue" between Shakespeare and Christian theology. On the one hand, theology can enable us to see more clearly what Shakespeare is doing with the Bible, doctrine, and religious controversies in the world of the long English Reformation. This is the direction taken by what has been called the "turn to religion" in recent Shakespeare study. But on the other, as a theologian, I shall be asking how the making of theology in our own time can be shaped by the reading of Shakespeare's texts and the viewing of his theater; this will be no patronizing of Shakespeare by treating his work as mere illustrations of Christian doctrine, but a genuine attempt to entertain the "more things" which may prove to be angelic messengers (Heb. 13:2), and which can actually *remake* doctrine. But first we need some context for Shakespeare's handling of religious issues. While we must not confuse Hamlet with his creator, there is a good case for finding the attitude revealed in Hamlet's appeal to "more things" within the plays themselves, in the effect they have on the audience.

A Confessional Scene

Recent historical inquiry into the early modern world of the Tudors and the Stuarts has offered two differing analyses of the religious situation, and to some extent there has been a shift between them in weight (and fashion) of scholarship. In the first place, stress has been laid upon a social and religious scene of multiconfessionalism. The theory of "confessionalization" concerns "the role of religious communities in the post-Reformation passage of Europe from the Middle Ages to modernity,"[6] and in its strongest sense it finds the holding of religious confessions to be an explanation of change in society. More generally it observes the significant part played by divisions in society caused by different religious identities. Brian Walsh cites a Venetian ambassador as reporting in the reign of James I that there were some twelve different religious parties in England, and this despite the attempt to impose a unifying "settlement" of religion by both Elizabeth I and her successor.[7] Critics of Shakespeare's plays then draw a number of different conclusions from the picture of a society fractured by religious confessions.

One is the attempt to show that Shakespeare aligns himself with one group or another on this scene, and a favorite identification in the last few decades has been Shakespeare as a Roman Catholic. Clearly, Shakespeare had no choice but formally to be a member of the Church of England—given the principle enunciated by Richard Hooker that to be a member of the commonwealth was to be a member of the English Church.[8] In his local parish church he heard the scriptures read in the folio Bishops' Bible, there he must have at least occasionally attended Holy Communion—to comply with the law—and there he was finally buried, having acquired the privilege of being interred in the chancel of Holy Trinity, Stratford, by leasing, as a shrewd financial investment, half of the tithes from agriculture and flocks in and around his town. The question is whether he was "secretly" a Catholic, either formally as a "recusant," or as a "church-papist" (attending the Church of England but secretly holding a Roman faith), or by simply keeping a nostalgic sympathy with what was—at least at an earlier point—his father John's religion.

The evidence for this allegiance has been presented many times, often centering upon a supposed continuing Catholicism of his father, John, who was listed as failing to attend Holy Communion at the parish church in

Stratford,[9] and whose name appears on a "Spiritual Testament" in the form of a Roman Catholic confession of faith recovered from the rafters of the Henley Street House in 1757.[10] To this has been added a claimed identification of the sixteen-year-old William with a young tutor and actor named William Shakeshafte at the Catholic household of Alexander Hoghton in Lancashire, named in his will.[11] However, any external evidence produced has been just as often refuted. John Shakespeare's citation for "recusancy" may well reflect absence from Communion in an attempt to avoid debt-collectors,[12] and the Spiritual Testament was a pro forma document designed by Cardinal Carlo Borromeo to which John's name may have simply been added by an unknown person.[13] As for William's supposed inclusion among servants at Hoghton Towers, Shakeshafte is a common Lancashire name, and anyway a recently arrived young man was unlikely to have become a beneficiary of a legacy.[14]

The most eloquent case for internal evidence for Shakespeare's faith within the plays themselves has been made by Richard Wilson, arguing for an "encoded" Catholicism.[15] Nevertheless, it is widely agreed that it is not possible to know what Shakespeare himself believed, and that there is no internal evidence for establishing it. This conclusion will be supported by studies of several plays in this volume, particularly *Hamlet* and *King John*. It is true that Shakespeare chooses to set several of his comedies in Catholic Italy, and populates the scenery with friars in a matter-of-fact way that shows none of the Protestant polemic of other plays of Shakespeare's time;[16] even though Friar Laurence in *Romeo and Juliet* is disastrously ineffective in his schemes, the prince reassures him at the end that "we still have known thee for a holy man" (5.3.270). The two lovers themselves share a sonnet which, in fusing erotic and religious language, uses Catholic imagery of pilgrimages and veneration of saints:

> For saints have hands that pilgrims' hands do touch
> And palm to palm is holy palmers' kiss. (1.5.98–99)

Yet at the same time there are counterindications: Juliet is encouraging veneration of *herself* as a saint, and she remarks in a Protestant voice that "Saints do not move," when—as Alison Shell points out—Italy was a place where miraculously moving statues of saints were commonplace.[17] In *Measure for Measure*, the Duke is able to move around incognito in an apparently Catholic Venice because it is simply an accepted part of the culture for a friar to provide spiritual help to a range of people, including prisoners under a death sentence. But on the other hand, he is not in fact a friar, and as an unordained person is offering services of confession and absolution that would be acceptable in a Protestant context of "confessing to one another" but would be a scandalous usurpation of the authority of the clergy in a Catholic one.[18]

Similarly, Pericles shows nostalgia for Catholic burial rites, complete with "aye-remaining lamps,"[19] in a play bearing his name which is presided over by a notably Catholic figure, the poet Gower (whose elaborate pre-Reformation tomb was close to the Globe Theatre);[20] but at the same time he desires to be left alone "whiles I say / a priestly farewell" to his apparently deceased wife, Thaisa. Brian Walsh points out the ambiguous effect of the adjective "priestly"; while it evokes a "sacramental aura," "we might say that a kind of post-Reformation priesthood of all believers is here claimed by Pericles."[21]

If a context of confessionalism prompts some critics to attribute a kind of Catholicism to Shakespeare, or at the least a mourning for a lost Catholic world,[22] it has led others to propose that Shakespeare's response is an essentially secular one. His evenhandedness with regard to distinct confessions is seen as evidence of an emergent secularity within the early modern theater. We might say that those who take this view suppose Shakespeare to be saying in effect with Mercutio, "a plague on both your houses." Stephen Greenblatt, for instance, has argued for an "emptying out" of doctrine and rituals in *King Lear*, a process in which "performance kills belief."[23] In my ensuing chapter on *King Lear* I will join those who have opposed Greenblatt's thesis, showing it to be a play full of echoes of the Reformation as well as biblical allusions. Others have taken a more moderate view of the theater as a "secularizing institution," recognizing that religious ideas and symbols still persist while being increasingly subordinated to the media of dramatic presentation.[24] One developing dramatic convention that is often singled out as an indicator of an early modern sense of the secular "self" is that of the soliloquy. Being and speaking alone, it is argued, is one of the markers of modernity.[25] My chapters on *Hamlet* and *Richard II* will demonstrate how much, nevertheless, soliloquies are embedded in a religious framework. Here we might only cite the final soliloquy of Richard in *Richard III*:

> Give me another horse! Bind up my wounds!
> Have mercy, Jesu!—Soft, I did but dream.
> O coward conscience, how dost thou afflict me?
> The lights burn blue. It is now dead midnight.
> Cold fearful drops stand on my trembling flesh.
> What do I fear? Myself? There's none else by.
> Richard loves Richard; that is, I am I.
> Is there a murderer here? No. Yes, I am.
> Then fly! What, from myself? (5.3.177–85)

We notice the emerging sense of the self as a distinct subject, where "myself" is moving from a reflexive form to the abstract noun "my self." But we cannot evacuate this speech of religious resonances, beginning from the ejaculation,

"Have mercy, Jesu!" which makes it possible to understand the following speech as conversing with Jesus, or with oneself in the presence of Jesus, even though "there's none else by." Richard recognizes his interlocutor as his conscience, and this cannot be entirely dissociated from the Reformation understanding of the conscience as in some sense the interior voice of God. Dictionaries of the time in fact define "soliloquy" as a "contemplative talking" with God.[26] Cummings, in his comments on the soliloquy, concludes that "far from existing as a form of solipsism," talking with oneself in medieval mystery plays is "a form of colloquium with God as silent witness," and that in the postmedieval theater "this is transferred to an implied presence beyond the self."[27] He adds that "the voice is caught in the expression of its own temporality and mortality," so arguing that it is confrontation with death that enables the development of the sense of a self, rather than the evolution of an individualistic, and nonreligious, consciousness.[28] "Talking alone" thus has the *potential* to be recognized by the audience as conversation with God in face of the boundary of death, though we do not have to read in a divine presence in order to feel the soliloquy as being open the other and meditative in quality. Just as Shakespeare cannot be pinned down to being either Catholic or Protestant, so he shows that there is no clear border between the sacred and the secular.

If we suppose that Shakespeare adopts neither a simply Catholic, nor Protestant, nor secular identity, another way of interpreting his approach is to propose that the plays encourage a toleration toward different religious parties in society. Jeffrey Knapp has argued that the early modern playwrights constituted a kind of "ministry" through which they sought to contribute to the cause of true religion, and in particular made it their mission to diffuse an Erasmian, latitudinarian spirit of inclusiveness.[29] Brian Walsh believes that there is no sufficient evidence that they approached their work from such a deliberate stance, but he judges that Shakespeare—and to some extent his fellow writers—dramatizes "the unstable dynamics of accommodating others," portrays what it might look like to "live with differences," and displays a tendency "to problematize and provoke thought about sectarian conflict rather than rendering it in binary terms with clear points of identification for the audience."[30]

This kind of pacific recognition of difference applies in Shakespeare not only to the binary of Protestant and Catholic, but to the divisions of Protestantism within itself, and notably to the confessional distinction between willing conformists to the new Church of England and Puritans who were not convinced that the Reformation had been taken seriously enough in England, in matters of worship, "oversight" (episcopacy), and discipline of life. Such Puritans existed *inside* and *outside* the state church.[31] Inside, they might be more concerned with moral stringency of life, more suspicious of "popery," and more opposed to ceremonial than others while still approving episcopacy, or they might form a pressure group seeking ultimately to put church oversight into the hands of a group of presbyters (elders) rather than bishops.[32] Outside, Puritans could take the form of radical "Separatists" who had illegally separated from the state church in order to live simply "under the rule of Christ" rather than under the rule of bishops appointed by the monarch, or even under the rule of a presbytery. Separatists held to a church order made by "covenant" with each other and with God in Christ,[33] and one important Separatist leader who developed the idea of covenant, Robert Browne, is named by Shakespeare. In *Twelfth Night*, Maria remarks of the pompous steward Malvolio, "sometimes he is a kind of Puritan," to which the absurd Sir Andrew Aguecheek replies, "O, if I thought that, I'd beat him like a dog." Later he comments that "policy I hate. I would as lief be a Brownist as a politician"—thereby giving his poor opinion of both.[34]

These passing exclamations give some hint that Shakespeare was well aware of the strains and fractions in and outside the newly established Church of England, whether or not he intends Malvolio to be identified as a Brownist kind of Puritan, as some have supposed he does.[35] Shakespeare's own estimate of Puritans of whatever sort must not, of course, be confused with that of the foppish and incompetent Sir Andrew. While the Puritan-seeming Malvolio is handled roughly by Olivia's household, the mistress herself evidently values him highly for both his character and function, and wants to include him in the renewed society at the end of the play, urging: "He hath been most notoriously abused"; Orsino concurs: "Pursue him, and entreat him to a peace."[36] That he may well remain excluded is a dark shadow on a bright morning. Angelo in *Measure for Measure* is presented more obviously as a Puritan: he is called "precise,"[37] one of the most common synonyms for "puritanical" in the period, and refers to himself as one of the "saints" (2.2.180–81), the self-designation of all Puritan and Separatist believers.[38] Given Angelo's vicious behavior toward Claudio and Isabella, the play might appear to be an anti-Puritan polemic,[39] but there are cross-currents which trouble this simple description. While the rigorous, capital laws against fornication do echo Puritan proposals in the period,[40] it is actually the Duke—who takes the identity of a Catholic friar and may well be intended to reflect well on James I as a quasi-omnipresent and quasi-omnipotent figure[41]—who has done nothing to reform "old" legislation. Nor is the harsh law alleviated by him at the end of the play, despite mercy given to Claudio and Angelo. The play certainly "provides a hint of a closure—however strained—for its Puritan figure that *Twelfth Night* denies"[42] and so for the audience may gesture toward the possibility of different Protestant groups living together in one culture. Yet, to introduce a balance once again, both Angelo's identity and his incorporation become uncertain at the end. After imagining that he has had sex with Isabella, he reflects on loss of self: "this deed unshapes me quite" (4.4.18). Walsh reflects that we are left wondering whether he can restructure his former Puritan self; "the end of the play leaves opaque who he is: a Puritan, a reformed Puritan, or an ex-Puritan. Also opaque is how, as any of these, he fits into mainstream society."[43]

The impossibility of pinning Shakespeare down on these interchurch tensions is magnificently demonstrated in the figure of Falstaff in the Henry IV plays, an unlikely and yet real contender as the third notable Puritan or Puritan-like character in Shakespeare. Modeled on Sir John Oldcastle, a well-known Lollard martyr commemorated by John Foxe,[44] his name in the plays was changed at the objection of his descendent, the fourth Lord Cobham, but in private performances, "Oldcastle" survived until at least 1638. Shakespeare is thus lampooning someone who was widely viewed as being not just proto-Protestant but proto-Puritan, and even proto-Nonconformist. Milton later said to Anglican churchmen that those who "were call'd Lollards and Hussites, so now by you be term'd Puritans, and Brownists."[45] One of Falstaff's characteristic speech patterns is a parody of the conventicle style—a "damnable iteration" of scripture (King Henry IV Part 1, 1.2.87), and use of such typical Puritan vocabulary as "saint" and "vocation" (1.2.88, 101). As Shaheen has pointed out, approximately half the play's scriptural citations are put in his mouth.[46] It has been suggested that in his speeches Falstaff is intentionally parodying the scriptural style of the sanctimonious Puritan, but David Scott Kastan, with Kristin Poole, go one step further in suggesting that Falstaff in his very self (not just in his periodic speeches) is "a parodic representation of a 'Puritan.'"[47] This may seem at odds with his bacchanalian appetites, but clerical authorities responded to the left-wing Puritan "Martin Marprelate" tracts attacking the national church by caricaturing their anonymous antagonist as a gluttonous and irresponsible figure, and this may have provided (as Poole suggests) some of the material for Shakespeare's portrayal. To add to the layers of complexity, it has been argued that Catholics, perhaps more than clerics of the Church of England, would have been delighted to see the mocking of one of the heroes of Foxe's Book of Martyrs.[48]

Yet the case of Oldcastle-Falstaff exactly shows that Shakespeare can be safely assigned neither to the anti-Puritan nor Catholic camp. Falstaff is one of the characters to whom audiences warmed—and still warm—most readily, for all his many faults, and his turning away by the newly crowned Henry V is felt as a tragic moment: "I know thee not, old man. Fall to thy prayers."[49] Falstaff's cavalier approach to "the laws of England" might well make his rejection a political necessity if Henry is to be a successful monarch, but the audience wishes it could have been otherwise, that he could have been included in this new birth of the nation: as Charles Williams reflects, "It is not the Prince who behaves badly to Falstaff—he at least had meant to do nothing else all along . . . it is we who have betrayed him because of our respectability."[50] Shakespeare's concern for the value of "unsettled toleration" is perhaps summed up in a passing comment of Lucio in *Measure for Measure*, "Grace is grace, despite of all controversy" (1.2.24–25), not least because the phrase is ambiguous. Playing on the words of Romans 11:6, that if grace results from works, "then grace is no more grace," Lucio seems to be making light of a major theological dispute between Catholics and reforming Protestants,[51] and so is apparently urging a tolerant spirit. But his words could also be taken to indicate a Calvinist view of irresistible grace, a resignation to divine predestination, and so Shakespeare escapes even the label of "tolerationist."

A BLURRING OF BOUNDARIES

So far we have been exploring one view of the early modern religious context in which Shakespeare was writing, that of an age of confessionalism. But there is a second overall view of the situation, to which many historians of the period have recently become inclined, that of blurred boundaries between confessional stances. It is suggested that while theologians of the different parties, and politicians who wished to exploit differences, might make sharp distinctions in belief and church polity, for most ordinary people, "their daily experience would have usually led them to understand that they had more in common than not."[52] A good deal of confusion must have been prevalent in the pews since in the space of twenty-five years they, or their parents, had experienced a movement from Catholicism to Protestantism, a countermovement back to Catholicism, and then a reversal once again back to a Protestant faith. Putting it another way, in one generation, from 1530 to 1560, they had experienced five different versions of official state religion, "five different and competing monotheisms":[53] Henrician Catholicism, Henrician mild Protestantism, Edwardian strong Protestantism, Marian Catholicism, and then Elizabethan "middle-way" Protestantism.

A popular sense of "unsettlement"[54] must have been exacerbated by what several recent historians have identified as a reluctance of the majority of the English to "settle down" as Protestants. They have stressed that a kind of residual Catholicism persisted throughout the sixteenth century and into the next, thus revising a previously held reading of the Reformation as starting an inevitable progression toward a fully Protestant world.[55] On the popular level there must have been a general resistance to the notion that grandparents in a family had been shut out of salvation due to their Catholic beliefs.[56] Walls between confessions were made even more porous by the concern of the liturgists and theologians in the new Church of England to retain a continuity with medieval Catholicism (though not with allegiance to the pope) through the retention of episcopacy and especially through the style of the new Prayer Book. Cranmer, in the first Prayer Book of 1549, had skilfully adapted substantial elements of previous Catholic liturgies: the Breviary was transformed into Morning and Evening Prayer, the Missal into Holy Communion, the Manual into services for baptism, marriage, and burial, and the Pontifical into the rites of confirmation and ordination (the "Ordinal"). Cranmer's creation was the model for all subsequent editions of the Prayer Book, and local congregations would have found a comforting familiarity in much of it, although the separate regional rites had now been replaced by "common prayer" in which the whole of the English church was intended to worship together with essentially the same words.

This approach was congruent with Elizabeth's deliberate policy to make the English church as comprehensive as possible, so that—in Barbara Everett's imaginative reuse of a phrase of T. S. Eliot's—it was a "draughty church" with the door left open for a variety of incomers.[57] For instance, the third edition of the Prayer Book, issued in 1559, altered the "Ornaments rubric" to allow use of old vestments, and removed the "black rubric" (1552) which had declared that kneeling at the communion indicated no adoration of bread or wine. Elizabeth's church was not of course *sufficiently* comprehensive to include Brownists, or other Separatists who were to fracture in the second decade of the seventeenth century into Baptists and paedobaptist Independents, all of whom were liable to imprisonment and worse under Elizabeth's anticonventicle acts which remained in force into the reign of Charles II. Two leaders of the Separatist church in London (which was actually highly suspicious of Robert Browne) had been hung, supposedly for circulating seditious books, in April 1593.[58] But people's identities often shifted between holding to a Puritanism inside and outside the established church, as was exemplified by the inconsistent career of Robert Browne himself, who was educated as an Anglican priest, formed a Separatist congregation in Norwich in 1581, failed to join the Presbyterian Kirk in Scotland in 1583, submitted to the Church of England and accepted a series of Anglican posts until about 1617, and was finally excommunicated as a Nonconformist in 1631.[59] There is much to be said for the view that "Dissent" as a coherent identity consisting of Independents, Baptists, Presbyterians, and Quakers existing as a block over against the Church of England resulted from the imposing of a more strict kind of conformity toward the reestablished church from 1660 onward. In short, it may be argued that the religious scene at the time of Shakespeare showed a "continuity of amicable, unsystematic religious thought in which communal harmony regularly trumped doctrinal purity,"[60] and in which the community at large held what Debora Shuger has called "a minimalist version of saving faith."[61]

The two perspectives on the religious scene at the time of Shakespeare I have identified—*either* viewing it as riven by distinct confessions *or* as a place of porous borders between confessions—may seem on first sight incompatible. Yet there is truth in both of them when they are not taken to extremes. We might adapt the image offered by Peter White of a "spectrum" of religious identities in the early modern era,[62] identifying degrees of difference and similitude rather than absolute polarities. But it matters where the emphasis lies between these views. Scholars such as Jeffrey Knapp and—more moderately—Brian Walsh situate Shakespeare's evenhanded approach toward different religious groups within a situation of confessionalism, and so find it to be a *reaction* against frictions caused in society by people's holding strongly to confessional difference. The plays are thus seen as demonstrating a deliberate intention of ameliorating conflict. My own approach in this book leans much more toward Shakespeare's using—even exploiting—a widespread uncertainty about boundaries of belief and practice. The religious material in the plays, avoiding partiality in the way I have illustrated, thus has its roots in a situation of blurred religious identities, and Shakespeare is taking advantage of this context for his own purposes.

By "taking advantage" of a situation of confused religious identity, I mean two things. In the first place, Shakespeare can be quite relaxed about referring to the Bible, Christian doctrine, and ecclesial practices as stuff—and especially a mine of metaphor—for making poetry and drama. He need feel no obligation to draw on this material for any particular polemical purpose. He need not fear that he will be recruited to one camp or another, or claimed by them, on the basis of references he makes. He can thus exploit ambiguities, even muddles in his audiences' minds, to pillage a rich seam of linguistic ore in the interests of nothing but a playful imagination. In the second place, as I argue in chapter 2, Shakespeare has a freedom to develop a kind of "general spirituality" devoid of dogma and appeal to specific doctrines. He can commend, though usually indirectly, a "spiritual" perspective[63] which remains open to the "many things in heaven and earth" urged by Hamlet.

It is well known that Shakespeare does employ well over a thousand quotations from, and allusions to, the English Bible, and in addition about 120 references to the Psalms, almost entirely from the Coverdale Psalter.[64] He must have owned and carefully read at least one version of the Bible himself, if for no other reason than that (as Shaheen has demonstrated) he makes more reference to chapters from Genesis, Isaiah, and Ecclesiasticus that were not "proper" first lessons in the Prayer Book lectionary than to chapters that were.[65] Thus his knowledge of the Bible cannot be attributed solely to hearing it read in Morning and Evening Prayer in church. Most of his references to the book of Revelation, moreover, are taken from chapters that were not appointed to be read in church at any time. Shakespeare's version was most probably the Geneva Bible, which was available in a handy and cheap quarto edition. While most of his references are common in their language to the family of English Tudor translations, including the Great Bible and the Bishops' Bible, the largest number of the references that can be attributed to a particular version are to the Geneva Bible,[66] and there are also references to Genevan marginal glosses. Since the Geneva Bible was not appointed for reading in church, this is further evidence for Shakespeare's owning his own copy. It is not impossible that Shakespeare also had an early quarto edition of the Bishops' Bible, but after 1584 it was only available in a heavy and expensive folio edition for church use, and the New Testament alone continued to be published in quarto (until 1618).

INTERTEXTUALITY IN SHAKESPEARE'S OWN PRACTICE

The many references to the biblical text, as well as quotations from the Prayer Book and the two books of Homilies,[67] combine with the many different voices which can be heard in the plays coming from Shakespeare's social and religious context—Protestant, Catholic, Puritan—to create a rich "intertextuality" which Shakespeare can exploit for his own purposes. In appealing to the phenomenon of intertextuality, as discussed successively by Mikhail Bakhtin, Julia Kristeva, Jacques Derrida, Roland Barthes, and Harold Bloom, I am not concerned with finding exact "sources" for the texts of Shakespeare's plays, but with exploring the way that a plurality of religious texts interact with them. Because the term "intertextuality" has been so variously defined, and—in the words of one theorist of intertextuality "cannot be evoked in an uncomplicated manner"[68]—I venture to advance my own working definition:

> "Intertextuality" is an interweaving or interplay of many texts within any particular text, where these "intertexts" may come from other specific written texts or circulate generally as discourse or ideology in society; where the implied author of a text uses other texts either intentionally or unintentionally; where written texts are part of the whole textuality of the world ("context"); and where text and reader together continually construct a new text.

Thus, in the case of Shakespeare, "intertexts"[69] may be particular written pieces that are quoted in the plays, or sayings and sentences that have circulated in the social context, or texts that are not inscribed on documents at all but which are "social texts" embodied in the attitudes of individuals, or groups in society, or in their customs and habits. In his early work on Dostoyevsky, Bakhtin observed that "a plurality of independent and unmerged voices and consciousnesses, a genuine polyphony of fully valid voices is in fact the chief characteristic of Dostoevsky's novels."[70] From this critique he developed a "dialogical" theory of literature in which no utterance, word, or text is ever spoken or written in isolation, but always calls to mind other utterances, words or texts which either precede it or come after it in response:[71] "The word, directed toward its object, enters a dialogically agitated and tension-filled environment of alien words, value judgments and accents, weaves in and out of complex interrelationships, merges with some, recoils from others, intersects with yet a third group: and all this may crucially shape discourse."[72] As Julia Claassens comments, "He argues that the text comes alive only by coming into contact with another text (with context)."[73] Thus, Bakhtin is of the opinion that the real meaning of a text develops on the boundary between texts: "The word lives, as it were, on the boundary between its own context and another, alien, context."[74] This context is essentially social, and here Bakhtin coins the word "heteroglossia" to recognize the numerous and different languages of social and professional groups, of classes and literary movements operating in society at any one time, and whose voices jostle with each other in any literary text, offering a threat to any unitary, authoritarian, or hierarchical conception of society.[75]

To this situation, aptly reflected in the many voices of Shakespeare's plays, Julia Kristeva is the first to put the word "intertextuality." Authors, she writes, compile texts from preexisting texts, so that a text is "a permutation of texts, an intertextuality in the space of a given text," in which "several utterances, taken from other texts, intersect and neutralize one another."[76] One particular contribution Kristeva brings to the discussion is to envisage texts always in the process of *production*, rather than as products to be consumed. Like Jacques Derrida, she thus protests against any view of texts as exchangeable objects of value, and so resists a social process of commodification.[77] In short, as Jacques Derrida insists, there is "nothing outside the text" since the whole of the material world is textual, carrying signs which signify some other reality, so that everything "signified" becomes in turn a "signifier" in an open chain: "That does not mean that all referents are suspended, denied, or enclosed in a book, as people have claimed, or been naive enough to believe and to have accused me of believing. But it does mean that every referent, all reality has the structure of a differential trace, and that one cannot refer to this 'real' except in an interpretive experience."[78] *Il n'y a pas de hors-texte* means "nothing else" than: "there is nothing outside context."[79] Every text is situated alongside or within another text, so that it has a "context" (a "with-text"). Particular groupings of signs form a text, but this is always connected to other texts in the movement of *différance*, or differential relation. A recent commentator on the development of intertextual analysis, Graham Allen, has neatly observed that "Individual text and the cultural text are made from the same textual material and cannot be separated from each other."[80]

In due course, I want to argue for an intertextuality between Shakespeare's plays in their period and theological texts *in the present*, following the final phrase of my working definition. But for the moment I simply draw attention to Shakespeare's creative association of preexisting religious texts in his plays and poems, exemplifying Roland Barthes's particular insight that the term "text" can stand for the "play" of the signifier within a work, a force which unleashes a disruptive, destabilizing, and yet playful writing.[81] The studies of the eight plays that follow will provide many examples of this kind of intertextuality, but for one witty instance, which also incidentally demonstrates Shakespeare's reliance on the text of the Geneva Bible, we might cite Shakespeare's allusion to Psalm 77 in his Sonnet 61.[82] Where the writer of the psalm appears to blame God's desertion of him for his anguish in prayer, so causing his lack of sleep, the Genevan gloss excuses God and explains that it is the Psalmist's own sorrows keeping him awake like "watchmen." Shakespeare turns the one in the psalm who has deserted him and caused his insomnia into the young man whom he loves, and he echoes the gloss by accusing his *own* love for keeping him awake, playing "the watchman":

> It is my love that keeps mine eye awake,
> Mine own true love that doth my rest defeat,
> To play the watchman ever for thy sake.
> For thee watch I, whilst thou dost wake elsewhere,
> From me far off, with others all too near.

The playful interaction of texts enables Shakespeare to open up meaning. The ambiguous reference to "my love" that keeps the poet awake, and the implied blame of his lover for being absent ("awake elsewhere") not only throws doubt upon his excusing of his lover, but also questions the Genevan gloss itself and suggests a different reading of the psalm. R. A. L. Burnet has drawn attention to the parallel between sonnet and psalm,[83] but Beatrice Groves points out the subtlety and daring of the intertextuality: "Shakespeare preserves in his allusion both the anxiety of the [Genevan] annotator and his own independent reading of the Psalm in which it is God who can be blamed for the speaker's condition."[84] The reference to the marginal gloss, incidentally, provides evidence for Shakespeare's particular use of the Geneva text, and makes it likely that it is the Geneva marginalia that Shakespeare has in mind when he has Horatio quip about Hamlet's interrogation of Osric: "I knew you must be edified by the margent ere you had done" (*Hamlet* Q2, 5.2.152), especially since the preface to the Geneva Bible repeatedly claims its version to be "edifying."[85]

Barthes insists that intertextuality is to be distinguished from a search for sources. He writes that "the intertextual in which every text is held, being the text-between of another text, is not to be confused with some *origin* of the text: to try to find the 'sources,' the 'influences,' of a work is to fall in with the myth of filiation," and he adds that "the citations which go to make up a text are anonymous, untraceable and yet *already read*."[86] He is using the word "text" in his own sense, not of a stable work (a "book" for instance) but of the disruptive force of "writing" within the work; yet, even so, his refusal to identify sources seems at odds with such examples as Shakespeare's use of Psalm 61 in the example above. Tracing the source there does not detract from the destabilizing effect of the text, but opens up subversive angles on both the psalmist's relationship with his God and the poet's obsession with his beloved. I suggest that it is better to follow Kristeva's insistence that the intertextual dimensions of the text cannot be studied as *mere* "sources" or "influences" stemming from what traditionally has been styled "background" or "context."[87] By the "myth" or "rhetoric" of "filiation" Barthes indicates the "death of the author," rejecting any notion that the text is the offspring, or owned object, of an authorial mind. We may agree that the meaning of a text is not to be *confined* to the intention of an authorial consciousness, as if the text releases a "theological message" of an author-God; but just as its intertextuality does not exclude identifying particular sources, so it surely does not exclude any authorial intention altogether, reducing it to a mere "tissue of quotations drawn from the innumerable centres of culture."[88] Finding how Shakespeare—or at least the notional author of Sonnet 61—is intentionally using Psalm 77 does not close down the meaning, but enables the reader to enter into the playfulness of the text, and to discover the "more things" that await in heaven and earth when nothing there is "outside the text." Thus, in my working definition, I allow for both intentional and unintentional uses of other texts by the author of a particular text.

The suspicion of Barthes and Kristeva about direct sources does, nevertheless, release us from the anxiety of attempting to prove conclusively that Shakespeare has deliberately taken a phrase or word from one particular source. The event of intertextuality does not require such forensic inquiry. Naseeb Shaheen tells that that some passages that appear to be clear references to scripture are "not biblical references at all." He references, for example, the witches' prediction that Macbeth could not be harmed by any "man that's born of woman,"[89] and notes that it seems to be a clear borrowing from Job 14.1 and its quotation in the Burial Service of the Prayer Book: "man that is born of a woman hath but a short time to live and is full of misery." He is surely right when he tells us that nevertheless "Shakespeare's source for these words was not Scripture, but the Macbeth story as he found it in Holinshed, and as Holinshed in turn found it in his sources, principally the *Scotorum Historiae* of Hector Boethius." Holinshed three times repeats the words that Macbeth would never be killed by "man born of any woman."[90] Shakespeare's "primary source," declares Shaheen, was not scripture.[91] But it is quite another matter to suggest that the phrase is not a "quotation" from scripture. Intertextuality is not merely about *sources*, but interplay between texts, including social texts. There is an interplay going on between scripture, Prayer Book, and Holinshed, for as Shaheen also assures us, "Job was a book that Shakespeare knew especially well, and he was no doubt aware that the witches' words were similar to Job and the Burial Service quotation of Job."[92] This interplay adds significantly to the drama of the moment; the resonance of the Burial Service, citing Job 14:1, introduces an ominous echo of impending death, at the very moment Macbeth is apparently being assured that he will escape death. This ambiguous note would be missing if the only intertext were Holinshed.

Again, Timon sends the message to Athens that "Timon hath made his everlasting mansion / Upon the beached verge of the salt flood."[93] There is a reference here to the familiar saying of Jesus in John 14:2, "in my father's house are many mansions," and yet the word "mansion" does not appear either in the Bishops' Bible (read in church) or in the Geneva Bible (most likely owned by Shakespeare), both of which have "dwelling places," actually a more accurate rendering of the Greek *monai*. The translation "mansions," influenced by the Vulgate *mansiones*, does occur in Wycliffe's translation, the Great Bible, the Rheims New Testament, and Tomson's revision of the Geneva Bible.[94] But we need not conclude that Shakespeare was remembering one of these translations, or even that Shakespeare's own quarto edition of the Geneva Bible was the popular Geneva-Tomson version (published after 1576). The phrase "many mansions" had no doubt entered everyday speech following its use by Wycliffe, and was circulating in the "social text."

It is often the case that the connection—if any—between a biblical or liturgical text and a proverbial phrase just cannot be traced. In four plays, for example, there appears to be an echo of the phrase from the General Confession (Morning and Evening Prayer) in the Prayer Book: "We have left undone those things which we ought to have done, and we have done those things which we ought not to have done," itself based on Matthew 23:23, which appears in the Bishops' Bible as "These ought ye to have done, and not to leave the other undone." The inclusion of the word "leave" in two of these four cases, such as "better to leave undone" (*Antony and Cleopatra*, 3.1.14), relates them quite closely to the Prayer Book and biblical text,[95] but the other two instances appear closer to a known proverb, "things done cannot be undone."[96] So Lady Macbeth simply states that "What's done cannot be undone" (5.1.67–68).[97] There is a play of texts going on here, and there is no point in arguing that one reference in Shakespeare's plays is a *direct* quotation where another is not. In the phenomenon of intertextuality, the "intertexts" outside Shakespeare's text are themselves intertextual constructs.

Using the poststructural language of Derrida and Barthes, we may say that these intertexts outside Shakespeare's text are not simply what is "signified" by "signifiers" which occupy his text; rather, they are themselves signifiers, pointing to yet other texts. Meaning happens within this play of signifiers so that, as Graham Allen puts it, "the signified is always, as it were, over the horizon."[98] Or, as Shakespeare's Hamlet tells us, there are always "more things in heaven and earth" than are dreamed of in our philosophy.

2

Shakespeare's "More Things" and Spirituality

*

S HAKESPEARE'S PRACTICE of intertextuality takes place against the background of a blurring of boundaries between religious convictions. To this point I have found his intertextual web to be characterized by a playful use of religious texts for the sake of poetry, character, plot, and interaction with the audience. But I have already hinted that there is a second dimension of Shakespeare's relation to religion, and I now want to follow up my earlier suggestion that the religious and ecclesial ambiguities of the time give him permission to develop what I am calling a "general spirituality," uncommitted to any particular Christian dogmas.

On the whole, recent critics have been reluctant to propose any connection of Shakespeare with "spirituality," fearing that it will either fence Shakespeare into a particular confession, such as Roman Catholicism, or constrict him within a theory of literature as moral education.[1] The kind of image of Shakespeare promoted by G. Wilson Knight, who presented him as a "prophet" to the nation, and his "total work as, in structure, another Bible" has fallen out of fashion.[2] However, recent criticism *has* been willing to take a view of Shakespeare as giving priority to what are identified as "communal values." Christopher Haigh paints a picture of "a largely habitual Christian" who recognized "the communal values of village harmony and worship,"[3] and David Kastan concurs, finding in the plays "an inclusive and theologically minimalist Christianity that resisted religious rigour and valued social accord."[4] My own inference from experiencing the plays is that we should expand "communal values" into more detailed content, while retaining "theological minimalism."

A Spirituality of Love and Death

I am not calling this ethos of the plays a "spirituality" because it points us to any sphere of life which is detached from, or even parallel to, the embodied existence which Shakespeare so rumbustiously celebrates. There is no dualism between spirit and flesh, or sacred and secular, in what I am proposing. Jacques Derrida is surely right that there can be no "transcendental signified," that is, no reality which is exempt from engagement in the bodily text of the world.[5] In speaking of "spirituality" I mean a sense of values which transcend that reality which can be proved and verified by merely empirical observation of the world and physical experiment. There is always excess, or in Hamlet's expression, "more things." In the words of the theologian Jean-Luc Marion, as we exercise our intuition upon the phenomena of the world, there is always "more, indeed immeasurably more" to be given to us.[6] But this does not *oppose* the spiritual to the empirical, as some who repeat Hamlet's phrase like to do. While these "more things" can never be reduced to physical existence or exhausted into it, their transcendence is always "immanent," always present in bodies and especially in relations between bodies, embedded into them, and only *knowable* by means of them. From a Christian, theological point of view, these values are a way of life that comes from participation in a God who is fully relational, and fully committed to physical creation—that is, a triune God. I will be unfolding this theological vision, initially in the next chapter and then in commenting on Shakespeare's plays in the following ones, but I do not suppose that Shakespeare himself would have held his convictions in so doctrinal a manner.

As a person of his time, no doubt Shakespeare would regard what I am calling "spiritual values" as *Christian* communal values, but I am keeping the phrase "general spirituality" because the reader in the present age can engage with it without assent to any religious propositions. Similarly, in his collection *Spiritual Shakespeares*, Ewan Fernie detaches "spirituality" from any *necessary* connection with religion, though he acknowledges it to be "religion's heart and inspiration"; Fernie defines spirituality as "the experience or knowledge of what is other and is ultimate," and suggests it has the political force of "a mode of opposition to what is," including offering an alternative to "radical materialism" or "a materialist status quo."[7] Spirituality is the sense of "excess" over materialism. A strong influence here has been Jacques Derrida's discovery of a spirituality of political "otherness" in *Hamlet*, focused in the figure of the ghost.[8] In his own essay in his volume, however, Fernie places spirituality elsewhere. The ghost is not really "other" as Derrida supposes, but far too much "the same" as Hamlet, trapped in the same ideologies that drive Hamlet's world.[9] Hamlet's spirituality, he suggests, is commitment to the "divinity that shapes our ends," which is a "special providence"; this is nothing to do with the traditional Christian God, but symbolizes a true otherness, a force of the absolute that challenges materialism and yet is thoroughly immersed in the "messiness" of human life.[10] In practice, this is a kind of "god of rashness" (Hamlet cries, "Praise[d] be rashness"),[11] motivating us to stake everything upon acting here and now in spontaneous, even reckless self-abandonment, to establish justice.[12] Here he cites A. C. Bradley's impression of the play *Hamlet*, that "In all that happens or is done we seem to apprehend some vaster power. We do not define it, or even name it . . . but our imagination is haunted by the sense of it."[13]

While appreciating Fernie's stress that an "excess" over materialism characterizes spirituality, I differ somewhat from him in that I do not think that spirituality can be separated from what Kastan calls a "theological minimalism" in Shakespeare's text itself, whatever might be in the mind of readers today. Expanding Kastan's reference to "communal values," this spirituality consists of at least the following elements: (*a*) loving relations take priority over institutions and social organization; (*b*) life must be lived in constant awareness that death presses in and limits it; (*c*) in some way, love nevertheless outlasts even death; (*d*) forgiveness is essential in view of the frailty of human life; (*e*) human justice is always imperfect, never an absolute, and so mercy is essential; (*f*) communal values are more important than political supremacy; and (*g*) people are in quest of a story to make sense of their lives. I will be continually returning to these aspects in my exploration of the chosen plays that follow, but their presence is scattered widely through all the plays. Here, for the remainder of this chapter, I aim only to introduce the themes, which Shakespeare constantly supports through intertextuality with the Bible and other religious texts.

First, the priority of love means a challenge to established conventions of society and traditions of culture. For example, in *Anthony and Cleopatra*, Anthony claims an intuitive vision of his love with Cleopatra in Egypt:

> Let Rome in Tiber melt, and the wide arch
> Of the ranged empire fall! Here is my space!
> Kingdoms are clay! Our dungy earth alike
> Feeds beast as man; the nobleness of life
> Is to do thus. (1.1.34–38)

Probably drawing on at least two biblical references—the kingdom portrayed as a figure with feet of iron and clay in Daniel 2:42 ("partly strong and partly broken") and the "dung of the earth" in Psalm 83:12—Anthony asserts that his love runs counter to the patrician and military values of Rome.[14] A few lines earlier, in response to Cleopatra's taunt that she could set a limit on how much Anthony actually loved her, he had asserted, "Then must thou needs find our new heaven, new earth" (1.1.7), echoing Revelation 21:1: "I saw a new heaven and a new earth," and giving a sense of transcendence to love.[15] Similarly, Romeo finds in the light of his intense love for Juliet that the social norms of a feud between two families are of no significance, and turns away Tybalt's insults with the soft answer, "[I] love thee better than thou canst devise."[16] Othello and Desdemona, too, overturn the conventions of white, Venetian society by a love that cuts so sharply across race and class that others accuse him of bewitching her, leading him to protest:

> She loved me for the dangers I had passed
> And I loved her that she did pity me.
> This only is the witchcraft I have used. (*Othello*, 1.3.168–70)

It is a tragic fact that Anthony, Romeo, and Othello all fail to hold faithfully to the vision of love they perceive at times, as we shall see in exploring the tragicomic "story" that Shakespeare is continually telling;[17] but this failure does not invalidate the supreme value of love in society as he presents it. Regina Schwartz insists that the love of Romeo and Juliet, for instance, must not be reduced to a "private passionate love affair," but that their "holy bond of love . . . dramatizes the impossible command to love the enemy, its cost as well as its efficacy."[18] Charity, in the sense of love toward neighbor, and erotic love are inseparable, as Shakespeare indicates in quoting from Romans 13:9–10 on two occasions.[19] He seems to have deliberately chosen the wording of this text from the Bishops' Bible, which places "love" and "charity" in parallel, where the Geneva and other versions have only "love": "Thou shalt love thy neighbour as thy self. Charity worketh no ill to his neighbour, therefore the fulfilling of the law is charity" (Bishops' Bible). Perhaps Shakespeare recalled the parallelism from a sermon. In *Love's Labour's Lost*, Berowne wittily adduces the text to justify breaking his vows of shunning the company of women for the sake of philosophy:

> It is religion to be thus forsworn,
> For charity itself fulfills the law,
> And who can sever love from charity? (4.3.137–39)

The life which love illuminates must, second, be lived in continual awareness of the boundary of death that awaits us all. Characters, as we have seen, often come to a sense of self-identity as they speak in soliloquies in which they face death. Macbeth muses in a few lines packed with metaphor:

> To-morrow, and to-morrow, and to-morrow,
> Creeps in this petty pace from day to day,
> To the last syllable of recorded time,
> And all our yesterdays, have lighted fools
> The way to dusty death. Out, out, brief candle.
> Life's but a walking shadow. (5.5.19–24)

The inevitable approach of death is sounded in three images woven densely together, as the passing of time is compared to a slow but inexorable treading of feet, to the reading of the pages of a book of words to the last syllable, and finally a funeral procession. Biblical resonances are there in the book of judgment, the dust to which all must return, the snuffing out of a candle and life as a shadow.[20] Macbeth comes to realization of his "foolishness" in supposing that taking action—any action, even murder—will stave off death, so that "here, upon this bank and shoal of time, / We'd jump the life to come" (1.7.1–7). He is forced to face his self-deception which, as Cummings suggests, is a fantasy generated by his own imaginative use of words.[21] The noble philosopher-lovers in *Love's Labour's Lost* are similarly given a cold dose of reality with the news that breaks into their games, "'The King, your father–' . . . 'Dead'" (5.2.714–15). Confronting this fact, the male lovers must come to self-knowledge, a hard process that cannot be completed in the mere hour left before the women leave; that would be "A time, methinks, too short / To make a world-without-end bargain in" (782–83), a phrase echoing the *Gloria* which closes psalms and canticles in the Prayer Book.

Another biblical image that portrays death as a boundary to life is that of a "span," found several times in Shakespeare's plays. Psalm 39:6 in the (Coverdale) Psalter of the Prayer Book runs: "Thou hast made my days as it were a span long," and there are four resonances with this text in the plays, such as in *As You Like It*, "How brief the life of man . . . the stretching of a span" (3.2.129–31).[22] In all this Shakespeare is employing the common theme of memento mori, but there is no conventional or dogmatic threat of hell; Hamlet, drawing on the established association of sleep and death, is troubled by the vague worry, "in that sleep what dreams may come." The spiritual gain of remembering death is an awakening of conscience ("conscience does make cowards"),[23] a "self-knowledge" that for the Reformation mind was an awareness of standing before the judgment of God.[24] Nobody in Shakespeare's plays prospers when conscience is neglected.

A third element of spirituality is made by putting the first two together. We must be warned that "All lovers young, all lovers must / Like chimney-sweepers come to dust," but nevertheless love has the power to overcome death, though *how* can hardly be defined. When Cleopatra exults that "I have immortal longings in me," and defuses the sting of death by comparing it to a "lover's pinch, that hurts and is desired,"[25] and when Romeo seals with his kiss a "dateless bargain to engrossing death,"[26] we believe that even death cannot extinguish love. We do not believe, however, in the picture Anthony gives us of a postmortem existence in which "Where souls do couch on flowers we'll hand in hand"; together with Cleopatra's matching cry, "I am again for Cydnus / To meet Mark Anthony," we are moved by expressions of confidence in an indestructible love rather than by a prediction of a literal state.[27] We can presume to say a little about the triumph of love over death: we may say that love creates a story that death cannot overcome, and creates a lasting monument to love, whether in the theater of Cleopatra's death ("give me my robes, my crown") or in the statue raised to Romeo and Juliet by their grieving family, or through Shakespeare's own lines of poetry, which he believes will survive when even brass and stone will be worn away:

> Or what strong hand can hold [death's] swift foot back,
> Or who his spoil o'er beauty can forbid?
>   O none, unless this miracle have might:
>   That in black ink my love may still shine bright.[28]

But there remains a mystery about the way that love outlasts even death, which exceeds any rational explanation.

In *Comedy of Errors* the mystery is portrayed as a kind of birth. At the end of the play, when the Abbess discovers her two long-lost children, she presents her lifetime's journey as a process of painful labor toward their delivery, and she invites the onlookers to share her joy at a feast like one to mark a baptism (a "gossips' feast")[29] after "nativity."

> Thirty-three years have I but gone in travail
> Of you, my sons, and till this present hour
> My heavy burden ne'er delivered.
> —The Duke, my husband and my children both
> And you, the calendars of their nativity,
> Go to a gossips' feast, and go with me;
> After so long grief, such nativity! (5.1.400–406)

While some editors regard the Folio text's repetition of "nativity" as a compositional error, the point is surely that the first occurrence refers to the twins' physical nativity, and the second to their spiritual nativity, being newborn to the Abbess. Though a careful reckoning actually makes it twenty-five years on from the shipwreck where she was parted from husband and twin sons, the Abbess speaks of it as "thirty-three," thereby evoking the life-span of Christ,[30] of whose birth there are also echoes in the religious term "nativity."

The audience knows that after thirty-three years Christ met death on the cross, and the Abbess must be close to the horizon of death given the life-expectancy of the time, closer to death than another woman long-supposed dead, Hermione at the end of *The Winter's Tale*; Hermione's separation from husband and child has been only sixteen years, and she is described as "aged" by a surprised Leontes (5.3.28–29). Yet this pilgrimage toward death can be experienced as a travail toward birth when love is present, the renewed love between Antipholus of Ephesus and Adriana, the new love of Antipholus of Syracuse and Luciana, and the restored love between the Abbess (Emilia) and her husband, Egeon. Arthur Kinney, referring to the twins' first birth, comments that "so short a play—actually Shakespeare's briefest—moves all the way from the Nativity to the Last Judgment."[31] Shakespeare's inter-textuality with the Bible is central here. The setting of Ephesus recalls the city which Paul visited according to the book of Acts, which like Shakespeare's Ephesus houses "dark-working sorcerers,"[32] and the play recalls at several points his discussion of marriage as it is presented in the Letter to the Ephesians.[33] It is love that turns death into birth, and it is love that is missing from the "Old Comedy" of Plautus,[34] whose plot has otherwise influenced Shakespeare. Adriana cites the author of Ephesians on the subject of the "one flesh" of marriage[35]—"we two be one"—in appealing to the sexually erring Antipholus, and *Ephesians* declares "so ought men to love their wives, as they love their own bodies," in the context of its appeal to all in the community to "walk in love," "redeeming the time."[36]

A SPIRITUALITY OF FORGIVENESS AND MERCY

This life, limited by death and yet unlimited by love, is morally frail and marred by errors, so that mutual forgiveness is essential in living together. This fourth element of spirituality is reinforced by many echoes of the phrase in the Lord's Prayer, which in the Prayer Book version runs: "Forgive us our trespasses as we forgive them that trespass against us." This exact phrase does not appear in the text of the plays, possibly because direct quotation from the Prayer Book ran the risk that its use on the stage would be deemed "disrespectful,"[37] but this would have been the prayer most familiar to Shakespeare. We find resonances not only in the general appeals for pardon and for sins to be forgiven,[38] but specifically in the reciprocity between forgiving others and being forgiven which the petition in the Lord's Prayer summarizes. Laertes with his dying breath asks Hamlet to "exchange forgiveness" with him, and similarly the dying Edmund in *King Lear* offers forgiveness to Edgar before Edgar asks him to "exchange charity."[39] The condemned Buckingham tells Sir Thomas Lovell that "I as free forgive you / As I would be forgiven," in a passage from *Henry VIII* that has been argued to be Shakespeare's composition.[40] The word "mercy" can at times carry the sense, like forgiveness, of a restoring of personal relations, and reference is made to the same petition of the Lord's prayer when Portia first asks Shylock, "how shalt thou hope for mercy, rend'ring none?" (4.1.88) and then urges him:

> we do pray for mercy
> and *that same prayer* doth teach us all to render
> the deeds of mercy. (4.1.96–98)

The former contemptuous behavior of Antonio to Shylock gives a personal depth to the legal mercy he is being asked to show. Other intertexts also echo in these passages, such as Jesus's expansion of the petition in Matthew 6:14–15; the beatitude of Matthew 5:7 ("Blessed are the merciful: for they shall obtain mercy"); the command in Luke 6:36 ("Be ye therefore merciful, as your Father also is merciful"); the wise sayings of Ecclesiasticus 2:2, 4 ("Forgive thy neighbour . . . so shall thy sinnes be forgiven thee also");[41] and the parable of the debtors in Matthew 18:32–35. Indeed, Shakespeare offers his own parable of the mutuality of forgiveness or mercy in an incident where Cambridge, Scroop, and Grey fail to show mercy to a man who had insulted King Henry V while drunk, and then plead in vain for mercy from the king when their own much greater treason is disclosed: "The mercy that was quick in us but late," retorts Henry, "by your own counsel is suppressed and killed."[42] His father, when Henry Bolingbroke, also references the petition from the Lord's Prayer about reciprocal forgiveness in the context of treason, although in this case with a positive outcome: "I pardon him, as God shall pardon me."[43]

The spirituality of mutual forgiveness is at times complex, as in Lear's fantasy in which he imagines himself repeatedly kneeling down and asking his daughter forgiveness, in an exchange with her request for his blessing—fantasy because he and Cordelia are after all in the violent hands of their enemies, "birds i'the cage."[44] Cordelia asks for blessing in the exchange, not explicitly forgiveness, but any viewer of the play is bound to ask whether she might not have handled more gently her honest rejection of his unreasonable demands at the beginning of the story.[45] Complexity is increased when, in the exchange of forgiveness between people, "God" or some unspecified higher power is often invoked or implied as participant; in addition to the examples above, in *The Winter's Tale* Leontes is reported as asking forgiveness of the childhood friend he tried to kill, Polixenes (5.2.50), having first been assured that he can be forgiven by "the heavens" (5.1.5–6).

The practice of reciprocal forgiveness thus has an intertextuality with phrases from the Bible and the Prayer Book, although it does not require any dogmatic belief in the mercy of God. It is an instance of what I have been calling a "general spirituality." This is also the case with a fifth element, which takes up a more forensic dimension of "mercy." The imperfections of human *justice* mean that mercy will always be required. A more theological version of this sentiment is that human justice is never an *exact* parallel to divine justice, but the image of God as supreme Judge need not be explicitly invoked to urge the tempering of law by mercy.

The play that most extensively explores this theme is *Measure for Measure*, where Isabella goes to Angelo to plead for her brother's life but finds Angelo obdurate, declaring, "Your brother is a forfeit of the law" (2.2.75), and, "It is the law, not I, condemn your brother" (2.2.84). Angelo cannot, it seems, be moved because he sees law as final and absolute in its own right, a kind of abstract process which is independent of the character of its administrator. Now, there are advantages in the independence of the law over the arbitrariness of the powerful. To be God's deputy, bearing the sword on God's behalf, meant that rulers themselves were to be accountable to the commands or law of God. Moreover, it was widely agreed that they should also respect and obey law made on earth, as an image of God's justice.[46] Yet the inexactness and spoiling of the image meant that personal morality had to play a part in discerning what was just: Shakespeare stands here with Erasmus, who declared in his *Education of a Christian Prince* that "there can be no good prince who is not also a good man."[47] The connection between the administration of earthly justice and the person of the judge—including the judge's own morality—is a theme that Shakespeare continually works at in dramatic form.[48]

Despite her own emotional inhibitions, Isabella urges this personal factor within the administration of justice: "I do think that you might pardon him / And neither heaven nor man grieve at the mercy" (2.2.49–50), she begins. However harsh the law, the judge has some discretion to interpret and modify the law, fitting it to the particular situation. The Duke had reminded Angelo precisely of this in handing over to him the power of "mortality and mercy," balancing "enforcing" the law with "modifying" it, "terror" with "love." These contending forces were to be balanced, urged the Duke, "as to your soul seems good," making clear the moral dimension of government (1.1.19, 44, 64–66). Angelo, as Peter Lake has shown, has conflated divine law to whose demands there are no exceptions (as understood by a Calvinist Puritan) with human law, in which it is incumbent upon the magistrate to distinguish between different levels of offense.[49]

Isabella thus advances a double argument for mercy: that mercy is the greatest attribute of human rulers, because it is most like to God's own, and that every ruler should be aware of human weakness and frailty, including his own. These arguments are given an extra, theological, dimension by appeal to the act of God in the atonement of human life, making reference to biblical texts. To Angelo's blunt statement, "Your brother is a forfeit of the law," she responds:

> Alas, alas!
> Why, all the souls that were, were forfeit once,
> And He that might the vantage best have took
> Found out the remedy. How would you be
> If He, which is the top of judgement, should
> But judge you as you are? O, think on that,
> And mercy then will breathe within your lips,
> Like man new made. (2.2.73–78)

This speech is full of echoes from Paul's Letter to the Romans, with its prom- ise of a new humanity ("man new made") and yet also its realistic psychology of a continuing struggle between the old man and the new man, a conflict between the old Adam and the man in Christ (Rom. 7:14–25).[50] "[W]hat I would, that do I not; but what I hate, that I do," confesses Paul, and it was a fundamental tenet of Reformation thought that the new man was "at the same time justified and a sinner" (*simul justus et peccator*). Angelo, however, fails to recognize his own frailty and sinfulness, and stands under Paul's ac- cusation: "in that thou judgest another, thou condemnest thy self: for thou that judgest, doest the same things" (Rom. 2:1).

The values held by Isabella ("More than our brother is our chastity," 2.4.184) make this what has been called "a problem play." As Ernest Schanzer points out, "She seems to imagine God as a kind of Angelo, a legalistic judge, who would sentence her entirely according to the letter of the law rather than its spirit."[51] But the whole situation of applying law and justice in a fallen world is a "problem" of conflicting values that has no neat solution. What *is* the "*lawful mercy*" to which Isabella appeals? (2.4.112). There is no easy reso- lution, but what resolution there is seems to lie in the character and wisdom of the judge, exercising the virtue of "moderation." This combines a number of elements—the classical virtues of Aristotle's "reasonableness" (*epikeia*) and Seneca's clemency (*clementia*),[52] together with the Reformer's idea of Christian "equity."[53] For all his ambiguity and spin-doctoring, the Duke is presented as a "gentleman of all temperance," mediating between extremes.

There is thus no *direct* application to human lawmaking of the act of par- don shown by God in the cross of Christ, despite attempts by critics and theologians to make the play an allegory of atonement,[54] with the Duke as a symbol for God or Christ.[55] In the quotation above, there is the clearest reference to God's initiative in atonement in any Shakespearean text ("He . . . found out the remedy"), and many biblical texts that deal with human fallen- ness and redemption are intertexts (in Romans alone, 3:23–25; 6:23, 5:8–10).

Nevertheless, the spiritual principle that no human law can be absolute, that mercy is essential, and so a merciful character needs to be developed, emerges without any need for doctrine.

A Spirituality of Authority

Just as no human law can be absolute, nor can any political or even monar-chical authority. A sixth spiritual principle we can discern is that values of living together in community outweigh the right of a ruler to exert power when he or she is abusing power to the detriment of society as a whole. With an Elizabethan view of the created world, Shakespeare was horrified at the consequences that flow from *loss* of order in the concentric circles of personal life, society, and cosmos, and the effect of disorder in any one of these spheres on the other. A definitive expression of order is offered by Ulysses in *Troilus and Cressida* under the label of "degree":

> O, when degree is shaked,
> Which is the ladder to all high designs,
> The enterprise is sick. How could communities,
> Degrees in schools and brotherhoods in cities,
> Peaceful commerce from dividable shores,
> The primogeneity and due of birth,
> Prerogative of age, crowns, sceptres, laurels,
> But by degree stand in authentic place?
> Take but degree away, untune that string,
> and mark what discord follows. . . .
> . . . The bounded waters
> Should lift their bosoms higher than the shores
> . . . .
> And the rude son should strike his father dead. (1.3.101–15)

But there are ambiguities here. The speaker is the wily Ulysses, who is using his rhetoric to manipulate his superiors and to goad the reluctant Achilles into action. A number of critics have suggested that Ulysses undermines his case about order and degree by losing order and control in this very speech, through an excessive use of accumulation of images, climax, and neolo-gisms.[56] David Bevington suggests that the play (in, for instance, portray-ing the relations between Achilles and King Agamemnon) reflects important social changes at work in late Elizabethan England, with a decline of feudal aristocracy and an increase in bourgeois mercantilism; those who were cling-ing to an outmoded social structure based on order and degree were finding themselves displaced by new wealth. Shakespeare did not, concluded Beving-ton, take sides in the conflict but "gave expression to many voices of anger and discontent in the England for which he wrote this play."[57]

Ulysses's speech on degree has in fact an intertextual relation to at least two of the homilies from the Book of Homilies.[58] The homily "Concern-ing Good Order, and Obedience to Rulers and Magistrates" links "perfect ordre" in "heaven, the earth, and waters" to Kings and Princes "in all good and necessary ordre,"[59] just as Ulysses conjoins "crowns and sceptres" with "the bounded waters," and the exclamation "Take but degree away" echoes the homily's "Take away ... ordre ... there must nedes folowe all mischief."[60] Ulysses warns that degree lost "the rude son should strike his father dead," echoing the Homily "Against Disobedience and Will-full Rebellion" with its warning "the brother to seeke, and often to worke the death of his brother, the sonne of the father, the father to seeke or procure the death of his sons."[61] Shakespeare's ambivalent, even ironic, approach to order thus touches not only state power but also church authority. Cleopatra, in *Anthony and Cleopa-tra*, similarly echoes the Tudor "doctrine" of monarchy in the Homilies when she bids Proculeius to tell Caesar that "I hourly learn / A doctrine of obedi-ence" (5.2.30–31), but it is clear that she speaks ironically, and plans to take her own path against Caesar's plan to lead her in triumph in Rome.

Shakespeare is in favor of order, but he seems sensitive to what *true* order might actually be, and does not *inevitably* equate it with the estab-lished order of the existing hierarchy. We glean from the plays the mes-sage that injustice can be resisted, even in a consecrated monarch. After all, Henry IV had deposed Richard II to produce the virtuous Henry V, victor of Agincourt. Henry Tudor had deposed the monstrous Richard III in order to establish the Tudor dynasty. Shakespeare is loyal to the Elizabethan settle-ment, but his plays draw coded warnings from history even for the present ruler about the consequences of tyrannical behavior in a society where sedi-tion was an ever-present danger. As we shall see in study of English history plays like *King John* and *Richard II*, there are reasons in Reformation theology for taking this nuanced approach to power, but for now I simply want to register Shakespeare's giving of priority to communal well-being—England itself, we might say—in envisaging good order in the state.

To comment on the condition of England, Shakespeare, with his fellow playwrights, turns to the classical world. Earlier than *Troilus and Cressida* (1601), *Julius Caesar* demonstrates the ambiguities of trying to discern what healthy order in the state might be. In a scene where the collaboration be-tween the conspirators is beginning to fall apart, Brutus accuses Cassius of taking bribes, and thereby undermining all the good that their assassination of Caesar might have achieved: "Did not great Julius bleed for justice' sake?"

(4.3.19). This justification, together with the accusation that he was killed "for supporting robbers," suddenly appears; earlier Brutus had specifically said that he knew of no corruption in Caesar (2.1.10–21), and the point had been to kill Caesar *before* he could turn tyrant, to *forestall* the fulfilment of the potential for corruption shown by Caesar's eagerness to take a crown. As the cynical Casca puts it, when he was offered a crown by the populace, "He was very loath to lay his fingers off it" (1.2.240–41). Brutus fears that Caesar will succumb to "Th'abuse of greatness" which "disjoins / Remorse [compassion] from power" (2.1.18–19). The point is not that the play shows the downfall of a dictator in the modern sense (Caesar is "dictator" in the classical sense of a special magistrate with extraordinary powers granted to him outside the constitution), and that Brutus and his fellow conspirators were thus justified when they "struck the foremost man of all this world," but that they and the audience are compelled to face the difficult decisions that the abuse of power brings, where there are no easy answers.

Aptly, Brutus begins the argument with Cassius with the cry "Judge me, you gods" (4.2.38). In the first place, this relates to Cassius's accusation that Brutus has wronged him, but as the scene develops it is clear that Brutus wants to be judged for his conduct toward Caesar as much as toward Cassius. The appeal "Judge me" is put in terms of a pre-Christian era of "the gods," but Naseeb Shaheen has made the tentative proposal that the cry may echo a well-known phrase from the Psalms. The expression "Judge me, O God" and variations of it such as "Judge me, O Lord" occur at least five times in the Geneva version of the Psalms, in 7:8; 26:1; 35:24; 43:1; and 54:1. Shaheen comments that "Since Brutus's words, 'Judge me, you gods!' have no parallel in Plutarch, Shakespeare may have borrowed that expression from Scripture."[62] The intertextuality has lost all specific reference to the God of the Psalms, and we are left with the reality that we always remain under judgment when we act, or fail to act, to confront power in the name of communal good. In this general spirituality, it does not matter whether there are gods to do the judging.

The Quest for a Story

The final element of spirituality to which I want to draw attention gathers together the rest. Giving priority to love, living in awareness of death, confident that love remains in face of death, making room for forgiveness in personal relations and for mercy in legal settings, and sensitive to ambiguities in the maintaining of order, means that all people are in quest of a story to make sense of their lives. The modern philosopher Martin Heidegger perceived that living "toward" the boundary of death gives shape to life, and makes a story out of what are otherwise contingent events.[63] Characters in Shakespeare's plays seek for a story, or fail to make a story, or are awarded a story by survivors. Enobarbus in *Anthony and Cleopatra* is content to stay with his general, Anthony, even though he has growing doubts about the loyalty of Cleopatra, as long as he believes there is a story to be inhabited:

> Yet he that can endure
> To follow with allegiance a fallen lord
> Does conquer him that did his master conquer,
> And earns a place i'th' story. (3.13.44–48)

The one who "conquers his master" is fate, and so the story can be crafted in face of all forces of contingency and chance. When Enobarbus does abandon the story, feeling it has fallen apart, all that is left is to seek a ditch wherein to die (4.6.40). Hamlet, on the brink of death, bids Horatio to remain alive "And in this harsh world draw thy breath in pain / To tell my story" (5.2.332–33). Just before he kills himself Othello tells a little story of his past nobleness of heart ("Set you down this, / . . . that in Aleppo once . . ."), and commands his hearers to "relate" the events of "one who loved not wisely, but too well" (5.2.342), although Gratiano immediately doubts Othello's version of the story, commenting, "All that's spoke is marred." Romeo and Juliet are to be remembered less ambiguously: "never was a story of more woe / Than this of Juliet and her Romeo" (5.3.309–10), and Juliet is to be awarded a gold statue, evoking the story of one who was "true and faithful." Macbeth, on the other hand, has lost all sense of what his story might be: "It is a tale / Told by an idiot, full of sound and fury, / Signifying nothing" (5.5.25–27). We can hear echoes in Macbeth's despair of several biblical texts, such as the Psalter version of Psalm 90:9, cited in the Burial Service, "we bring our years to an end, as it were a tale that is told," and the Geneva version of Ecclesiasticus 20:18, "A man without grace is as a foolish tale which is oft told." But more general discourse in society also reflects the central place of story in life, such as the proverb "A good tale ill told is marred in the telling."[64]

Some stories, such as those in Shakespeare's last romances, are frankly fabulous, and—as Paulina tells us—"should be hooted at / Like an old tale." But they still seem to offer clues to the story we seek for ourselves, for as Paulina continues, "it appears she lives."[65] Moreover, it is important at the end of a comedy for the participants who have lived through the confusing events to tell each other—usually offstage—all the details of the story they may have missed, to have the opportunity "where we may leisurely / Each one demand and answer to his part / Performed in this wide gap of time."[66] Malvolio, though apparently excluded from the happy ending of *Twelfth Night*, must be pursued because there are wrinkles in the fabric of the story that only he can unfold: "He hath not told us of the captain yet" (5.1.374). Although there has been a denouement and truth has come to light, this is never enough, and there is a sense that the story continues even as it is being told.

I have already suggested that telling a story of love is one way in which death can be overcome; in the time they have left (which turns out to be minimal), Lear proposes that he and Cordelia, celebrating their renewed love, will tell tales from a God's-eye point of view:

> so we'll live,
> And pray, and sing, and tell old tales, and laugh
> . . . .
> And take upon's the mystery of things
> As if we were God's spies. (5.3.10–17)

How we might take a theological leap, and find that the story people seek is finally nothing less than a participation in the story of God, will be the task of the next chapter.

THE SHAPE OF THE STORY

Shakespeare makes clear that the story in which human beings play their part is neither simply comedy nor tragedy but a tragicomedy, showing us that comedy and tragedy are two views of the same universe.[67] If all stories remind us that we, the readers and audience, are in quest of a story for our lives, he makes clear that it is neither simple comedy nor tragedy. Reduced to their barest levels, a comedy has a happy ending and a tragedy has a sad one; we approve the ending of one, and regret the other, wishing it could have been otherwise. But our reaction to such drama as Shakespeare's is a mixture of feelings; the plays demand a perpetual and sometimes bewildering reorientation of "modes of attention."[68] Our response is like that of Duke Theseus when the inept players in A Midsummer Night's Dream promise him a "most lamentable comedy" (1.2.11) and "very tragical mirth": that, he replies, is "hot ice" (5:1.57–59), and yet the hot ice of tragicomedy is what Shakespeare is always offering us.[69]

In a comedy, confusion is the means of working toward a resolution in harmony and reconciliation, often marked by feasting, wedding, and dance.[70] It is what the Abbess of The Comedy of Errors names "a sympathized one day's error,"[71] which prepares the way for a baptismal celebration of new birth. As You Like It opens with a younger brother who complains that his elder brother is undeservedly treating him like the prodigal son of the Gospel parable,[72] and it ends with the elder brother repenting and joining the "fair assembly" of restored exiles, taking his story one step further than that of the biblical elder brother, of whom we are not told whether he joins the feast or not. Yet in the midst of joy, Shakespeare introduces a note of doubt; a shadow falls. Nearly always, for instance, there is someone excluded from the charmed circle of the dance; there remains an outsider who cannot or will not be reconciled, a witness to the darker strains of life which cannot be tidied away. There is Malvolio, vowing, "I'll be revenged upon the whole pack of you." The melancholy Jacques excuses himself from returning to the gaiety of the court, "to see no past-time, I." Shylock does not belong, despite his enforced baptism: "I pray you give me leave to go from hence."[73] Don John refuses to be integrated into the carnival of Messina, vowing, "I had rather be a canker in the hedge than a rose in his grace; let me be that I am and do not seek to alter me," and the very last line of the play promises he will be cast out with "brave punishments."[74] Like Caliban in *The Tempest* he remains testimony to the fact that some exclude themselves from human nurture. The dance is never complete, and its patterns are the poorer for those who are absent.

But there are other shadows too. Deep emotions have been aroused during the course of the action, and strains shown up in relationships which threaten to break out into new trouble in the future. Such couples as Claudio and Hero, Antipholus and Adriana, Jessica and Lorenzo, will need to be wary. Jessica's contribution to the "such a night as this" speech at the end of *The Merchant of Venice* seems only half-joking, characterizing Lorenzo as "Stealing her soul with many vows of faith / And ne'er a true one" (5.1.18–19). The silence with which Isabella twice meets Duke Vincentio's twice-offered marriage proposal[75] also does not bode well for their future life (if we assume they are to have one together),[76] while Don Pedro seems constitutionally unable to find his life's partner ("Prince, thou art sad—get thee a wife, get thee a wife!").[77] Above all in the comedies, the shadow of death presses in. Despite all the harmonies that art and music can give, the final boundary remains, giving urgency to passing time and bringing to nothing even "the great globe itself, / Yea, all which it inherit."[78] We are constantly reminded that death breaks the dance. We have seen that even in a farcical comedy like *The Comedy of Errors*, the ravages of time are underlined; the reuniting of a mother with her lost children seems like a new birth, but it cannot wipe out thirty-three years of birth pains and extended labor.

Conversely, we find that Shakespeare's tragedies end with a touch of triumph amid the dark. Death is presented there as the final disorder of life, the last enemy, yet it can be made to serve the promise of life, if it is approached in the right way. Tragedies end with a waste of life and expense of spirit that we regret. We wish that things could have been otherwise, though we have also been convinced by the progress of the drama that in practice they could not. The tragedy of Classical Greece highlights a sinful flaw, such as hubris, in an otherwise exceptional person, while medieval tragedy tended to emphasize the wheel of Fortune. According to accepted theory of tragedy, the plunging to disaster of an important person, such as a king, universalizes the tragedy and helps to release the emotions of pity and fear in the audience. In particular, we may say that watching the public death of a great human personality enables us to face up to the fact of our own death, which is likely to be insignificant and accidental.

Shakespeare's tragedy consists, not so much in a fall from greatness to disaster, as in a failure to live successfully in the tension between self and society. His tragic heroes are people who have a certain freedom over against their environment, in perceiving some truth or value which challenges custom. They have a vision of how things are which contradicts appearance and convention, and they create friction with their surroundings for a while; but they are unable to hold to the vision they glimpse, or to build anything substantial upon it. The love-tragedies provide the most obvious example of a conflict of values between hero and society. As in the comedies, the insights of love can penetrate beyond merely superficial appearance, but in the tragedies the protagonists fail to sustain them in face of the hostility of their society. The circumstances are unpropitious. Further, the love-tragedies exhibit a particularly intense form of this pattern of conflict; in a kind of swinging movement, the hero begins with a new vision which is at odds with his society, relapses back into the old perspective, and then attempts unsuccessfully to recover his former height of vision. It is the relapse that prompts the catastrophe, since the characters cannot live on two levels of worldview at once, and each destroys the other.

For example, when Othello woos and marries Desdemona, his love challenges the outward forms and conventions of his society. He is a Black African, a commoner and a soldier, while she is a white Venetian, and a sophisticated noble lady. Her father can only explain an act which seems to him "against all rules of nature" (1.3.101) in terms of witchcraft. The tragedy of Othello lies in his failing to hold to his intuitive perception of Desdemona, and relapsing into the prevailing view of his world; prompted by Iago, he accepts the verdict that the match is such an unlikely one that she is bound to betray him in the end, and he lets the outward evidence of his senses (the handkerchief) convince him against the inner knowledge of his faith. Judging that Desdemona's love for him is "nature, erring from itself" (3.3.231), he capitulates to the surface view of things expressed by Iago:

> Not to affect many proposed matches,
> Of her own clime, complexion and degree,

> Whereto we see in all things nature tends;
> Fie, we may smell in such a will most rank,
> Foul disproportion; thoughts unnatural. (232–37)

Well may Iago exult that Othello is "much changed" and that now, after his duplicity, "He's that he is," deceitfully adding that "if what he might, he is not / I would . . . he were" (4.1.270–72). Iago might as well have said, "He is not what he was," as he had said of himself earlier, "I am not what I am" (1.1.64). There is surely an ironic echo here of God's self-naming in the book of Exodus, "I am that I am,"[79] so that Othello's collapse into Iago's view of the world is effectively a denial of his own being.

Similarly, Romeo, from the perspective of his love for Juliet, begins by challenging all the conventions of his feuding society by tolerating the insults of Tybalt. But he loses his grasp on the new vision when Mercutio is killed, exclaiming: "O sweet Juliet, / Thy beauty hath made me effeminate" (3.1.112). He capitulates to the old vendetta between the houses of Montague and Capulet, kills Tybalt and so catapults himself into tragedy. From that relapse flows all the haste which brings them finally to the "dateless bargain with engrossing Death."[80] Juliet too has a reversion into old habits when she hears of the death of her cousin Mercutio, condemning Romeo as a "serpent's heart hid in a flowering face" (3.2.73), but she soon recovers her trust in their love, and her slip into conventional loyalties does not have any effect on the mechanism of the tragedy that is now in movement.

Likewise, Anthony begins with the intuitive vision of his love with Cleopatra in Egypt, claiming, "Here is my space," on whose biblical resonances I have already commented. But he betrays his vision when he swings back to Rome to recover the old values of political power, complaining that, "These strong Egyptian fetters I must break / Or lose myself in dotage" (1.2.122–23). The political bargain he makes by marrying Caesar's sister will mean tragedy when he swings back again to Egypt and Cleopatra, as he must. As Wilson Knight perceives about both Anthony and Cleopatra, there is "a strange seesaw motion of the spirit, an oscillating tendency, back and forth."[81] After the disastrous sea battle of Actium when Cleopatra retreats with her fleet, she dallies with Caesar's messenger, looking for a way out of her dilemma. But then she swings back to Anthony, protesting her love despite all appearances, and appropriately using the biblical imagery of the plagues of Egypt to underline her vows: if she is cold-hearted toward him, may she be—"together with my brave Egyptians all"—smitten by hail, afflicted by a plague of flies and suffer the loss of her first-born! (3.13.163–72).

So all these tragic characters oscillate from one side to another, "to rot [themselves] with motion."[82] They lose their balance, alternately asserting their freedom and capitulating to the limits of their environment. What is needed is not for them to ignore all limits in a confident freedom of vision; that would be the tragic pride of forgetting creaturely finitude.[83] What they fail to do is to keep the vision clear while taking account of their boundaries as they are. We cannot altogether blame them, for the pressures of their world make their fall practically inevitable. Yet death, when it comes, gives an opportunity to affirm the vision they have lost. At the very moment of catastrophe we find again in Shakespeare's plays the moving boundary between tragedy and comedy. Death is a waste, and yet there is a moment of triumph in it.[84] As Othello stabs himself, he recalls his valor in the little story of his smiting of the Turk, presents himself as one who loved "too well," and reasserts his love for Desdemona:

> I kiss'd thee ere I killed thee, no way but this
> Killing myself, to die upon a kiss. (5.2.356–57)

Thus, in the act of dying he affirms the values of valor and love that he had perceived beneath the surface and now admits that he has failed to live by. As the critic Helen Gardner puts it: "But the end does not merely by its darkness throw up into relief the brightness that was. On the contrary, beginning and end chime against each other. In both the value of life and love is affirmed."[85] Significantly Othello presents himself to posterity as one:

> Perplexed in the extreme; . . . one whose hand,
> Like the base Judean, threw a pearl away
> Richer than all his tribe. (344–46)

Shaheen cogently argues that we should read "Judean" with the First Folio text over against "Indian" in the First Quarto; in this case, Othello is recalling the biblical story of Judas, who in betraying Jesus threw away the "pearl of great price" (as in the parable of that name in Matthew 13:46) which was richer than the whole tribe of Judah, from which both Jesus and Judas came.[86] Then the kiss with which Othello dies evokes the kiss with which Judas betrayed Jesus (Matt. 26:49). The audience would have recognized this self-identification with Judas not as an assertion of villainy but as a sincere confession and repentance, indicating the return of Othello to his former noble self.

Similarly, Anthony and Cleopatra, while betraying their love for each other in life, attain fidelity to each other in death: now, claims Cleopatra

> I am marble-constant: now the fleeting moon
> No planet is of mine.

. . . .
The stroke of death is as a lover's pinch
Which hurts, and is desir'd. (5.2.238–39, 294)

Anthony, despite being lured to a premature suicide by the false report that
Cleopatra is dead—spread by herself—reclaims his vision of love in the last
moments of his life: "the long day's task is done" and all that is left is to lay "of
many thousand kisses the poor last" on Cleopatra's lips (4.14.35; 4.15.21). The
final affirmation of his virtue is made by others who employ a series of biblical images from the book of Revelation: for the guards he is the star fallen
from heaven (Rev. 8:10), and his death brings an end to all time (Rev. 10:16);[87]
for Cleopatra herself, he is like the angel of Revelation 10:1–5, his face like the
sun, his voice like thunder, and his legs bestriding the ocean. Echoing Revelation 14:15–16 in this catena of quotations, his generosity was like a harvest to
be reaped.[88]

Of course, we must get matters into perspective, as the Clown does at
Cleopatra's own theatrical death, remembering that he once knew a woman
"something given to lie," which is a similar judgment to Gratiano's on the death
of Othello. Dolabella joins the critics by responding to Cleopatra's question,
"Think you there was or might be such a man / As this I dreamt of?," with the
blunt answer, "Gentle madam, no."[89] Yet, since the tragic hero is to die, or had
died, nothing can really spoil the affirmation he or she is making, or others
make. Truly, if it were not for death's coming, the hero might betray the vision
again; Cleopatra would again "pack cards with Caesar," and Othello would let
jealousy "perplex" his reason, and Anthony would try to play power politics at
others' expense. But this is just the point: since death *has* come, it can be used
to fix the vision into a monument of art which will survive death itself.

With regard to Romeo and Juliet, Beatrice Groves has proposed that the
shared tomb in which they make their final pledges of love to each other is
presented on stage like the tombs in church which were decorated as if for
the sepulchre of Jesus on Good Friday, and which were used as the liturgical burial place of the consecrated host in the Easter ceremonies.[90] From
this "Easter sepulchre," the host would be raised out on Easter morning to
represent the resurrection of Christ. The embrace of Romeo and Juliet in
the tomb also suggests, Groves notes, an alchemical promise of death and
resurrection.[91] Groves makes clear that in the play any literal hope of resurrection remains "illusory," and the only afterlife of the pair is confined to
a golden statue. Yet this intertextuality with liturgy enhances the "comedic
form of the tragedy," in which "sacrifice itself is part of the comic matrix." The
lines between comedy and tragedy are blurred, and "through the Easter allusions Shakespeare maintains the viability of a happy ending."[92]

Death, we may say, can be used to defeat itself; the mutability of time is overcome in the moment of its apparent victory as death makes the story immortal. Whereas comedy acknowledges the threat of passing time and death, tragedy suggests that to die well, in a way that summons up those values by which one wanted, but failed, to live is to make death serve one. It is to find the "more things" that are present in excess and ready to be given.[93] It is to make a pattern and a story that will heal time itself.

3

Shakespeare's "More
Things" and Theology

✳

"A ʟʟ I Really Need to Know I Learned from Shakespeare." This subtitle
of a book by a serious Shakespeare scholar, Laurie Maguire, exemplifies a recent trend in the study of Shakespeare that another critic has dubbed
"presentism": this, he explains, is a form of criticism whose "centre of gravity
is . . . 'now' rather than 'then.'"[1] As Maguire testifies about her life in 1999: "I
broke my heart and had a delayed adolescence. My investments plummeted
and I went down with pneumonia. To cap it all, my cleaning lady threw out
the handwritten manuscript of my new book. . . . I read my way through the
entire self-help section of my local bookstore. And that's when I realised that
I had read it all before: in Shakespeare. . . . I had my very own life coach."[2] She
thus begins her book by asserting that "Shakespeare offers us strategies for
survival and success," and she goes on to write, "My father was dying; I read
Hamlet." In a similar vein, Stephen Greenblatt confesses that he wrote his
book *Hamlet in Purgatory* as a way of saying *kaddish* for, and laying to rest, the
"ghost" of his own dead father.[3] And he develops a critical theory of Hamlet
in which the play inherits the cultural function of purgatory as a means of
keeping the living in touch with departed, or maintaining contact between
the present generation and its predecessors.

The style of "presentism" has met with the criticism that it dissolves historical differences, and my own interest in Shakespeare is not in any kind
of "self-help guru" (to quote Maguire again). But this book is nevertheless
"presentist" in a modified kind of way, in exploring the way that Shakespeare's
text might help theologians in the present *to do* theology. This, I suggest,
takes historical difference seriously. As a basis for asking how living in a selection of Shakespeare's plays might shape theology here and now, I propose
each time to engage, in the first place, in the historical task of investigating
the way that the text of the plays *employs* theology. In both historical and

"presentist" concerns, a connection is being made with the way that theology has developed over the years, and so we find ourselves naturally in the area of intertextuality.

INTERTEXTUALITY AND THE AFTERLIFE OF A TEXT

In considering what is meant by intertextuality, I have so far limited our view to the play of texts that lies *behind* the construction of any text, in Shakespeare's case unpicking some of the network of references to the Bible and the Prayer Book, as well as to phrases circulating already in the "social text." This intertextuality gives Shakespeare material for making poetry, and for developing what I have been calling a "general spirituality." Now, however, with the help of formative theorists of intertextuality, we can consider what lies—to borrow a phrase from Paul Ricoeur—in *front* of the text. Ricoeur agrees with Jacques Derrida that stories and poems do not refer directly to the world around us; they are not mere imitations. But they do refer to the "real world," says Ricoeur, that is, to the world as it can be. The world of the text is referring to a world less "behind" than "in front of" the text.[4] For Ricoeur, human being is *possibility itself*, and out of this fecund capacity the imagination can create genuinely new possibilities which are not simply repetitions of the past and present; symbol and myth refer to a reality which is yet to come and which they help to create. "Fiction changes reality," maintains Ricoeur, "in the sense that it both 'invents' and 'discovers' it."[5] Similarly Ewan Fernie asserts, defending presentism, that "insofar as it is singular and creative, the Shakespearian text is also irreducible to history. And the creativity of literature is a concrete revelation of the possibility of change."[6] In this book we are concerned with what is to be "invented" (Ricoeur's term) by the plays of Shakespeare in one specific area: the making of modern theology. So theology can count itself among the recipients of the "more things" that are to come from a text which is open in meaning,[7] even as it explores what is transcendent, or the "more things" that are "excessive" to everyday existence.

Further light can be thrown on the way that texts from the past shape texts in the present from the thought of several theorists of intertextuality. Since, for Julia Kristeva, the text is a *practice* and *productivity*, its intertextual status means that it exists within the whole text of society and history. Any particular text displays an interweaving structure of words and utterances that not only existed before the text, but will *go on after* the moment of utterance, and so are, in Bakhtin's terms, "double voiced." If written texts are made up of fragments of the social text, then the ongoing ideological struggles and tensions which characterize discourse in society will continue to reverberate in the text itself over the years, and the text will also make its own impact on society and on other writers.

Kristeva thus understands intertextuality as a "permutation," or "transposition," of texts. Any text is a "translinguistic area" in which the speech-forms and sign-systems of different cultures are being constantly transferred and redistributed in a process to which there is no end.[8] This is a dynamic movement which is intensified in poetic texts—such as the work of Shakespeare—by the upsurge of deep-laid rhythms in the body, whose source is a prelinguistic, or "semiotic," state of drives and impulses in which the emerging consciousness is still embedded in the life of the mother, and which Kristeva names the *chora*.[9] This breaking out of the "semiotic" in poetry (as well as in the birthing of a child) disrupts and revolutionizes the "symbolic" order of social communication which is shaped by a patriarchal culture.[10] Kristeva thus contributes something totally original to the "intertextuality" discerned by Bakhtin, in addition to the word itself. The linguistic phenomenon is rooted in a psychoanalytic account of the growth of subjectivity, a crossing from early bodily life into the world of language. The disturbing entrance of the "semiotic" into writing in later life prompts and enables intertextuality as the exchange of texts which belong to different symbol systems.

Further, Kristeva picks up the element of the "carnival," or the "grotesque," that Bakhtin finds in the interplay of the many voices of a text. Just as the growing subject finds a "strangeness" in leaving behind the *chora* and entering a society characterized by symbols, so any writer finds the text she is writing grows strange to her as it becomes the place of transposition. There is a *signifiance* she does not intend, an "unlimited and unbounded generating process" which becomes a *jouissance*—an ecstatic, even erotic pleasure—for her.[11] With this idea of the "strange," Kristeva avoids the total death of the author: the text is still in some way connected with her but is no longer familiar or under her control. I suggest that this account generally accords with the working definition of intertextuality I offered in the first chapter: the interweaving of texts is both intentional and unintentional, and the unintended continues through the "afterlife" of the text in its social context as it is read and reread.

Roland Barthes builds on Kristeva's account of *jouissance* as "the pleasure of the text,"[12] and on *signifiance* as signifying what cannot be represented, but he extends them into the *total* self-loss of the author into the text. The afterlife of the text, beyond its authorship, is now everything. Picking up Kristeva's word "intertextuality," he understands it to mean that the reader of a text is also its writer. The text is made of multiple writings, entering into mutual relations in dialogue, but the place where this multiplicity is focused is not the author but the reader. "The birth of the reader must be at the cost of the death of the Author," he writes: "The reader is the space on which all the quotations that make up a writing are inscribed without any of them being lost."[13] Intentional borrowing or reference by an author is therefore of no interest at all in considering the "play" of the text: textual analysis "tries to say no longer *from where* the text comes (historical criticism) nor even *how* it is made (structural analysis) but how it is unmade, how it explodes, disseminates—by what coded paths it *goes off*."[14]

This interest in the "destination" of a text rather than its origin[15] finds a kind of apotheosis in the account of intertextuality by Harold Bloom. For Bloom, nearly every author is afflicted by an "anxiety of influence," an anxious awareness that his or her work is necessarily both an imitation and a mis-reading of precursors, together with a refusal to accept this state of affairs. Every text is "a relational event," and most authors are driven by conflicting desires: a desire to imitate previous texts, and the desire to be original and de-fend oneself against the knowledge that all one is doing is imitating previous writers.[16] This is true of literature in general, thinks Bloom, but particularly true of poetry, where the "meaning of a poem can only be . . . another poem," even if the new poet has never read the other poem.[17] "Source study is wholly irrelevant here," insists Bloom, since "primal" images and associations have sunk deep into the culture. In more recent work Bloom has made an excep-tion for several writers whose texts are certainly intertextual, but who are examples of "facticity"—that is, being of such originality that they are not afflicted by the same anxiety as most writers and can never be avoided by later writers.[18] In *Shakespeare: The Invention of the Human*, Bloom argues that Shakespeare is the most factitious writer in history, and we live out our lives in images and figures which originated in Shakespeare's work: "Shake-speare did not think one thought and one thought only: rather scandalously, he thought all thoughts for all of us."[19]

INTERTEXTUALITY AND THEOLOGY

Thus, in different ways, Kristeva, Barthes, and Bloom include within "inter-textuality" the way that a particular text both *contains* other texts and be-comes the *ingredient* for other texts in ceaseless interchange. My own study of the texts of Shakespeare is, however, more restricted than the widespread de-stabilization of meaning proposed by these critics. In difference from all three, but especially from Barthes and Bloom, I *am* interested in the historical ques-tion of how Shakespeare uses previous texts, and in particular the Bible, the Prayer Book, and doctrinal ideas of his time, in order to create poetic drama and to express what I am calling a "general spirituality." Of course, I recog-nize the truth of Barthes's perception that each reader "writes" or partially constructs a text's intertextual dimensions. In fact, the dialogue I am stag-ing between Shakespeare and theology means that theological insights and concerns make me, as a commentator, more sensitive to intertextuality with scripture and doctrine in Shakespeare than nontheologians would be, and so there is an unavoidable element of readerly construction. But I am still taking the risk of making some historical judgments about Shakespeare's intentions, while recognizing both unintentionality and the fact that there is an openness to the text which prevents our *confining* its meaning to what might be intended.[20] One reason for taking this risk might be that to make the reader the *sole* focus of intertextuality, as Barthes does, seems only to replace the divinity of the author with that of the reader.

There is another risk involved, too, in trying to write about what Shakespeare is doing with texts. The Shakespeare about whom I am writing is the kind of personage whom one critic, Jakob Lothe, has called "the implied author."[21] He is not a person I am excavating from historical documents other than the plays and poems themselves; I am not myself attempting any kind of biography of the Shakespeare of Stratford-upon-Avon, though I do not think it an impossible task, and some have done it well. The "Shakespeare" I refer to is the author implied by the work, the one whom we find by reading it. However, as soon as we appeal to this "implied" author's use of other texts, we are engaged in "context," and I have in fact already explored in my first chapter some of the ecclesial, theatrical, and generally social context of the period in an attempt to throw light on the intertextuality of Shakespeare's work. There is a necessary tension, then, between the "implied author" and "actual context," which has to be admitted. Perhaps we can resolve this slightly by proposing that the text implies an author who lives in a specified period, and this period can be examined with the tools of history and sociology; this is part of the author's identity as formed by the text itself, and it underlines the point made by both Jacques Derrida and Barthes that we cannot be certain about what is inside and outside a particular text.[22]

There is another way, too, in which I am not following the particular track laid down by Barthes. My interest in the creative engagement of a theological reader in the text of Shakespeare is not to make a playful and imaginative exegesis of Shakespeare from the viewpoint of the reader. It is rather to consider the way that reading Shakespeare might, in Bloom's sense of "facticity," make an impact on another text, and I mean the theological text. It is to place Shakespeare in the intertextuality of *theology* itself. As well as asking how Shakespeare is using theology, I am asking how the result of this inquiry might help to *make* theology. Following the insights of our three theorists of intertextuality, we must say that any theological text, including the one I am writing in this book, already has intertextual relations with the text of Shakespeare as it is embedded in Western culture. Any text of theology will be intertextual, and those intertextualities cannot avoid what Bloom calls the "facticity" of Shakespeare. It is an illusion to suppose, though some theologians do,[23] that Christian theology is a unique kind of "grammar" which gives rules for the speech of the Christian community, and that this is a "language-game" that is specific to that community, sealed as it were within its boundaries of meaning. Christian theology does indeed have the form of a grammar, although it is one that is porous to other grammars which function as rules in other communities and which interpenetrate each other. But beyond this existing state of inevitable intertextuality, I am proposing to make *new* intertextual connections myself in the course of this book. I am staging a dialogue in which intertextuality, in Kristeva's sense of "transposition," can happen.

In previous studies I have set out what I believe to be a fruitful method of "dialogue" between creative literature and the work of the doctrinal theologian.[24] There I have proposed a relationship of mutual influence without confusion where, first, doctrinal thinking can provide a perspective for the critical reading of literary texts, for, as E. H. Gombrich aptly puts it, "the innocent eye sees nothing."[25] Awareness of the historical development of doctrine can make the theologian sensitive to an intertextuality which may well be missed by historians and literary critics who have little theology. Further, without imputing religious intentions to the author where they do not exist, the attempt of theologians to achieve a coherent grasp of patterns of human experience can make readers sensitive to aspects of experience within and beyond a text of poetry, novel, or drama that they might otherwise miss in reading it.

Second in this dialogue, images and stories of literature can help the theologian to make doctrinal statements.[26] This claim may seem harder to justify: the two areas seem vastly different. Poetic metaphor and fictional narrative rejoice in ambiguity and the opening up of multiple meanings; doctrine, by contrast, will always seek to reduce to concepts the images and stories upon which it draws—including those within its own scripture. Literature emphasizes the playful freedom of imagination, while doctrine aims to create a consistent and coherent system of thought, putting into concepts the wholeness of reality that imagination is feeling after. Of course, doctrinal statements are bound to go on using symbol and metaphor since it is not possible to do without analogies in speaking of God as infinite and transcendent Reality. But doctrine uses metaphor in an attempt to *fix* meaning, to define and limit a spectrum of possible interpretations. In short, literature *tends* to openness and doctrine to closure.

It is thus easier to see how creative writing can *interrupt* doctrine, as Kristeva finds poetry disrupting the symbolic language of society by the "semiotic." Because no doctrine of God can be absolute or final, it needs to be constantly broken open by the impact of image and story in changing times and situations. My interest goes further, however, into the actual *making* of doctrine. How might this work? On the one hand, through the history of the development of doctrine alternative ways have emerged in which the multiple meanings of the metaphors and stories of faith can be fenced around by concepts; sometimes minority views have been violently discounted and dismissed as heresy. Reading poetry, novels, and plays can enable the theologian today to make choices between alternatives, and to listen to suppressed voices. Such judgments become possible because novels and plays such as Shakespeare's enable theologians to enter other worlds than their own, to extend their range of experience as they vicariously live other lives in a narrative which has "reconfigured" (as Paul Ricoeur puts it)[27] the time and sequence of their everyday life. In exalting Shakespeare as "the greatest of writers," Iris Murdoch notes that "the pages of Shakespeare abound in free and eccentric personalities whose reality Shakespeare has apprehended and displayed as something quite separate from himself";[28] readers, too, must learn to respect the "contingency" of "real character[s]" who are "not oneself."[29] In this new time and space, through multiple consciousnesses which are depicted in the story, theologians can test out what certain doctrinal concepts feel like if they are embodied in flesh and blood, and can trace out the consequences to which they give rise. At the same time, the theologian is exploring the way that the concepts of faith "correlate" with the concerns of human culture,[30] as expressed in the symbols and stories of art, and can assess the adequacy of these concepts for effective correlation. All this will enable a theologian to make choices between ways in which doctrines such as creation, redemption, and consummation may be formulated.

"Making" doctrine, on the other hand, exceeds choosing between existing alternatives, and here poetry has a particular effect. Poetry—and I include the poetic drama of Shakespeare—aims to compress a great diversity of human experience into a small span, and provides an intense opportunity for the theologian to immerse herself into alterity. It also offers a wealth of metaphors and similes which expose connections between objects and persons in the world, both revealing an underlying unity between different things and putting them together in new and unexpected ways. Metaphors both console and startle, having a vitality which, as Coleridge asserts, "dissolves, diffuses, dissipates in order to re-create."[31] Poetry alerts the theologian to the impact that metaphors make, both those which have a place in church tradition and those outside it, and it thus enables the theologian to create new ways in which metaphors can interact with concepts, and perhaps also to create new metaphors, opening long-established doctrines out to new meaning.

INTERTEXTUALITY AND REVELATION

For a theologian, the suggestion that the intertextuality of Shakespeare's poetic drama with theology can actually make *theology* (rather than, say, religious experience) is a particular kind of claim. The discipline of "theology" has a credal element within it. Theology, as distinct from much religious writing, is "God-talk," that is, a *deliberate* and conscious reflection on divine revelation which is received in the context of human history and diverse human culture, and which shapes the development of the Christian community.[32] In "revelation," Christian theologians think they are concerned with the self-disclosure of God's own being (God's word or self-expression), to which biblical writers respond in a human way in their own context, and which comes to a focus in the event of Jesus Christ. To stage meaningful intertextual interactions between theology and Shakespeare, literature outside the Bible must thus be associated in some way with divine self-revelation. I am suggesting that images and stories on the one hand, and concepts on the other, are all to be understood as *responses* to revelation. None are *identical* with revelation, for in revelation we are concerned with the self-opening of God's own life, not with the transmission of some kind of divine message or bundle of propositions or laws. Wherever God opens God's own self to draw human persons into relationship with the divine life, there will be response of varying kinds, including that of the imagination. Only this universal self-opening of God can justify for a theologian the making of intertextual connections between theology and other "writings" in our culture, of whatever kind.

We observe that in poetry, drama, and novel the imagination reaches out toward mystery, toward a reality for which we feel an ultimate concern, but which eludes empirical investigation. As Jacques Derrida proposes, the consciousness transcends itself toward something other than the world which it treats so often as an object to be dominated; it is open to something "other" which both promises and threatens to "come" into our present moment without ever being possessed.[33] With Kant, we might regard this movement toward the absolutely Other merely as a plumbing of the depths of our own feelings. But we might also regard this Other as the mystery of God, and think that our very capacity for self-transcendence is being prompted by the self-opening of the mystery to us. As Paul Tillich expresses it, we have ultimate concerns because what is ultimate—God as Being itself—is already participating in our existence. We are already seized and held by a "spiritual presence," so God is in our asking of questions about meaning as much as in the answers.[34] Symbols thus open up a way into a final reality which is already present in our experience, though in a hidden way.[35]

Similarly, Karl Rahner observes that the human spirit appears to have a natural openness to the infinite. A person experiences himself or herself as a "transcendent being," able to go on asking questions endlessly about existence: "the infinite horizon of human questioning is experienced as a horizon which recedes further and further the more answers man can discover."[36] In fact, however, Rahner maintains that this openness to mystery can never be separated from God's own openness to us in gracious self-communication. The movements of grace and nature are always bound up together, so that God's offer of God's self to us is prior to all human freedom and self-understanding.[37] To be a person is actually to take part in "the event of a supernatural self-communication of God." There is a theological perspective here upon the sense of mystery which we articulate in image and story: the work of the creative imagination is one kind of response to revelation.

There is, then, a universal revelation giving rise to a knowledge of God which is nonconceptual and nonobjective; Rahner identifies this as "transcendental" revelation, a "pre-apprehension" (*Vorgriff*) of God which happens in the human orientation toward mystery. By contrast, there are also moments when the self-giving of God takes form in historic events and gives rise to deliberate concepts (what Rahner calls "categorical" revelation).[38] Some events "stand out" as decisive moments of disclosure, insisting that they be noticed and calling for a whole reorientation of life from the participant. They also demand conceptualization in an attempt to understand them. At the center of particular revelation like this, Christian theologians find the decisive revelation of God in the life of Christ and the historical events surrounding it, a moment in whose light all other revelations are to be interpreted.

All creative writing, since it is concerned with human experience, is occupied with themes that also occupy Christian faith and theology. The movement of the human spirit toward self-transcendence is bound to overlap with the theological understanding of the human spirit as being grasped by transcendent reality.[39] As long as we do not pretend that a secular writer is actually making the jump from one dimension to the other, then the Christian perspective upon revelation allows a theologian to interweave *any* writer's use of metaphor, symbol, and story into those from the Christian tradition, together with the Christian concepts which (as we have seen) are used to organize and limit them. In the case of Shakespeare, there is a deliberate spirituality in the text which a theologian will interpret as response to revelation; such a response can also be found in the Bible with which Shakespeare is in intertextual relation, and in the theology which is being made in a complex intertextual network with Shakespeare and the Bible.

The Bible and Other Texts

The text of the Bible thus stands in relation both to texts of creative literature—in this case, plays of Shakespeare—and to texts of theology; the intertextuality is multivoiced, since texts of the Bible which are taken into Shakespeare have already been enlisted into a dialogue with theology, and texts of Shakespeare that can help to shape theology are already in relation to the Bible. To understand this complex interplay, we need to think theologically about the relation of scripture to other texts in the world.[40]

In his essay "How Is Christianity Thinkable Today?" (1971), the Jesuit philosopher Michel de Certeau challenges the idea that scripture provides any unified and self-contained authority. He has in mind those who claim there is a "world" of scripture that absorbs the everyday human world into itself and simply shapes it from within the particular space of the text.[41] Rather, every form of authority in Christian society—whether scripture, tradition, or councils—is "stamped by the absence of that which founds it," and so the founding event of Christ gives rise to a plurality of authorities, leaving behind a "multiplicity of signs, a historical network of interconnected places, rather than a hierarchical pyramid."[42] In this network of texts, which is interconnected but not unified, the plural is maintained and "differences permit the other." In the New Testament each writer of a text, for example, offers a distinct treatment by speaking in his own way of faith in the dead and risen Jesus. This plurality of narratives is increased by interaction with the reader, which undermines attempts by any authority to own the "letter" of the text.[43] Widening his gaze beyond the intertextuality of scripture itself, Certeau finds that scripture also exists in a world of many narratives: "From morning to night, narrations constantly haunt streets and buildings. . . . Captured by the radio (the voice is the law) as soon as he awakens, the listener walks all day long through the forest of narrativities from journalism, advertising, and television, narrativities that still find time, as he is getting ready for bed, to slip a few final messages under the portals of sleep."[44]

Certeau's stress on alterity, and his resistance to unitary authority, are characteristic of the circle of late-modern thinkers in Paris of which he was a part from the 1960s onward, and among whom ideas of intertextuality emerged. Indeed, we can begin to understand the relation between the one text that is regarded as Holy Scripture within the Christian tradition, and the many other texts in the world, if we consider the way that the self always reads signs in the world through empathy with *others*. In his reflections in *Oneself as Another*, Paul Ricoeur perceives that an authentic encounter with a text occurs when the reader meets with another person through it, and reads the text *through other eyes*. In general, he affirms, we only come to understand ourselves by understanding others, by internalizing other people, their stories, and the signs they present us with.[45] This is also true of reading texts: "hermeneutics is thus, explicitly or implicitly, self-understanding by means of understanding others."[46] Later in his book, Ricoeur confesses that, writing strictly as a philosopher, he recognizes an "aporia of the Other" in which "philosophical discourse comes to an end"; engaging with the other (and we must assume that he includes an encounter with the other through written texts), he can neither assert, nor deny, that he is confronting the Other who is "the living God."[47]

Taking up Ricoeur's insights, we may say that, reading the Bible, we meet with other persons through the text, and read with their eyes. Christian theologians will want to add that through these human authors of scripture we are faced by the address and summons of an infinitely Other. But if we find this to be true of reading scripture, it *must* be the case, in some way, of all texts. When we read as another, seeing with their eyes and hearing their voices, we can suddenly find that we are addressed by an infinitely Other. The "aporia," or impasse, to which Ricoeur draws attention cannot be restricted to a single text, and there are several reasons for this. The first is the nature of revelation itself: if revelation is the disclosure of a self-revealing God, as I have suggested, then this God must be free to unveil the divine self (or utter the divine word) wherever God wills, and this means through a variety of textual media.[48] Second, as Ricoeur himself stresses elsewhere when he is writing a deliberately religious essay, the referent of all textual worlds—including scripture—is God, who is "at once the coordinator of these diverse discourses and the vanishing point, the index of incompletion, of these partial discourses."[49] Third, if the "other," including the "other" we meet in literary texts, is understood in an ethical way as making an *unlimited* demand upon us and upon our responsibility for others, then—as Emmanuel Levinas insists—we touch at least a trace of the "infinitely Other" in and through all others, and in all "faces."[50] We recall here the meaning of spirituality offered by Ewan Fernie, who discerns in Shakespeare's plays a spirituality of being confronted by "others" in a way that challenges a materialistic status quo.[51]

Yet for all this, a Christian theologian will claim a unique place for the Bible, an inclusive uniqueness within a wider field. This is the body of written material most closely connected with the life of Jesus and the birth of the early church, whose own scriptures were the Hebrew Bible, and this is the compound text which has shaped the life and practices of the Christian community most intensively through the ages. Early theologians drew limits by creating a "canon" of sacred texts, and yet I suggest that this very establishing of frontiers is what enables intertextuality. In the first place, the edges create a textual space, within which the reader or hearer can discover places of the self-disclosure of God. But then the boundary of a canon invites comparison of this particular text with literature beyond its frontiers. The enclosure of a certain area of material by a community should not result in reading it in *exclusion* from other texts, but always in reading it in *relation* to others. The notion of canon obliges us to bring it into conjunction with other territories. It is as if *all* writings are near neighbors, as if all lie on the immediate further side of the boundary, and their proximity cannot be ignored. In Certeau's understanding of the Christian canon of scripture, its internal differentiation and plurality open it to other later texts which multiply its meaning beyond the control of ecclesiastical authorities: "If the corpus of the testament is closed (i.e. limited) it is because it has to allow, *outside* of itself and after itself, other compilations: patristic, liturgical, theological and so forth, which will become multiple and often more and more different. The 'closing' of the New Testament makes such differences possible and even preserves the necessity of such differences."[52]

However, Certeau is apparently referring here only to other texts within the Christian church. He views the "limit" of the Christian community and its canon as a sign of "lack" (echoing Jacques Lacan, of whose psychoanalytic seminar de Certeau was a member),[53] and this is a recognition that there are "unknown spaces" beyond the church's own narrative resources which have no connection with its own space. My proposal is rather different—that the limit of the canon precisely *links* it with all other texts in the world-archive. Derrida perceives that every text is potentially connected with every other; its "hymen," or boundary, always opens its inside to the outside, and to a universal "grafting" of one text onto another (whether a text written on a page or on a body).[54] The Christian claim for scripture is that, in the myriad ways of interconnecting the different members of the world-archive of texts, the canonical text is always to be included where this involves the flourishing of human life. Until quite recently this has in fact been the position of the canon of the Hebrew-Christian scriptures in Western culture; it has been, in the words of William Blake, "the great code of art," the text by which all creative works are to be interpreted.[55] David Ford writes that a Christian wisdom (*sophia*) is always in dialogue with the text of scripture, and that a sapiential approach to exegesis means that "nothing can be ruled out as unrelated to scripture and its understanding—no people, experience, history, culture, event, institution, sphere of knowledge or religion. How they might figure in the process of the Spirit leading into all truth is not predictable. . . . The confidence is that the Word is already involved with them."[56]

A church theologian will nevertheless give a certain privilege to canonical texts. While she is obliged to bring them into contact with other texts, she is also committed to exploring them internally for herself. The identity of a community is shaped by owning and transmitting a certain, defined body of material, and especially significant narratives;[57] thus members of the community have an obligation to engage with it. They cannot ignore it. The boundary marks out an area, sets up a space, in which investigation is required.

With regard to the Christian community, as long as people count themselves part of it, they have a demand laid upon them to read, interpret, and wrestle with its canon in a manner that no other texts ask from them. It is *not* an obligation to accept the words of the writers of scripture as correct or infallible; it is to enter into relation with them. It is to stand where they stand, to attempt to enter with empathy into their "otherness," and to hear the word of God in company with them. To some extent this will be an experience of what John Macquarrie calls "repetitive revelation,"[58] or what Barth identifies as the "contingent contemporaneity of the Word,"[59] where the self-unveiling of God in the past is reactualized in the present.

In his frequent references to the Bible, Shakespeare is participating in this common practice of members of the Christian community; it is simply part of their identity to engage with their scripture. Shakespeare himself then becomes a text from which Christian theologians will gain an enrichment of their theology. This is a web of intertextuality that is created by revelation, and by the multiple interconnections between the Bible and other texts that is the source of "more things in heaven and earth" than can be contained in any dogmatic system.

Text and Trinity

Above I cited the comment of Ricoeur that God is the "coordinator" of diverse discourses in the world. In the light of the theological approach to intertextuality I have been developing, I want to add "coauthor" and "cocreator." Christian theology has traditionally affirmed that God is author of the whole physical text of the world. Augustine envisaged a book of nature alongside the Bible,[60] and confessed: "you have stretched out the firmament of your book 'like a skin,' that is your words which are not mutually discordant," and that in the heavens "there is testimony to you, 'giving wisdom to infants.'"[61] A modern theological view will want to ascribe a coauthorship of the text to created beings, understanding that God as the only "uncreated creator" gives a radical freedom to others to be "created creators" of the universe. Through written and social texts, human beings respond to the self-disclosure of God, and the physical textuality of the world has been shaped by the activity within it of animate beings, whether or not human, responding to or resisting the creative spirit of God.[62] Christian theology will conceive of God as the coauthor of the text of the world, in the sense of being the one who initiates creativity, while being fully aware that "author" is a metaphor.

In any written text, the human author is both absent and present. While the author has absented herself from her work by producing the artifact of a text, she remains present within it to a limited extent, insofar as it exhibits her intentions as the author. But this intention has to be related to the internal authority of the text itself, and to the interpretation which the reader brings to it. It is an "intentional fallacy" to suppose the meaning of a text is exhausted by, or even subordinate to, the purpose of the author. Some who have developed theories of intertextuality, such as Barthes, have stressed the absence of the author to the point of excluding her presence and intentions altogether. The author is completely banished from the text; it no longer belongs to her but only to itself and to us who read it. A more nuanced view, such as Kristeva presents, hears the voice of the author as still present in the text, but estranged, diffused through a collection of signs which require to be given meaning by others. Ricoeur thus maintains that writing "frees itself" from its author, but offers the clarification: "Not that we can conceive of a text *without* an author; the tie between the speaker and the discourse is not abolished, but distended and complicated."[63]

Considering the relation between God as author and world, Derrida takes a leap of empathy and puts himself into the mind of Levinas, who—unlike Derrida himself—wants to continue to speak of God and not simply of an absolute "Other." If we *were* to do this, Derrida maintains, then it would be better to think of God primarily as *writer* of a world rather than *speaker* within it (as Levinas does), since this divine Other must be absent: "The writer absents himself better, that is expresses himself better as other, addresses himself to the other, more effectively than the man of speech. . . . The thematic of the trace . . . should lead to a certain rehabilitation of writing. Isn't the 'He' whom transcendence and generous absence uniquely announces in the trace more readily the author of writing than of speech?"[64]

In a moment I want to affirm Derrida's image of "*writing* the world," but Christian theology will question his insistence on absence. With human authors we must certainly say that they are present and absent from their texts at the same time. With regard to God as author, however, we cannot speak of a duality of presence with *absence*, since a Creator must indwell creation in a more immediate way than any artist does her painting, sculpture, or book.[65] Theology must think rather of God's *hidden* presence. God is always present, but hidden even as God reveals God's self, veiled at the same time as unveiled.[66] God is present in the world through signs, filling them to bursting with the divine glory, so that they seem infinite, unfathomable, and inexhaustible. But the Creator remains hidden within them, veiled as well as unveiled, because they are still finite and created things. As Hans Urs von Balthasar puts it, "no appearance of God is more overwhelming than this non-appearance."[67]

Now, Christian theology has a set of images for thinking of this presence of God in the textuality of the world, in a way that affirms physical signs and enables created beings to become authors and creators of the text themselves. It is called the doctrine of the Trinity.[68] This ancient formula, first developed by the Church Fathers, refers to "three persons (*hypostases*) in one essence." They did not intend to speak of three "persons" in the modern sense of three self-conscious individuals, as if asserting that these were also, by some paradox, one individual being as well. This would fall into the trap of making the being of God a mere projection of finite being, even if at the top of an ontological tree (what Heidegger dismissed as "ontotheology").[69] Rather, they aimed to speak of a divine life which was rich in relationships and which escaped literal description. By *hypostasis* the Fathers meant a "distinct reality" which has being, and the *hypostases* were entirely characterized by being in relation with each other and the world that God had created. Athanasius, for example, responding to the skeptical Arian question as to what the difference could be between the persons if they were one in divine essence (*ousia*), gave an answer using a different kind of vocabulary: the Father is "other" (*heteros*) in that he alone begets the Son, the Son is "other" in that he alone is begotten, and the Spirit is "other" in that he alone proceeds from the Father.[70] These realities are different in the way that they are related to each other, notably in their origin. This doctrine of relations was taken up by the Cappadocians in the East—who spoke of paternity, filiation, and spiration (begetting, being begotten, and being breathed out)—and by Augustine in the West.[71] Trinity then is a vision of God as three interweaving relationships of ecstatic, outward-going love, giving and receiving.

However, I suggest that we should go even further in the direction of a relational understanding of God than this, and think of the "persons" in God as not simply *formed* by their relations, but as *being* no more and no less than the relations themselves.[72] The *hypostases* are "distinct realities" *as* relations, and the *perichōrēsis*, or "co-inherence,"[73] in which they have communion is an interweaving of relations. This idea was already hinted at by Augustine when he declared that "the names, Father and Son do not refer to the substance but to the relation, and the relation is no accident."[74] Aquinas then gave formality to the notion with the term "subsistent relations," stating that "divine person signifies relation as something subsisting. . . . [R]elation is signified . . . as hypostasis."[75] We can, however, free the idea of subsistent relations from its Neoplatonic and Aristotelian settings in Augustine and Aquinas. Taking a clue from Barth's insistence that "with regard to the being of God, the word 'event' or 'act' is final,"[76] we may speak of God as an event of relationships, or three *movements* of relationship subsisting in one event. Focusing on relations rather than personal agents who *have* relations takes us from an ontology of substance to one of event. This does not mean that the final reality of God is *reducible* to relations, which remain, of course, an analogy for God, drawing language from human relationships we know; the point is that the metaphor "person" can only be understood as a relation, and that this is the most appropriate language that we have for God.

With this perspective, talk of the triune God ceases to be a language of observation and becomes one of participation. For of course it is not possible to visualize, paint, or etch in glass three interweaving "relationships" without any personal agents who exercise them. We cannot "see," even in our mind's eye, three movements of being which are characterized by relationship. But then this ought to be a positive advantage in thinking about God, who (as Kant pointed out with regard to *noumena*)[77] cannot be an object in the world. Talk of God as Trinity is not the language of a spectator, but the language of a *participant*. It only makes sense in terms of involvement in the complex network of relationships in which God happens. To refer to God as "Father" thus does not mean to represent or objectify God as a father-figure, but to *address* God as Father, and by using this invocation to enter into a movement of a relationship which, by analogy, we can say is like a relationship between a son and a father. The Christian practice of prayer is one place where this participation comes alive. The cry of "abba, Father" in prayer fits into a movement of speech like that between a son and a father; our response of "yes" ("Amen") leans upon a filial "yes" of humble obedience,[78] glorifying the Father, a response which is already there.

At the same time, we find ourselves involved in a movement of self-giving like that of a father sending forth a son, a movement which the early theologians called "eternal generation" and which has its outworking in the mission ("sending") of the Son by the Father in history to achieve the reconciliation of all things. In this moment we discover that these movements of response and mission are undergirded by movements of suffering, like the painful longing of a forsaken son toward a father and of a desolate father toward a lost son; here Jürgen Moltmann speaks of God as "the event of Golgotha" and to the question, "can one pray to an event?" rightly answers that one can "pray *in* this event."[79] These two directions of movement, sending and response, are interwoven by a third, as we find that they are continually opened up to new depths of relationship and to the new possibilities of the future by a movement for which scripture offers impressionistic images—a wind blowing, breath stirring, wings beating, oil trickling, water flowing, fire burning. The traditional formulation that the Spirit "proceeds from the Father through the Son" points to movement which renews all relations "from" and "to" the other. In the language of the New Testament, we are praying to the Father, through the Son, and in the Spirit.[80]

Thus, through our participation, we can identify three distinct movements which are like speech, emotion, and action within relationships "from father to son," "from son to father," and a movement of "deepening relations." They are mutual relationships of ecstatic, outward-going love, giving and receiving. Actively they are such moments as originating, responding, opening; passively they are moments of being glorified, being sent, being breathed. So far in describing them I have followed the form of address that Jesus himself taught his disciples, "Abba, Father" (Matt. 6:9), offering the image "from son to father" for the movement of response that we lean upon. But these movements of giving and receiving cannot in themselves be restricted to a particular gender, as is quite clear with the images for the movement of Spirit. They must also, in appropriate contexts, give rise to feminine images; for instance, the nature of our participation may require us to say that we are engaging in a flow of outward-going relationships like those originating in a mother (cf. Isa. 49:14–15),[81] or like those which characterize the response of a daughter to a parent, or a woman to a lover. There is a long Jewish and Christian tradition in which God's outward expression of wisdom is like a woman (wisdom, *hokmah*, *Sophia*), going forth into the world from the being of God.[82]

A theology of participation in God now enables us to think of the relation between the world-as-text and its uncreated creator. It has the form it has because it exists in God, in the flow of relationships of love that we name as "persons." Materiality is shaped and impressed by the divine movements of relation, and it is sign-bearing because it shares in movements of being which are eternally self-expressing and self-interpreting. As the theologian Eberhard Jüngel puts it, God is always speaking the truth about God's self and interpreting God's self: "The doctrine of the Trinity is the interpretation of God's self-interpretation."[83] According to the symbol of the Trinity, a "Father" eternally sends out a "Son" from his being in the power of the Spirit; this is a story about the self-expression of God, about God's speaking out a word of creative love and costly reconciliation. In this Word, the "Son," God interprets *what God is* as creator and redeemer of the world. All signs in the world exist in this act of divine self-communication, of divine signing. All human interpretation of signs exists in this act of divine self-interpretation. Interpretation is, in fact, one mode of response to the self-disclosure of God which, as we have seen, characterizes all written texts.

There will be a variety of metaphors which theology proposes for participating in the sign-giving flow of God's life. As supreme mystery which cannot be known as we know an object in the world, it is not possible to talk literally about God, but it is quite consistent to think that all metaphors point to a reality which is of "ultimate concern" to us,[84] and that some metaphors and analogies are more appropriate than others for this situation. "Flow" and "movement" are themselves metaphors, and another is "voice," which has traditionally been associated with the image of the Logos, or "Word." Derrida is opposed to giving any priority to voice in the interaction between self and others, as he thinks it encourages the idea of a projection of the self in order

to dominate others. He criticizes Christian theology for having privileged
the image of voice, with the result that a theology of "mediation" has been
developed in which the spoken "Word" of God becomes a mediator between
a purely spiritual realm of being and the world of matter.[85] God, according
to Derrida, is therefore detached from physical signs, as a "transcendental
signified" floating free from the world of signs, present even when there are
no signifiers, and self-excluded from the semiotic chain in which the signified
becomes a signifier in turn.[86] If (like Levinas) we insist on referring to God,
then for Derrida voice should be replaced by writing: "our writing, certainly,
but already His ... starts with the stifling of his voice."[87]

But there is no need to "stifle" the image of the voice. If we envisage a textual world as existing in God, then we are rejecting any idea of a cosmic "mediator," such as was developed in the "Logos doctrine" of the early Church
Fathers,[88] and we are replacing it by "participation." Many metaphors for the
mutual participation of God and the world will then be valid, including—but
not prioritizing—the voice. Human participation in the interweaving relations of God might be imagined as a sharing in plural voices of conversation,
an image stressed by Oliver Davies in his work *The Creativity of God*:

> The nature of the sign as referring is held ultimately in the act of Trinitar-
> ian address: signs only refer because they are part of a world which is itself
> constituted as the issue or outflow of an act of communication between
> God and God. God as Trinity is therefore implicated in the very ground of
> the world. As one who speaks, who enables speech, and is himself spoken
> of, God moves at a central point in human history. The Eucharist is the
> making present in the everyday of that redemptive inhabiting of the text of
> the world by the divine voice, as Author of that world.[89]

However, there is no need to privilege voice over text as Davies tends to do.
Voice is only one metaphor for the movement of self-giving in God; voice is a
form of pattern of relations, but it is only one pattern. Using Derrida's image,
the shaping of materiality by God's creative action can also be envisaged as
"writing" a text, while the text can be continually "revoiced" by the presence of
God in it, and not least by the voice of the Jesus of history as preserved in the
Gospels. Here the metaphor of a drama becomes appropriate, since a written
text is revoiced in the theater; the sharing of created beings in the life of God
can thus be envisaged as the immersion of the drama of human life into the
drama of God. As Hans Urs von Balthasar affirms, "It is a case of the play
within the play: our play 'plays' in his play."[90]

The Christian symbol of the Trinity is thus not only a further theological
validation for the intertextuality of the world, alongside the phenomenon

of revelation and the contiguity of the biblical text to all texts. It expresses the theatrical experience of participation, about which Stanley Cavell writes in his study of Shakespeare's *The Winter's Tale*. Reflecting as a philosopher that knowledge is an uncertain venture, he finds that Leontes comes to know the truth of the situation—that there is a life beyond the limits of his own life—not by observation but through "participation" in the awakening of Hermione.[91] Moreover, Cavell reflects that this is a mode of knowing in which we as the audience are being called to share: "A transformation is being asked of our conception of the audience of a play, perhaps a claim that we are no longer spectators, but something else, more, say participants."[92] The theology of the Trinity I have been outlining means that this experience of being drawn into the drama of a play is not merely an *analogy* for human participation in God. When a play exposes the spirituality of love, justice, and forgiveness (as in Shakespeare), to participate in its action is actually to be drawn more deeply into the life of the triune God, as a "play within a play."

God's Commitment to Text

Concepts of "pan-en-theism," or "everything in God," are often dismissed by theologians as too easily lapsing into pantheism (everything as God). But the "trinitarian panentheism" I am proposing guards against this. Everything exists in God only because God is an event of triune relations, and so there are always relations of love and justice that are wider, more capacious, more generous than our own relations. This is the spirituality of "excess," or of "more things," that we can discern in Shakespeare, though there it is without any dogmatic content. For theology, the experience of "excess" is finding oneself in a "force-field" of relations that cannot be reduced to human relations.[93] Participating in the triune God means discovering "more things" that support human flourishing, because there is always "more" in the relations that characterize the divine life. Again, this is well expressed by Balthasar, whose theology is about "the sheer exuberance of the 'always more' which is God."[94] For Balthasar, human existence is a mystery just because "wherever there is some actuality, the knowing mind stands before a gift that no amount of reflection can thoroughly digest and systematize." There is an "excess transcending all we can grasp by conceptual analysis" because there is "an eternal 'more' belonging to every being."[95] This endless self-giving of beings is grounded in the ecstasy of the triune God, in whose mutual and out-going relations there is infinite gift.[96]

We may see room, then, in this kind of panentheism for degrees of engagement in the "more" of God. In everyday life we participate in relations with others at different levels of intensity, and this analogy can help to interpret our participation in God. Everything, by its very existence and creation, exists in God: through God's own desire to be a creator, God makes room for it to dwell within the divine *perichōrēsis* of relations. But this dwelling is not homogeneous. Created things and beings will have different capacities for depths of relation, with animate beings having a greater capacity than inanimate objects, and conscious beings having even more possibilities. Moreover, among conscious beings, there will be opportunities for persons to engage more deeply, aligning themselves with patterns of love and justice, that some will take and others will neglect. Here is the space for responding to the self-disclosure of God that I have suggested is characteristic of the creative imagination, and being drawn into a "play within [God's] play" will provide other moments when persons can travel deeper into God's life.

Hans Urs von Balthasar locates even deliberate human rejection of God within the network of divine relations. Since, he argues, "there is nothing outside God," there is only one place where the human "no" to God *can* be spoken, and that is—ironically—within the glad response of the divine Son to the Father. The "no" is a kind of "twisted knot" within the current of love of the Son's response. So Balthasar writes, "The creature's No, its wanting to be autonomous without acknowledging its origin, must be located within the Son's all-embracing Yes to the Father, in the Spirit."[97] The drama of human life can only take place within the greater drama of the divine life. "The creature's No," Balthasar affirms, "resounds at the 'place' of distinction within the Godhead"[98]—that is the difference between the persons in God, to which we shall shortly return.

I conclude from God's commitment to textuality that we can only know these transcendent relations (always in "excess") through immanent relations in the physical world. Participation in the relations of the Trinity undermines any concept of God as the kind of "transcendental signified" opposed by Derrida. The triune God cannot be a remote mind that stands beyond the signs in the world and their differences from each other. Talk about God as Trinity begins from encounter with God in the world. We can only experience divine relations in and through the multiple relations we find in the world, whether human or in the wider context of nature. In the present, Trinity-talk begins from Christian practices such as prayer, and from engagement in the lives of others. In the memory of the church it begins from a person, Jesus, who is fully open in trust to God his Father in a responsive life, that becomes revelatory of the love of God as it is seen to fit uniquely into patterns of relation in God. His life refers to a "signified" which in turn becomes a signifier, offering signs upon which human sign-creating relies.

There can thus be no God as Trinity other than the one who opens the divine *perichōrēsis* of relations for human beings to participate within it. In creation and redemption God opens space within the interweaving of movements of relation, so that the created universe exists "in" God, immersed into the flow of divine love. There is no way of getting "behind" this God who is disclosed to us as one who desires to be a creator and author,[99] and who is thus inseparable from the text of physical creation. God, we may say, is committed eternally to writing text, and voicing the text. Being inseparable does not mean being identical: it is still God's own desire and will as the only uncreated reality to get this process of writing started. But this being God's intention, there is no "before" in the choice since, as Barth tells us, God *is* what God wills to be, and "God does not will to be Himself in any other way than He is in this relationship to us."[100] We may conclude (though Barth is not so definite) that God is no "transcendental signified," if this means existing and being present even when there are no signifiers.

Late-modern theories of textuality propose that the signs which make up texts have their meaning through being in relation to other signs, and particularly in a relation of "difference." Inventing an example, we might say that the meaning of the signifier "book" is not established by any similarity of the sound "book" or the shape of the word "book" on the page to the actual physical appearance of a book. It is established through its difference from such signifiers as "newspaper" or "magazine" or "DVD." Taking its origin from the structuralist work of Ferdinand Saussure,[101] this focus on difference has become more radical in our late-modern period, making the securing of meaning into an endless open process.[102] From a trinitarian perspective, the world with its complexity of signs exists within a communion of love in God which is entirely characterized by difference. Aquinas thought that, although there might be a kind of "conceptual commonness" in the word "person" when applied to the *hypostases* of the Trinity, the particularity of each person in relation to the others meant that there could be no "real commonness."[103] Karl Rahner thus suggests that for Aquinas the single word "person" is only a stopgap, as it were; one really needs the three different words "Father," "Son," and "Spirit" to do justice to the difference between the distinct modes of being in God.[104]

Heribert Mühlen rightly considers this difference in the context of love, observing that in human relationships we only become truly close to someone when we experience the other person as different from us. As our encounter with someone deepens, we become more and more aware of the uniqueness of the other, and only from the awareness of this difference from ourselves can the relationship take on a new depth of nearness. So by analogy in God, who is perfect love, Mühlen suggests we may say that: "The distinction of the divine persons, in so far as they are distinct modes of being, is so great that it could not be conceived of as greater, while their unity is so intensive that it could not be conceived of as more intensive."[105] That is, the modes of God's being are so closely united with each other that they must be infinitely different from each other. Hans Urs von Balthasar similarly suggests that "God as the gulf of absolute love contains in advance, eternally, all the modalities of love, of compassion, and even of a 'separation' motivated by love and founded on the infinite distinctions between the [persons]—modalities that may manifest themselves in the course of a history of salvation involving sinful humankind."[106] In the difference between the persons, in the distances between the movements of love, there is the "eternal more" which is reflected in the excess of "glory" which shines out of each created form. But at the same time, there is also room to take in the painful experience of relationlessness in death. God can enter with empathy into the human experience of the breaking of relations because God lives in relationships which have a difference and otherness about them.

For Derrida, the Christian symbol of the Trinity denotes a circular, harmonious rhythm of suffocating closure.[107] With Robert Magliola, I suggest that Derrida could have taken Trinity as "difference" more seriously.[108] The Trinity, Magliola argues, is constituted by "negative or relational differences" as "a God of perpetual alterity."[109] But because this is a difference within relationships of love, the Christian vision of dwelling in God offers a blend of closure and openness, in contrast to the sheer openness of meaning in much late-modern thinking.

STAGES OF AN INTERTEXTUAL HERMENEUTIC

If all texts are held in the interweaving relations of a triune God, then there is bound to be intertextuality, since all texts are connected finally in God. Moreover, in the way that the borders of a particular written text create its particular character and yet at the very same time link it with other writings in the world, we may find an analogy with the human body. Both written text and body are networks of signs; both have boundaries which bestow an individual identity and create a density of meaning within their enclosures; and in both the boundaries also open and connect this identity with others. As Merleau-Ponty puts it, the body is about touching and being touched, about being "enfolded" in a kind of embrace which has no horizons, and where the divisions between our body and that of others collapse.[110] Through the body we participate in the widest possible space, and engage in self-giving relations with others rather than protecting our own boundaries. While this is an analogy between text and body, it is more than an analogy, since the body is itself a text on which society inscribes its habits and demands.[111] Further, from a trinitarian perspective, these text-bodies are also interconnected in the widest context of the relational life of God.

On the one hand, then, our discussion of text and Trinity provides a sustained justification for the intertextual project of drawing on the plays of Shakespeare to make theology, which is a particular kind of "presentism." But more than this, as the following chapters map the connectedness of the plays of Shakespeare to the Bible, to other religious texts of his time and to the making of Christian theology today, we can see that there is the same dynamic at the heart of both intertextuality and spirituality. There is an openness to the "other" which challenges the mere status quo of materialism and every kind of oppressive, unitary authority. This "otherness" and "difference," I have argued, is grounded in the very life of God in which all texts are held and shaped. There are always "more things" to come from a text because there is always "more" in the otherness *of* God and *within* God.

In presenting the eight plays that follow, I will thus cover the following three stages of an intertextual hermeneutic, explained successively in the first three chapters of this book, and indicated earlier in my working definition of intertextuality. First, in commenting on the plays, I shall trace biblical and other religious texts which lie "behind" the Shakespearean text (expanding chapter 1). Second, I will discern a "general spirituality" which Shakespeare seems to be commending (expanding chapter 2). Third, I will move "in front" of the text to suggest ways in which reading a Shakespearean text might help us to make Christian doctrine today (expanding chapter 3). At all three stages—which I do not intend to take in a strict sequence, and which are in fact interconnected—there are always "more things" than can be contained in any system of thought or religion.

4

A Midsummer Night's Dream
and Seeing with the Eyes of Love

＊

IN HIS famous diary, Samuel Pepys recorded the following in September 1662: "[I] went to the Kings Theatre, where we saw Midsummer Night's Dream, which I have never seen before, nor ever shall again, for it is the most insipid ridiculous play that ever I saw in my life. I saw, I confess, some good dancing and some handsome women, which was all my pleasure."[1] We might be inclined to say that Pepys was not seeing clearly, since all he could see was dancing and some good-looking women. It seems that seeing things properly is not at all straightforward. Indeed, this is what Helena says in the play about love:

> Love looks not with the *eyes*, but with the *mind*,
> and therefore is wing'd Cupid painted blind. (1.1.234–35)

In Renaissance iconography, Cupid was depicted wearing a blindfold, because love's sight does not depend upon the senses;[2] there is a kind of see-ing, a kind of perception which transcends the evidence of the senses and reason, and even seems to contradict it at times. These are the eyes of the *imagination*, which Pepys apparently lacked, and perhaps the most important kind of such inner sight is the seeing of love.

LOOKING WITH THE EYES OF LOVE AND THE LIMITS OF REASON

In preparation for her image of blind Cupid, Helena explains what she means about love-sight:

> Things base and vile, holding no quantity,
> Love can transpose to form and dignity. (1.1.232–33)

"Beauty is in the eye of the beholder"—or more exactly, the eye of the be-
holding lover. To see with the eyes of love, the eyes of the heart, may appear
to be going blindfold as far as the eyes of the senses are concerned. The rational person certainly thinks so. Duke Theseus, the preeminent man of reason
in the play, disparages this kind of imaginative sight; when Hippolyta comments, "'Tis strange, my Theseus, that these lovers speak of," Theseus replies:

> More strange than true. I never may believe
> These antique fables, nor these fairy toys.
> Lovers and madmen have such seething brains,
> Such shaping fantasies, that apprehend
> More than cool reason ever comprehends.
> The lunatic, the lover and the poet
> Are of imagination all compact. (5.1.2–8)

Theseus and Pepys would, it seems, have agreed with each other's theater
criticism. But there is no reason why we should think that the Duke is right,
however wise a ruler he might be (and the play gives us cause to find his limits); indeed, his bride-to-be, Hippolyta, immediately contradicts him, asserting that the lovers' story witnesses to more than "fancy's images" and "grows
to strange constancy." Shakespeare is constantly concerned with the theme of
appearance and reality: he knows that what is real often does not appear on
the neat surface of reason.

In fact, the play opens with a problem that reason, even the Duke's reason,
cannot solve. Duke Theseus of Athens is looking forward to his marriage, in
four days time, to Hippolyta, Queen of the Amazons, whom he has defeated
in battle, and with whom he now hopes to make peace in bed. There comes
before him Egeus, a prominent citizen of Athens, with a complaint: Egeus
wants to marry his daughter Hermia to a young man, Demetrius, who is in
love with her. But she is refusing him, being in love with Lysander, who is
not favored by her father. Egeus requests the Duke to give judgment, that
either she must obey him or by the Laws of Athens must die. Hermia pleads,
"I would my Father look'd but with my eyes" (1.1.56). The Duke replies in
similar terms: "Rather your eyes must with his judgement look," but as she
cries later to Lysander, "O Hell! to choose love by another's eyes" (1.1.140).

These appeals to the "eyes" in the opening scene herald a play which is satu-
rated with references to the visual: eyes, images, pictures, looks, and gazes.[3] It
is clear right from the outset that this is a play about seeing properly, which
means seeing with the eyes of love and not merely cold reason. Now, the per-
vasive imagery of "eyes" in the play has a biblical ring to it. The Hebrew Bible
contains several hundred examples of phrases which invoke the eyes, many

of which have now passed into common speech: for instance, "doing what is right in one's own eyes," "finding grace/favour in your eyes," "lifting up eyes," "being hidden from your eyes," "eyes being enlightened," "eyes being opened," "your eyes shall see," "what is pleasing in your eyes," "eyes being darkened," and "eyes consumed with grief." In other plays of Shakespeare there are numerous usages of these biblical "eye" phrases,[4] and while in this play none of his references to the eyes seem to be such *exact* quotations, the biblical resonances drive home the need for true sightedness. Later, when Puck lets magic flower-juice "sink in apple of his eye" (applying it to Demetrius's eyes), there is a definite echo of Psalm 17:8, "make me the apple of your eye," the phrase "apple of the eye" also appearing in four other places in the Hebrew Bible (Deut. 32:10; Prov. 7:2; Lam. 2:18; Zech. 2:8). Shaheen notes that the phrase was probably being used in daily speech by Shakespeare's time, but he judges that most people would still have become familiar with it through reading the Bible.[5] Though he does not mention this, if the memory of the Latin Compline lingered on after Compline and Vespers had been joined together to form Evening Prayer in the English Prayer Book, then people would also have been acquainted with the phrase "make me the apple of thine eye" from the antiphons. Among these biblical references to eyes, we shall come in due time to the most important for Shakespeare's spirituality, the direct quotation (or misquotation) from 1 Corinthians 2:9–10 by Bottom: "things that eye hath not seen . . . God hath prepared for them that love him."

It is possible that the classical reference of Cupid's being depicted blind would have reminded Shakespeare's original audience of a significant scriptural reference to spiritual blindness—Jesus's rebuke of the Pharisees in the Fourth Gospel when they had criticized him for healing a blind man on the Sabbath: "And Jesus said, I am come unto judgement into this world, that they which see not, *may* see: & they which see, might be made blind. And some of the Pharisees which were with him, heard these things, and said unto him, Are we blind also? Jesus said unto them, If ye were blind, ye should not have sin; but now ye say, We see: therefore your sin remaineth" (John 9:39–41). As Cupid is blind as a sign that he sees with the eyes of love, so if the Pharisees had *admitted* they were blind, they would not have been guilty of failing to see spiritually. The religious leaders—like Theseus, and perhaps Pepys—were far too confident that they could see. This Gospel scene and conversation seems to have been in Shakespeare's mind, since he makes explicit reference to it in another play from this early period of his writing. King Henry VI is presented with a man, supposedly born blind, who claims that his sight has now miraculously been restored. The king comments that "by sight his sin be multiplied" (2 *King Henry VI*, 2.1.74), echoing the words of Jesus, "now ye say, We see, your sin remaineth." Henry probably means that seeing will provide the occasion for greater sinning, though the comment turns out to be truer than the king expected: it transpires that the man has only been feigning blindness and so the healing of his sight.

Faced with the brave constancy of Hermia's love-sight, or her "fantasy," as Theseus calls it, Theseus is able to do nothing else but administer the laws of Athens; reluctant though he is, his reason is bound by the law, and all he can do in this impasse is to take the gentler sentence the law ordains; if in four days Hermia has not consented to her father's choice, she must enter a nunnery for the rest of her life and give up any ideas of marriage at all. Her answer is to be given on Theseus's wedding day, and so the whole direction of the plot moves toward the marriage celebration. It is clear that Shakespeare wrote this play for entertainment at a real marriage ceremony (probably in 1595, possibly one where Queen Elizabeth herself was present),[6] and the play celebrates the fulfilment of love in marriage in a more concentrated way than in any other of the comedies.

Theseus's harsh judgment prompts a sequence of images from Hermia which relate sight and love in a way that evokes the biblical text more profoundly than echoes of eye-phrases. When Lysander comments on the change in her appearance—"why is your cheek so pale? / How chance the roses there do fade so fast?"—Hermia replies that she will remedy the watering of the roses by "the tempests of her eyes" (1.1.131), leading to the exclamation, "O hell, to choose love by another's eyes!" (140). This hell is, she continues, the cross of love:

> If then true lovers have been ever crossed,
> It stands as an edict in destiny.
> Then let us teach our trial patience
> Because it is a customary cross,
> As due to love as thoughts, and dreams and sighs (1.1.150–54)

The traditional "cross" of fate from which "star-crossed" lovers[7] suffer ("O cross!," 1.1.136) is here transformed into a cross of patience which is "due to love," neatly fusing at least two biblical references. The "customary cross" recalls Jesus's warning that his followers would need to bear a cross "daily": for example, "If any man will come after me, let him deny him self, and take up his cross *daily*, and follow me" (Luke 9:23).[8] There is an echo of the "customary cross" also in *Richard III*, 3.1.4, "our crosses on the way." The "patience . . . due to love" recalls "Love suffreth long" in 1 Corinthians 13:4,[9] and perhaps the patience of Job (Jas. 5:10–11). The scriptural allusions create the sense that seeing with the eyes of love is a costly business, involving sacrifice. In the conversation between Lysander and Hermia at this point, Lysander laments that before one can see ("Ere a man hath power to say 'Behold'") mutual love in its brightness and vitality—called a "sympathy in choice" which is "quick" and "bright"—darkness has blotted it from sight (1.1.141–49).

Reason at the beginning of the play cannot find a way through the crisis provoked by the imaginative sight of love. Reason, is, it appears, forced to do what is inhuman and wasteful—banishing a young woman to a nunnery. Now, this inner perception of love can, however, go badly astray. The vision of love can be irrational in a *positive* manner, going further into reality than reason can; but it can also be irrational in a *destructive* manner. So far is Theseus right when he distrusts the "tricks of strong imagination." Intuition can err, and it does so with Demetrius, and also with Helena and Titania, all of whom I shall come to in a moment. The eye-imagery of this first scene makes us aware of this double-sidedness of love-sight, since the Renaissance image of blind Cupid is ambiguous; while Neoplatonists found it to be a symbol of a higher love than the material, others read it as a sign of love's notorious unreliability.[10] In the same speech where Helena celebrates love as seeing not with physical eyes but with the mind, she also laments:

> Nor hath Love's mind of any judgement taste:
> Wings and no eyes, figure unheedy haste.
> And therefore is Love said to be a child
> Because in choice he is so oft beguil'd. (1.1.236–39)

The three, Demetrius, Helena, and Titania, have fallen into a disorder of the intuition of love: they are all in the state of "doting," as Shakespeare puts it.[11] Demetrius, before he saw Hermia, had paid vows of love to Helena, a childhood friend of Hermia. Again, eye-imagery appears when we learn that he now dotes "on Hermia's eyes";[12] we believe that indeed Helena is his true love and that his attachment to Hermia, though favored by her father, is a wild aberration. Helena laments the disorder caused in her former friendship with Hermia by his behavior, again using images of eyes: while "my ear should catch your voice, my eye your eye," this is no longer the case ever since Demetrius has treated Hermia's eyes as "lodestars" (1.1.183, 188).

In loving Demetrius, Helena is certainly not doting; but she is doting when she chases after him, losing all her dignity, clinging to his legs like a pet dog. When love is not returned, it is clearly disordered behavior to go on clinging, crying, "I am your spaniel, and Demetrius, / The more you beat me I will fawn on you." Prompted by her hopeless infatuation with Demetrius, Helena tells him of Hermia's plan to elope with Lysander to escape the Duke's judgment. Lysander and Hermia have fled into the wood nearby Athens in order to make their way to refuge. Demetrius, mad with love for Hermia, follows them; and Helena follows Demetrius. So Shakespeare gets the two couples into the essential wood where magic is to happen.

There are others, too, with a disturbed love-vision in this (somewhat over-crowded) wood. As well as the human lovers there are Titania, the Queen of the Fairies, and her consort Oberon, the King of the Fairies, who have come separately with their fairy retinues to bless the house and the bed of Theseus at his marriage. They have come separately, since they are at war with each other, Titania having forsworn Oberon's "bed and company." The cause of the quarrel is that Titania is keeping for herself a little Indian (changeling) boy whom Oberon wants to make a Knight in his own retinue. There is the strong hint here that Titania's attachment to the boy is a disorder of love, an obsession: "She perforce withholds the loved boy / Crowns him with flowers and makes him all her joy" (2.1.26). But *both* Titania and Oberon seem ob-sessed with the boy in a less than healthy way.

THE CONFUSIONS OF COMEDY AND THE HEALING OF DISORDER

So the first major theme of the play—the eyes and the vision of love—is sup-plemented by a second theme: order and disorder. The situation is disordered at the beginning of the action, before any of the comic confusions which are to delight the audience have yet happened. The wood is still fairly quiet: but things are already upside down in the world. As with all Shakespeare's com-edies, the play begins with things out of harmony: here there are disorders of reason *and* of the imagination.

For an Elizabethan, order was the supreme desire at every level of the cosmos—in the individual life, in the state, in the universe.[13] Disorder at any level bred lack of harmony everywhere: here it is not only the lives of the lovers and the fairy couple which are out of joint—the brawling of Ti-tania and Oberon has had cosmic repercussions: "contagious fogs," an angry moon, flooded rivers, strong winds, mud everywhere, and an alteration in the very seasons themselves have meant that "The fold stands empty in the drowned field," and crows have grown fat on sheep who have died of disease (2.1.90–105).[14] We have already noted in Ulysses's speech about order echoes of the Homily "Concerning Good Order,"[15] and here there is an extensive reversal of the Homily's statement that "The Earth, Trees, Seedes, Plants, Hearbes, Come, Grasse, and all maner of Beasts keepe themselues in order."[16]

It is the technique of Shakespearean comedy to heal the disorders of life through further disorder: through comic confusions, mistakes, deceits, dis-guises and mistaken identities, disorder is turned into order. It seems that the only way to restore harmony is to make everything *more* confused; the movement is disorder through extra disorder to order. We might ask why it is that the confusions of comedy have a healing function: probably it is because confusion breaks open the surface of things. Like an explosion it blows open the surface appearance and so forces the participants—and with them the audience—to look beneath for the reality which is there. As the philosopher and novelist Iris Murdoch put it: "Philosophy aims to clarify. . . . Literature is full of tricks and magic and deliberate mystification."[17] Human relationships, human personalities are too complex for surface investigation: comic confusion turns things upside down and mines deeply below the surface for the truth. The art of comedy confuses things, because only through this confusion can one clearly see the truth that the situation was wrong all the time, and the way to put it right.

Usually in Shakespearean comedy, the healing confusion is a matter of change and mistake of identities. Either somebody pretends to be somebody else—for example, Viola in Twelfth Night assumes the identity of a page boy, and Portia in Merchant of Venice disguises herself as a lawyer—or a false identity is thrust upon somebody else. Somebody is made to play a role. Benedict and Beatrice in Much Ado about Nothing are fooled into playing the role of lovers to each other, because each is told by their friends that the other is dying for love of him/her; so they play the role of lover out of pity (they say). In the complex "gull" of As You Like It, Rosalind assumes the appearance of a young shepherd, Ganymede, and in that role persuades Orlando to woo her by pretense, as if she were Rosalind. These exchanges offer a dense and ambiguous exploration of sexual identity and relations: in the last case, a boy (the actor) is playing a girl (Rosalind) playing a boy (Ganymede) playing a girl (Rosalind).[18] In Midsummer Night's Dream, the participants are not tricked into playing a role: they are magicked into it. The role is thrust upon them (not very expertly) by the use of magic juice.

The person dispensing the magic chaos here is Oberon. One day, he says, he happened to see Cupid miss his mark with one of his bow-shots and saw where the arrow fell:

> It fell upon a little western flower,
> Before milk-white, now purple with love's wound;
> And maidens call it "love-in-idleness." (2.1.166–68)

He commands his servant Puck, a mischievous goblin, to fetch the flower, explaining that its juice "on sleeping eyelids laid / will make or man or woman madly dote / Upon the next live creature that it sees."[19] Love-potions are usually drunk, but this one is applied to the eyes, continuing the chain of imagery about seeing. While Titania is asleep, he streaks her eyelids with the juice, so that she will madly love the animal she "sees" when she awakes—lion, bear, wolf, or bull. This is not just revenge on Oberon's part: he thereby hopes to heal what he regards as her possessive fixation upon the Indian boy. However, we may observe that he fails to notice his *own* obsession with the same boy, and so it is not surprising when things go wrong. What Titania does see when she awakes is—as all the world now knows—Bottom the Weaver in an ass's head.

Bottom and his "fellow-mechanicals," or manual labourers, have entered the wood (extremely crowded as it is) to find a quiet spot to rehearse a play which they hope to present before Duke Theseus on his wedding day. They are preparing to do, in fact, precisely what Shakespeare himself is doing with this play for a noble household. Puck gives Bottom an ass's head as being, he thinks, most appropriate for his character. His fellow guild members/actors run away in fright at his transformation, but he considers they are only doing this "to make an ass of me." Singing to keep up his spirits in the eerie wood, he awakens Titania, who greets him "as wise as you are beautiful" and enlists all her fairies to garland him with flowers, stuff him with grass, and scratch him in the right places—for an ass. So by magic Titania is made to play the role of lover to an ass, and Bottom is made to play the role of an ass (or would have been, were he not one already). They have been propelled into a parody of the kind of transformations Ovid writes about in his *Metamorphoses* and Apuleius in his tale of *The Golden Ass*, probable sources used by Shakespeare, and their hilarious confusion thus has a dark, bestial disorder within it: as Leonard Barkan puts it, Bottom "has had an experience simultaneously beastly, human and divine."[20]

Distressed by the scene Oberon overlooks of Helena chasing a reluctant and increasingly angry Demetrius, he commands Puck to use up the rest of the flower-juice by "anointing" the eyes of the now sleeping Athenian, who is lying in the wood with the exhausted Helena nearby. So, he plans, Demetrius will love Helena again. Yet another biblical resonance surely inheres in this command of Oberon's to "anoint" the eyes of the disdainful Athenian youth (2.1.161). This would be an odd term for what is portrayed as the *dripping* of a liquid, but it becomes entirely appropriate when we recall the command of Christ to the Laodiceans in Revelation 3:18 to obtain "salve to *anoint* your eyes so that you may *see*." Demetrius is intended to see Helena with a true love-sight.

But Puck finds the wrong Athenian: Lysander and Hermia have been asleep together in the wood, lying at such a chaste distance from each other that when he wakes up, Lysander sets eyes first upon Helena and is consumed with love for her. Puck, with a little advice from Oberon, hastily tries to rectify his mistake by anointing the eyes of Demetrius as well, with the consequence that when he sets eyes on Helena on awakening, he is consumed by love for her. Helena, who before had no men at all after her, now finds herself hotly pursued by two. Hermia had gone to sleep wildly loved by two men: she wakes up to find that Helena is now the center of attention and nobody cares for her at all. Most hurtfully, Lysander, her own true love, now seems to hate her. Helena is in fact no better off than she was, for she is convinced that the two men have made an agreement to mock and humiliate her by *pretending* to love her.

Bottom's Eyes

So the theme of love's inner sight, supported by imagery of the eyes through the motif of the magic juice, is closely bound to the technique of comic disorder. The irrationality of love is made *more* irrational. Those who began by "doting" on somebody (Titania on the boy, Demetrius on Hermia) have ended up in a more extreme, even fanatical form of dotage. The disordered imagination has been deepened. The confusions run deeply into that intuitive, subconscious area where love-sight operates, so that when Bottom finally awakens from his nightmare he is right to think that the dream was a profound one. He expresses his sense of the mystery of the night in a wonderful bungling of St. Paul: "The eye of man hath not *heard*, the ear of man hath not *seen*, man's hand is not able to *taste*, his tongue to conceive, nor his heart to report what my dream was. I will get Peter Quince to write a ballad of this dream; it shall be called 'Bottom's dream' because it hath no bottom" (4.1.209–12). This speech brings to a climax all the previous references to eyes, and all the previous biblical allusions, with its muddled declaration: "the eye of man hath not heard." The original disorder came from the eyes and it has been deepened through the eyes, as anointed by the love juice. But through that very disorder comes healing. Bottom is right to think his dream is a deep one. Somehow he feels that the confusions of his dream have had ultimate meaning, if only he could work out what it was. John Joughin comments that "Bottom's initiation into the world of the spirit forgoes the conventional criteria for 'knowing'; it is unrepeatable ('no man can tell what'), absolutely singular." There is a "transfiguration" of the world of the senses; something new is happening, "threading together the *aporia* of the embodied and non-embodied, the visible and the non-visible," resulting in a theatrical performance of "hidden visibleness."[21]

St. Paul had actually written: "As it is written,[22] the things that eye hath not seen, neither ear hath heard, neither hath come into man's heart, are, which God hath prepared for them that love him. But God hath revealed them unto us by His Spirit, for the Spirit searches all things, yea, the deep things of God" (1 Cor. 2:9–10). This translation is from the revised Geneva translation of the Bible, and the Bishops' Bible translates similarly, while being slightly closer to Shakespeare in its phrasing, "the eye hath not seen"; Shakespeare could have known either, or both, of these readings. But the earliest edition of the Geneva Bible published in 1557 followed Tyndale's translation prepared by Thomas Matthew (1537) in reading the last phrase as "the Sprite searcheth all things, yea, the *bottom* of Goddes secretes," and although this was changed in all subsequent editions to "the deep things of God," it is possible that—as some scholars have argued—the "bottom" wording lingered on in popular jokes.[23] Shakespeare's audience would then have relished his own version of the joke that "it shall be called 'Bottom's dream' because it hath no bottom." At the same time the dream is truly bottomless, since "it is itself without foundation or prior fixity and yet . . . 'unfathomably profound.'"[24]

Bottom's quotation, or misquotation, from the Bible is, on the one hand, part of a series of biblical allusions that simply give Shakespeare material for his dramatic poetry. Bottom, as Frank Kermode points out, is being portrayed as a "wise fool," such as Paul celebrates in 1 Corinthians 3:18:[25] "If any man among you seem to be wise in this world, let him be a fool, that he may be wise." The eye-imagery allows Shakespeare to develop the plot of tensions and confusions between the characters. But the intertextuality also expresses what I have been calling a "general spirituality," of which I have identified the first element as the priority of love over institutions and social organizations. Capping all the previous references to seeing with the "eyes" of love, Bottom awakens the hearer to a kind of seeing and knowing which is more far-sighted even than imagination. After all, imagination itself can become distorted. Shakespeare thus hints that there is a healing which is deeper than dramatic comedy, and a love which is more profound even than human love. It is a spirituality in challenging the merely material, and in arousing a sense, and bringing to embodiment, an "other" which cannot be contained within objective forms of knowing.[26] Reflecting on the speech of Bottom, Joughin urges that the experience of play encourages us "to learn to live together, exploring the boundaries of blissful boundless love," offering us a taste of "the invention of the wholly other."[27] Theseus speaks more truly than he realizes in referring to the "poet's *eye*" as bringing forth "the form of things unknown."[28] Hamlin further makes the acute comment that: "Bottom's experience could be said to be even more transcendent than the one described by Paul. In Paul's description, the mysteries of God's love are beyond anything the eye has seen or the ear has heard; in Bottom's description, his dream goes beyond what we can conceive, let alone experience, since we simply cannot imagine eyes hearing, ears seeing, or hands tasting. Bottom's dream is extrasensory."[29]

It is a dream, and a spirituality, of *love* first because it reflects on an ecstatic experience which is highly erotic while also strangely religious. Second, the

Pauline text declares that the mysteries it invokes are "prepared for those who love" God. But there is another dimension of intertextuality here. The widely read Renaissance text *The Praise of Folly* by Desiderius Erasmus, which existed in an English translation at the time of Shakespeare, ends by citing this very text of 1 Corinthians 2:9–10.[30] Erasmus here claims that the spiritual experience of being granted a foretaste of "eternal felicity" in heaven, or being "ravished" by the Spirit of God, is a kind of madness ("sweet rauying"…"a certaine passion muche lyke vnto madnesse"). This state he then associates both with love and a dream. Plato, he asserts, "didde euin than dreame of suche a thyng, whan he wrote, *that the passion and extreme rage of fervent louers was to be desired and embrased, as a thing above all others most blissfull.*"[31] Again, such an experience was granted to holy men "as it were through a cloude, or by a dreame."[32] The implication is that there is not only a similarity, but a basic affinity between the two states of knowing divine mysteries and love.

This is a spirituality of love which challenges not only materialism, but human authority, as Hermia had done by appealing to her "eyes." It is significant that in the verses immediately before Paul's appeal to what "eye hath not seen" he declares that the "princes of this world" had failed to see the true vision of glory (1 Cor. 2:7–8): "But we speak the wisdom of God in a mystery, even the hid wisdom, which God had determined before the world, unto our glory. Which none of the princes of this world hath known: for had they known it, they would not have crucified the Lord of glory." While Louis Montrose finds that this is being read as a political statement, since it is Bottom, a manual worker, who has had the "rare vision" rather than the figures of power who appear in the play,[33] I suggest that—if indeed this verse is in Shakespeare's mind—the stress falls more on the priority of love over established structures of power. Moreover, the Pauline text prompts us to think that there is a parallel to the confusions of comedy, or tragicomedy, within the Christian story itself. In both drama and Christian theology, the healing of human eyes issues from confusion, but perhaps the theological account is even more ironic. As St. Paul puts it, the rulers of this age did not understand the wisdom of God, and so (humanly speaking) they were confused and made a terrible error in crucifying Christ. Nevertheless, God has used the situation to bring about human transformation, and so, while the wise of the world count the cross as folly, God has "made the wisdom of this world foolishness" (1 Cor. 1:20).

LOVE'S KNOWLEDGE

So far I have been exploring the intertextuality of Shakespeare in terms of what he himself is doing with his art: he is using religious images and echoes for dramatic purposes, and he is thereby opening up a general spirituality. But in considering the scope of intertextuality theoretically, I have suggested that Shakespeare's text might be allowed to shape the texts of theology today, "in front" of the texts of the plays. St. Paul, in 1 Corinthians 1–2, declares that a new knowledge of the way things are develops out of human confusion, and—in the imagery of *A Midsummer Night's Dream*—this is a seeing with the eyes of *love*. It is love's knowledge. As Joughin comments, Bottom's vision contradicts the "conventional criteria for knowing"; there is a startling epistemology, whose logic is one of a "surplus economy." In this, while "nothing is untranslatable (there is always more)," yet at the same time "the true nature of the sharing or communion in question remains secret."[34]

Entering the embodied space of the play, the theologian will thus be enabled to explore the particular kind of knowledge which love is. Embedded deeply in the Christian tradition is the connection between *scientia* (knowledge) and *sapientia, or sophia*—the latter being a "wisdom" which is rooted in the love of God.[35] Philosophers such as Martha Nussbaum have similarly insisted, though from a nontheistic perspective, that love is not merely an emotion but a kind of knowledge. Nussbaum stresses that love is not an unthinking movement, a tide by which we are simply pushed around. As an analytic philosopher she understands this knowledge as "evaluative cognition" of what and whom a lover loves—we evaluate, reckon the worth of one we love, and so love is knowing.[36] But she notices that this can lead to problems—among them the desire to satisfy our own needs at the expense of others and attempts to master and control the love-object. Somehow, she thinks, elements of wonder and compassion must enter love's knowledge.[37]

Late-modern philosophers, such as Jacques Derrida and Emmanuel Levinas, have alerted us even more acutely to the problem that knowledge easily becomes domination. In knowing others we want to make them part of the total universe that revolves around us, to treat them as mere objects of our subjective minds. "Seeing" the world becomes a matter of controlling it.[38] But as we enter the play-space of such dramas as *Midsummer Night's Dream*, we find that we are experiencing a blend of loving and knowing which blocks all attempts to objectify the other, and this is precisely because this love's knowledge is open to mystery. It is a seeing with which "no eye has seen," a translation into words of an experience which remains secret. In making theology, this can lead the theologian to develop the kind of doctrine of God in which God is never objectified, since with God, it is always a question of "What no eye has seen, not ear heard."

Kant set theology a challenge when he pointed out that *noumena*, such as freedom, God, and the subjective self, could not be known like other objects in the world. God cannot be known as an *object* of perception, since

God is not a phenomenon in the world to be presented to the understanding through the senses. For Kant this meant that God could not be *known* at all, but that religion could nevertheless provide a motivation for moral action and moral struggle, with the *postulation* of a God as the supreme moral lawgiver of the universe.[39] The making of theology after Kant was the story of trying to deal with Kant's challenge in ways that did not reduce religion to morality, though theologians were quick to insist that they had themselves for many years insisted that God could not be placed under any category by which objects in the world could be classified. One powerful answer to Kant in the twentieth century was provided by Karl Barth, who accepted that God could not be an object of *human* knowledge, yet asserted that through God's self-revelation, human beings could share in *God's* own knowledge of God's self. According to Barth, the symbol of the Trinity tells us that God knows God's self as an object—the Father knows the Son through the Holy Spirit—and so God makes God's-self an object to us.[40] "As knowledge of faith," Barth assures us, "the knowledge of God is just like any other knowledge in that it also has an object." But since this object is "the living Lord of the knowing man," then "Certainly we have God as an object but not in the same way as we have other objects." We do not, for instance, "have God at our disposal." God "posits himself" as the object and "always gives himself to be known."[41] Thus, knowledge of God is always "bound to the Word of God," and this word is Jesus Christ as the act of God's speaking.[42] In the becoming-flesh of God in Christ, God finally lowers God's self to be known in time, and is known in "creaturely objectivity" in the world.[43]

Barth is surely right that all knowledge of God, and indeed all theology, depends on participating in God's own self-knowledge. He also makes the important point that *when* God unveils God's self through taking material objects in the world as a place of encounter with us, at the same time God must remain veiled, as no object in the world can contain or fully express God. Revealing is re-veiling; the wisdom of God is "hidden" in the very moment of self-opening.[44] This is what Barth calls the "mystery" of the Word, and it includes the veiling/revealing of God in the humanity of Jesus. But, starting from this agreement, we may then pursue a different track from Barth: we can speak of participating in God's knowing, and the revealing/hiding of God *through* material objects ("the sacramental principle"), but without thinking that God *becomes* an object of our perception. Indeed, if we allow our standing in the play-space of *Midsummer Night's Dream* to shape our theology, we will resist any thought that God can be the object of our subjective knowing.

The alternative, I suggest, is that love is a form of knowing that need not involve a subject-object relationship if we envisage participating in the infinite, interweaving network of giving and receiving in love that theologians call the Trinity. I have earlier proposed an understanding of "persons" in God where the word "person" indicates a dynamic relationship, and where talk of relations only becomes meaningful in the very act of participation in the "flow" of love.[45] This is, we may say, both an ontology and an epistemology of relations, a way of being and a way of knowing. We cannot observe God, even in our minds; the way of love exceeds even the imagination. God can be neither object nor subject, as these descriptors trap God in some kind of life as a being, or as three beings. Talk of three "personal" relations in God without persons who *have* relations is a way of saying that is also an unsaying, a kataphatic mode which is also apophatic. As theologians, we must learn to develop ways of speaking which are participatory and not observational. Bottom has already achieved this, in his foolish wisdom of exclaiming that "The eye of man hath not *heard*, the ear of man hath not *seen*, man's hand is not able to *taste*," a mode of speech which defeats imagination even in the act of using words.

There is no access to these movements of relation in God that always offer a "surplus" except through relations which are embodied in materiality. So we "know" the hidden God *through* objects in the world, but not *as* an object. In the first of these assertions we may commend Barth, while in the second rejecting his talk of God as object and leaning more heavily on his perceptions elsewhere that "we always understand God as event, as act, and as life."[46] He affirms that God is "personal being" (not "a" personal being) in "the originality and uniqueness that is applicable only to him," and this can only be expressed in the dynamic formulation: "God is the one who loves in freedom."[47] This is the expression, not of an essence, but a happening.

I have been arguing that the triune symbol means that knowledge of God, as love and through love, cancels out the subject-object relationship. However, God is unique and incomparable. Knowledge of finite things and people in the world will always, by contrast, include an element of objective knowing, but we can begin to learn not to dominate others as we experience the love of God. Participating in the interweaving relationships of love which are always "more," always excessive, we are helped to give up control of others by our subjective self. Entering the dramatic space of this Shakespearean play within God's "play," we practice sitting more lightly to a structure of knowledge which is characterized by subject and object, the kind that Theseus represents. We seek for a knowing that arises within a rich network of loving relations, since empathetic participation in the lives of others is also knowledge. So Lysander, in a flash of insight, calls love a "sympathy in choice" (1.1.141). I am not, of course, suggesting that reading Bottom's speech in the context of the whole play will simply *create* from nothing this theology of trinitarian participation. I suggested that literary texts might "make theology" in the sense of persuading us to accept one formulation of theology on offer rather than another; trembling with Bottom in the face of an ecstatic experience of the "deep things" of God (1 Cor. 2:10) will be just one of the moments of art that contributes toward a theological decision. But it is not a trivial one.

THE MECHANISM OF HEALING: EXPOSING THE TRUTH

Bottom is reaching after a meaning he cannot grasp. It is a meaning which has healing at its center, for through the trick of anointing and confusion, disorder has been brought to order. In the mechanism of a Shakespearean comedy, the maneuvering of someone into playing a role has led to the truth of the situation's being exposed.

In other comedies of Shakespeare, truth comes to light through confusion partly because the tangled situation gives opportunity for a new kind of speech. Love and understanding actually develop through the tangles of the situation, which has been produced by a trick or a set of mistakes. The confusion within which characters are caught enables them to express their feelings in a way which is powerful and creative through being indirect rather than clear and open. The ironic way they speak copes with the complexity of their emotional responses and enables them to explore each other's minds. Viola, disguised as a page boy, can speak of her love to the Duke with a depth and subtlety that communicates with him at an intuitive level, and prepares him for the moment when she is revealed as his "fancy's queen":

> VIOLA   My Father had a daughter lov'd a man
>   As it might be, perhaps were I a woman,
>   I should your lordship.
>
>   . . . .
>
> ORSINO   But died thy sister of her love, my boy?
>
> VIOLA   I am all the daughters of my father's house,
>   And all the brothers too: and yet I know not.
>   (*Twelfth Night*, 2.4.107–22)

As Viola confesses something she "knows not," so do Beatrice and Benedict in their conversation with each other:

> BENEDICT   I do love nothing in the world so well as you: is
>   not that strange?

BEATRICE   As strange as the thing I know not. It were as
            possible for me to say I loved nothing so well as
            you, but believe me not; and yet I lie not; I
            confess nothing, nor I deny nothing. (*Much Ado
            about Nothing,* 4.1.267–72)

Within the framework of their misapprehension they are feeling for a truth
with their intuitive senses that their conscious minds will not acknowledge;
in their ambiguous use of the word "nothing" they could either be saying that
they value each other at nothing, or more than anything, and they are moving
within themselves from one meaning to the other. It seems that love cannot
be recognized without a bit of chaos, for love does not operate with normal
sight and rational intellect.

Demetrius in *Midsummer Night's Dream* also admits that "I know not"
how he has come to know himself and Helena more truly (4.1.163), but we
catch a glimpse of the process in the hilarious scene when both Lysander
and Demetrius have been anointed (or afflicted) with the love-juice. Helena
comes to realize the truth about her behavior when faced by a Demetrius
who is no longer despising her, but who now apparently desires her in an extravagant way. Faced by a Demetrius playing the role (haplessly) of the fanatical lover, sadly she sees the uselessness of her pursuit of someone who does
not respond to her love. She resolves to go quietly, bearing "her folly back"
to Athens, and leaving a "foolish heart behind" with Demetrius (3.2.315–18).
She is thus prepared to receive Demetrius back at the last as a true lover,
when confusions are over. Confronting a Lysander also absurdly in love with
her, she invokes biblical texts about finding the truth—being weighed in the
scales and being found too light: "Weigh oath with oath and you will nothing
weigh."[48] Another to face the truth is Titania, who recognizes the reality of
the situation when she realizes she has been tricked. When the role is lifted
from her by Oberon's applying the antidote plant to her eyes in sleep, she
enters a dance of reconciliation with him. This need not mean that she is
the only one in this fairy marriage who is at fault, only that she is the one who
realizes—through the experience of loving an ass—that their love has been
disordered.

Perhaps of greatest interest in this regard, there is Demetrius. He realizes
where his heart's true home is, *without* the magic trick's being canceled. When
the two pairs of lovers have collapsed in sleep after their exertions in the
woods, Puck applies the antidote only to the eyes of Lysander. The anointing is never removed from the eyes of Demetrius. Does this then mean that
his recovered love for Helena is only a fraud, a cheap magic trick worked by
Puck—hardly a sound basis for the lifelong contract of marriage? Not at all.

Demetrius has been tricked into playing a part which, in essence, is really his true part all the time, but he has been too blind to see it. Shakespeare uses the same device in other comedies, though without the magic. When Beatrice and Benedict in *Much Ado* discover they have been tricked into playing the part of lovers, they do not mind at all: it was only this way that they discovered they really had loved each other all the time.

So Demetrius says in wonder to the Duke that he does not know by what power it has happened, but his experience has been like recovering from a sickness: "But as in health, come to my natural taste" (4.1.173). Demetrius never awakes from the dream, yet the audience feels that it was before the dream that he had really been asleep. Indeed, only this kind of dream-perception, looking with Bottom's eyes, can solve such problems of relationship as are presented at the beginning of the play. Demetrius's recovery to an imaginative love of Helena resolves the impasse for the Duke that reason could not remove. Faced by a Demetrius who is no longer willing to wed Hermia, he feels he can in reason now override the claim of Egeus, even though before he had insisted that the laws of Athens must stand. It seems that even the law bends to grace through the power of the imaginative vision of love.

Truth, in Shakespeare's comedies, is thus exposed *through* confusion and clashing discord, and it is this that brings healing to broken relationships. This process must have an impact on the Christian theological view of the human comedy, as a Shakespearean play is allowed to shape the making of theology "in front" of the text. It would, of course, be absurd to draw any therapeutic conclusion that we should play tricks on each other in order to find the truth of our relationships; dramatic comedy uses this technique so that we can experience confusion vicariously, and so come to a sharper awareness of our own hidden feelings through an exaggerated situation. I have already suggested that, in the divine irony and mercy, even human confusion and errors can be used by God to bring about reconciliation: "If they had known, they would not have crucified the Lord of Glory." But this situation inevitably raises a question of theodicy: why should confusion and disturbance be present *at all* in a creation which is supposedly good? The question becomes even more acute for theology when we see the suffering caused to all sentient life by the chaos that seems endemic to the universe as we know it.

Living in the play-space of Shakespeare's comedies, such as *Midsummer Night's Dream*, a theologian cannot dismiss the chaos, confusion, and discord of the universe as entirely due to evil and human sinfulness. We experience the "fairies" as random factors in the action that are not under the control of the human participants. Christian theology has, of course, attempted to lay all disorder at the door of human sin, with a dogma of the creation of a perfect universe spoiled by a fall at one point in primeval time.[49]

I suggest that it is necessary to have a theodicy in which various dimensions or strands of disturbance—or what Elizabeth O'Donnell Gandolfo calls "wildness"[50]—can be discerned, though never separated. Some of the tragic elements of wildness, some of the discord of the universe, can be envisaged as a part of God's good creation. We can think of God as having loving aims in creation without this being a unilateral activity on God's part, or an intervention in the processes of nature. We can envision the persuasive love of the divine Trinity surrounding an immature creation, not yet perfected, winning response and cooperation from created beings and other entities at every level of created reality. In this process, some chaos, involving suffering, seems inevitable for the evolutionary development of life, just as it does for the emotional and moral growth of the lovers in this play. We cannot envisage a free creation, able to be co-creative with God, without some elements of the random which are bound to cause pain and suffering to creatures.[51] For *this*, God must ultimately be held responsible, and there can never be a finally satisfactory theodicy because we are bound to ask, with Ivan in Dostoyevsky's novel *The Brothers Karamazov*, "Is it worth it?"[52]

But this divine intentionality cannot account for the whole of the *dark* side of the wildness. It does not explain the superfluous and outrageous suffering that we see in the world, which far exceeds the part that suffering plays in the growth of sentient beings. Whether this excessive suffering is felt by human beings or by other members of the natural order, whether it arises from disease, war, or natural disaster, it prevents the flourishing of life and the gaining of satisfaction. We surely have to speak about some mysterious slipping of creation away from the good. The term "evil" is appropriate, as denoting a turning from the ultimate good toward nothingness. Again, God must be held ultimately responsible, as creating a universe (or universes) in which there is freedom to slip back toward nonbeing. The question is put memorably by Dostoyevsky's Ivan when he asks, "Is the whole universe worth the tears of one tortured child?" It is a step of faith, reasonable but not reducible to the rational, to answer "yes."

The "free-will defense" of suffering is often advanced, arguing that for human beings to be truly free persons rather than automata or puppets, they must have the possibility of choosing evil as well as good. They must, it is said, have the possibility of refusing God's purposes for a flourishing life.[53] But human beings are embedded in wider organic life, and for this argument to have any effect it must include the possibility of other sentient beings than the human resisting the creative movement of the Spirit of God in their own way, suitable for their capacities of response. This scenario is imaginable,[54] but it still leaves God responsible for creating a situation in which evil is not only possible but likely. While human beings cannot evade their responsibility for the way they conduct their life within the created world, God is ultimately responsible for the existence of that creaturely world with all that it implies.

Throughout his classic book *Evil and the God of Love*, John Hick argues that for this kind of ultimate responsibility to be consistent with a God of love, it must be the case that the good attained through suffering—that is, the creation of "souls" or persons in relation with God and others—could not be reached by any other means than by the risks of evil and suffering. Given that the process of making personalities is often frustrated in this life, he also urges that theodicy requires that evil play a part in a divine aim that is working toward a fulfilment beyond human time, in a future "Kingdom of God" where all evil will be overcome.[55] But even if these criteria can be shown to be satisfied, I suggest that it still does not answer the question posed by Dostoyevsky's character Ivan, "Is the whole universe worth the tears of one tortured child?" Even if persons can be created only through suffering, and all persons will be fully formed in eternity, the question remains: is it *worth* it? There can thus never be a complete theodicy, since this question calls for evaluation, and so for a leap of faith. Yet careful thinking can build a platform from which the leap can reasonably be made, and this requires, I suggest, another criterion. With many other theologians today, I judge that a God of love must participate in the risk that created beings endure. Only if God suffers in God's own self is it credible to trace suffering to the free will of the creation. A loving God who commits created beings to the hazards and contingencies of freedom will accompany them on the way with the deepest solidarity and empathy, and this must mean a co-suffering with them.[56] This is not a situation forced on God by an external necessity, but one that flows from God's own loving desire to be a creator.[57]

This is the kind of doctrine of God that will be shaped by immersion into the comedic world of Shakespeare, in which confusion is the context for healing. It is, however, the risk of creation, that created beings will try to resolve their anxieties by false means, falling from the good into greater estrangements. This is paralleled in the dramatic comedy of Shakespeare, where the devices of "pretense" have a dark underscoring to them. Here we cross once again the boundary between comedy and tragedy, for in the comedies as well as the tragedies, people get hurt even by the pretenses that are meant to be genial. There is a dangerous side to "practising," not only when undertaken by comic villains like Don John, or by tragic villains like Iago, or by half-hearted villains like Iachimo, but even when it is used for the best intentions by romantic heroes like Viola. She confesses: "Disguise, I see thou art a wickedness, / Wherein the pregnant enemy does much."[58]

A New Kind of Order

Bottom is to preside over the final act of the play. The simple workmen put on their own play to entertain the Duke and his court. Their choice is the Tragedy of Pyramus and Thisbe—doomed lovers, torn apart by their families. In the story, a wall between their families' houses separates them, and through a chink in the wall they tell each other their love. Later, Pyramus supposes that Thisbe has been killed by a lion and so kills himself. Discovering him dying, Thisbe takes his sword and kills herself too. Snout the Tinker represents the crucial wall in his own person, and summarizes the plot, leading the Duke to enquire sarcastically, "Would you desire lime and hair [constituent parts of a wall] to speak better?" and Demetrius to reply, "It is the wittiest partition that ever I heard discourse" (5.1.166).

The play of Pyramus and Thisbe they present is evidently a parody of *Romeo and Juliet* that Shakespeare had completed the year before, and also echoes the situation of Lysander and Hermia; they are all star-crossed lovers, opposed by their families. This burlesque contains a reference to the New Testament text as significant as Bottom's earlier muddled quotation of St. Paul. As Pyramus and Thisbe lie dead on the ground, the Duke continues the nobles' joking commentary on the play by observing to Demetrius that "moonshine and lion are left to bury the dead," and Demetrius adds, "Ay, and Wall too." At this point, Bottom leaps up from the floor and declares with great emphasis, "No, I assure you; the wall is down that parted their fathers" (5.1.343). This is an echo of *Romeo and Juliet*, where the fathers are ancestors of the two hostile families, but even more importantly, it is the second major echo in the play of a letter attributed to St. Paul.[59] In Ephesians 2:14–16 the author describes the effect of the cross of Jesus on the ancient feud between Jew and Gentile, between the primeval fathers of the two races, describing it as the breaking down of a wall: "For he is our peace, which hath made of both one, & hath broken the stop of the partition wall, In abrogating through his flesh the hatred, that is, the Law of commandments, for to make of twain one new man in him self, so making peace, And that he might reconcile both unto God in one body by his cross, and slay the hatred thereby." This translation from the Geneva Bible actually uses the word "partition," echoed surely in Demetrius's reference to the "wittiest partition," where the Bishops' Bible translates "he hath broken down the middle wall that was a stop betweene us." The word "partition" appears four times in Shakespeare's plays, but only once—here—meaning a wall as in the Pauline text.[60] Indeed, the wall is down that parted their fathers. Beatrice Groves remarks that Bottom leaps up "to explain the redemptive aspect of the plot to the spectators," and further proposes that his recovery—as Pyramus—from death exhibits the paschal motif of death and resurrection that she also finds in the deaths of Romeo and Juliet.[61]

For the author of Ephesians, the broken wall is partition between peoples, and its abolition has happened through an event which, according to Paul in 1 Corinthians 1–2, seems mere confusion to the wise of this world, the "folly" of the cross of Jesus. The two major New Testament references in the play thus converge on the effect of the cross; both passages conjoin the cross, reconciliation, and mystery. In 1 Corinthians 2:7–9 it is the love displayed at the cross that undermines any knowledge that depends on rational observation; something has happened whose "bottom" human wisdom cannot reach. The passage on the breaking of the "partition" in Ephesians 2 is immediately followed by a meditation on the "mystery" of God in Christ, which was previously hidden but is now made known to both Jews and Gentiles who have become members of the one body (Ephesians 3:1–6). In its use of the texts from 1 Corinthians 2 and Ephesians 2, the play thus shows a double movement from disorder to reconciliation, marked by the Duke's word "concord" on both occasions (4.1.142; 5.1.60). The first sequence is with the drama of the nobles in the wood, and the second with the "most lamentable comedy" of the workmen. Each time a scripture text witnesses to human confusion brought to divine concord.

My point here is not that Shakespeare is promoting Christian doctrine: the scriptural images of seeing more clearly and breaking down a wall have given him metaphors for poetic drama. They have also enabled him to express a spiritual vision: that relations of love are more important than human hierarchies such as divide families, or a patriarchal social order that sanctions the repression of a daughter's choice in love. It is part of Shakespeare's spiritual outlook that while he generally supports the order in the cosmos that Elizabethan philosophers and politicians aimed to preserve, and he wants to see disorder brought to order, his plays also continually question the accepted order. One critic observes that none of the four social worlds of the play (rulers, lovers, fairies, artisans) takes the central place, and that they exist only in balanced relation to each other.[62] Sukanta Chaudhuri adds that the balance is shifting and precarious, and judges that "the play advances a series of challenges to patriarchy which are defeated yet never quite dispelled." So, in what Chaudhuri calls a "comedy of compromise," Shakespeare assumes "a deliberate inconclusiveness that deflects all questions and ambiguities in the comic-romantic close," and "the value-structure supporting the narrative is undermined but never quite toppled."[63]

The mood of festivity in the play, bolstered by reference to three religious feasts,[64] enhances a spirituality which questions hierarchy, since it recalls the allowance on such days for a ritualized subversion of order. Bakhtin, in his study of carnival, notes that the authorities tolerate a conventional breaking of convention, but only in order to absorb forces that might have otherwise destabilized the social order.[65] Nevertheless, such moments of an allowed "riot of disorder" can foster ideas that will grow under the surface and in time become genuinely threatening to the status quo. Chaudhuri raises the question, for example, as to how far the audience would have shared in the patronizing attitudes of the courtiers to the artisan-actors, as they greet their dramatic efforts with supercilious comments. A good proportion of the playhouse audience would have been artisans, and actors would have been regarded in essentially the same social bracket. Shakespeare, suggests Chaudhuri, is reflecting "ambiguous cultural and class relations between his own actors' cohort and its elite patrons," while at the same time lampooning amateur actors who lacked the professional skills of his company.[66] Bottom, the wise fool, is not intimidated by the snide comments of his social betters, and while there is no manifesto for a political revolution in *Midsummer Night's Dream*, there is just a hint here that social order might take new forms.

Shakespeare's equivocation over order is remarkably demonstrated by his treatment of Queen Elizabeth, whose presence continually hovers between the lines. Her mystique is divided between four characters—Theseus, the Fairy Queen, the "fair vestal throned by the West," and the moon which symbolizes Diana, the virgin goddess. Theseus and the moon recall her part in the preservation of good order in the state. The moon rules the monthly rhythms of the tides and so prescribes order in the cosmos, marking the four nights during which Theseus and Hippolyta have to wait for the consummation of their love (1.11.1–11). So the moon, "the governess of floods," is pale with anger at the quarrel between Oberon and Titania which causes such disorder in nature (2.1.103), as Queen Elizabeth might be envisaged as being angry at disorder within her kingdom. Yet these are not straightforward compliments to Elizabeth, who might well have been present at the play on its first performance at a court wedding. Theseus is the guardian of order in this play, arbitrating between Hermia and Egeus, and yet in his "backstory" in Shakespeare's sources there are dark shadows of violence, even sexual violence, toward women, including his conquest of Hippolyta.[67] The moon is also portrayed in equivocal terms, the adjective "fruitless" (1.1.73) linking virginity with frustrated love, and "watery" (2.1.162; 3.1.189) carrying the overtones of weakness. "Titania" is another form of the name "Diana," and Spenser had already celebrated Elizabeth as Gloriana, the Fairy Queen. Shakespeare, however, underplays the connection compared with Spenser, and Titania has negative features—she is victimized and dominated by Oberon (who in Spenser represents Henry VIII), she is tricked into being "enamoured of an ass," and shares Oberon's unhealthy obsession with the

Indian boy. The "fair vestal throned by the west" stands as a relatively complimentary symbol of Elizabeth, as Oberon recalls the incident of the creation of the magic flower:

> But I might see young Cupid's fiery shaft
> Quench'd in the chaste beams of the watery moon;
> And the imperial votress passed on
> In maiden meditation, fancy-free. (2.1.161–64)

The political message seems clear: the inviolable virgin Queen who is able to resist even the fiery shafts of Cupid (with the aid of the chaste moon, that is, herself)[68] is certainly able to keep order in the state. Moreover, since the arrow of Cupid falls upon the crucial flower and changes it into the potent charm of love, Elizabeth's virginity is effectively written into the plot as the source of the magic herb which finally brings harmonious order between the couples.[69] But, taking the four symbols together, Chaudhuri persuasively concludes that "Across the play Shakespeare works a nuanced, *ambiguous* critique of the royal icon."[70]

Shakespeare is therefore offering no simple endorsement of royal power in the state, such as underwriting a divine right of rule. The authorities have an ambiguous status, and in this ambiguity there is an affinity between the human court and the court of the fairies, linked by the association of Elizabeth with the Fairy Queen. The identity of the fairies is complex, uniting rural traditions of nature spirits with a courtly image more akin to the divinities of the classical period that inhabit the pages of Ovid's *Metamorphoses*. While some religious writers of the time—including James I—associated them with witchcraft,[71] and there was a tradition of "Robin Goodfellow" (alias "Puck") as a minor devil,[72] the fairies in this play are neither obviously good or evil, and are more like the class of spiritual beings described by Cornelius Agrippa as neither angels nor demons.[73] Shakespeare is creating a new image of fairies as mysterious forces which are at work behind the scenes, beyond our control, with capacity for danger and destruction as well as the blessing which Puck offers at the end of the play. In the plot of the play they link together the classes of courtiers and artisans into one shared drama. They seem, then, less a parallel spiritual world alongside our everyday world than forces which we encounter *within* the world, and they bear some resemblance to what St. Paul called "principalities and powers."[74] We shall come across this idea again when we consider *The Tempest*, but the key point is that for Paul these are spiritual powers which operate within the fabric and structures of the state, with capacity both for keeping order and inflicting oppression. The implied yet presiding figure of Elizabeth—a female patriarch like

Theseus, Virgin Queen, Diana the huntress, and Fairy Queen—reminds us that flesh-and-blood powers can bless and destroy in the civic order, bringing life and death to its inhabitants. The play enables us to see this more clearly, and yet we are also given the hope that love finally conquers as the greatest power of all.

Such is Shakespeare's own spirituality, which a theological perspective helps us to discern, but his text can also help to *make* theology. As the theologian enters this embodied play-space, she begins to see that harmony need not mean the kind of inflexible order in the cosmos that theologians have often worked with. I have already suggested that if a loving creator gives freedom to created persons and other sentient beings to be co-creative, this must mean an element of the chaotic and the random *within* structures of order, a discord within the harmony of the cosmos that has been exacerbated to an intolerable extent through a slipping away from the Good. It is ironic that, in Christian tradition, the redemptive activity of God, healing this situation, has also often been depicted in terms of strict order and hierarchy. "The wall is down" announces Bottom the Wise Fool, evoking for his audience the words in Ephesians 2 and 1 Corinthians 2 about the effect of the death of Christ, which is baffling to those who count themselves wise. Yet this breaking down of divisions has been depicted by theologians in hierarchical, even patriarchal terms: a father-God has been portrayed as demanding punishment for the breaking of his laws, with a divine son offering satisfaction on behalf of a submissive humanity. *Midsummer Night's Dream* does not offer any kind of doctrine of atonement, but living in the ethos of the play should turn a theologian away from any transactional theory, such as is often called "penal substitution," toward ideas of redemption in which the revelation of God's love in the cross of Jesus has power to transform human lives through evoking a response of love.

The theme of "seeing with the eyes of love" in this play can help to make a theology in which the influence of love takes prominence in ideas of salvation. The Western, or "Latin," doctrine of atonement has been strongly shaped by the thought of Calvin, inheriting Anselm's idea of a "debt" owed by humanity to God, but taking it out of Anselm's context of relationships of loyalty between human beings and God (expressed most strongly in a life of prayer and worship) and replacing it into a Roman view of criminal law.[75] St. Paul's affirmation that Christ was immersed, in death, into the human predicament of estrangement from God,[76] was also converted from a theology of empathy and identification into one in which punishment becomes the key issue. While Calvin rightly saw in his time that it was essential for monarchs and princes to be subject to the rule of law rather than following their own arbitrary wishes, he created a theology in which God is made subject to a principle of law, and thus loses the freedom to dispense with retribution. Punishment has to be inflicted on *someone* in order to satisfy demands of law. Love, of course, has a place within this scheme: God's love is understood as *motivating* the substitution of Christ's punishment for human damnation, and those who have faith in Christ *respond* in love to God out of gratitude, entering on a life of obedience.[77] But love is either prologue or epilogue in this drama of atonement: it is not central to the dramatic action in itself.

Theology in intertextual relation with this play of Shakespeare will restore love to its central place, as Abelard did—for example—in declaring that "everyone is made more righteous, that is more loving towards God, after the passion of Christ."[78] This not merely a matter of subjective "moral influence," in which spectators of the cross imitate the self-giving love of Christ, as Abelard's approach has often been dismissed, from the time of St. Bernard onward;[79] rather, Abelard envisaged love as an active energy, where the love of God manifested in the life and death of Christ "enkindles" love in our hearts, "incites" love, and "inclines" us to love.[80] Abelard is attempting, though not with complete success, to express something objective: that the divine love has power to *generate* love within human beings. The theology which is to be made "in front of" *Midsummer Night's Dream* will find some integration between this transformation of persons through love, and a similar theology of transfiguration—*theosis* (deification)—which has consistently characterized the Eastern church.[81] The text of this play should help this construction of soteriology by enabling the reader and viewer to live through an experience in which, through love's knowledge, all hierarchies of domination dissolve.

ART, LIFE, AND RITUAL

The fact that Demetrius, in effect, never awakens from the dream prompts us to consider the relationship of art and life in *Midsummer Night's Dream*. In this play, as in others of Shakespeare, the borders between so-called dream and so-called reality are blurred. The dream proper of the title is the action that takes place between the two sleeps of the lovers and the two sleeps of Titania: in the first the juice is put on, in the second it is taken off. Titania wakes to the sound of Oberon's voice and the lovers to the sound of Theseus's hunting horn. But the edges of the dream are more vague than these neat borders. The lovers, when awoken at last, all testify to their experience that they still seem to be dreaming. Demetrius confesses:

> These things seem small and indistinguishable,
> Like far off mountains turned into clouds.

Hermia replies:

> Methinks I see these things with parted eye,
> When everything seems double.

And Demetrius adds:

> Are you sure
> That we are awake? It seems to me that yet we sleep
> We dream. (4.1.186–94)

So our thoughts move from the dream simply as the magical interlude of the night to the dream of the whole play, a dream of art from which the audience apparently wakes at the end. This, indeed, is what Puck suggests to the audience in his epilogue:

> If we shadows have offended
> Think but this and all is mended,
> That you have but slumbered here
> While these visions did appear,
> And this weak and idle theme
> No more yielding but a dream.

But we protest that we *have* seen the play, that *we* were not in fact asleep. So the barriers between art and life are being broken down; if the play we have experienced was a dream, then so is the whole of what seems reality to us. As Prospero declares in *The Tempest*:

> *We* are such stuff as dreams are made on
> and our little life is rounded by a sleep.

Thus, what the lovers experience at night is a dream (their confusion) within a dream (the play) within a dream (life itself).[82] The effect is that we become receptive to what art might have to show us in our daily lives, not just in a particular artifact; we can learn to see others with the eyes of love in our own drama, and Bottom's earlier words take on new meaning: "Let the audience look to their eyes" (1.2.22). The dissolution of neat boundaries opens up the possibility of seeing the "more things" than are "dreamt of" in our philosophy.

This transgression of the borders between the theater and life outside the theater is also prompted by the dramatic performance of the simple workmen. The effect of viewing this absurdly inept play within a play is to heighten the reality of what surrounds it. We join the audience onstage, and thereby we as the theater audience consent to the reality of the outer play, *Midsummer Night's Dream*, to which the onstage audience belongs. We are amused at the attempts of the artisan-actors to create the illusion of reality (the moon) and their unwarranted fear that the illusion will be *too* real (the lion) for the ladies in the audience to bear; yet because our awareness that these actors are destroying the illusion of reality by explaining it away is shared with the onstage audience (as they show by their gibes), we have the sense that we are sharing the *same* reality. We know with our minds that the whole play is an illusion ("the best in this kind are but shadows," declares Theseus, 5.1.210), but we are the more ready to suspend disbelief and to accept that the illusion, when skilfully done, exposes what is real.

Yet another way in which Shakespeare convinces us that art can reveal the truth of life is in his use of ritual. In ritual we put our deepest feelings into some kind of outward drama, and it is often only ritual that can express and explore the reality that lies beneath the surface appearance of things. Shakespeare uses ritual constantly in this play, which is suitable for an *occasion* of ritual, a marriage. In other comedies Shakespeare uses the convention of the Pastoral,[83] having his characters leave the court or town for a period in the country, and then returning to town after having absorbed some of the virtues of the country. In *As You Like It*, for example, the characters lodge for a while in the Forest of Arden and believe they find "tongues in trees, books in the running brooks, / Sermons in stones, and good in everything" (2.1.15–18). But in *Midsummer Night's Dream* Shakespeare makes the two-way journey between the court and the wood into a briefer ritual, like a movement in a liturgy, a procession in church. Two of the three festival days mentioned in the play have such ritual actions associated with them. Lysander, as he arranges to meet Hermia in the woods when they elope, names the meeting place as "where I did meet thee once with Helena / To do observance to a morn of May" (1.1.167), and when the Duke stumbles upon the two pairs of lovers in the early morning as he is out hunting in the woods, he finds a ready explanation in this rite: Egeus anxiously wonders what they are doing lying there together, but the Duke suggests they had no doubt woken up early to celebrate May morning—"to observe / The rite of May" (4.1.131–32)—and had fallen asleep. In the May game, people would ride into the woods to collect dew and the May flowers, and then would return to crown a young man and woman as the King and Queen of the May, celebrating fertility and the renaissance of life after the death of the winter. The title of the play evokes a second ritual game, when on Midsummer Night young people would sleep the night in the woods and once again gather plants in the early dawn which would have rejuvenating powers.

All this is of course definitely not Christian doctrine, but it is not exactly pagan religion either. Rather, it evokes a general spirituality of new life marked by love. There is a startling example of this nondogmatic spirituality in the lament of Titania that her discord with Oberon has resulted in such disturbances in nature that "human mortals want their winter cheer, / No night is now with hymn or carol blessed" (2.1.101–2). Here the breaking up of *fairy* festivity is simply associated with practices that are part of the *Christian* liturgical calendar. The songs in the play, such as Oberon's final blessing, take the form of prayers: the lullaby sung to Titania, for example, is a kind of exorcism against the threat of evil. The fairy anointing of the eyes of the lovers also has a ritual quality, evoking all the echoes of anointing in Scripture—for coronation, ordination, and healing; I have already drawn attention to the intertextuality with the phrase from the book of Revelation, "anoint your eyes that you may see."

Supporting this general spirituality of the renewal of life, through seeing with the eyes of love, is an even-handed reference to Catholic and Protestant festive practices, or what Phebe Jensen calls "Shakespeare's inclusive calendrical vision." She maintains that, instead of simply validating either a Catholic or Protestant liturgy, the play creates its own kind of "festive fictions" of dancing, singing, and blessing, investing them "with the power of a religious ritual that encompasses Catholic as well as Protestant rituals."[84] She does, nevertheless, judge that the fairy ritual of the final moments "is more associated with England's old religion than with its new one," agreeing with Greenblatt that it "appropriates" Catholic practice to the stage.[85] But I suggest that Shakespeare's impartial approach continues here too. The final blessing of the marriage-bed by Oberon, after the preparation of the chamber by the dance of the fairies, explicitly recalls the prayer in the Marriage Service in the Church of England Book of Common Prayer, petitioning God for fertility of the womb ("that they may both be fruitful in the procreation of children"):

> And the issue there create
> Ever shall be fortunate.
> So shall all the couples three
> Ever true in loving be. (5.1.395–98)

Shakespeare has already alluded to the promise of both man and woman in the Marriage Service to love each other "as long as you both shall live" ("Whom I will love, and will do till my death," 3.2.167) and the promise to remain faithful "till death us depart" ("With league whose date till death will never end," 3.2.373). The command of Puck, "With this field-dew *consecrate*" echoes the phrase in the service that God has "consecrated the state of Matrimony." On the other hand, Oberon's intention to sprinkle the marriage-bed with holy water (in this case, dew), recalls the pre-Reformation Catholic rite to promote fertility, which had been discredited after the Reformation.[86] The continued repetition of the word "bless" by Oberon also has a Catholic ring to it.[87] However, balance is preserved even here: the ritual action is being performed by persons (Oberon and Titania) who are not priests, preventing it from being a Catholic "sacramental." The grace is, after all, "fairy grace" (5.1.389).

Through ritual which dramatizes a *general* spirituality, rather than a particular confessional belief, we are thus being prompted to cross the boundaries between art and life. It has been suggested that much of the Puritan rejection of the playhouse was a reaction to the way that the theater was becoming a rival to the church, providing another drama to replace the drama of the Eucharist. With the Reformation insistence that the Eucharist was not a miraculous transubstantiation but only a *representation* of the body and blood of Christ, it was open for others—including actors—to offer other *representations* of reality.[88] The church could no longer appeal for exclusivity to a miracle that only it could perform. Today, if the text of the play is allowed to *make* theology, it will be possible to get beyond any rivalry of church and theater and find that the ritual of the play, with its New Testament echoes, issues in the writing of new Christian liturgy. One example is available in print, published by "Arden Shakespeare," in a liturgy called "Seeing with the Eyes of Love."[89] Here the text of traditional liturgical elements interacts and intertwines with Shakespeare's own text from *A Midsummer Night's Dream*.[90] This liturgical intertextuality should help to open the art-form of the liturgy into the daily life which Orthodox theology has come to name as "the liturgy after the liturgy."[91]

In *Midsummer Night's Dream* an intertextuality with scripture and other religious texts provides images for poetry, expresses a general spirituality of order and love, and can help to make a theology of God's relation to the world. Some dark shadows nevertheless remain at the end, typical of Shakespeare's kind of tragicomedy. As René Girard has suggested, the relation between the lovers is one of "mimetic love," each male in competition with the other, *copying* what the other desires, and ending up in self-alienation.[92] Girard has proposed that the whole life of society is characterized by mimetic desire, each person wanting the same goods and benefits that others desire.[93] Although the tension so generated can be released by ritual acts such as sacrifice, the relief is only temporary, and conflict will build up again unless society takes on new values altogether—which, in his later work, Girard identifies as the perspective of a nonviolent kingdom of God.[94] In this play, reconciliation and a new kind of order are won out of the disordered situation through the healing power of comedy, for the sake of a new life founded on love.

The question is whether the future relations of the lovers can avoid the destructiveness of mimetic desire to which they have succumbed before, and at least a doubt that they can hangs over the ending. Nevertheless, the whole drama moves toward the marriage of the three pairs of lovers: Theseus and Hippolyta, Lysander and Hermia, Demetrius and Helena. And hovering behind these three is another pair—the couple for whose entertainment the play is written, who watch it as the Duke and his friends watch the play of Bottom and his company. The play urges us to watch it more clearly than Pepys did, so that our sight can be cleared for the drama of life.

5

The Merchant of Venice
and the Covenant of Love

✳

ANY SUGGESTION that *The Merchant of Venice* offers a "general spirituality" and can assist in the making of a modern theology immediately runs into the problem of its perceived anti-Semitism. While Shakespeare cannot be entirely excluded from the prejudices of his age, and traces of anti-Semitism cannot be excused, I want to suggest that the *emphasis* of his approach to Jewishness lies elsewhere, and that this makes it beneficial to explore an intertextuality with theology. The place to begin is near the very beginning of the play, which provides a piece of exegesis of a biblical text which sets the focus for what is to come.

THE BIBLICAL STORY OF JACOB: CALCULATION AND RISK

In the third scene of act 1, Shylock refers to a long passage from the Hebrew Bible (or Old Testament). For modern audiences it is an obscure piece of scripture, and may well be cut by a producer's blue pencil as being too difficult to follow, and yet it foregrounds the basic theme of the play. The text, from Genesis 30, is an episode in the life of Shylock's ancestor, Jacob, and concerns his management of the flocks of sheep and goats of Jacob's uncle Laban. The way the story is read by the two characters concerned, Antonio and Shylock, makes clear that this is not essentially a play about Jews and Christians, but about law and grace; put another way, it is about a contrast between the "old covenant"—or rather, as we shall see, the old covenant read *in a certain way*—and the "new covenant," illustrating the words of the Apostle Paul that "the law kills while the Spirit gives life" (2 Cor. 3:6).

The play, I want to maintain, is not at its core anti-Semitic, but antilegalist, and the play itself makes abundantly clear that legalism can be found among Christians as much as among Jews. James Shapiro protests against the reading of Shylock as "theological" rather than racist, rightly pointing out that in the Elizabethan period it is precisely theology that helps produce racism.[1] But my case is not that antilegalism can be entirely separated from anti-Semitism, rather that when the theological critique of legalism is mounted widely beyond Jews to Gentiles, antilegalism does not *necessarily* become anti-Semitism. There is, of course, always the danger of this happening, and Shakespeare cannot be entirely excused of falling into the trap himself, though this is contrary to the basic direction of his thought revealed by this piece of scriptural interpretation, early on in the play.

The context of the textual reading is Antonio's request to borrow three thousand gold ducats from the Jewish moneylender, Shylock, in order to finance his young friend Bassanio's venture in journeying to a distant city, Belmont, where he hopes to woo and marry the wealthy and beautiful Portia. Antonio lacks ready cash as he is engaged in a venture of his own, having no fewer than six ships at sea embarked on trading missions. The exegesis of the text turns precisely on the difference between the kind of "venturing," or risk, to which Antonio and Bassanio are committed, and the kind of calculation on which a usurer like Shylock could rely. According to the text, Jacob and Laban agree that Jacob should keep, in lieu of wages, all the lambs and goats that are born with striped or piebald-colored coats. While Laban obviously thinks this a good deal, he reckons without Jacob's wiliness: while the animals are in the act of mating, Jacob faces them with wooden poles that have been partly peeled of their bark, and the ewes and does apparently take the hint and conceive lambs and kids with multicoloured coats (Gen. 30:37–43). Shylock tells this story as a defense of money-lending at interest, since the way he reads the text is that Jacob is blessed in multiplying his assets, making his possessions work for him, in breeding more wealth, receiving what he deserves. Shylock asserts that he is likewise making his money work for him, and concludes: "This was a way to thrive, and he was blest: / And thrift is blessing, if men steal it not" (1.3.85–86). This is a legalistic exegesis: profit comes from skilful exploitation of assets, and work is always rewarded. Moreover, as Lawrence Danson has suggested, Shylock is advancing a parallel between an "artificial" device of breeding in this story, and an "artificiality" about the generation of money through usury.[2] However, Antonio immediately responds by offering a different exegesis of the story:

> This was a venture, sir, that Jacob served for,
> A thing not in his power to bring to pass,
> But swayed and fashioned by the hand of heaven.
> Was this inserted to make interest good?
> Or is your gold and silver ewes and rams? (1.3.87–91)

Shylock replies with a joke, "I cannot tell, I make it breed as fast," but Antonio's point is quite the opposite. He reads the story as an example of risk-taking, of "venturing," or hazarding, for which Jacob was dependent, not on his skills in breeding, but on the grace of heaven. Jacob could not guarantee the outcome of his act of sympathetic magic with the peeled rods. Antonio was launched upon such a venture in his trading enterprises, hazarding all upon the toss of the ocean with a risk that no moneylender had to take. Bassanio was about to venture forth on a quest of love to Belmont; but above all, Antonio was hazarding for the sake of love and friendship in putting himself into the power of Shylock's bond, with a stake which was to be nothing less than his own life. For Shylock was to offer to lend the three thousand ducats interest-free for three months, but the penalty for failure to repay at the end of that time would be a pound of Antonio's flesh. Antonio agrees to this "merry bond," taking up the hazard of love to raise the money for Bassanio to make his journey of love.

There is a dense intertextuality here, interwoven with the basic biblical text from Genesis. As John Drakakis points out, the discussion reflects a social situation where two forms of circulation of wealth in society were increasingly coming into conflict: the exchange of goods for money represented by the merchant (Antonio) and financial exchange where money itself was increasingly a commodity (represented by Shylock, the usurer).[3] Mercantilism inevitably involved risks from which money-lending at interest was exempt, as Luther pointed out in his tract *Trade and Usury*.[4] There was a potential civic instability here which could not easily be resolved by reference to divine law, which was assumed in some way to underlie the laws of society. Biblical texts were involved and were ambiguous. The Deuteronomic law of the Old Testament forbade usury in the case of fellow-nationals, but allowed it for dealings with foreigners (Deut. 23:19–20), and there is an allusion to this prescription when Antonio bids Shylock, "lend it rather to thy enemy" (1.1.130). Usury, however, was often argued[5] to be entirely ruled out for Christians by the New Testament text Luke 6:30, 35,[6] although Calvin had allowed it under certain circumstances, and an English Act of Parliament of 1571 legalized it with a limit on interest of 10 percent.[7]

The societal tension between merchant and usurer is further sharpened and confused by ethnic conflict between Christians and Jews, the latter adopting the practice of usury widely in Europe as propertyless exiles. Moneylenders in England were not actually Jewish (Jews having been expelled in 1290), unlike the situation in Italy, but reference to money-lending in plays and stories tended to attract a Jewish stereotype.[8] While Antonio complains about Shylock's practice in loaning money at a high rate of interest, and Shylock bears a grudge against Antonio for his undermining of the credit and interest market by making loans free of charge, this economic conflict is thus darkly underscored by ethnic hatred. Antonio does not contradict Shylock's assertion that "you call me misbeliever, cut-throat dog, / And spit upon my Jewish gabardine" (1.3.107–8). When Shylock comments that Antonio "hates our sacred nation" (1.3.44), this appears to be a reversal of the words in Luke 7:5 about another Gentile that "he loveth our nation."[9]

However, Shakespeare is taking these social and ethnic divisions and using them to express what for him seems a more basic contrast, between the mathematics of commerce, and the generous risks of love. Antonio is warned by Gratiano that he too, as a merchant, can fall into a frame of mind driven by mere calculation of profit: those who seek to gain the world "lose it that do buy it with much care" (1.1.75), echoing Matthew 16:26,[10] "For what shall it profit a man though he should win the whole world, if he lose his own soul?" but with the twist that the world too is lost. I suggest that John Russell Brown misses the point by finding an imagery of the "commerce of love" to be an alternative to the commerce of business;[11] rather, commerce and systems of exchange are altogether set against the venture or risk of love. Setting this out in a piece of Old Testament exegesis makes clear what Shakespeare's contemporaries would have perceived immediately, that it is also a contrast between law and grace. This is a theme taken from St. Paul and revived in the Protestant Reformation. The question of the time is this: *what place does the law of God, as contained in the Old Testament and summarized in the Ten Commandments, have in a life which has been redeemed by the grace of God received through Christ?*

Framing the question this way opens up a more nuanced view of the theological issue than a simple contrast between Old Testament law, supposedly represented by Shylock, and New Testament grace to which the Christians in Venice at least aspire. Two complications here, usually neglected by literary critics,[12] are: first, that the old covenant as identified by the Apostle Paul is not simply equivalent to the book called the "Old Testament," which contains a range of literature apart from law-codes (although in late Judaism the whole of the Hebrew Bible had come to be called *Torah*, i.e., law or instruction, not simply the Five "Books of Moses"). Shakespeare himself appears to be drawn especially to the Psalms and the wisdom literature. Second, the old covenant of God with Israel is itself not simply a matter of law; in Paul's view, it can be read as God's oracular promise ("oracles of God," Rom. 3:2),[13] and the theology of Shakespeare's time, Protestant and Catholic, offered a whole range of theological assessments of what was sometimes called a "covenant of works," as we shall see. But Shylock as a Jew can certainly stand as a symbol for all those who live by relying on the old covenant *read only* as a matter of law, rather than reading it as a promise of the true righteousness that comes by faith and grace. He is the "Jew" of the Apostle Paul's arguments about condemnation by law and justification by grace in the Letter to the Romans (chaps. 3–4). More precisely, we should say that Shylock is depicted as the *kind* of Jewish believer who reads the law without perceiving the grace of God which it signifies, just as he represents Christians who have the same hermeneutic.

Whatever the view of Antonio, the play itself does not condemn Shylock's *ethnicity* but his *theology*. For when none of Antonio's ships come home safely to Venice at the end of three months and he cannot repay Shylock, his opponent insists on the demands of the law. Antonio has entered into a legal agreement, and he must be called to account. As Shylock points out, the whole system of law on which Venice and its commercial wealth depends is put to the test by this instance:

> The pound of flesh which I demand of him
> Is dearly bought; 'tis mine, and I will have it.
> If you deny me, fie upon your law:
> There is no force in the decrees of Venice.
> I stand for judgement: answer, shall I have it? (4.1.98–102)

I am not suggesting that *The Merchant of Venice* is a religious allegory, in which the requirements of the civil law stand as a cipher for divine law.[14] In Shakespeare's time the two kinds of law are inseparable while not being identical; the law of the state was understood as reflecting the law of God, although—as I have already suggested—a play like *Measure for Measure* demonstrates that human law can only approximate to God's law.[15] Nevertheless, according to the Reformers, the monarch or magistrate carried a commission from God to make law that would resist evil in the state. It is not possible, then, to separate an attitude of legalism in religion from an attitude of legalism in the state; both are characterized by lack of attention to the moderating of strict demands of the law by mercy. Shylock's inflexible invocation of the law of Venice is presented as part of a way of life which has religious implications, and may indeed issue from them.[16] So he swears to keep his legal bond "by our holy Sabaoth" (4.1.36, First Quarto), by which Shakespeare probably means "Sabbath," although it is not impossible that we are meant to hear the scriptural resonance of "the Lord of Sabaoth,"[17] and he insists that "An oath, an oath I have in heaven" (4.1.224) which he must respect, echoing Ecclesiastes 5:3–4.[18]

In line with my suggestion that Shylock in this play stands for "the legalist," whatever religion he or she holds, Luther identifies a general legalistic approach to life that he finds exemplified in Papists, Jews, and Mohammedans alike. He maintains in his commentary on Galatians that, although their rites may differ in outward form, the same *ratio*, or the same *opinio*, belongs to them all. This is the argument of reason[19] that "to live unto God you must keep the law," and that "the work of God in saving a person depends on personal worth."[20] In the *Jew of Malta*—which is generally recognized as having had some influence on the genesis of Shakespeare's play—Marlowe had similarly depicted a Jew as typical of Christian mores, but in this case legalism was not the issue; Drakakis writes that "one of the evident objectives of the Jew of Malta was to submerge the difference between Christian, Jew and Turk in a Machiavellian ethic that was universally applicable to them all,"[21] and Greenblatt identifies a "disturbing perception of sameness" that is a characteristic feature of the Christian-Jew relation in Marlowe's play.[22] By uniquely focussing on the attitude of legalism which is common to different religions and ethnic groups, Shakespeare is able to express a contrasting spirituality of the risks of love and forgiveness, and is also able to develop—as we shall see—a difference *within* sameness.[23]

So far we have been exploring one line of the plot—Shylock's flesh-bond—but we can now see how this fits into a second, the wooing and winning of Portia by Bassanio. Antonio has hazarded his life for the sake of raising capital for Bassanio's journey to distant Belmont, and the action of the play alternates almost scene by scene between these two places—Venice and Belmont, one a place of commerce and the other a setting for love. If Venice typifies the making of bonds which are sanctioned by law, Belmont is the place in which the bonds of love and marriage are made and consummated. While Shylock insists that "I stand here for law" (4.1.141), Portia declares "I stand for sacrifice" (3.2.57). As Hamlin suggests, she is the sacrifice of her father's will, but at the same "Shylock and Portia 'stand' for opposed values of Justice versus Mercy."[24] However, he polarizes the situation too much when he immediately goes on to add that they stand "for the Jewish and Christian principles, respectively, of Law versus Sacrifice," even if he adds in a footnote that "this is the Christian perspective of course."[25] We shall see how the play, drawing on scripture, has a more nuanced view of "the Law" than simple equation with Jewishness.

In Belmont: Love and the Caskets

During the three months that Antonio's agreement with Shylock is running, Bassanio journeys to Belmont and wins the hand in marriage of the beautiful, intelligent, and fabulously rich[26] lady Portia. At the same time her companion, Nerissa, agrees to marry Bassanio's friend Gratiano. But, following the theme that Shakespeare has already established with the story of Jacob, Bassanio can only gain Portia as his wife by "hazarding" for her.

In the game of three caskets devised by Portia's deceased father, the risk is not only in the choice but the consequences, since suitors must vow on their honor never to marry anyone if they choose wrongly. The gold casket carries the inscription, "who chooseth me shall gain what many men desire" (2.9.24), the silver the motto "who chooseth me shall get as much as he deserves" (36), while the lead casket carries the threatening words: "who chooseth me, must give and hazard all he hath" (21). The first two inscriptions correspond approximately to those on the gold and silver caskets in the story from the well-known collection *Gesta Romanorum,* but the third is quite different; in the source, the motto on the lead casket reads: *Thei that chese me, shulle fynde [in] me that God hathe disposed.*[27] Shakespeare has thus deliberately introduced the notion of hazard, and underlines it when Portia tells Bassanio that he must "hazard" and "venture" for her (3.2.2, 10), using terms that occur eighteen times in the play. As well as contrasting with the calculation of commerce and the fixed returns of law, hazard reaches deeply into Shakespeare's method of comedy.

The unlikely outward form of the dull lead contains inside the portrait of the lady, exemplifying a topos that Shakespeare invokes in all his comedies, the relation between appearance and reality. As we have already seen, Shakespeare's comedies are filled with mistakes, deceptions, confusions, and disguises. Shakespeare plunges us into the confusion in order to achieve a healing of relationships; it is because appearances are deceptive in life that we can only reach what is real by breaking up the surface of things, making what appears to be the case more confusing than it already is, in order to get to the truth. So the members of the audience are asked to hazard themselves no less than the characters in the comedy, to expose themselves to the dangerous experience of chaos, with the hope that order will—like love—finally reign. In this case, the surface of worthless lead hides the reality beneath. The one who chooses correctly has to enter a world of risk in which values seem to be subverted. This is a hazard beyond the two Princes who make their hapless and derided entrances, but Bassanio achieves it. The test of the caskets thus exemplifies the principle which has emerged from the story of Jacob's breeding of sheep: Shylock in his exegesis relies upon the power of the *outward* appearance of the stripped wands which the sheep and goats imitate, while Antonio know that this surface appearance achieves nothing without the grace of heaven and so the need to hazard.

Now, the theme of the character of law in this play is intertwined precisely with that of appearance. Legalism is preoccupied with the outward appearance and form of things, as the Apostle Paul stresses in 2 Corinthians 3:6–8: "6. [God] has also made us able ministers of the New testament, not of the letter but of the Spirit: for the letter killeth, but the Spirit giveth life. 7. If then the ministration of death written with letters and ingraved in stones, was glorious for the children of Israel could not behold the face of Moses for the glory of his countenance (which glory is done away) 8. How shall not the ministration of the Spirit be more glorious?"

There have been two streams of tradition in the exegesis of this Pauline text. The older, stemming from Origen, is hermeneutical, concerned with finding a meaning ("spirit") which exceeds the surface sense of any written text. The second, stemming from Augustine, is concerned with salvation and the opposition between law and grace.[28] But the two streams have often been interfused: legalism which undermines grace gives attention only to the outer letter of the text rather than the spirit *within* the text. So for Shakespeare, it seems that love and forgiveness have to penetrate beyond the surface of mere law, whether it is written on parchment like Shylock's bond, or cut into the stone of Moses's tablets. Bassanio, prompted by the "outward" form of the lead casket, muses on these issues of appearance and reality.

> So may the outward shows be least themselves,
> The world is still deceived with ornament.
> In law, what plea so tainted and corrupt,
> But, being seasoned with a gracious voice,
> Obscures the show of evil? In religion,
> What damned error but some sober brow
> Will bless it, and approve it with a text,
> Hiding the grossness with fair ornament? (3.2.73–80)

Shaheen comments that much of this speech about deceitful show "has biblical overtones, but much of it is also proverbial."[29] Some of the resonances he detects are 1 John 2:15–16 (listing "all that is in the world" as "the lust of the flesh, the lust of the eyes and the pride of life") and the citing of scripture by the devil in Matt. 4:6 and Luke 4:9–11, so approving error with a text (cf. 1.3.98). A more explicit scriptural reference on the same theme is the inscription of the scroll in the golden casket: "gilded tombs do worms enfold,"[30] recalling the words of Jesus in Matthew 23:27 about "whited tombs, which appear beautiful outward." The same scriptural reference had indeed already been associated with the gold casket in the "Morall" appended to the story in the *Gesta Romanorum*.[31] What is significant for our purpose here, beyond mere source-hunting, is that Shakespeare's intertextuality, whatever the text, enables him to present Bassanio as passing easily from critique of the text of civil law to religious texts, underlining the multivalent meaning of "law" in this play.

The story of the three caskets is a very old one, although in *Gesta Romanorum* it takes the form of a woman choosing the right casket to win a man, the son of the emperor of Rome.[32] There is a source for Bassanio's wooing of

Portia in another collection, *Il Pecorone* (where the hero Giannetto wins the hand of an unnamed lady, mistress of Belmont), and the same story includes the flesh-bond demanded by a Jew, the lady of Belmont's disguise as a lawyer, and the final trick with the rings. Most of the pieces of *The Merchant of Venice* are thus in this tale, but the wooing of the lady of Belmont is based on a totally different test: she (not her father) has made a law that "whoever arrives here must sleep with her, and if he can enjoy her, he must take her for wife."[33] No suitor has yet succeeded, since she administers a potion of drugged wine to them before bed. No source has yet been discovered which links the three-caskets story to the wooing of a lady of Belmont;[34] this original move by Shakespeare, together with the alteration of the inscription on the lead casket, has enabled him to link the theme of "hazarding for love" with reflection on the place of law in human life, civil and religious.[35] Through successive episodes, and through the use of intertextuality, he is building a contrast between (on the one side) law, regard for outer appearances, and a literal reading of a text, and (on the other side) love, risky self-giving, and a regard for the inner spirit and open meaning of a text. This is the spiritual approach to life that Shakespeare's play commends, and it is the theme that Shakespeare carries through into the climax of the judgment before the Duke of Venice.

The interesting case has been made by John Klause that Shakespeare has been influenced in his stress on "hazard" by the writings of the Roman Catholic poet Robert Southwell,[36] and others have also argued generally for a connection between the two writers, pointing to a large number of what are claimed to be verbal parallels.[37] It is certainly striking that Southwell stresses the qualities of "hazard" and "venture" in the Catholic spirituality he is commending, using the terms nearly thirty times in his *An Epistle of Comfort* alone, as also in his *An Humble Supplication to Her Maiestie* and *Marie Magdalens Funeral Teares*.[38] The words are, as might be expected given the situation, related to the selfless giving of martyrs, who "to so open hazarde, ventured themselves,"[39] often connecting this attitude with love for God and others. Klause finds that the phrase "to adventure the hazard" is "formulaic in Southwell," and though he admits that such formulas are "hardly unique to Southwell," he claims that it was Southwell's uses that lingered in Shakespeare's imagination.[40] This proposal is part of Klause's larger argument that the play reflects Protestant-Catholic conflict of the time, and that Shakespeare is following Southwell in using the figure of the hated Jew to further an anti-Protestant polemic. I have already insisted that it is not possible to pin Shakespeare down to such loyalties, but it is feasible that Southwell has played a part in introducing the language of "hazarding" oneself for a religious cause into the social text, even if Shakespeare has not directly read him, and that Shakespeare has constructed a more general dialectic of hazard and calculation from such a mood and textual echoes.

The Law, the Bond, and the Judgment

The world of Belmont comes to Venice as Portia and Nerissa pretend to be a lawyer from Padua and his clerk, who have come to judge the case which Shylock brings against Antonio. The plot of Portia's disguise, as well as her successful quibble that the flesh must be taken without blood and to the exact weight, all come from *Il Pecorone*. But Shakespeare brings to this his reflection on the relation between law and mercy, in the context of the need to travel beyond mere appearance to the heart of reality. The monarch's sceptre, says Portia in her speech on mercy, is only an *external* display of power:

> His sceptre shows the force of temporal power,
> The attribute to awe and majesty,
> Wherein doth sit the dread and fear of kings,
> but mercy is above this sceptred sway;
> It is enthroned in the heart of kings,
> It is an attribute to God himself (4.1.186–91)

Within Shakespeare's pattern of the comedy of confusion, adopting a disguise and so making appearance even more deceptive gives Portia the opportunity to penetrate the surface of law and bring everyone, Jew and Christian, to face reality. Portia's speech in the Duke's court is a tissue of intertextuality with scripture and other ecclesial sources, the result of which is to offer a spirituality of mercy in the face of human failings which is surprisingly light in doctrine. She pleads:

> The quality of mercy is not strained:
> It droppeth as the gentle rain from heaven
> Upon the place beneath: it is twice blest:
> It blesseth him that gives, and him that takes. (4.1.180–83)

Like love, mercy and forgiveness take risks. While Shaheen and Drakakis refer the first three lines to Ecclesiasticus 35:19 ("mercie . . . is like a cloude of rayne"),[41] there is surely also a resonance with Jesus's words in Matthew 5:45 that "God . . . sendeth rain on the just, & unjust"; the latter text makes clear that mercy takes no strict account of deserts, and it also hints at an element of sheer contingency, or divine hazarding. Jesus's reported words that "it is more blessed to give than to receive" (Acts 20:35b) are consequently recalled in the light of this and are radically changed into a double blessing of givers and receivers. Portia goes on to paraphrase St. Paul on the nature of justification by grace and condemnation by the law, though without explicitly mentioning the Christian story:

> therefore Jew,
> Though justice be thy plea, consider this,
> *That in the course of justice, none of us*
> *Should see salvation:* we do pray for mercy,
> And that same prayer, doth teach us all to render
> The deeds of mercy. (4.1.193–98; my italics)

A strong echo of Romans 3:20–21—"By the works of the Law shall no flesh be justified in [God's] sight. . . . But now is the righteousness of God manifest without the Law"—leads into reference to the clause in the Lord's Prayer ("that same prayer"), "And forgive us our sins: for even we forgive every man that is indebted to us."[42] When Portia urges that "mercy . . . is an attribute to God himself," she awakens echoes of far too many scriptural texts about the mercy of God than can be easily listed,[43] but the word "attribute" readily recalls the prayer in the Communion Service, "Thou art the same Lord, whose *property* is always to have mercy." Her opening plea to Shylock, "How shalt thou hope for mercy, showing none" (4.1.88), again echoes the clause on forgiveness in the Lord's Prayer, but is also an "interrogative version" of James 2:13, "for he shall have judgement without mercy, that hath showed no mercy."[44] Perhaps there is also in the background Jesus's parable of the Two Debtors (Matt. 18:23–33) when the lord of the unmerciful debtor asks the question, "Oughtest not thou also to have had pity on thy fellow, even as I had pity on thee?"

Shylock, however, decides to stand by the law, and replies: "My deeds upon my head! I crave the law, / The penalty and forfeit of my bond" (4.1.202–3). His first phrase echoes the words of the crowd before Pilate, "His blood be on us and on our children,"[45] especially in view of Shylock's reference to Barabbas some lines later (4.1.296–97). However, the story of the cross of Jesus remains implicit here in Portia's version of St. Paul. This is apt, because *both* Christian and Jewish believers can be urged to read their Scriptures as witness essentially to a God of grace and not a God of strict legalism. As Paul declares in the key intertext of Romans 3:21, the righteousness of God which is revealed "without the Law" has the "witness of the Law and of the Prophets." John Gross rightly insists that "the notion that Judaism has an inadequate concept of mercy is a travesty."[46] There is a far denser mesh of intertextuality with scripture here than in the speech of the judge to the vengeful moneylender in Munday's *Zelauto*, which is thought to have had some influence on Portia's plea; but Munday's version of the speech has explicit references to the judgment of God on sin and to "that blessed body, which bare the burden of our manifolde sinnes."[47] In Shakespeare a more general spirituality is emerging for all believers and nonbelievers: the importance of mercy, in which risks will have to taken beyond the strict limits of any written codes.

As with St. Paul, it is a matter of reading for the spirit rather than the letter in the written text, for (as he says) "the letter brings death, but the spirit gives life." Legalism insists upon a literal reading, and this is what Shylock does with his bond; he is constantly asking the audience whether what is asked of him is explicitly *in the text*. Portia asks, for example, that Antonio be permitted here and now to repay the money three times over, but the strict letter of the bond says it must be done within three months, and Shylock regards deviation of this as "perjury" of his "oath in heaven" (4.1.224–25). Portia asks that Shylock allow a doctor to stand by to try and save Antonio's life when the flesh is cut, but Shylock refers again to the written text: "Is it so nominated in the bond?" (4.1.255). Portia replies, "'It is not so express'd, but what of that? / 'Twere good you do so much for charity" (256–57). But Shylock is remorseless: "I cannot find it, 'tis not in the bond" (268).

As Shylock vows to live by the law, so he is condemned by the law. Those who will not take the risks of love and forgiveness will find that the law brings death. Portia encourages him to take up his knife and cut, but then at the last moment points out the full implications of the letter of the law. The bond allows a pound of flesh, but there is no mention of taking any blood with it. The bond states one pound, so Shylock must not take one tiny scruple less or more than the weight stated. If Shylock fails to take the exact pound, or sheds any blood, then he must pay the penalty of having all his goods confiscated and must himself die. Such a task is of course impossible, and, having made his decision, Shylock cannot now show mercy and retrieve the amount owed to him. Kastan comments that the "hyperliteralism" of Portia's reading of the contract is then compounded by the revelation of a statute that has not to this point been mentioned,[48] and that might have deterred Shylock had he known of it, or realized it applied to him: the law of Venice condemns him as "an alien" for having plotted against the life of a citizen, and may fine him up to the limit of one half of his estate, the other half being due to the defendant as compensation, with his life at forfeit. Shylock is now dependent on the mercy of the Duke and Antonio, who offer him his life and the use of half his estate until his death, on the condition that he is baptized as a Christian. After his death this half is to be passed to his daughter Jessica, who has fled Shylock's house to marry a Christian, Bassanio's friend Lorenzo. How "merciful" (4.1.374) all this might be is a matter to which I intend to return.[49]

The trick of turning the wording of the text of the bond against the money-lender is already contained in a number of analogues and possible sources for Shakespeare's play: among others, it is found in *Il Pecorone, Zelauto,* the *Ballad of Gernutus,* Alexander Silvayn's *The Orator,* and the Middle English version of the *Gesta Romanorum.* But Shakespeare has arranged the event so that, as Daniela Carpi has argued, "The struggle between Shylock and Portia is a struggle for the act of reading."[50] Like Christian interpreters of Paul's passage on "the spirit and the letter,"[51] Shakespeare has combined the issue of how to read a text with the theme of law and grace, exposing a contrast between the mathematics of gain and the absurdly gratuitous generosity of love. We have been alerted to all this by the rather obscure story of Jacob and the flocks of his uncle Laban, which raises the question about how to read a text, and so how to live a life. Did Jacob rely on the law of multiplication, or did he hazard for love? And so the audience is compelled to ask itself: are we to take our own risks in reading the stories of Jacob and Shylock, to look for the spirit or the letter?

The story of Jacob and Laban is even more appropriate than appears at first, for Jacob was not just hazarding for his wages. He was working for Laban for seven years without proper wages in order to pay the bride-price for Rachel, the loved wife of his heart. He had been tricked by his scheming uncle into taking her elder sister Leah on his wedding night, and to gain Rachel as well he had to serve seven more years.[52] Those who knew their Old Testament would realize that *Jacob* was also, like Antonio and Bassanio, on a venture of love. Shakespeare drops a rather broad hint about this when we learn in passing that Shylock's now dead wife was called *Leah.* It was the ring that Leah had given him before their marriage that his daughter Jessica steals and sells when she elopes with Lorenzo. It is the crowning indignity that Jessica exchanges Leah's ring for a pet monkey, as Shylock laments: "I had it of Leah when I was a bachelor. I would not have given it for a wilderness of monkeys" (3.1.110).

WHO ARE THE LEGALISTS?

We must try and catch something of Shakespeare's subtlety in his attack on legalism in the cause of grace. It is far too simplistic to see it as a Christian criticism of Judaism, although the play certainly reflects the anti-Semitism of Shakespeare's time, despite the situation that the few Jews living in London at the time were almost entirely converts to Christianity.[53] But though the play *portrays* this, does it *commend* it? It would be unrealistic to excuse Shakespeare entirely from anti-Jewish feeling, as a child of the religious and social prejudices of his time. But he does go a remarkably long way to *expand*

the category of legalism in support of the spirituality of mercy and forgiveness he is offering.

I have been arguing that contrast of calculation and risk running through
the play can be read as an echo of the Reformation contrast between old covenant and new covenant. Commentators have often proposed such a contrast,
but have usually presented it as a simple dialectic, with Shylock representing
the old covenant, and the Venetian and Belmontian Christians—especially
Antonio and Portia—standing for the new. However, there is a much more
complex intertextuality here, and a more nuanced treatment by Shakespeare
of the doctrinal dispute; awareness of this will help us to answer the question, "who are the legalists?" in this play.

It is an irony that Portia overturns Shylock's claim by a piece of sheer legalism, a quibbling on the precise letter of the text—no mention of blood,
and an exact pound. There is what Eagleton calls "a ruthless precision about
her sense of the text" and a "crassly literal" reading which ignores the spirit
of the law,[54] and which actually echoes Shylock's insistence on having the
letter of his bond. The point of Portia's argument is a theological one, that
to live by law and neglect mercy is to die by the law, and Neville Coghill—in
a famous essay of the 1940s—defends Portia's tactic simply on the grounds
that the theology calls for it.[55] The one who appeals to the law for his righteousness will end by being condemned by it.[56] But the play (*pace* Coghill)
is not a theological allegory, and Portia is arguing her point with legalistic
methods that have no place in Paul's rhetoric or elsewhere in the New Testament. Even if the quibble is necessary to save Antonio's life, it positions the
Christians on the ground of the old covenant. Moreover, it is clearly not necessary for saving Antonio to move onto the further legalism of a statute not
previously mentioned, and which depends on defining Shylock as an "alien."
Kastan raises the question as to whether Shylock would have considered
himself an alien in Venice, and in any case the law "ultimately assumes . . . a
Christian life is worth more than a Jewish one, at least in the sense that an
'alien' who seeks a Christian's life is punished more harshly than a Christian
seeking an alien's."[57] No doubt the requirement on Shylock to be baptized
would have seemed a charitable attempt to save his soul from eternal death
to Shakespeare's contemporaries, but Kastan remarks that theologians of the
time would have questioned whether forced conversion was a true or "willed"
conversion at all.[58] The insistence on the baptism of Shylock to avoid being
executed "seems a lot like the Jewish letter,"[59] a matter merely of what Bassanio had called earlier "outward show."

The spreading of legalism among all the participants is further ramified
by the identity of Shylock himself. He is certainly ethnically a Jew, but some
in the audience might well have glimpsed in his face the visage of Christians

accused of being legalists, either Roman Catholic or Protestant. After all, in *Zelauto* both plaintiff and defendant in the case of the flesh-bond are Christians. I have already drawn attention to the parallel that Luther draws between Jews and Papists, with regard to living by the rationality of law. Roman Catholics were widely accused by the new Protestants of trying to secure salvation by obedience to "the works of the law," the target being the theology of gaining merit through a whole system of good works. Luther graphically takes up the question of the Jew depicted in Galatians 3:19, asking, "wherefore then serves the law?," and puts it into the mouth of a typical Catholic cleric who is faced by theology of justification by faith alone through grace: "Of what profit has it been," he supposedly asks, to have lived under vows for many years in a monastery and to have undertaken arduous religious practices, if "a maidservant sweeping a house [is] not only our equal, but even better and more deserving?"[60] The Homily *Of Good Works* (1547) remarks that "Neuer had the [J]ewes in their most blindnesse, so many Pilgrimages vnto Images, nor vsed so much kneeling, kissing, and sensing of them, as hath bene vsed in our time."[61] Protestants might well see in Shylock's attitude an excessive veneration of the divine law by Catholics, and a number of commentators on the play have perceived a "Catholic Shylock."[62]

On the other hand, Catholics might well regard Puritan Protestants as maintaining with Shylock that "I stand for law." John Klause points out that Robert Southwell draws a parallel between Jews and Puritans, calling the church of Luther and Calvin the "sinagogue of antichrist," and he suggests that it is Catholic-Puritan conflict that is the reason for the oddly passionate nature of the doctrinal hostility depicted between Christians and Jews in the play, which hardly reflects the actual situation of the time.[63] Forced baptism, Klause argues, also makes more sense in the case of Christian heretics, who had already seared their consciences. With Richard Wilson, Klause finds a Roman Catholic spirituality depicted in Portia, who explains her absence from Belmont as an intention to lodge in a monastery (3.4.31) and who is described as straying about "By holy crosses where she kneels and prays" (5.1.30). Both find her to reflect the matriarchal lay-Catholicism which preserved the faith in England, represented by Lady Magdalen Montague, grandmother of Shakespeare's patron the Earl of Southampton; one of the family's houses was actually Belmont in Hampshire, famed as a "mass-seat" in England.[64] Klause thus maintains that there is coded Catholic attack on Puritans in the way that Shylock is presented, confronted by a Catholic voice in Portia, the lady of an estate that seems to live by Catholic customs.[65] Wilson is more circumspect, suggesting only that "the mercy of the Catholic mansion redeems the mercenariness of the Protestant market" in Venice.[66]

A Catholic would certainly resist the accusation of legalism, maintaining with the Council of Trent that there is a "cooperation" between works, grace, and faith in gaining salvation: works alone cannot avail.[67] This in fact had been Luther's own view in his earlier Catholic days, when he had seen an overlap between the old covenant of law and merit and the new covenant of grace and faith, works of merit "preparing" for the coming of the grace of God.[68] It was an irony that Puritans were often perceived by contrast as legalists, calling for a life strictly regulated by the laws of God as summarized in the Ten Commandments. Thereby they attracted a comparison with Jews, one prominent image on the stage being the Puritan "Rabbi" of Ben Johnson's play *Bartholomew Fair*. There lay behind this kind of attack a complex dispute between Protestants themselves about the relation of the old covenant to the new covenant, differences not only between Lutheran and Reformed theology—of which Calvin was the major representative—but differences within Reformed theology itself. Popularized versions circulated in sermons, making any simple distinction between a Jewish old covenant and a Christian new covenant unlikely in *The Merchant of Venice*. As I intend to make clear, this contemporary theological argument also explains why Puritans could be understood to be legalists.

In his mature thought Luther had replaced the old dualism between "old" and "new" covenant with a sharp distinction between "law" and "gospel." Living by faith in Christ and under the regime of grace, the Christian person—the "new man"—was entirely free from the law. Law was only relevant in two areas—for keeping evil at bay in a state which was not entirely composed of "new" human beings, and for bringing sinners to an awareness of their need of salvation and their perilous situation before a righteous God.[69] However, nobody was totally a "new man": even those living by faith were *simul justus et peccator*, and so law was necessary to continue to remind Christians of sins to be repented. But law was not given as a way of *living* by obedience to God after justification.[70] By contrast, Reformed theology was developing a theology in which the old covenant was a "covenant of works," contrasted with the "covenant of grace" in Christ. This first covenant had been made with Adam before the Fall, and was intended by God to bring Adam to salvation through obedience to the law and so the gaining of merit; after the Fall it became impossible for the "covenant of works" to achieve this state. After, however, somebody by faith alone had entered the new "covenant of grace" in Christ, established by Christ's atoning death, the old "covenant of works" could come back into play as a means of living a life obedient to God. According to the Heidelberg theologian Zacharia Ursinus, translated into English in 1587, "the lawe is to bee taught, that it may bee the leuil, squire and rule of our life and actions."[71] The "covenant of works" was useless for achieving salvation, but still of use in the Christian life, where it could be finally fulfilled, and fidelity to it was a mark of assurance in being one of the elect (a theology often called "experimental predestinarianism").

The doctrinal situation of the time was not, therefore, at all straight-forward. It has been argued that Calvin himself never subscribed to the idea of a prelapsarian covenant of works, but maintained there was only one cove-nant, a covenant of God's grace, existing in two historical periods and under two conditions, the same covenant in its old and new forms.[72] Those who lived under the old covenant "participated in the same inheritance and hoped for a common salvation with us by the grace of the same Mediator."[73] What matters is how the old covenant is read, and Calvin himself developed the hermeneutical duality of "the spirit and the letter."[74] The "double covenant" of works and grace, it is said, was an invention of neo-Calvinists develop-ing a "federal" theology, whose roots lay more in thought of Zwingli and the Zürich Reformed theologians, with some influence from Melanchthon's view of the legitimate place of merit.[75] Other scholars do find a "covenant of works" in Calvin's thought, laying stress on what he calls a "covenant of law," and in God's primordial, sovereign intention to "bind" God's self to human beings in a bond of mutual obligations.[76] What is clear is that many Puritans in England at the time of Shakespeare, such as William Perkins,[77] did sub-scribe to a "covenant of works," more in the line with the Reformed theology of Zürich than Geneva, and the ordinary person would be well aware of the high profile which Puritans subsequently gave to the need to regulate their lives in accord with God's commandments. It would not be difficult to dis-cern a "Puritan Shylock."[78]

In all these different doctrinal packages, whether Catholic or Protestant, grace was acknowledged to lie in the old covenant, and even (where such an idea was held) in the "covenant of works." There was no absolute dialectic between a covenant of law and a covenant of grace. Where law is criticized, it is about the way it is being read, missing the element of promise. Real theological differences began to emerge about the place of law within the *new* covenant: was it only a means of exposing sin, or was it the "rule of our life and actions"? When Shylock declares, "I stand here for law," his attitude might then be understood by different hearers as being typical of the Jew (by all Christians), or a Roman Catholic (by all Protestants), or a Protestant Puritan (by Roman Catholics and also by some other Protestants, especially of a Lutheran disposition).

Shakespeare does not take sides in this dispute, as is typical of his even-handed approach, but the discussion in the air about the place of law in Christianity does enable him to be critical of all participants in the drama. When Portia arrives in the Venetian court, her seemingly innocent inquiry, "Which is the Merchant here, and which the Jew?" (4.1.170), has far-reaching implications. It has a social and economic edge, since mercantilism and usury are both means of exchange, and there is a sense in which they imitate each other in building wealth. But Shakespeare is also to surround the query with another kind of "mimetic desire"[79] as all, including Portia, succumb to legalism. Shylock's own brand of Jewish legalism is underlined early on by his insistence on keeping the Jewish food-laws: "I will not eat with you, drink with you, nor pray with you" (1.3.33); but this pronouncement stands in a particular context; it caps an ironic refusal to eat pork, which Shylock justifies by the Gospel story in which Christ "conjured" demons into pigs (Matt. 8:32–34). Shylock is thus using a refusal to share a meal to turn the rhetoric of demonization against his accusers: they are accusing him of being the devil, drawing on Matthew 4:6 (1.3.98–99, "the devil can cite Scripture for his purpose," cf. 3.1.2), but, he implies, they "literally ingest the devil each time they eat pork."[80] Shylock in fact on another occasion does eat with Christians (2.2.17–18). Again the audience may have also heard a resonance with Puritans who, as Milward points out, points out, were known for their religious exclusivism.[81]

Shylock exposes the hypocrisy of those who urge mercy upon him, and yet use no mercy themselves in the way they treat their slaves, as if they were no more than "asses, dogs and mules." They make them sweat under heavy burdens, and do not allow them to marry. Christians say "the slaves are ours, we bought them." So, says Shylock, "The pound of flesh which I demand of him / Is dearly bought, 'tis mine and I will have it" (4.1.98–100). Shylock is making clear that the Christian citizens of Venice are appealing to the same letter of law as Shylock is doing: they all think that they *own* human flesh because the law has made flesh a matter of commerce.

Shakespeare is not making one person or one ethnic group the target; it is legalism and an attraction to what lies on the surface that he is exposing, wherever it occurs. The singing of the angels and of the "young-ey'd cherubin" in Lorenzo's speech on celestial harmony (5.1.60–65) echoes the crying aloud of the angels and the "Cherubin and Seraphim" in the Te Deum, which followed the first lesson in Elizabethan Morning Prayer. But, though this speech is supposedly pointing up a contrast with the "muddy vesture of decay" in human life that prevents us from seeing the harmony, in finding a metaphor for the stars Lorenzo himself is more attracted to the external appearance of the "patens of bright gold" than the eucharistic bread that the patens contain. As Kastan comments, "Lorenzo finds the language for what is precious in the golden plates of the communion service rather than in the mystery of the Eucharist itself, that is, in what has a price rather than what is priceless."[82] Whether the audience can look beyond the surface is the spiritual challenge that emerges from the play.

The Body, Flesh, and Blood

Being preoccupied legalistically with the mere surface of things magnifies the ethnic and religious difference between Jews and Christians. The "Jewish gabardine" marks Shylock out as the "other" and is the target for Antonio's venom—indeed, spittle. The body itself, "flesh and blood," can also be regarded as a marker of difference, and several characters in the play treat Jessica's body in this way. Janet Adelman notes how characters insist that Jessica remains racially bound to Shylock and to Judaism through her body even after her conversion to Christianity.[83] Launcelot Gobbo[84] asserts that she cannot be saved, even if she marries a Christian (Lorenzo), *unless* Shylock were not physically her father in the first place and she had been born illegitimately from a non-Jew (3.5.5). The Second Folio assumes this is actually Launcelot's belief, by reading "did" in the earlier First Folio line, "If a Christian do not play the knave and get thee, I am much deceived" (2.3.11). Launcelot backs up his jocular assertion that Jessica is damned by her own body with a biblical text, that "the sins of the father are to be laid upon the children," a quotation from the second commandment (Exod. 20:5) as it appears in the Communion Service of the Book of Common Prayer.[85] Shylock too insists from his own point of view on Jessica's bodily identity with Judaism, declaring, "I say my daughter is my flesh and my blood" (3.1.33), even after she has eloped and he wishes her dead. Salarino continues the presumption that difference is established by the body when he denies an identity between "thy flesh and hers," finding a distinction between their bloods like that between red and white wine (35). Salarino's image is a rhetorical one—Janet Adelman calls it a "fantasy";[86] he can only mean that that she behaves *as if* she were begotten from a different body, and she herself takes the same line by insisting that "though I am a daughter to his blood / I am not to his manners" (2.3.18–19). She, however, has another reason for thinking that she is no longer of the same body as Shylock: "I shall be sav'd by my husband, he hath made me a Christian!" (3.5.19–20). This echoes the Apostle Paul's assurance that "The unbelieving wife is sanctified by the husband" (1 Cor. 7:14), which assumes the Hebrew background of understanding husband and wife to be of "one flesh" (see 1 Cor. 6:16), as is shown by the Apostle's consequent comment, "else were your children unclean."

All this seems to insist that the body is a marker of difference, but there are indications that Shakespeare wants us to question this assumption. The phrases "all flesh" and "flesh and blood" are widespread throughout the Hebrew Bible and the New Testament to indicate simply being human.[87] The fact that "flesh and blood" became a common expression in everyday speech does not mean that it would not still have sounded biblical when

Shakespeare used it,[88] and in the Hebrew text, as Terry Eagleton notes, "the body is not in the first place a physical object, but a form of relationship, a principle of unity with others."[89] Lancelot's legalism of the flesh, and probably Salarino's too, is meant to be comedy, and Jessica does not simply submit to her husband as the savior of her body; indeed, she dares to mock his lack of sincerity (5.1.18) with the accusation, "Stealing her soul with many vows of faith / And ne'er a true one," which has an uncomfortable ring to it. Nowhere is this questioning of the body as a *separator* of identity more apparent than in the wager of the flesh-bond itself. We can, in fact, with Eagleton, view the bond as a kind of cry for Jewish flesh to be recognized as equal to Christian flesh.[90] Shylock stands within a long history of the abuse of Jewish flesh by Christians (see 1.3.101–26); revenge certainly motivates his claim on a pound of Christian flesh, but the very agreement gives Shylock a kind of gruesome intimacy with Antonio, or what Eagleton calls "a grotesque parody of eucharistic *fellowship*."[91] What stands between them is not the mere currency of financial exchange, but flesh itself. Flesh is what they have in common, and when Antonio faces the payment of the forfeit, it is with a curious intensity that Shylock calls Antonio's flesh "my flesh" (4.1.100). This recalls his claim earlier upon "what is my own" (1.2.113), perhaps echoing Matthew 20:15, "Is it not lawful for me to do as I will with my own?" Now what is his "own" is not just money, but flesh. At the point of death it is all too clear that we have a common humanity, a fact that Antonio himself has denied in his behavior toward Shylock. Shylock's great speech in defence of Jewish humanity affirms that what we all have in common is the body:

> I am a Jew. Hath not a Jew eyes? Hath not a Jew hands, organs, dimensions, senses, affections, passions? fed with the same food, hurt with the same weapons, subject to the same diseases, healed by the same means, warmed and cooled by the same winter and summer as a Christian is?—if you prick us do we not bleed? If you tickle us do we not laugh? if you poison us do we not die? and if you wrong us shall we not revenge?—if we are like you in the rest, we will resemble you in that. (3.1.52–61)

Since this speech ends with a cry for revenge, there are some limits to its power to awaken sympathy, but that is not its aim. Its purpose is to urge the "sameness" of the body.[92] Shylock's bond, then, is not so much a strictly legal instrument as a means for forcing us to recognize that Christians and Jews have a common body, exposed to the same life and death. And so we may return again to the story of Jacob and his uncle's flocks, which sets the tone of a common heritage; Antonio and Shylock can discuss the passage because they share the same spiritual ancestor. Though Shylock calls the Christian Launcelot "Hagar's offspring" (2.4.43), a descendent of Abraham's woman slave-servant rather than of his free wife, Sarah, this is only a reversal of Paul's allegory in Galatians 4:21–31, where it is the adherent of the "covenant of Sinai" or law (the Judaizer) who is the son of Hagar. Shylock's insult underlines, for those who catch the echo of Paul's image, that both Jew and Christian are claiming descent from Abraham, the father of those who live by faith (Rom. 4:1–18).

Nevertheless, a stress on sameness of body may also raise problems for healthy relationships in society. Late-modern philosophers such as Emmanuel Levinas and Jacques Derrida have analyzed the tendency for the human subject to project itself on others, failing to recognize and respect their true "otherness" and instead to view them as extensions of the self and so objects to be possessed, used, and dominated.[93] Similarly, the novelist and philosopher Iris Murdoch has insisted on the need for the self to give proper "attention" to the other.[94] The negative side of Shylock's insistence that Antonio's flesh is "my flesh" is the belief that he therefore owns it, and cannot give attention to Antonio for who he is in himself. The reader or viewer of the play thus experiences the need to affirm otherness as well as sameness, or identity in difference.[95]

The conclusion of the play, the trick with the rings, underlies the danger of *possessive* sameness. When Portia and Nerissa, wearing their disguise, succeed in begging from Bassanio and Gratiano the rings they have themselves given their husbands, they have the makings of a great deal of fun at the men's expense as well as material for some sexual innuendo on everyone's return to Belmont. Once again, as in all Shakespeare's comedy, reality lies beneath the surface appearance of literal words: Nerissa speaks truth when she confesses that she has already lain in bed with the lawyer's clerk the night before (5.1.261–62). Moreover, there is an even more direct connection with the theme of law and grace. Bassanio has bound himself to Portia with the bond of marriage, just as Antonio is bound to Shylock by the bonds of credit. Portia had stipulated and Bassanio had agreed that the sign of this bond, the ring, should never leave the finger of Bassanio. Like Shylock's bond, this one involves the body, as Portia makes clear when she demands to see Bassanio's finger toward the end of the play, describing the ring as "a thing . . . riveted with faith unto your flesh" (5.1.168–69). No bond, no bargain, could be more serious. Yet even this, the trick makes clear, cannot be held legalistically. It is right for the bond to be broken when love requires it, the love of Antonio for Bassanio. The joke with the rings has a profound theological meaning: there is no earthly legal bond which must rigidly be upheld against the stronger demands of love and mercy.[96] But it seems that this company of Venice and Belmont will never learn the lesson: the play ends on a sexual double-entendre by Gratiano, laying claim as a husband to the possession of Nerissa's body: "Well, while I live, I'll fear no other thing / So sore as keeping safe Nerissa's ring." The metaphorical association between "ring," "honour," and "vagina" was an Elizabethan commonplace,[97] and the final jest here underlines the commodification of women's bodies. Karen Newman comments that when Portia gives herself to Bassanio, she "objectifies herself."[98]

Curiously, the "identity in difference" which can both accept and respect the "other"—whether Jew, Catholic, or Protestant Puritan—is hinted at in the parody of Isaac's blessing of Jacob which is played out in the scene between Launcelot and his father, Old Gobbo (2.2). Having begun the play in biblical intertextuality with one story of Jacob, Shakespeare gives us an earlier episode in Jacob's life, already alluded to in the first with the words "as his wise mother wrought on his behalf" (1.3.69). What Rebecca had done for him was to help him to disguise himself as his elder brother Esau, and so deceitfully receive Esau's inheritance along with a blessing from his blind father, Isaac (Gen. 27:5–38). Deceit is also at the center of the action between Launcelot and his own blind father, with Launcelot pretending to be a gentleman and telling his father that his son has died; confusion multiplies as, confessing his true identity, he asks his father to bless him, and Old Gobbo fails to recognize him, believing him indeed to be dead. Touching the body of the son plays a key part in both this incident and the biblical story—as, amusingly, does the mistake of feeling a hairiness on it.[99] Lowell Gallagher suggests that Launcelot has lost his identity through his comic tricking of his father, and that this is only restored when Launcelot associates himself with both Jew and Christian, insisting, "I am Launcelot, the Jew's man, and I am sure Margery your wife is my mother" (2.2.90). Gallagher calls this a proclamation of "equivalent intimacy with a Jewish paternal body and a Christian maternal body," and concludes that "Two bodies are . . . summoned into a glancing type of union."[100] The union, he suggests, is symbolized in the dish of doves that Old Gobbo brings as a present for the Jew, and then transfers at Launcelot's request to Bassanio. Doves are presented in the sacrificial rituals of the Old Testament, but in the New Testament a dove is chiefly associated with the baptism of Christ. This image of transference from Jew to Christian could, he admits, be read as Christian triumphalism and supersessionism, but he thinks these attitudes are ruled out by the sheer spirit of the gift: echoing Derrida, he maintains that "the spirit of Gobbo's gift is the impossible thought of unconditional giving."[101]

In discussing this disclosure of "the transfiguring claims of the Other within the Same," Gallagher asks the penetrating question, "Where is the body of Christ?"[102] Commentators have tended to identify the Christic body with Antonio, prepared for sacrifice. Despite dismissing the once-popular fashion of finding Christ-figures everywhere in Shakespeare's plays, Hamlin is prepared to find echoes of Christ in Antonio.[103] But Gallagher is surely right to find the eucharistic body distributed more widely in this play, wherever there is a trace of kenotic self-giving, and wherever "the Other and the Same subsist in a profound though precarious intimacy."[104] These are observations that take us some way into our final task of reflecting on the intertextuality of this play with a theology "in front" of it, or into the making of theology through reception of the play.

MAKING THEOLOGY: INCLUSIVISM AND THE COVENANT

The spirituality that emerges out of *The Merchant of Venice* presents the audience with a number of questions, of which we become aware as we explore the intertextuality "behind" and "within" the play. Do we hazard for love, or calculate for what we can gain? Will we allow legalistic attitudes to be moderated by mercy? Do we respect all flesh, or only our own kind? In fact, these are three ways of putting the same question—which is "what kind of 'bond' holds us together?" As we now take another direction and consider the relation with theology that lies "in front" of the text, any of the three questions could be a shaping influence on the theologian as she lives in the play-space of the *Merchant*. In our time, however, it will perhaps be the third form of the question that has the greatest resonance. The Christian characters in the play seem to exhibit a kind of "hard supersessionism" with regard to Judaism,[105] the belief that a new covenant in Christ has not only fulfilled the promise of the old covenant made with Israel, but has superseded and replaced it; so the only way of including the Jew within Venetian society is by conversion. The horrifying truth that became evident in the twentieth century was that such a traditional Christian attitude is at root anti-Semitic and needs to be repented of, since the end point of such an argument, in the kind of world in which we live, is the Holocaust.

If we allow this third form of the question to make its impact, Launcelot Gobbo and Jessica, the characters most living on the boundaries of different religions, step out of the shadows of being a subplot and become central to the whole picture. We gather from their stories that if the varied social groups of Venice are to live together in the "harmony" that Lorenzo optimistically celebrates, flesh will need to be recognized as the "same" and yet also "other." We see too that this is the same issue as the "bond" or the covenant: old and new covenant are the same and yet different. Positively, their sameness is in offering a pattern of life which participates in the movements of love in God's own life; negatively, it is in a proneness to legalism. Taking a more modern perspective, religions—and *religio* means the tie, or "bond," of a society—must be respected as both the same and yet other. Inclusion cannot mean the suppression of difference. Living imaginatively through the experience of the play and taking seriously *both* the question, "which is the merchant, which is the Jew?" and the assertion, "I say my daughter is my flesh and my blood" should thus cause the theologian to reexamine doctrinal accounts of relating Christianity to other religions.

One approach may be called "inclusive relativism," and has been advocated by John Hick under the title of "a new Copernican revolution." Like planets circling the sun in our solar system, the many world faiths express many revelations of One God, relative to particular times and contexts: we have to realize, asserts Hick, that "the universe of faiths centres upon God, and not upon Christianity or any other religion. He is the sun, the originative source of light and life, whom all the religions reflect in their own different ways."[106] Though Hick thinks that the "different ways" will always prevent the assimilation of the world's religions into a single religion,[107] it is clear that he regards difference as relating only to "the cultural and philosophical form" of what is in essence the same truth. Living in the play-space of the *Merchant*, with its intense "doctrinal passion,"[108] Hick's universe seems to err on the side of sameness at the expense of otherness. But a second approach to the question of multiple faiths, traditional "exclusive absolutism," fails to take sameness seriously. The archetypal expression of this view was made at the Council of Florence in 1438, that "outside the Catholic Church no one, neither heathen nor Jew nor unbeliever nor schismatic, will have a share in eternal life."[109] A more moderate version of this doctrine holds Christianity to be a "supernatural" fulfilment of "natural" knowledge of God in other religions, but this distinction assumes that such natural endowment is not a "saving" knowledge in itself, and so leads inevitably to supersessionism and its worst consequences.

The Catholic Church now takes a very different approach from the Council of 1438, with the statement of the Second Vatican Council of 1965 that the "plan of salvation" includes "first that people to which the covenants and promises were made, and from Christ was born according to the flesh" (i.e., the Jews), and then, "those who acknowledge the Creator, in the first place amongst whom are the Moslems: these profess to hold the faith of Abraham."[110] This statement is interpreted by Hans Küng as recognizing that the world's religions are the "ordinary" way of salvation in a universal salvation history, while the way of salvation in the Christian church appears as something "extraordinary."[111] However, Küng apparently considers the "ordinary" way to be provisional: non-Christians' right and duty to seek God within their own religion is only "until such time as [they are] confronted in an existential way with the revelation of Jesus Christ."[112] They are, Hick judges, "called and marked out to be Christians," and so this approach remains "the old Ptolemaic system" where the Christian faith is the center of the universe.[113] The same critique can be leveled against Rahner's recognition of adherents of non-Christian faiths as "anonymous Christians."[114]

How can a theologian respond to the experience of the *Merchant*, that on the one hand there is only "one flesh" in all humanity, and yet on the other that religious groups want to insist that "I say [she] is *my* flesh and *my* blood" and that there is an otherness here to be respected? Perhaps the least unsatisfactory approach is that which has been dubbed an "inclusive uniqueness," in which Christian theology will find a unique revelation of God in the life of Jesus Christ, but will also understand this revelation as being thoroughly inclusive of other faiths which do not acknowledge such uniqueness. In dialogue, of course, Christians will respect those who make the same claim for uniqueness in their own religions, while preserving the integrity of seeing the world in a Christian way. The Catholic theologian Raimundo Panikkar has worked this approach out thoroughly, as expressed most fully in his study *The Unknown Christ of Hinduism*. The heart of his argument is that Jesus Christ is the meeting place between Christians and those who hold to other faiths, because adherents of all faiths meet in the life of God, and for a Christian the triune God must be inseparable from the Christ who "mediates" God to the world. Such an elaboration of the "meeting ground," Panikkar hastens to add, "does not seek to win the acquiescence of the Hindu, but only his understanding of it."[115] Hence, for Christianity, "Christ is already present in Hinduism. The Spirit of Christ is already at work in any Hindu prayer. Christ already present in every form of worship, to the extent that it is adoration made to God."[116]

Thus there is salvation—or transformation of human life—without explicit or conscious allegiance to Christ. "Conversion" does not mean a change from one culture to another, but a changing "in" the culture—"a changing into a new life, a new creation, a new existence which is precisely the old one—and not another—but transformed, lifted up, risen again."[117] This approach takes "otherness" seriously, in that Christians will expect to learn more about their *own* faith through a mutual encounter with God with others; they will not just be communicating faith but exploring it. Articles of faith are only "expressions, manifestations, explicit examples of a mystical act of Faith" in which a Christian encounters others "because it is Christ who inspires."[118] Christians will especially learn more about their Christ from the form he takes in the life and faith of others, since "Christ is not yet 'finished,' not yet 'discovered,' until the 'last moment.' ... The process itself is still open-ended."[119] To affirm that there is a "hidden Christ" is not the same as supposing there to be "anonymous Christians"; as Panikkar puts it, "the great thing is to overcome this tribal Christology by means of a Christophany that would

permit Christians to recognize the work of Christ everywhere, without pretending to monopolize the mystery."[120]

Making the *Merchant* an intertext with theology will, I suggest, nevertheless show up a problem with Panikkar's approach. Panikkar suggests that the
presence of Christ in a religion like Hinduism is up to the present only that
of the cosmic Christ, the Logos or Reason at work in creation and renewal of
the world. Other religions, he claims, lack the "historical and concrete dimension of Christ which is yet 'inseparable' and 'indivisible' from his divinity and
cosmic action." Christ then "has not completed his mission there"; he must
"grow up" bodily in the other religion, and "he still has to be crucified there . . .
in order to rise again, as the same Christ (who is already in Hinduism)."[121]
Though he asserts that Christ has lived, died, and risen in Judaism, it would
surely be coherent according to his own logic to say that Christ has only done
so within Christian Judaism, rather than within the historic fabric of Judaism as a whole. But then, the question appears from a critic of the *Merchant*
(Gallagher), "where is the body of Christ" in this play? The name of Christ is
mentioned by Shylock, and his person is implied in the existence of Christians, the speech of Portia, and the rite of baptism. If the play makes us, the
audience, think of the Christ in whom God has shown the mercy to which
Portia appeals, its reflection on flesh and blood makes us also think that he
must be embodied in Jewish flesh as well as in Christian flesh, in Shylock
as well as in Antonio. A modern poet, Micheal O'Siadhail, echoing Portia's
words about the mercy that "droppeth as the gentle rain" ("compassion's fluid
laws"), puts these words into Shylock's mouth:

> I hazard broader love when I ask you
> Has not a Jew these eyes, these hands? If this
> Is true of Jews, then surely it's true too
> Of all that breathe. Your hate's a Judas kiss
>
> Betraying us both as I respond with hate.
> My pound of flesh is what I'm asking for;
> From a Christian bringing down my rate
> I'll have my bond and therefore speak no more.
>
> I would be friends with you and have your love—
> But too enamoured of a loathing myth,
> Of centuries you cannot rise above,
> Forgetting stains that you have stained me with . . .
>
> There stop my speech! Transcend these tragic flaws,
> Apologise and shower us both with grace

To juice us with compassion's fluid laws.
Do you dare see your Christ in Shylock's face?[122]

We cannot therefore, having lived in the play-space of the *Merchant*, say with Panikkar that "Christ is there in Hinduism, but Hinduism is not yet his spouse. . . . Christ appears there to the eyes of Christians, somewhat as a prisoner in a body which still has to die and rise again, to be converted into 'Church' in the precise theological sense of the word."[123] This presents a picture of Christ who is to be met as a kind of transcendent spirit rather than as actively *expressed* through bodies in the world, but I suggest that we *can* meet the risen Christ taking form in bodies within Hinduism, other world faiths and indeed in the secular world. We can give a positive answer to O'Siadhail's final question, "Do you dare see your Christ in Shylock's face?" This does not mean that we shall see a recapitulation of the story of Jesus of Nazareth, but we may expect to see *patterns* of love and justice exhibited that were typical of the life of the historical Jesus in his particular context. As Panikkar himself makes clear, the Christian conviction that the Logos or Wisdom of God can never, after the resurrection of Jesus, be separated from the Jesus of history does not mean that the Logos is exhausted into Jesus.[124]

This universal enfleshment of the risen Christ, released from historical particularity, fits in with the image of Trinity as movements of relation that I have already developed.[125] In his earlier work, Panikkar refers to a theology of mediation, in which Christ is understood to be a connection between a spiritual and a material world. Panikkar suggests that to meet "in God" is to meet "in Christ," because Christ is the only "link, one mediator between God and the rest."[126] This picture, however, depends on a Platonic worldview, in which there are two separate worlds (often regarded as unchanging "being" and transient "becoming") and some kind of bridging principle between them. The early church, though not the New Testament,[127] tended to adopt this philosophical picture, which inevitably implied that God the Father was absent from the world in himself, and relied on mediation.[128] This kind of picture unfortunately lends itself to a disembodiment of the Logos, except in the particular situation of incarnation in Christ. Later, however, Panikkar writes of our "participating in God," and the experience of being "in" a God who is "movement and energy . . . life as constant dynamism . . . God understood as a force that is not based in ourselves."[129] This picture of participating in a triune God, indwelling in relationships that are inexhaustible, is an alternative to mediation, and leads to a Christology of inclusive uniqueness. I mean that for a Christian the "movement," or "rhythms," of the life of Jesus fit more exactly into the movements in God than other finite lives, but that all life shares to some degree in this same dynamic. So all the speech of

Jesus, all the ways he sees the world, all his acts fit exactly into the movement in the Trinity that we recognize as being like a son relating to a father, and that we may call "Christic."

The relation of the human person Jesus Christ to the one whom he calls his heavenly father can be mapped exactly onto the relation in God which is like that between a son (or daughter) and a father (or mother). The historic Jesus fits the eternal Christ with a match that for Christians is unique.[130] His prayer, saying "Abba, Father," his cry of desolation, "My God why have you forsaken me," and his offering a welcome to the outcasts of society: all these fit into the movements of the Trinity which are like speech, suffering, and generous love. But when we recognize this, we can find the same patterns in all other bodily life, within all religions and none. Wherever people share in the self-giving love of the triune God, the body of Christ will become visible, not only in individuals but in social structures. The form of the material body of the risen Christ will not be *simply* the same outside the church as in the church, since within the church it is characterized by the preaching of scripture, the gift of the sacraments, and the lifestyle of Christian disciples, and Christ will be met in a particular way in word, sacrament, and ecclesial *koinonia.* Yet in this difference the body is still the same, as the dwelling in the world of the risen Christ who was Jesus of Nazareth. This vision of embodiment accords, I suggest, with the duality we experience in *The Merchant of Venice,* that all flesh is the same ("which is the merchant, which is the Jew?"), and yet that Shylock's insistence "I say [she] is my flesh and my blood" is to be respected.

This sameness and difference can, in the history of religions, be described as covenantal. The Hebrew Bible and the Christian New Testament present us with a range of covenants that God makes with different social and ethnic groups in humankind. They are the same, yet different in context and aim.[131] This note is sounded in the Hebrew Bible's account of primeval history, with the covenantal declaration of God to Noah that: "I am establishing my covenant with you . . . and with every living creature that is with you, the birds, the animals and with every creature of the earth. . . . I will remember the everlasting covenant between God and every living creature of all flesh that is upon the earth."[132]

Much later, the prophet Hosea has the same breadth of vision of covenant when he relates the promise of God that "I will make for you a covenant on that day with the wild animals, the birds of the air and the creeping things of the ground, and I will abolish the bow, the sword and war from the land" (Hosea 2:18). Mark Brett has proposed that we can see a "Priestly imaginary" in the universalism of the Noahic covenant, a vision of God's relation to all creation by the Priestly School of theology which is setting itself over against a restrictive view of a merely national covenant and national sovereignty.[133] The participation of the whole universe in God means that we should think of a diversity of covenants between God and creation, not leveling all these relations out by one common denominator. It does not mean from the Christian point of view that all humanity and all religions live in the same covenant as if they were some kind of invisible church, a view toward which Jürgen Moltmann tends in identifying a "church of the poor and oppressed,"[134] and to which Panikkar seems to aspire in his vision that all religions can take the final form of "church." Nor do we have to think that God's many covenant partners have been always faithful to the covenant; both the history of Israel and the church, for instance, tell a different tale. But because there is a history of covenant between God and others that a particular religion may not know, we can expect that listening to the story of others in interfaith dialogue will deepen the grasp of each participant on their own story of faith.

Both Jewish and Muslim thinking recognizes such a diversity of divine covenants. Within Judaism there is, in particular, the tradition of the Noahic covenant as a universal reality. The modern Jewish scholar and rabbi Naftali Rothenberg, expounding the Mishnat Rabbi Eleazer 6 on this covenant, concludes that "This is the beginning of a possible partnership between Jews and non-Jews," because "there is essentially a shared covenant and mission" and there is "the consequent possibility of accepting the Other as one of the righteous of the nations."[135] He stresses that "the Jew remains a Jew" and "The Others remain Other,"[136] but at the same time they are partners in covenant. The principle of a diversity of covenants remains, as to a Jew the Abrahamic and the Mosaic covenants are exclusive.[137]

In Islam, the Qur'an records covenants with the Jewish people,[138] Christians,[139] and finally (normatively) with Muslims.[140] While the Qur'an does not portray a covenant with Noah in which different covenants are all grounded, it may be argued that it presents another universal covenant, a mysterious primordial, pre-Adamic covenant. Many commentators link sura 7:172 with the theme of covenant, picturing as it does a moment before the creation of the world when all human beings, in a preexistent state, testify before God that they acknowledge him. The point is that no one will have the excuse of ignorance on the Day of Judgement.[141] Less literally, Fakhr al-Din al-Razi in his commentary on the Qur'an in the twelfth century takes the verse to be a metaphorical account of a covenantal event that takes place in the life of all persons as they reach full maturity and the moment of accountability before God.[142] Thus the theme of covenant in the Qur'an explains the universal responsibility of humankind before God, and gives unity to the gradual unfolding of revelation to each prophet in sequence, throughout the story of Judaism, Christianity, and Muhammad himself, in a "covenant of the prophets."[143] Of course, Muslim accounts of covenant will interpret all covenantal relations in the light of the final covenant with Mohammed, and Jewish accounts will find the primal covenants with Abraham and Moses normative. My account of the new covenant in Christ leading to the bodily presence of Christ in all religions, and none, is similarly a Christian theological view of the world, and a Christian will not expect this viewpoint to be accepted by non-Christians.

Recent Jewish exegesis of *The Merchant of Venice* has suggested that, in the figure of Shylock and his fate, Shakespeare is recognizing the need for some structure of law that will support justice. One conclusion from Shylock's story, it is argued, is that religious tolerance cannot be fostered—and anti-Semitism overcome—by privatizing religion in a modern liberal manner;[144] another is that in a situation of racial conflict the use of mediating words is bound to fail without the particular verbalizing of law.[145] Yet Shakespeare's spirituality is characterized, as we have seen, by the conviction that law must always be limited by mercy and forgiveness. The idea of "covenant" may offer the theologian a way forward here. As well as offering a way of recognizing God's relation to all religions, it may also offer a model for society in which there is both corporate consent to law and a strong defense of individual human rights. As the Jewish scholar David Novak has suggested, a society which sees itself as bound by a "covenant" based on the scriptural paradigm recognizes mutual commitments between its members, and the rights of individuals and communities are understood as flowing from God's covenantal promises, which function as irrevocable entitlements.[146] There are thus no covenantal duties that are not backed by correlative rights, and this covenantal context will also encourage the operation of mercy and compassion within society.

What matters is that the texts of covenants, whatever form they take, or texts of corresponding documents in non-Abrahamic religions, should not be read legalistically. This is the imperative that emerges from living in the world of the *Merchant of Venice*, with its implied appeals to the old covenant and new covenant, given voice in the contentious word "bond." In the *Merchant* a start is made on reading for the spirit of a text, reaching beneath the surface, interpreting with mercy and with love, "to juice us with compassion's fluid laws." In the play this process is brought to an abrupt end by the Christians themselves, but the theologian, in front of the text, is encouraged to continue what has been begun on the stage.

6

King Lear and a Journey to Nothingness

*

"NOTHING WILL come of nothing." So King Lear pronounces to his youngest daughter, Cordelia, when she has failed—in a way satisfactory to him—to express her love in effusive terms. "Speak again," he commands, but to the word "nothing" she can only add, "I love your majesty / According to my bond, no more nor less" (1.1.92–93). Lear's dictum has respectable classical authority,[1] and by Shakespeare's time it had become proverbial.[2] Shakespeare's audience would have recognized it from the "textuality" of common speech. But there are other texts, those in the Christian tradition, which would, or should, have prompted them to question it. The mainstream theological accounts of creation increasingly insisted that God had created "out of nothing" (*creatio ex nihilo*);[3] at the very beginning of all things, *something*—indeed all things—had certainly come of nothing. The scholastic theologian Thomas Aquinas had been obliged to counter the common opinion that *ex nihilo nihil fit* (nothing comes out of nothing) precisely in order to establish the doctrine of creation from nothing.[4] Right at the beginning of the play the audience is thus confronted with a conflict of texts, and the play will force it to ask whether something *can* come from nothing.

For Lear's progress is to be a journey to the "nothing" which he invokes in his opening judgment on Cordelia. The play is a journey to absolute zero; it is the story of a man reduced to nothing, the passion story of a man stripped bare. As the Fool tells him, "Now thou art an O without a figure," that is, a zero with no number in front of it to give it value: "Thou art nothing" (1.4.183–85). The action proceeds remorselessly until Lear has nothing left that people usually build upon in their lives. And the "nothing" is accompanied by two other negatives, "no" and "never." Lear, driven insane, dies of a broken heart with the dead body of Cordelia in his arms, holding in the embrace of death his sole faithful daughter with whom he had just before been tenderly reconciled.

> And my poor fool is hanged. No, no, no life!
> Why should a dog, a horse, a rat, have life
> And thou no breath at all? O thou'lt come no more,
> Never, never, never, never, never. (5.3.304–7)

Lear's lament echoes and intensifies the repetition of "no more" in the text of Job 7:9–10: "He that goeth down to the grave, shall come up no more. He shall return no more." Shakespeare's fivefold "no" ("No, no, no life! . . . no breath . . . no more") and the fivefold "never" underline an end which a chorus of characters compares to the terrors of the end of the world and the Last Judgment:

> KENT.   Is this the promis'd end?
>
> EDGAR.   Or image of that horror?
>
> ALBANY.   Fall and cease. (5.3.261–62)

Although wrongs have been set right and the kingdom restored to Lear, he and the guiltless Cordelia must still die. It seems a profoundly pessimistic vision of the world. Lear has come to the final "no" and "never." He has entered apocalypse now. Yet the question posed to the audience is whether something can after all come out of this dread nothingness.

In this book I am proposing a threefold relation between Shakespeare and theology, set up by his intertextual practice. In the first place, Shakespeare picks up a whole range of imagery and ideas from the Bible and from the theology of his time, using them for the purposes of poetic drama. So in *King Lear* Shakespeare presses Christian images of the end, of apocalypse and of divine judgment into the uses of poetry, not dogma. The Christian story of the world has an ending to it. Each little story of a human life comes to an end in death; and the grand story of history comes to an end with new creation. In this play Shakespeare is making a poetry of endings, and to do so he makes his own appeal to scriptural texts. While his main source play, *The True Chronicle History of King Leir* (first played 1594, printed 1605), has multiple biblical references, Naseeb Shaheen judges that none of these are used by Shakespeare;[5] his intertextuality is his own. In the second place, I have been arguing that a general spirituality emerges from Shakespeare's drama, not a set of doctrines but a spiritual way of looking at the world. In this play there is the need to take death seriously, with the hope that something will outlast even the ravages of time and death. What that "something" might be we must wait to see. Then, in the third place, we can allow this play to make an effect on the making of theology, "in front" of the text. But for the moment let us trace Lear's journey to the end, a voyage to nothingness.

A Journey to Nothingness: Images of Disintegration

In considering the impact of the ending of any story, the critic Frank Kermode has suggested that the end of a narrative is what unifies it.[6] Kermode has argued that the ending of a narrative creates a pattern for the action within it, unifying past, present, and future in a way that overcomes the mere successiveness of time as measured by the clock. The sense that the story is working toward an ending turns mere *chronos* into moments of *kairos*, or points of time filled with the significance of being part of a larger story. Thus all fiction, he argues, provides "paradigms of concord"; it encourages us to think that our lives, too, can be a whole, despite their appearance of fragmentation. In accord with this proposal, I suggest that the ending of *King Lear*, the "no" and the "never," integrates the whole process of the plot.

Lear's path to tragedy begins with the mistake he makes in the first scene of the play, when he deprives himself of royal power in a foolish way, and so propels himself toward the nothingness of the end. The plot simply works out the action that begins when Lear "divests" himself of his crown, and the shape of the play is a dissolution to nothing. In the very opening scene Lear strips himself of the garment of power, shaking "all cares and business from our age" so that he might "*unburdened* crawl towards death." This unburdening is to result in the scene on the heath when Lear in madness tears off all his clothes, "Off, off, you lendings; come unbutton here!," and it reaches its climax at the end with Lear desperately trying to get some breath into Cordelia dead on his lap: "Pray you, undo this button." As the fool says, Lear has put down his own breeches (1.4.165).

Lear's mistake is not so much the political error of divesting himself of authority; it is the manner in which he has done it which unlooses the apocalypse. He has chosen the recipients of his kingdom by making love a commercial matter of bargaining, and has thereby stripped himself of what matters most—the fellowship of those who love him truly. He has divested himself of his daughter Cordelia and his faithful servant Kent, as he decides to distribute his lands and rule among his three daughters and his sons-in-law according to the degree to which the daughters can swear they love him. The two selfish daughters find no difficulty in flattering the old man and drawing their payment, but Cordelia (whom Lear loved most) is unable to play this numerical game and compute her love by arithmetic:

CORDELIA.   What shall Cordelia speak? Love and be silent.

. . . .

LEAR.   What can you say to draw
         A third more opulent than your sisters? Speak.

CORDELIA.   Nothing, my Lord.

LEAR.   Nothing?

CORDELIA   Nothing.

LEAR.   Nothing will come of nothing: speak again.

CORDELIA.   Unhappy that I am, I cannot heave
             My heart into my mouth; I love your majesty
             According to my bond; no more, no less. (1.1.62, 85–93)

Shakespeare is to offer a series of images in the play which express a reduction to nothing, all of which have resonances with biblical texts and the wider Christian tradition. In this speech there appears the first image, the untying of a bond. The "bond" Cordelia respects is the harmony that ties together the elements of the universe in the thought of the time. The bonding that unites her to her father is the opposite of the divesting and dissolution which is the action of the play; Lear's world comes apart because he has neglected this great creative bond by appealing to the text that "nothing will come of nothing." By despising Cordelia's bond Lear has unlinked the Great Chain of Being, as in savage anger he orders her exile from the kingdom, and the result will be to propel himself into nothingness, into "no" and "never."

We have already come across Shakespeare's playing with the word "bond" in *The Merchant of Venice*, and there it stands not simply for the old covenant but for the reading of the covenant in a particular, legalistic way. Here the word "bond" is framed in more positive terms; Cordelia explains that it means that she will "Obey you, love you and most honour you"—echoing the words in the Marriage Service of the Book of Common Prayer, "to love, cherish and obey." She is speaking of her bond with her father, but uses a phrase which includes the word "love," thus adding "love" to the injunctions in Exodus 20:12 ("Honour thy father and thy mother") and Ephesians 6:1–2 ("Obey your parents. . . . Honour thy father and mother") of which there are also resonances here. Indeed, the Marriage Service offers a prayer following the giving of the ring which deliberately defines "covenant" (the bond) in terms of "perfect love." The bond that holds all things together is nothing less than love. It is significant that when Goneril later despises Albany for his scruples, calling him a "Milk-livered man," she accuses him of having "a cheek for blows" (4.2.51). The phrase echoes and rejects the new commandment of Jesus in the Gospels, "unto him that smiteth thee on the one cheek, offer also the other" (Luke 6:29), expanding the call to "love your enemies" (v. 27).

Lear has, however, made love a matter of commercial exchange, and his daughters repay him in kind. They break their bond, as Edgar/Mad Tom indirectly points out ("obey thy parents," 3.4.78), by progressively stripping him of whatever power and ceremonial dignity he has left. Since he has made love a matter of arithmetic, he ought not to be surprised when they start doing the sums. They reduce his retinue of knights in rapid calculation, and to begin with Lear accepts the logical equation of love and quantity. When Goneril cuts his hundred knights to fifty, he denounces her as a "marble hearted fiend," and curses her into sterility, but when Regan cuts the fifty to twenty-five, he vows to return to Goneril after all: "Thy fifty yet doth double five and twenty, / And thou art twice her love" (2.2.448–49). Lear is still calculating love by numbers, and ought not to be as astounded as he is when Goneril replies, "what need you five?" and Regan concludes the theorem, "What need one?" Lear begins to see the point when he replies, "O, reason not the need! Our basest beggars / Are in the poorest things superfluous" (453–54). Eagleton proposes that Lear's appeal "reason not the need" indicates that there is always a "surplus" of meaning over sign. It is a mark of being human that we transcend ourselves; in every area of culture there is a "capacity for a certain lavish infringement of exact limit," and so our very language will always be superfluous to exact need of sense.[7] Love, we gather, has the same superfluity, as Mark Anthony perceives in declaring, "There's beggary in the love that can be reckoned," in response to Cleopatra's Lear-like request, "If it be love indeed, tell me how much."[8] This is the excess, the "more things in heaven and earth" which Hamlet urges us to notice. But Shakespeare is portraying a journey into nothingness, a path into the void, launched from Lear's angry assertion of the doctrine of equivalence: "Nothing will come of nothing." He has made love into mathematics, and the total of the sum is nothing.

Lear is finally thrown out by his ungrateful daughters, the doors barred against him, to wander bareheaded and increasingly mad in the wind and rain of the open heath. His only faithful daughter, Cordelia, returns from exile in France with an army to restore him to his throne. Although the sisters are to be finally defeated, it is to be too late for Lear and Cordelia, as Cordelia is captured and murdered in a temporary defeat of her forces, and Lear himself is to die of a broken heart. The plot of the play is thus one of a progressive stripping away of status, possessions, health, and sanity from Lear.

A second image of disintegration and dissolution is that of unclothing, or stripping bare; humanity is to be reduced to a state of nakedness. The Bible is full of images of nakedness and lack of clothing as a symbol for human life in its most basic condition. Paul as he faces death is anxious that when he has lost his body he will "be found naked," and expresses his desire that "we would not be unclothed, but would be clothed upon, that mortality might be swallowed up of life" (2 Cor. 5:3–4). As Job reflects in the midst of his suffering, the nakedness of death is matched by that of birth: "Naked came I out of my mother's womb, & naked shall I return thether" (Job 1.21). When they meet on the heath, Lear reminds Gloucester of this experience of leaving the womb:

> We came crying hither:
> Thou knowest the first time that we smell the air
> We wawl and cry. (4.6.174–76)

There is probably some resonance here with Wisdom 7:3, "When I was born, I received the common air . . . crying and weeping at the first as all other do," but the pairing of birth and death in Job 1:21 is central to the theme of the play, as Lear moves toward his death. In a mesh of intertextuality, 2 Corinthians 5:3–4, Job 1:21, Wisdom 7:3, and also Wisdom 7:6 ("All men then have one entrance unto life, and a like going out") seem to resonate with each other in the memory of the playwright. The image of unclothing, which begins with Lear's intention to "divest" himself of rule, finds its most vivid example in the figure of Edgar, who assumes the role of the naked madman Tom, and accompanies Lear in his mad ravings on the heath. Edgar is in fact the loyal son of the Earl of Gloucester, who has been forced to go into hiding through a plot against him by his illegitimate half brother, Edmund. Ironically, it is meeting the supposed madman Tom that drives Lear deeper into his own real madness; Lear sees in Tom the image of humankind reduced to absolute nothing, and in his frenzy seeks to imitate Tom by tearing off his own clothes, stripping to "the [bare] thing itself" (3.4.105): "Why, thou wert better in a grave than to answer with thy uncovered body this extremity of the skies. Is man no more than this? Consider him well. Thou ow'st the worm no silk, the beast no hide, the sheep no wool, the cat no perfume. Ha? Here's three on's us are sophisticated; thou art the thing itself. Unaccommodated man is no more than but such a bare, forked animal as thou art. Off, off you lendings: come, unbutton here. [Tearing at his clothes]" (3.4.99–107). Hamlin traces here what he calls an "intertextual constellation" linking King Lear with Job in this image of unclothing.[9] Not only is there an echo of the naked body of Job 1:21, but in his *Sermons on Job* Calvin writes many times of God's stripping men naked: for instance, "I say, it becommeth us too suffer God too strippe us out of all, even to our bare and naked skynne, and to prepare oure selves to returne to our grave in the same state."[10] This book of sermons was accessible to Tudor readers in a translation by Arthur Golding (1574), who was also translator of one of Shakespeare's most used sources,

Ovid's *Metamorphoses*. Regina Schwartz notes that the book of sermons was adopted by several parishes for the use of parishioners, and that it "was surely one of Shakespeare's sources."[11]

The catalogue of animal donations to human adornment in Lear's speech is often noted as being similar to a passage from John Florio's translation of Montaigne,[12] but Hamlin argues that even closer is a sentence from the Catholic Robert Parsons's *A Booke of Christian Exercise*, adapted by the Protestant editor Edmund Bunny (1584). In the same context as Parson quotes Job 1:21,[13] he writes of "robbing" animals to adorn our bodies: "From one, we take his wool: from another, his skin: from another, his fur: and from some other, their very excrements; as the silk, which is nothing els, but the excrements of woorms."[14] There is in fact a strong case for the relationship between the stories of Lear and Job. It is possible that the Queen's Men played both Richard Greene's *The History or Tragedy of Job* and *King Leir* in the same year (1594), and Hamlin argues that the same actor may have played both leading roles: "If Shakespeare saw both plays this may have given him the germ of the idea for a play in which these two were drawn into parallel."[15] Following his reflections on human borrowing of apparel from animals, Parsons cites Job 27:19–21:[16] "When the rich man dieth he shal take nothing with him, but shal close up his eies, and find nothing. Povertie shal lay hands upon him, and a tempest shal oppresse him in the night: a burning wind shal take him away, and a whirl wind shal snatch him from his place." Both "rich men" Lear and Job are exposed to the whirlwind. In God's answer from the whirlwind, Job finds "nothing" in the sense of receiving no answer to his problem, except the assurance of the presence of God. In the tempest on the heath Lear receives "nothing" by way of answer from the gods, but whether he ultimately receives anything at all we must leave for the moment.

Pointing to the unclothed body of Tom, Lear asks: "Is man no more than this? Consider him well" (3.4.101). Again there is a significant biblical resonance here, since the author of the book of Hebrews quotes Psalm 8:4 in asking, "What is man, that thou shouldest be mindful of him? Or the son of man that thou wouldest *consider* him?" (Heb. 2:4).[17] It has been suggested that "consider him well" is another borrowing from a phrase in Montaigne, in Florio's translation: "a wretched, weake and miserable man: whom if you consider well, what is he[?]"[18] But Montaigne himself is probably citing the scriptural verse. Whereas Psalm 8:4 expresses admiration for human life, which is not the sense of either Lear or Montaigne, Hebrew 2:4 is making an ironic reversal of the Psalm since the author goes on to admit: "But we yet see not all things subdued unto him" (Heb. 2:8–9).[19] Quotation of the verse is therefore quite in tune with the tenor of Lear's speech.

A third major image of dissolution is that of water, not the life-giving refreshment of the river of life, but the death-dealing waters of chaos. Again this is a profoundly biblical image. Lear compares the storm on the heath in which he is caught, unprotected, with the primeval flood come again. Recalling the biblical texts about Noah's flood, the cataracts of heaven are opened from above, and the depths of the earth are broken open from below, so that the water pours into the world from every side (Gen. 7:11–12):

> Blow, winds, and crack your cheeks! Rage, blow!
> You cataracts and hurricanoes, spout
> Till you have drenched our steeples, drowned the cocks!
> . . . .
>
> . . . and thou, all-shaking thunder,
> Strike flat the thick rotundity o' the world,
> Crack Nature's moulds, all germens spill at once
> That make ingrateful man! (3.2.1–9)

The report of a knight in 3.1.5–6 that Lear "Bids the wind blow the earth into the sea" echoes Psalm 46:2–3, "though the earth be moved, and though the mountains fall into the middes of the sea." But even more potent than this storm outside is the storm within Lear's mind, and here the flood of water is a matter of tears. The whole play conspires to make Lear weep, for Lear has vowed never to do so (1.4.293–94; 2.2.471–75); when he cries, he will have finally come apart, and so he fights continually against tears (5.3.23–25). He regards tears as a sign of humanity reduced to its most basic, naked state, as he instructs the blinded Gloucester:

> If thou wilt weep my fortunes, take my eyes.
> I know thee well enough, thy name is Gloucester.
> Thou must be patient. We came crying hither:
> Thou knowst the first time that we smell the air
> We wawl and cry. I will preach to thee: mark me.
> . . . .
> When we are born we cry that we are come
> To this great stage of fools. (4.6.172–89)

But Lear does weep after all; at the end, with Cordelia dead in his arms, he associates weeping with the same "cracking" of the cosmos as the flood produces, crying:

> Howl, howl, howl, howl! O, you are men of stones!
> Had I your tongues and eyes I'd use them so
> That heaven's vault should crack. (5.3.255–57)

His crying is the sign of the final disintegration of his personality; when he cries, he dies. He is reduced to absolute zero, to humanity as a piece of earth, to mere dust. So Kent aptly inquires as Lear weeps: "Is this the promised end?" (5.3.262). The return of the primordial flood is a mark of apocalypse, and when Edgar adds to Kent's words, "Or *image* of that horror," there is a resonance with the query of Jesus's disciples about the "sign" of the end of all things, "Tell us when these things shall be, and what sign shall be of thy coming?" (Matt. 24:3).[20] Gloucester reflects, meeting Lear, that "this great world / Shall so wear out to naught," linking an image of the end to the clothing image ("shall so wear out"), and recalling Psalm 102:26, which laments that heavens and earth "shall perish ... even they all shall wax old as doeth a garment: as a vesture shalt thou change them."

A fourth image of disintegration is the fragmenting of human passions into animal forms, into a whole pack of wild beasts. Human emotional unity is scattered into animal diversity, or as Edgar preaches in his feigned madness, "hog in sloth, fox in stealth, wolf in greediness, dog in madness, lion in prey" (3.4.91–92). At the end point, these negative passions are depicted as demonic, and Shakespeare has drawn upon a contemporary tract about witchcraft and demon possession, Samuel Harsnett's *A Declaration of Egregious Popish Impostures* (1603) for some of the most vivid vocabulary which he puts into Tom's mouth. Harsnett, for example, portrays the demons of the seven deadly sins as taking animal form, among them the dog and the wolf.[21] According to Albany, Goneril's passions have taken on a deadly life of their own, so that "humanity must perforce prey on itself / Like monsters of the deep" (4.2.50–51). The Great Chain of Being is becoming unlinked, and so Lear complains over the dead Cordelia: "Why should a dog, a horse, a rat have life / And thou no breath at all?" While Harsnett is a primary text for this image of fragmentation, Shakespeare has added scriptural allusions of his own to support it. References to the serpent (1.4.280, "sharper than a serpent's tooth," and 2.2.349–50, "her tongue / Most serpent-like") echo Psalm 140:3, "They have sharpened their tongues like a serpent." Mad Tom's reference to "the prince of darkness" (3.4.139) derives from Harsnett,[22] but it also recalls the "princes of darkness" of Ephesians 6:12 (Geneva version). Alongside Albany's portrayal of Goneril as having degenerated into a cannibal-like fish, he places a more scriptural image of dissolution:

> She that herself will sliver and disbranch
> From her material sap, perforce must wither,
> And come to deadly use. (4.2.35–37)

Goneril retorts, "The text is foolish." Foakes assumes that the "text" refers to biblical injunctions to honor father and mother,[23] but it surely here refers more directly to Jesus's words in John 15:6, "If a man abide not in me, he is cast forth as a branch, and withereth: and men gather them, and cast them into the fire."[24] While Jesus is warning his disciples about the "deadly" consequences of separating from himself, like a branch splitting from a trunk, Albany is warning Goneril of the danger of spurning her origin in Lear. Continuing animal imagery, Cordelia laments Lear's journey to nothing as the route of the prodigal son, reduced to the level of pigs: "To hovel thee with swine and rogues forlorn" (4.7.39; cf. Luke 15:15–16).[25]

A JOURNEY TO JUDGMENT: A BIBLICAL PERSPECTIVE

Alongside all this biblical imagery that marks the journey of Lear to the state of zero, there is the biblical idea of human beings under judgment. Human beings are brought to nothing under the verdict of God. This idea is expressed, though ironically, in three mock trials in which Lear plays at judging his two ungrateful daughters, and these three fantasies of judgment mark out progressive stages on his journey to nothingness.

In the first of these scenes, which takes place in the raging storm of the open heath, Lear realizes for the first time the state of the naked poor. He calls upon the gods to show justice to the poor and to have vengeance upon their so-called judges who have exploited them:

> Let the great gods
> That keep this dreadful pudder o'er our heads
> Find out their enemies now. (3.2.49–51)

Significantly, at this point he includes himself as chief among the oppressed: "I am a man / More sinn'd against than sinning" (3.2.58–59). Lear has had a glimpse of humanity in its basic state, and he expects the thunder of heaven to intervene on the side of the poor and himself.[26] He is still confident about justice, and wants it applied. Albany later in the play has the same assurance: hearing of the assassination of the Duke of Cornwall while in the act of blinding the Duke of Gloucester, he exclaims: "This shows you are above, / You justicers, that for our nether crimes / So speedily can venge" (4.2.79–81), echoing words of Jesus in Luke 18:7–8: "Shall not God avenge his elect? . . . I tell you he will avenge them quickly." Later, Lear is to realize the futility of *demanding* this kind of vengeance: "the thunder would not peace at my bidding" (4.6.101–2). So Lear realizes he is not the Christ who "rebuked the wind," commanding "Peace and be still" (Mark 4:39).

In the second of these mock trial scenes, sheltering in a farmhouse near the castle, the journey to nothing has gone a further stage. Now Tom, the Fool, and Lear play out a court scene where Regan and Goneril are accused; so the poor and the justices have their roles reversed; the beggar and the fool change places with the judges (3.6.37–38). We have gone further than demanding that the law should be applied justly for the poor; the whole order of judges has been supplanted by the poor and the mad.

In the third trial scene, out in the open country again, there is now no human judgment at all. Lear realizes that in their basic state all people are equally guilty, all sinners. He calls for the court officer who lashes the back of the whore to halt his hand, for "Thou hotly lusts to use her in that kind / For which thou whipp'st her" (4.6.158–59). While small vices easily become apparent through the tattered clothes of the poor, "robes and furr'd gowns hide all" (160–61). We recall the words of the Apostle Paul, "Therefore thou are inexcusable, O man, whosoever thou art that judgest: for in that thou judgest another, thou condemnest thyself: for thou that judgest, doest the same things" (Rom. 2:1). This vision of universal sin also echoes Paul's assertion in Romans 3:23, "All have sinned and are deprived of the glory of God," but Lear does not quote this text directly. Instead, he refers to it in reverse, creating in his madness an apparently anti-Pauline text. He pronounces, "None does offend, none I say, none" (4.6.170) and acquits everyone:

> I pardon that man's life. What was thy cause?
> Adultery?
> Thou shalt not die—die for adultery? No!
> The wren goes to 't, and the small gilded fly
> Does lecher in my sight. (4.6.108–12)

Thus he works out in his own way Paul's conclusion in Romans 3:23: "there is no difference." Since all are guilty, none are guilty; no discrimination can be made between them. The death sentence against adultery, as in the Old Testament, must not be sustained (Lev. 20:10; Deut. 22:22); Christ's words in the case of a woman caught in adultery, "neither do I condemn thee" (John 8:4–5), are to be universally applied. All are equally guilty; all are equally innocent. We have arrived at nothing. As Gloucester perceives, echoing Psalm 102, "This great world / Shall so wear out to naught [nothing]" (130–31).

Lear's appeal to scripture makes it argue for universal innocence, against its overt meaning. For him, all is nothing. Yet the effect for the audience is more ironic: it is to make those who are inclined to judge others realize the actual fact of universal guilt and so their own guilt. Shakespeare uses just such a device in *Measure for Measure*, where the title comes from a text which presented a problem to the rulers and lawyers of the Elizabethan age: "Judge not, that ye be not judged. For with what judgment ye judge, ye shall be judged, and with what measure ye mete, it shall be measured to you again" (Matt. 7:1). Elizabethan jurists coped with the direct command of Jesus, "Judge not," by making a distinction between private and public spheres of life. Princes and other rulers were "Gods by office" not "Gods by nature."[27] But Jesus's perplexing command not to judge cannot be resolved so rationally. It opens up a space between divine and earthly justice which can only be bridged by imagination and sympathy for the accused, as *Measure for Measure* demonstrates in its plot.[28] With his dictum "None does offend," Lear reverses a text of scripture ("All have sinned") with the same effect for the audience, as he does with his reflection on those who had flattered him: "To say 'ay' and 'no' to everything that I said! 'Ay,' and 'no' too, was no good divinity. When the rain came to wet me once and the wind to make me chatter, when the thunder would not peace at my bidding, there I found 'em, there I smelt 'em out" (4.6.98–102).[29] Actually, the texts he is quoting *do* make saying "aye" and "no" a "good divinity," in the context of not resorting to oaths or breaking one's word. James 5:2 has, "Let your yea, be yea, and your nay, nay," and Matthew 5:37, "Let your communication be, Yea, yea: Nay, nay." With his apparent contradiction of these texts ("no good divinity") Lear startles us into thinking that there might be a use of "yes" and "no" which is not so profitable: flatterers say "yes" and "no" merely in order to reinforce what the other person hopes to hear. It seems that Lear's descent into "nothing" may be yielding a "something" for the audience; it remains to be seen whether it offers anything to Lear.

A General Spirituality: A Journey to Look on Death

Through an intertextuality of reference to biblical texts and wider Christian ideas, Shakespeare is progressing the plot and imagery of the play. Further, however, a general spirituality is emerging from this play. Viewing it, we feel the need to face the reality of death as an ending to life, to take death and the passing of time seriously. We have traced the way that Shakespeare propels one man, Lear, into the abyss of nothingness. He is reduced to humanity at zero, basic man with no clothing to hide his nakedness. Recognizing such an ending organizes and unifies our time, as the philosopher Heidegger insisted, giving us a horizon within which to live with a meaningful story.[30]

Some have suggested that Lear is redeemed through his experience; through his passion story, as with Christ, life has come out of death.[31] He has gone the furthest into death's other kingdom, and come forth in resurrection. Such commentators point to Lear garlanded in flowers like Christ wearing a crown of thorns, and they find evidence of Lear's sanctification in his reconciliation with Cordelia. But this is a fantasy; Lear is not redeemed; he is still, as he admits, a "very foolish, fond old man" (4.7.60). Lear is not redeemed, but he does *learn*. He looks steadily upon what humanity is like. He looks upon humanity at bare minimum, reduced to its basic elements, and he invites us to look too. Through his passion story his eyes are at least cleared. At the end Lear carries in Cordelia, dead in his arms, and he pleads with us:

> Do you *see* this? Look on her, look, her lips,
> Look there, look there! (5.3.310–11)

Some critics have suggested that Lear dies believing that Cordelia is alive after all; he is asking the bystanders to look on her lips which he believes are moving with breath, and so he dies in a final delusion to crown all his others.[32] I believe this is the wrong interpretation. Lear is simply asking us to look, to contemplate a piece of humanity, a piece of earth. This is a human being in the face of death. "Do you see this?" Lear presents Cordelia to us as the prime example of what a man or woman is; in himself, in herself, this is all. The very finest, the most faithful, the most loving—dead. This is "the thing itself," as Lear said earlier of the naked Tom.

The play as a whole invites us to "consider" this, humanity at zero. Lear's error from the beginning—like the lovers in *Midsummer Night's Dream*— has been a failure of sight. He has looked upon the outward appearance of words and flattery rather than being able to see to the heart of Cordelia. He has said, "Nothing will come of nothing." Continually in Shakespeare's plays, lovers suffer failure of inner sight; they do not trust the inner, intuitive vision of love and are deceived by the outward appearance of the senses. They reduce the meaning to the sign. Othello loses trust in Desdemona because of the flimsy proof of a lost handkerchief, while Claudio (in *Much Ado about Nothing*) shamefully rejects Hero because of the so-called evidence of an overheard conversation at a window. In the last mock-trial scene when Lear meets the blind Gloucester, it flits into Lear's mind that Cupid is depicted wearing a blindfold, and he recollects:

> I remember thine eyes well enough. Dost thou squiny at me?
> No, do thy worst, blind Cupid; I'll not love. (4.6.133–34)

As became evident in our reading of *A Midsummer Night's Dream*, Cupid is portrayed blindfold in Renaissance iconography to indicate that people in love see each other not with the outer senses but with an inner sight that transcends mere reason:

> Love sees not with the eyes, but with the mind,
> And therefore is wing'd Cupid painted blind. (1.1.234–35)

Lear is still neglecting this deeper love-sight. "You see how this world goes," he says to the blind Gloucester (4.6.143), but Gloucester has only come to see how things really are through his physical blinding by Lear's enemies as a punishment for supporting the old king, and Lear has some way to go before he sees with eyes of love.

The scene of the gouging out of Gloucester's eyes is a horrifying piece of theater, but only through this drastic piece of surgery to his moral sight does Gloucester come to see the truth.[33] He confesses that "I stumbled when I saw." We are reminded of the words of Christ to the Pharisees in the Fourth Gospel, alluded to elsewhere by Shakespeare: "now ye say, We see, your sin remaineth" (John 9:41).[34] The trick that the good son Edgar plays on his now blind father is painful to watch; Gloucester has become suicidal and wants to kill himself, so Edgar pretends that they are high up on the edge of the cliffs of Dover. It is only when Gloucester thinks he has thrown himself off the top of the cliff, and finds himself still alive, that he discovers the value of life, and the need for patience; he comes to agree with Edgar that

> Men must endure
> Their going hence, even as their coming hither:
> Ripeness is all. (5.2.9–11)

As in Shakespeare's comedies, the truth emerges here through a confusion which has healing power. The Fool is always doing this; he turns things upside down so that the audience can see that the world was the wrong way up all the time. His jokes reverse the normal order of things, and then we suddenly see that things were disordered anyway. When Lear is beginning to suspect a dislocation between his outward appearance to the eyes of either himself or others ("Where are his eyes?") and his real identity, he asks: "Who is it that can tell me who I am?" (1.4.217–21). The Fool replies,[35] "Lear's shadow." If this is a reply to the question "who can tell me . . . ?," then the Fool is claiming that only the shadow, the reverse side of things, can enable us to see clearly. This is the function of the Fool, and he disappears from the play with one more joking reversal of fact: "And I'll go to bed at noon" (3.6.88), so speaking truly of his untimely death.

The need for Lear to see clearly is linked with his need to weep, for tears are the natural emotional response to seeing clearly, the feeling part of the sight pattern. Cordelia both sees and weeps, saying at the end of the first act that she leaves her father with "washed eyes," washed with tears and washed clear of the specks of dirt in the eye that Jesus draws attention to in a well-known saying to the Pharisees of his time (Matt. 7:3–4). In the scene of reconciliation with her father, while Lear maintains a Stoic attitude, her eyes are full of "holy water." In his meeting with the blind Gloucester a little earlier, when Lear had asked with irony, "you see how this world goes," Gloucester had replied, "I see it *feelingly*," and Lear had added, "If thou wilt weep my fortunes, take my eyes" (4.6.145, 172). And at the last Lear both weeps and sees; he sees with feeling as he cries, "look here, look here." He sees the sheer fact of death which cannot be avoided if we are to give attention to other human beings. The chain of "sight" and "eye" images in *Midsummer Night's Dream* is associated continually with the need to see with the vision of love. In *King Lear* this love-sight is linked to the need to see death, or at least the need to recognize the condition of a life which is orientated toward death.

The Bible constantly urges us to take death seriously. It asks us to face the finality of death for human life, that is, to regard it as the end of the whole person, and not just the cracking of an outer shell of flesh so that the butterfly of an eternal soul can emerge. The modern biological view of psychosomatic unity fits in with the Hebrew understanding of the human being as a body *animated* by the "life" or "breath" given by God rather than the Greek view of a *soul imprisoned* within a body. The Hebrew view of a human person knows nothing of the dualism between soul and body that Christian tradition has absorbed from Platonism. According to the Hebrew Bible, the *nephesh*,[36] or "life" (often translated "soul"), may certainly be distinguished from the "flesh" (*basar*), but not as an independent entity, or "ghost in the machine" that inhabits the body and could exist outside it as a personal consciousness. At death the *nephesh* is described as being breathed out, or poured out like water that has been spilt on the ground and cannot be gathered up again (Job 11:20; Isa. 53:12; 2 Sam. 14:14). Having lost all the vitality, purpose, and emotions represented by the *nephesh*, the body is in the very weakest state and is thought to inhabit *Sheol* as a kind of shadow ("shade") of its former self.[37] It is as if the air has been let out of a tire and it has gone flat. The description of human vitality as *ruach*, or "breath," within the body pictures the wholeness of the human being in a similar way, although *ruach* tends to carry stronger psychical functions of intellect and will.

Death cannot be finally escaped. To be "rescued from Sheol," a phrase that occurs many times in the Psalms, means to return to health and so only to put off dying; the *nephesh* or *ruach* begins to drain out of the body in illness, so that ill people stand on the very borders of Sheol from which they can be said to "return" only if the *nephesh* returns to their body and they recover their strength (Psalm 30:1–3). For almost the whole period of the Hebrew Bible Israelite faith thus had no concept of a meaningful life beyond death, asking "can the Shades praise Yahweh?" (Psalm 88:10–12). The Christian hope for life beyond death begins with recognizing the impact of death; there can be no self-justification in terms of possessing a survival capsule—an immortal soul—but any hope lies in the creative activity of God.

The Reformation Context: Being Brought to Nothing

However, far from being a biblical play, some commentators have found this to be an essentially *pagan* play. It shows, they argue, either a disillusioned atheism or a rejection of any likelihood that a God or gods will intervene beneficially.[38] Susan Snyder, for instance, writes of Lear's sense of the "uncaring" heavens, as a typical indicator of the process of dying.[39] Certainly, the progress of the mock-trial scenes is marked by an increasing doubt about the thunder of heaven: in the last of these scenes Lear remembers "when the rain came to wet me once and the wind to make me chatter, when the thunder would not peace at my bidding" (4.6.100–102). Lear is no longer confident, as he was earlier, that the thunderbolts of the gods will strike at the guilty and vindicate the innocent. Gloucester offers one interpretation of this, taking a view of the nature of divine behavior as arbitrary, unpredictable and cruel, an opinion that was common in the classical world: "as flies to wanton boys, are we to the Gods; / They kill us for their sport" (4.1.38–39). Yet there is a growing sense, reflected (for example) by Alison Shell,[40] that the play must be set in the context of Reformation theology, rather than reading it anachronistically. It can be argued that Lear's doubts about the transparency of divine providence are not pagan—or therefore Gloucester's—at all, but reflect a thoroughly Reformation position.

One way of understanding this is to stress the Calvinistic context of belief in an inscrutable divine Providence. In this theology, human discernment of God's judgments in the storm of life and the whirlwind of suffering is always fallible, since God's plans are unsearchable by human beings. This, Shell suggests, is Shakespeare's intention, as embodied in Lear's responses to what befalls him.[41] She argues for a congruity between classical ideas of fate and high Calvinistic providence which could be exploited by playwrights. This fortuitous parallel, she argues, allowed a dramatist to explore emotional reactions to determinism, evoking either personal despair in the face of God's mysterious sovereignty, or optimism in the face of what appeared to be the justice of these decrees as they were worked out in events. Similarly, Hamlin takes a passage in Golding's introduction to his translation of Calvin's *Sermons* on Job, and compares it to the speech in which Edmund mocks the idea of astrological causes for disasters (1.2.118–33). Golding bids us to "look up to the hand that smiteth us" in God's inscrutable providence, rather than "impute [afflictions] to the influence of the skies."[42] God, thinks Calvin in one of the sermons, need not even act according to his own declared law, but simply according to his "secret justice"; God might not be punishing Job for any particular sin but testing him for his own good.[43]

If the message of the play were that, in line with Calvin's sermons on Job, one should simply submit to a mysterious divine providence, this would fit well with the well-known topos of the "patience of Job." A text from the Epistle of James had imprinted the idea of Job's patience on the Christian consciousness and made it proverbial, part of the common textual stock: "Ye have heard of the patience of Job, and have known what end the Lord made" (James 5:11). Lear does indeed vow to be "the pattern of all patience" (3.2.37), and Hamlin suggests that this wording recalls not only the text in James but more specifically the introduction by Golding to Calvin's *Sermons*, in which Golding describes Job as "a perfect patern of patience."[44] Falstaff makes a joking reference to the patience of Job in *Henry IV Part 2*, admitting, "I am as poor as Job, my lord, but not so patient" (1.2.101). In *King Lear* itself there are altogether eleven references to patience or being patient, including Lear's injunction to Gloucester: "Thou must be patient. We came crying hither."

But for all this I do not think that the spirituality conveyed by this play is the need to live patiently, under submission to mysterious divine providence. Lear shows himself as *impatient* under his tribulations as Job himself in the actual Hebrew poem, rather than in the summary of it in the Letter of James. A careful reader like Shakespeare could not fail to notice that the Hebrew Job is full of protest against God, and that he is not condemned for this attitude by the final divine speech from the whirlwind.[45] Hamlin himself admits that "what seems at first a contrastive allusion—Lear suffers as Job does, but not patiently—turns out to be more complex,"[46] but I suggest that there is no "contrastive allusion" at all. Nor is the theological fulcrum of the play the mystery of God's decrees, as Shell and Hamlin suppose. The Reformation context for this play lies somewhere else, in Luther's opposition to a "theology of glory," or belief in a God who could be demonstrated from the appearance of the world.[47]

King Lear shows agnosticism toward natural theology, that is any attempt to prove the existence and justice of God from the state of the world. But this is a typically Reformation "agnosticism." Luther finds God not as openly displaying himself in "thunder," but hidden in the suffering of the cross of Jesus Christ. The *deus revelatus* (the revealed God) is the *deus absconditus* (the hidden God) veiling divine power and glory in weakness. To the "theology of glory" there is opposed the "theology of the cross." I am not suggesting that Shakespeare is promoting Lutheran doctrine, but that the theological debates of the period provide the background for a more general spirituality of facing the reality of death. This appeal to a hidden God does have some association with what Calvin called God's "secret" justice, and it *could* be used to reconcile divine providence with the obvious injustices of everyday life, asserting that God operates by a principle of justice we cannot comprehend. Calvin certainly thinks in this way. But Luther, with his appeal to the hiddenness of God in the cross of Christ, opens the way to a different spirituality, in which God can be found hidden in the weakness of human suffering and mortality. This is the Reformation theme that suffuses King Lear, not the ineffable sovereignty of God.

Lear's doubts, like Job's, are not just about whether the nature of God's providence is self-evident, but about whether providence is active at all. The poem of Job itself offers no solution to the problem of human suffering. When God speaks to Job from the whirlwind it is not to make Job understand that God has a secret reason for inflicting suffering on Job. It is to draw attention to the scope, complexity, and elusiveness of the world that only God fully comprehends (chaps. 38–41), and so to underline that the human mind cannot solve the mystery of suffering.[48] Job is satisfied, not by an answer, but by assurance that God has not deserted him: "now my eye sees thee" (Job 42:5). Luther's concept of the "hidden God" is in fact closer to this witness of Job; he is not as dogmatic as Calvin about an absolute divine will or "secret justice" of God working itself out. The hidden God is to be found in the crucified Jesus, and so the believer is being encouraged to trust God in the face of suffering that may remain mysterious to reason. While Luther certainly condemns the "evil eye" that accuses God of injustice, he stresses that God's ordering of the world escapes the strict boundaries of any human rational arguments[49]—and among those, we may say, are the arguments that Calvin advances to *explain* the suffering of Job. The question is what an audience of Shakespeare's time would have felt the effect of the play to be. There would, no doubt, have been some who would have concluded that Lear was the object of inscrutable divine decision. Others, however, may have stood closer to a widespread modern theological perception which stands in the heritage of Luther: that no theological argument about suffering is finally going to prove convincing, and that the most effective theodicy is the practical one of fellowship with the Christ of the cross, in whom—in some sense—God is crucified.[50] It seems clear that the spirituality that Shakespeare is commending is not a dogmatic account of providence, but simply the need to face suffering and death realistically. And this means looking "nothingness" in the face.

This takes us to another dimension of the Reformation context of the play; *King Lear* echoes Reformation thought in seeing humankind as reduced to nothing *in itself*. Lear's conclusion in his last scene of madness on the heath, "None does offend, I say, none," removes moral differences between people as does the Pauline text, "all have sinned," but it has a greater shock value than the expected text. It indicates that no true justice, values, or moral order can be built on human nature acting *on its own*. This does not mean that there is no spark of goodness at all within the natural person; few Reformation thinkers—including Calvin—would have insisted on *that*, and most thought

of the image of God in humankind as being marred rather than totally destroyed.[51] Rather, the nothingness which Lear is driven to recognize is to be
seen in Reformation perspective as clearing the ground ready for something
to built upon it. We are meant to feel that Lear is altogether wrong when he
says that "nothing will come of nothing."

For the Reformers, humanity is reduced to nothingness in judgment as a
prelude to justification by grace through faith alone, and not by human actions. As Luther puts it, "God destroys all things and makes us out of nothing and *then* justifies us."[52] Again, in his commentary on the Psalms, Luther
reflects: "For what can [a person] reach, who hopes in God, *except* his own
nothing? He came from God and from His nothing (*suo nihilo*)."[53] He goes
on to write that God "reverses and disturbs the proud, *driving them back to
nothing*," forcing them to seek divine mercy, "having laid aside their arrogance
in their righteousness" since "the cross of Christ is the only learning of the
words of God, and the purest theology."[54] Later he repeats in his lectures
on Romans, that God's "strange work" (*opus alienum*) is "first to destroy and
tear down whatever is in us" before he does his "own work" (*opus proprium*)
of "giving us good things."[55] Nor is Luther alone in this perception. Calvin
writes similarly, commenting on Romans 4:17, that, "when we are called God
we arise out of nothing . . . we must completely die to ourselves. The condition of our divine calling is that the dead are raised by the Lord, and that
those who are nothing begin by his power to become something."[56] Luther,
however, uniquely merges the hiddenness of God and God's work of raising
from nothing in the cross of Jesus, where the *opus alienum* of God is displayed and in which the believer can participate. The play itself does not take
the step of moving from the "nothing" to the "something" which is "creation
from nothing," but it creates an open space for the audience to take this step.
At the end we, who sit watching the play, feel that something more must be
said, and the play leaves room for the audience to say it.[57] As Hamlet assures
Horatio, there are always "more things" to come.

Any biblical allusions that associate Lear with Christ in the play are thus
not in the service of making Lear a "Christ-figure" or the play into an allegory on redemption. The hint that Lear is sharing in the sufferings of Christ
does not identify him with Christ, but with all human beings who encounter
the hidden God of the cross in suffering. When Lear exclaims about Edgar
in the guise of Mad Tom, "Is man no more than this? Consider him well"
(3.4.102–3), I have argued that we hear an echo of the text in Hebrews 2:5,
where we are called to "consider" the state of the human being. The allusion continues as Lear appears, wearing a crown of weeds; instead of being
"crowned with glory and honour" which is God's intention for human life
according to Hebrews 2:7, *this* man, Lear, is crowned with weeds. Cordelia

describes him as "Crown'd with rank fumiter and furrow-weeds, / With burdocks, hemlock, nettles, cuckoo-flowers, / Darnel and all the idle weeds" (4.4.3–5). Shaheen here finds a reference to the homily "Of the Misery of All Mankinde," "We . . . bring foorth but weedes, nettles, brambles, briers, cocle, and darnel," comparing the human disordered state to an unweeded garden.[58] But it is the Hebrews' text that provides the image of the crown, as well as the lament that we do not yet see humanity wearing this crown as intended: "we yet see not all things subdued unto him."[59] The author of Hebrews then goes on to say, "But we see Jesus crowned with glory and honour, which was made a little inferior to the Angels, through the suffering of death, that by God's grace he might taste death for all men" (Heb. 2:9). When Lear does appear, wearing the crown of weeds, Edgar exclaims, "O thou side-piercing sight!," evoking the piercing of the side of the crucified Christ with a spear,[60] and so perhaps also the crown of thorns. But while Lear's suffering is like that of Christ, he is not a Christ-figure. The Christ-image is invoked simply to give the audience assurance that *something* can come of nothing; as Luther puts it, in the experience of "driving back to nothing," "the cross of Christ is the only learning of the words of God." Here, however, there is nothing dogmatic being said about the something that can emerge.

The same kind of resonances are awoken when Gloucester reflects that in the storm "I such a fellow saw / As made me think a man a worm" (4.1.35). It is just a couple of lines later that he continues, "As flies to wanton boys are we to the gods, / They kill us for their sport,"[61] but the reference to a "worm" is quite distant from the pagan ethos of the comment about "flies." The book of Job contains two texts that may be in Shakespeare's mind: "How much more man, a worm, even the son of man, which is but a worm?" (Job 25:6) and "I shall say to corruption, Thou art my Father, and to the worm, thou art my mother and sister" (Job 17:14).[62] But the best-known biblical reference to humanity as a worm comes from Psalm 22:6, "But as for me, I am a worm and no man." This is the Psalm which the church understands from its earliest years to be a prophecy of the crucifixion of Christ, and the speaker in the Psalm ("But as for me") is taken to be Christ himself; he calls himself a worm because he is scorned, despised, and mocked by people (vv. 6–8). If any association is being made between Christ and Edgar, it is for the same purpose as with Lear: to evoke the possibility of something emerging from all this nothing.

A General Spirituality: The Love That Lasts

It is the same story with the Christological associations that are made with Cordelia, though in her case Shakespeare gives the largest hint about what the "something" might be which comes from what Luther calls "driving us back to nothing," and which adds to the general spirituality of learning to face the nothingness of death. For most of the play Lear will not cry; he fails to see; he will not love. But through his reduction to nothing he is brought to tears, to sight, and, I suggest, also to love. The something which comes of nothing in this play is not only a clear view of death, but some glimpse of love.[63] In all Shakespeare's tragedies, something is affirmed at the end; even in the midst of the wreck of lives, something of value is rescued, held up for us to see and then fixed forever in story by the event of death. The story of it will last forever and so overcomes death. Here, at the end, Lear is reduced to gazing upon a human being reduced to nothing; but I suggest that we are drawn into feeling something else that has the seeds of possibility within it. Transfusing this nothingness is Cordelia's love for Lear and his for her in the face of death. It is love with no reconciliation to come, no eternal happiness promised. This is love in the face of bare mortality; yet humankind reduced to zero can still learn to love. Shakespeare's spirituality is to encourage hope in the potential of the power of love to survive and transform even death, though no details of this conquest can be given.[64] This is the "something" more which the nothingness provokes us to hope for, and which finally proves Lear wrong with his anticreation dictum: "Nothing will come of nothing." Instead, there are "more things in heaven and earth" than are dreamed of in his philosophy of strict remuneration.

Thus we are presented with the final tableau of Lear with Cordelia dead upon his lap. Helen Gardner perceives that this is a secular version of a *pietà*; where artists have conventionally depicted the sacred subject of Mary with the dead body of Christ in her arms, Shakespeare now gives us Lear with Cordelia in his arms.[65] It is a pose of faithful love. This is the "something" that comes of nothing. "My poor fool," says Lear, "look on her lips," and this is not a hopeless delusion that she is breathing, but a command that awakens all the echoes of love songs we have known where lips are the place for the kiss of love.[66]

Cordelia takes the part of Christ in the *pietà*, but this is not an allegory in which Cordelia represents a "pure redeeming ardour" which is divine.[67] It is simply a symbol of the excessiveness of human love, and the Christological reference points us to the "more" that can emerge from nothing. In this modest light we can recognize other instances where there is an intertextuality of Cordelia with the story of Christ. Before the first battle with Lear's enemies, she exclaims, "O dear father, / It is thy business that I go about" (4.4.23–24), echoing the words of Jesus in Luke 2:49 that "I must go about my father's business." Foakes comments that this reference is deeply ironic,[68] since Cordelia's "business" is to fight to restore Lear's right to be king, where

Jesus's business was to attend to God's affairs in the temple. But there is no allegory here, in which there might be a detailed, consistent parallel between the stories of Cordelia and Christ. The Christological hint simply directs us to expect something out of nothing, which is human love, flawed and fallible though it is. It might even, following Foakes further, be a love which mistakenly thinks that Lear *wants* to be restored to his kingship by this stage in the play.[69]

When Lear runs from the heath in madness, fearing he is being captured although his own supporters have arrived, a Gentleman comments: "Thou hast one daughter / Who redeems nature from the general curse / Which twain have brought her to" (4.6.202–3). The "twain" here in immediate context are Goneril and Regan, who have broken the bond of nature. But behind them stand another twain, Adam and Eve, whose fall, in much Christian thinking, had brought a curse upon the natural world,[70] and in that story the one who redeems is Christ. The logic is set out by Paul, though he restricts his thought to one man, rather than a human pair: "if through the offence of one, many be dead, much more the grace of God, and the gift by grace, which is by one man Jesus Christ, hath abounded unto many" (Rom. 5:15). Cordelia is once again being associated with Christ in the Gentleman's assertion, but once again too there is no allegory of redemption. It is Paul's "much more" and "hath abounded" that the audience feels, in the sense of the excess of love represented by Cordelia, that refuses to be bound by the calculation of the twain. The audience feels that if the bartering of love represented by these two has brought a curse into the world of Lear, much more will the unbounded love of one bring something out of nothing.

THE THEOLOGIAN IN THE PLAY: CHRISTIANITY AS A TRAGIC FAITH

To this point I have been exploring Shakespeare's own art. I have been suggesting that he draws on intertextuality with the Bible and theology for the uses of poetic drama, and that out of this network of reference he commends a kind of general spirituality of facing death and sustaining love. A Christian theologian should be especially sensitive to what Shakespeare is doing here—she may notice it when others miss it—but it is all the playwright's work. *Now,* however, as in my previous chapters, I suggest that something else can happen "in front of the text" (employing Ricoeur's phrase) for the *making* of theology.

Shakespeare, through Lear, is bidding us "look," and the theologian will respond by looking on two realities. First, she sees human suffering in all its seriousness. She recognizes what Donald MacKinnon has called the "intractability" of evil and suffering in everyday life.[71] MacKinnon maintains that the literary form of tragedy, such as *Oedipus Rex* or *King Lear,* is a form of discourse which expresses "as does no available alternative"[72] the "irreducibility" of evil and suffering in everyday life.[73] Tragedy as a literary form deals with contingencies and resists any resolution in a broader system of explanation or justification. It resists the drawing of any moral or metaphysical point which might soften its impact. If theology is shaped by the tragedy of *King Lear,* it will insist that there be no easy metaphysical consolations for these mysteries, no grand theories that can be foisted onto human misery, no guaranteed happy ending. In the second place, the Christian theologian who looks at human evil and suffering is bound to look at the cross of Jesus, insisting that we take the forsakenness and death of Christ with utter seriousness, forbidding us from any superficial alleviation of *Christ's* suffering. What is meant by affirming that "God is revealed in Christ" can only be grasped in the total desolation of Gethsemane and Calvary.[74] In these two ways, in these two dimensions (the passion of Christ, the passion of the world), theology learns to look with Lear, and develops what may be called a tragic theology.

Now, suppose that the theologian allows theology to be shaped by a celebration of the "something" that comes from nothing, the "more thing" which *King Lear* prompts us to expect. In the play itself this is only an intimation, not developed dogmatically. But the theologian is bound to have a fuller vision of this "something" than the slight clue about love to which the play itself rightly points us. The theologian is going to have the same view of God's grace in Christ that Luther and Calvin had, and that is going to be the explicit hope in resurrection that is missing in the play. This is where love of God for created beings, their love for each other, and their love of God will lead. In the words of the Fourth Gospel, "God so loved the world that he gave his only Son" so that people "may not perish but may have eternal life" (John 3:16, NRSV).

But what might be the nature of this "eternal life"? In underlining the seriousness of death in the Bible, I drew attention to the Hebrew conviction about the psychosomatic unity of the human being. This meant that for almost the whole Old Testament period Israelite faith had no concept of a meaningful life beyond death, asking, "can the dead praise Yahweh?" (Psalm 88:10–12). So when hope for a future life began to develop late on in Jewish belief, it had to be in terms of resurrection; that is, the whole person must be raised to life in a new bodily environment. There was no question of just a disembodied soul surviving death. The history of Jewish thought shows that death cannot be escaped by some kind of survival capsule; it could only be conquered—by resurrection of the body. This is the perspective that Christian faith inherited. The deaths of Jesus and Socrates have often been compared in this regard, Socrates urbanely discussing philosophy with his

friends while the poison was taking effect, Jesus in a bloody sweat in the garden and crying out on the cross. As the theologian Oscar Cullmann points
out, the difference was that Socrates thought of himself as stepping into immortality, his soul released from the prison-house of his body, while Jesus as
a Jew could only feel the onset of death as an attack upon life.[75] The finality
of death must be felt, in the Apostle Paul's words, as "the last enemy" which
has to be conquered by resurrection and a new creation. The Christian belief
was that this had indeed happened for the first time in Christ.

However, this belief raises the question, can Christian thinkers really look
at life from the viewpoint of Shakespeare's *Lear* at all? *Lear* encourages us to
cultivate "something" in the face of nothing, but in moving to a greater "something" in the form of the resurrection, would we cancel out the tragic vision
of the play altogether? The critic George Steiner, in effect, thinks we would.
He robustly asserts that "Christianity is an anti-tragic vision of the world. . . .
Christianity offers to man an assurance of final certitude and repose in
God. He leads the soul toward justice and resurrection."[76] Again he writes,
"Real tragedy can occur only where the tormented soul believes there is no
time for God's forgiveness."[77] So his claim is that there can be no such thing
as Christian tragedy, and the Christian faith is one key factor that has led to
the "death of tragedy" as a literary form in the Western world. Some Christian theologians have agreed with Steiner that the Christian story cannot be
seen as tragic, and have appealed as he does to the possibility of forgiveness
held out by the Christian faith. Brian Hebblethwaite believes that if tragedy
means "*ultimate*, eternal failure and an *absolutely* unredeemable corruption of
the good,"[78] then tragedy must be countered by the hope of universal salvation, or *apokatastasis*. Thus he opposes MacKinnon's contention that tragedy
is ineradicable from Christianity. He believes that while it is certainly hard to
apply the ultimate Christian hope to situations of unspeakable tragedy without the appearance of trivializing suffering, the fact that tragedies in life have
not so far been resolved "has no bearing whatsoever on the characteristically
Christian faith that, in the end they *will* be resolved, in the sense that their
victims *will* participate in resurrection, transformation and consummation of
all things."[79] The question, he thinks, is whether these failures, tragedies, and
horrors are "ultimate, irredeemable facts" and so whether the people involved
in them are "for ever unforgivable, unchangeable and unresurrectable."[80] Only
if they are, can tragedy be said to be "ineradicable" from Christian faith; but in
fact, the Christian faith as he understands it (and I agree with him) contests
the irredeemability of anyone or any thing.

King Lear calls us to look, but it is said that neither reality at which the
theologian looks—the passion of Christ nor human suffering—can be seen
as tragic in the perspective of the overall Christian story. The passion of Jesus,

it may be argued, is undermined by the *resurrection* of Jesus. The light of Easter must surely cancel out the darkness of the cross. This means also that the terrible reality of general human suffering is alleviated by the hope of eternal life based on the triumph of Christ. Nevertheless, I want to argue that *King Lear* demands that we develop a tragic theology, and shows us the way to do so. The impact that *King Lear* makes on theology is to urge it to conceive of the "something" (the "more") in a way that does not undermine the tragedy of human suffering. Lear holds together a realistic facing of "nothing" with allowing room for something to emerge. Living in its world should prompt the theologian to achieve the same kind of counterpoint in the rhythm of experience, even while giving the "something" much firmer definition than the play can do.

"Looking" at the death of Jesus, we see that the glory of the resurrection *follows* the cross in the Christian story. This is not the reversal or cancellation of the tragedy of the cross: it is an event of a completely different order. Death is not overcome by finding some inner meaning of the event, making it less final, but by new creation. It is just because death *is* serious—deadly serious—within this old order of creation, and Christ meets nothingness head-on, that God has to do something new in the face of death. We cannot lessen the desolation of the cry of Jesus, "My God, why have you forsaken me?" There is no secret survival strategy within this experience. In itself, the cross has no meaning: but it can acquire meaning.[81] From the other side of Easter, Christian theologians can now affirm that God was in it and using it as a final reconciling act of love. They cannot make this affirmation, however, unless they allow their very doctrine of God to be affected by it. If "God was in Christ," and so was in some way totally identified with this human being, then forsakenness and desolation entered into the very center of the communion of relations that is God. I have argued elsewhere that this must mean that the event of the cross of Jesus brings something unknown into the experience of God;[82] the theologian must say that God could not know, in terms of exact prediction, what would be the result of allowing the nothingness that Jesus encountered in the cross to enter the divine being and disturb its interweaving of relations of love. This could not be an ignorance forced upon God from some outside force, but a self-limitation willingly assumed by God's own desire to be creative and redeeming. God, to be God, must certainly have known the power of love to overcome evil, but what new creation would be like had to emerge from the actual victory of God over the "nothing."

This is why the story of the cross remains relevant for a suffering world. As Eberhard Jüngel affirms, contesting the "death of God" movement, God is not dead precisely because God has exposed God's being to death and overcome it by embracing it: there is a "death of the living God," a death that belongs to the being of God because God has taken it into God's self without being destroyed by it. Thus God is not "dead" to the world, just because God has experienced death in solidarity with human beings.[83] The symbol for the overcoming of death is "resurrection." This is a metaphor, picturing a "rising" as if from sleep, and cannot be a literal description since it refers to a new creation and we only have the tools of language of the "old" creation. As Wolfhart Pannenberg writes about the Hebrew concept, "speaking about a resurrection is metaphorical. The familiar experience of being awakened and rising from sleep serves as a parable for the completely unknown destiny expected for the dead."[84] Again, we see that hope for "resurrection," which Christian theology affirms has only happened so far, uniquely, in Christ, does not cancel out the cross. Language of death and suffering does belong properly to the world as it is, but "resurrection" is language of a different order, pointing to a reality that cannot be described literally. Living in the world of *King Lear* requires the theologian in these ways to develop the Christian "something" and the "more" while not undermining the reality of "nothing."

THE THEOLOGIAN IN THE PLAY: HOPE AND HUMAN SUFFERING

To find the "something" without underplaying the "nothing" applies not only to the event of the cross of Christ, but to the other reality that Lear commands us to see: all human suffering.

Richard Wilson has argued that the characters in the theater of human suffering on view in the play are not universal but specific, representing Catholics in England. He suggests, for example, that various references to "fools," including Lear's "we are come to this great stage of fools," echo Thomas More's reported words on the scaffold that he rejoiced to "play out the last act" as one of "God almighty's fools."[85] Lear's appeal to Cordelia to "sing like birds i'the cage" is, he urges, a recitation of Southwell's *Epistle of Comfort* enjoining Catholics to imitate the birds that "in the cage sing sweetlier and oftener than abroad," as well as to exchange roles with their jailers by becoming "gods spies" (cf. 5.3.9, 17).[86] He points to the evidence of the play's being produced in a Catholic household in the Pennines as evidence that Catholics owned it as "their" play, and recognized coded references to their plight in it.[87] However, some doubt as to whether contemporary Catholics did regard Shakespeare as giving special attention to their suffering is raised by a poem attached to the beginning of an edition of the martyr-narrative of the Catholic priest Edmund Jennings, published in 1614.[88] Alison Shell draws attention to this prefatory poem, which appears to contrast the "fictional" grief ("feyned passions") portrayed in King Lear unfavorably with the "true" grief evoked by the exceptionally cruel execution of Jennings.[89] Of the author of "King

Liere," the poet writes, "He hath applause," implying it is all that interests him. It seems then better to regard *King Lear*, not as a partisan account of selected suffering, but as what Foakes calls "a kind of objective correlative for the spiritual journey through life of suffering Man."[90] In this case, the "wheel of fire" (4.6.33–34) on which Lear feels himself to be bound is unlikely to be a direct reference to the instrument of torture and death to which the legendary Catholic saint Catherine was tied, as Wilson proposes,[91] but rather an image of the general human condition.[92]

The question is whether, in the Christian worldview, this universal suffering *can* be tragic if it is subject to an eschatological hope based in the resurrection. If *King Lear*—and indeed the book of Job—is allowed to make its impact, there can be no question of supposing that meaning can be *inherent* in suffering. Just as meaning is "acquired" by the cross of Christ so, as Hans Küng declares, "In the light of Jesus' definitive passion, his suffering and death, the passion of each and every [person] . . . *could* acquire a meaning."[93] The insight that meaning needs to be "acquired" does not demean the reality of suffering. But what of Steiner's challenge (and Hebblethwaite's) that tragedy cannot include any elements of forgiveness and reconciliation? *King Lear*, with its concluding *pietà*, might well cause us to question this, at least in regard to the kind of tragedy Shakespeare is writing.[94] It is surely possible for Christian theology to conceive of final consummation and final tragedy belonging together, in the reaping of a harvest of what A. N. Whitehead called a "tragic beauty."[95]

Apokatastasis, or reconciliation of all things, need not exclude elements of tragedy, as Steiner and Braithwaite assume, insofar as future transformation and new creation is an open concept. The new creation of created persons does not imply the making of a standard product, but the raising to a new level of reality of a personality that has been shaped by all the decisions and actions of this life. One might then envisage that there are values and experiences which were within the potential of a person but have tragically not been actualized, some goods which were within the grasp of a person that have been neglected. With Lear we might lament, "Thou'lt come no more: never." There has been, in short, evil as "lack of good" (*privatio boni*),[96] and this makes human persons what they are. It makes Shakespeare's tragic heroes who they are.

While we can only speak of new creation in images and metaphors rather than literally, we might expect that persons who experience future redemption will be totally satisfied with their vision of God, and will be unaware that they lack some unfulfilled potential. Objectively their beauty will include an aspect of tragedy, but it is likely that this lack of fulfilment will be known only to God, who will know that persons are not entirely what they could have been. The God who feels and values the worth of every life will thus (as Charles Hartshorne puts it) be open "to the tragedy of unfulfilled desire."[97]

In this sense, God will be the only one who experiences tragedy eternally, and we might conceive this to be an aspect of the divine humility. In self-limitation God allows created reality to make an impact upon God's very self, enhancing divine satisfaction and causing divine suffering. Scholastic thinkers (and in particular Aquinas) presumed that God's *aseity*—or self-existence—would be infringed if the being of God owed anything to any other reality outside itself;[98] God, it was asserted, can only be the origin and primary cause of all contingent realities if God's own being were totally unconditioned by the world. But God's experience of tragedy, including the "unknown" of the cross, can add something to the divine life without infringing God's aseity if we distinguish self-existence from self-sufficiency. There is no reason why a God who depends upon nothing else for very existence should not choose to depend on others for some aspects of the *mode* of existence. A God who is self-sufficient with regard to the very fact of existence is not thereby prohibited from electing not to be self-sufficient as far as the ongoing richness and value of divine life is concerned.[99] A vision of God as Trinity allows us to think of broken human relations being taken into eternal relations of love and (as Hans Urs von Balthasar puts it), deepening the difference and separation between the divine persons into a tragic gulf of estrangement,[100] as well as expanding divine relations by the embrace of human relations.

Such a God, one might think, is revealed in the passion of Christ, participating with infinite empathy in every human passion. Such a God is not the eternal victim of the universe, disabled and broken by suffering, since passionate love can absorb suffering and transform it. Indeed, we may judge that *only* suffering love has the power to persuade reluctant human wills toward the Good, and so overcome evil. Poetically we may dare to say that there is "an eternal cross in the heart of God."[101]

Such a vision of consummation, including tragedy, is—I suggest—true to the world of *King Lear*, though the play does not attain this vision itself. It also may enable the theologian to come to a conclusion in a theological dispute about the very nature of hope for the future.[102] The question has been posed: do the seeds of the future which God intends lie entirely in God or in the human situation in the present? Eberhard Jüngel takes the first view, appealing to Luther's affirmation that "justification" means that God raises human beings to something from nothing (*ex nihilo*).[103] The whole Aristotelian tradition (in which the text "nothing will come of nothing" has a place)[104] assumes the priority of actuality—what is here and now—over possibility. But the doctrine of justification, Jüngel argues, makes possibility prior to actuality, as we *become* righteous in God's sight before we *act* righteously. The hope we have in the future is thus not in the development of present actualities, but hope in God who distinguishes the possible from the impossible. In the death of Christ, affirms Jüngel, God "makes impossible the impossible," that is, God negates the nothingness of sin; and in the resurrection of Jesus, God makes possible the possible. Those who are justified have faced up to the nothingness revealed in the death of Christ, and they trust in the promise of the resurrection that God will bring new possibilities to the world from beyond it. The possible world to which Christian language testifies is generated from without, by God in the freedom of divine love.[105] This possibility has ontological priority over whatever we make through our own activity.

A similar view is taken by Jürgen Moltmann, who argues that the possibilities of the new creation come entirely from God's future, expressed as the future coming of Jesus. Moltmann's characteristic formulation is that they come from *adventus* and not from *futurum*.[106] Hope must be in the God of resurrection who does altogether new and unexpected things; there is no true hope in calculating or forecasting from present possibilities, which would only be an extension of the present and not a real future. The future (as *adventus*) can only be imagined, drawing on symbols such as resurrection, because it is the future of God.

By contrast, Paul Ricoeur understands hope to be based in the "surplus" which is always present in human existence. Like Jüngel, he affirms the priority of possibility over actuality, and he sees this possibility to be disclosed by God's action in the resurrection of Jesus; like Moltmann, he finds in the resurrection a revelation that even fulfilment of promise is not an ending, but open to yet more fulfilment to come.[107] Yet he sees this priority of possibility to be rooted in the basic structure of human existence, as itself being full of possibilities.[108] In the "world of the text" there is an overflowing "surplus" of meaning in language, rooted in the surplus of being in humanity itself. Human existence is orientated forward in a passion to be, and this is the true basis of hope.[109] Here he picks up the idea of a "surplus," or "excess," of meaning from Derrida, but gives it another direction from the endless straying and playing which Derrida commends; the result of the surplus in human life is not to *defer*, but to give us *hope*. Ricoeur finds that texts are eschatological because they express possibilities rather than actualities; they describe not how things are, but how they *might be*. For Ricoeur, human being is *possibility itself*, and out of this fecund capacity the imagination can create genuinely new possibilities which are not simply repetitions of the past and present; symbol and myth refer to a reality which is yet to come and which they help to create. Imagination offers possibilities to the will which adopts them and forms *projects* which are not dependent upon conditions in the present. In accord with Moltmann, he affirms that such projects are not unreal just because all the conditions for them do not exist here and now; but his reason, unlike Moltmann, is that the world includes "what *is to be done* by me." Human existence means that "the possible precedes the actual and clears the way for it."[110] This is why, to adopt Hamlet's phrase, "there are more things in heaven and earth" than are dreamt of in any philosophy held in the present moment.

If we live in the world of a tragedy, especially a tragedy as complete as *King Lear*, do we in fact find what Ricoeur affirms—a possible world arising from a surplus of meaning in human existence itself? On the one hand, Lear seems to bring us instead to a blank "nothingness" which demands something "more" which *theology* defines as a new creation through the Word of God. Though the play does not get this far, there is a slight anticipation of it in a comment of Edgar to his blinded father, encouraging him to turn away from suicidal thoughts and to have some hope for the future; he urges him to "Think that the clearest gods . . . make them honours / Of men's impossibilities" (4.6.73–74). That is, the gods gain renown by doing what is impossible for human beings to do. A number of critics find here an echo of Matthew 19:26, "With men this is unpossible, but with God all things are possible," and Luke 18:27, "The things which are unpossible with men, are possible with God."[111] It seems then that reading the play must cause a theologian to side with Jüngel and Moltmann. But on the other hand, there is the "surplus of meaning over sign" detected by Eagleton,[112] the question mark which the play itself places against Lear's dictum, "nothing will come of nothing," and what I have been calling hints about the "surplus of love," which arises from the characters themselves; the ending of the play calls for the audience to find a "something" in human existence which cannot be suppressed and which opens up the possibility of redescribing the world.

The possibility of bringing "something from nothing" in *King Lear*, together with a resolute facing of the "nothing" in human existence, might well challenge the theologian to try to combine the insights of Jüngel and Ricoeur. That there is something altogether new about the future in God's new creation is not incompatible with there being some continuity with the present. On the one hand, hope must be more than the actualizing of what is potentially present in human life; it is hope in God who is the source of the creation of new possibilities in the face of nothingness. But, on the other hand, my argument that tragic elements must be present in any future consummation requires that loss in the present (*deprivatio boni*) is being carried forward, even into resurrection. If there is continuity with loss, we should expect also a continuity of gain. We may detect a surplus of being and meaning in human existence, not as a natural phenomenon which is independent of God but as evidence of the pressure of divine grace already there at the foundation of personal and social life. There is an "excess of the gift" everywhere in existence.[113]

This is the basis of spirituality, and Hamlet evokes it in his urging us to notice "more things in heaven and earth" than we might dream of in our narrow philosophies. Indeed, dreaming *about* them in our imagination will alert us to their presence. "Look," urges Lear, "Look here." The theologian will be bound to see things that Shakespeare himself does not see, but the play succeeds if we are willing to look, and it goes as far as it possibly can to *make* us look.

7

Hamlet, Hesitation, and Remembrance

T HERE IS a mystery at the heart of *Hamlet*, centering on the enigmatic yet
compelling personality of its main character. Why does Hamlet delay
in killing his uncle, Claudius?[1] The result of this delay is that—in addition
to Claudius—seven people die who need not have done so: Polonius, Ophelia, Laertes, Gertrude, Rosencrantz and Guildenstern, and Hamlet himself.
The gravedigger (whom we meet during the course of the play) need have no
fear of unemployment, even if—as he claims—the houses he makes "last till
doomsday." Setting ourselves to answer this question will reveal the extensive
intertextuality with the Bible and theology in which the play is embedded.
David Kastan has judged that "In no other play, with the possible exception
of *Measure for Measure*, is there such a sustained engagement with religious
issues and in which religious language is so prominent."[2] Reviewing the narrative sources on which Shakespeare seems to have drawn,[3] Naseeb Shaheen
concludes that "almost all of the numerous biblical and liturgical references
that Shakespeare makes in *Hamlet* originated with him as part of his own
design for the play as he reshaped and augmented his sources."[4] Tracing this
original intertextuality of Shakespeare will not only inform possible answers
to the question, "Why does Hamlet delay?" but will bring to light the particular spirituality which emerges from Hamlet's lack of action, and which
is summed up in the title to this book, *More Things in Heaven and Earth*.
Finally, as in previous chapters, we shall ask what impact the play might make
on theology "in front" of the text.

Perhaps the word "delay" on its own will not do to characterize the plot, as
it implies a deliberate postponement of an event to another time by the main
actor; it needs to be qualified by the ideas of "hesitation" and "uncertainty," as
a summary of the plot will indicate. The play begins with a demand for Hamlet to act, issued by an apparition claiming to be his dead father and urging
vengeance on his brother Claudius for having murdered him and seized both
his throne and his wife, Gertrude. Hamlet hesitates to do what the ghost

orders, spinning out the time by pretending to be mad. Most crucially, he fails to take the opportunity to kill Claudius when he finds him conveniently alone at prayer, and goes off instead to harangue his mother, Gertrude, in her bedroom. During this scene, by mistake he kills the aged counsellor Polonius, who has been listening behind the curtains once too often. This leads to the suicide of Ophelia, who is Polonius's daughter and the one whom Hamlet has professed to love deeply in the past. Her suicide is also prompted by Hamlet's now seemingly mad and cruel behavior towards her. This in turn leads to a plot between Claudius and Ophelia's brother, Laertes, to kill Hamlet. On return from a truncated voyage to England, Hamlet himself still takes no action.

In the denouement of the play, Claudius and Laertes fix a fencing match as a trap for Hamlet, poisoning the tip of Laertes's sword. Having been fatally struck by the poisoned sword-tip, Hamlet strikes down Laertes with the same weapon. Gertrude drinks by mistake a poisoned cup of wine which Claudius had prepared for Hamlet as an insurance in case the poisoned sword trick failed to work, and then Hamlet forces Claudius to drink from the same cup. A new character, Fortinbras, the prince of Norway, arrives to find the ground strewn with bodies, and immediately takes the opportunity to claim the kingdom for his own. The hesitation and delay of Hamlet has thus led to the killing of Polonius, the suicide of Ophelia, the doubly fatal vengeance of Laertes, and a failure to carry out the ghost's explicit instructions—which were to avoid any harm coming to Gertrude while disposing of Claudius. On the way, Hamlet's treacherous friends Rosencrantz and Guildenstern have suffered the execution by the king of England which was intended by Claudius for Hamlet. Claudius is not killed by any planned action of Hamlet, but has only been carried off in the end amid mass carnage: his punishment has been spectacular but hardly economic.

The plot, driven by hesitation, forces us to ask, why does Hamlet delay? Four main answers can be offered to that question, and three of them are relevant to our concern about the relation between Shakespeare's plays and religion.

THE MENTAL STATE OF HAMLET

The first explanation that has been given is that the character of Hamlet is indecisive because he is psychologically disturbed. Hamlet's very ability to see deeply into issues, to contemplate the truth that lies beneath the surface, makes him unable (it is said) to take the specific action required of him. His own words are taken as the key to the whole play:

> Thus conscience does make cowards—
> And thus the native hue of resolution

Is sicklied o'er with the pale cast of thought,
And enterprises of great pitch and moment
With this regard their currents turn awry
And lose the name of action. (3.1.82–88)

Many have followed the judgment of Coleridge that Hamlet "vacillates from
sensibility, and procrastinates from thought, and loses the power of action,"
his "everlasting broodings . . . throwing a mist over all commonplace actualities."[5] Psychological analysis of Hamlet since then has proved a very popular
art, and he has been attributed with all kinds of neuroses, from an overactive
conscience to an Oedipus complex. Under the heading "The heart of the mystery," John Dover Wilson notoriously wrote: "We are driven to conclude . . .
that Shakespeare meant us to imagine Hamlet suffering from some kind of
mental disorder throughout the play."[6] But I do not think that this will do.
To make this view of Hamlet persuasive, he would have to be understood as
a permanent neurotic or psychotic throughout the action (or lack of it), and
this takes away the whole impact of the scenes in which Hamlet is clearly
only *pretending* to be mad.

   Of course, it is fashionable for producers to present Hamlet as laboring
under a constant psychological handicap, so that the mad scenes appear entirely consistent with his usual character. Instead of a man with sufficient
presence of mind to adopt and sustain a very difficult masquerade, we are
presented with somebody who is constantly on the border of a mental break-
down, and sometimes right over the edge. But the text requires us to conceive
of a Hamlet who is *playing* at being mad: he has taken on a role. We must
feel "but this is not the real Hamlet," and the text prompts us to do this because of the extravagant manner in which the madness is adopted: Ophelia
describes his neglected clothes, physical collapse ("pale as his shirt, his knees
knocking each other," 2.1.78), his hysterical gestures and deep sighs: the queen
describes him as "mad as the sea and wind when both contend" (4.1.7).

   The modern stage Hamlet tends to be at least slightly psychotic all the
time, but the Hamlet of the text is at times perfectly sane, and at others perfectly lunatic, putting—as Hamlet says himself—"an antic disposition on"
(1.5.170). It is clearly a role that Hamlet is playing. Dr. Johnson commented
that "the pretended madness of Hamlet causes much mirth," and that "He
plays the madman most, when he treats Ophelia with so much rudeness."[7]
Hamlet indeed expresses the wish to have been an actor; he lectures the players who come to the court on the proper mode of acting, telling them: "suit
the action to the word, the word to the action . . . hold, as 'twere, the mirror
up to nature" (3.2.17–22).

   Admittedly, the fact that Shakespeare presents Hamlet as naturally having a melancholic temperament does lend some ambiguity to the madness

scenes. Even before Hamlet puts on his actor's mask (as it were), he is lamenting the unsatisfactory state of life:

> O that this too too sallied flesh would melt,
> Thaw and resolve itself into a dew,
> Or that the Everlasting had not fixed
> His canon 'gainst self-slaughter. O God, God,
> How weary, stale, flat and unprofitable
> Seem to me all the uses of this world!
> Fie on't, ah, fie, 'tis an unweeded garden
> That grows to seed. (1.2.129–36)

But we must not confuse Elizabethan melancholia with modern psychosis: to be melancholic was to have a certain introspective and intellectual temperament: melancholics could be men of action and were not necessarily psychologically handicapped: indeed, the melancholic politician was a most dangerous animal.[8] Shakespeare's Julius Caesar preferred to have plump and smiling politicians around him and distrusted the lean and hungry look (1.2.193). The fact that Hamlet is melancholic does not mean that he is naturally slightly insane.

Here we must pay attention to intertextuality. The resonances with scriptural texts and church homilies in Hamlet's speeches about the "weariness" of the world tend to bring an audience familiar with them into sharing his perspective, or at least finding it reasonable rather then pathological. In the soliloquy of 1.2.129–36, the desire that "flesh" would "resolve itself into a dew" echoes St. Paul in Philippians 1:23–24 on the necessity of living "in the flesh," but "desiring to be loosed and to be with Christ."[9] Hamlet's word "resolve" is equivalent to "dissolve" in the homily "Against the Feare of Death," which comments on Paul's text, explaining that "Paule hym selfe declareth the desyre of his harte, which was to be dissolued and leused [loosed] from his bodye, and to be with Christe."[10] Hamlet does not, in accord with Shakespeare's nondogmatic approach, give us any reference to "being with Christ," but then he is also echoing the Hebraic sense of the weariness of things as notably expressed in *Ecclesiastes*, a book with which Shakespeare shows considerable familiarity; with the "unprofitable . . . uses of this world" we may compare Ecclesiastes 1:14, "I have considered all the works that are done under the sun, and behold, all is vanity, and vexation of the spirit." When Hamlet goes on to compare life to "an unweeded garden," Shakespeare probably has in mind the homily "Of the State of Matrimonie" echoed elsewhere in the play, which urges, "Though it bringeth forth weedes . . . apply thy selfe to weede out by little and little the nosysome weedes of uncomely maners."[11]

Hamlet's expostulation to his former friends Rosencrantz and Guilden-stern that "Man delights not me" draws upon a scriptural text in praise of human beings in Psalm 8, only to refute it with another text (which I place in italics): "What a piece of work is a man—how noble in reason; how infinite in faculties, in form and moving; how express and admirable in action; how like an angel in apprehension; how like a god; the beauty of the world; the par-agon of animals. *And yet to me what is this quintessence of dust?*" (2.2.269–74). We readily hear the resonances of Psalm 8:4–6. In the Coverdale version this reads: "What is man, that thou art mindful of him: and the son of man, that thou visitest him? Thou madest him lower than the angels: to crown him with glory and worship. Thou makest him to have dominion of the works of thy hands: and thou has put all things in subjection under his feet. All sheep and oxen: yea, and the beasts of the field." The Genevan version of the Psalms, however, has "Thou has made him a little lower than God" in place of "lower than the angels." Both readings of the Psalm may be in Shakespeare's mind as Hamlet exclaims, "how like an angel . . . how like a god," or it may be that he is recalling the Genevan version both of the Psalm ("like a god") and the quotation of the same Psalm in Hebrews 2:6–7: "Thou madest him a little in-ferior to the Angels" ("how like an angel"). The Hebrews text fits better than the Coverdale translation of the Psalm,[12] as human beings are celebrated in Hamlet's speech as "*like* an angel" which is closer to "[only] *a little* inferior to the Angels" than "*lower* than the Angels" (Coverdale).

If there are echoes of the text from Hebrews, as well as from the Genevan version of the Psalm, then it is even more suitable for Hamlet to follow on with a more negative verdict, "quintessence of dust," also echoing scriptural and liturgical texts. The author of Hebrews, like Hamlet, refutes the Psalm text: though God has made human beings to be crowned with glory because all things are subjected to them, in fact this is not the case at present: "But we yet *see not* all things subdued unto him." Hamlet's gloomy view thus has scriptural support.[13] The phrase "quintessence of dust" evokes scriptural texts such as Genesis 3:19, "Thou art dust, and to dust shalt thou return," and Ec-clesiastes 3:20, "All was of the dust," as well as the pronouncement from the Burial Service, "earth to earth, ashes to ashes, dust to dust." Dust reoccurs with Hamlet's answer to the query as to what he has done with Polonius's body, "Compounded it with dust, whereto 'tis kin" (4.2.5). A little later in the scene he declares, "The King is a thing . . . Of nothing" (25–27), recalling Psalm 144:4, "Man is like a thing of naught."[14]

Hamlet's melancholia thus reflects a strain within scripture, though in an exaggerated manner. The scriptural echoes would tend to make an audience hesitate before judging him to be *actually* mad, and this would be further alleviated by the particular *kind* of madness that Hamlet assumes: it is an extravagant form of folly in the form of a court jester's foolishness. The jester was the "allowed fool" in a great man's household, permitted to poke fun at serious matters and to turn matters upside down in his jesting. He was permitted to do this because it was felt that truth often emerged by reversing the state of the world—it was as if only by seeing it this way could one perceive that something was amiss all the time. It is a distorted form of the court jester's humor that Hamlet adopts: for example, the king asks anxiously about the play that the actors are to put on, and whose plot Hamlet has designed to mirror the actual crime Claudius has committed. Hamlet has got the actors to play out a scene in which a man pours poison into the ear of a sleeping king, the very way that Claudius has murdered his brother. This is what Hamlet calls a "mousetrap," and by the way that Claudius reacts to the scene he intends to test the truth of what the ghost has revealed about his death. Claudius inquires: "Have you heard the argument? is there no offence in't?" Hamlet replies, "No, no, they do but jest. Poison in jest, no offence i' th' world" (3.2.226–29). In saying the opposite of what is actually the case (for in fact, poison is a deadly offense) the truth emerges, which is that Claudius has been behaving as if poisoning were a matter of no serious account at all.

Hamlet assumes the pose of a fool, so that the truth should be known. As in others of Shakespeare's plays, the man who *plays* the fool is partnered by the person who *is* a fool in reality and yet speaks wisdom. In *As You Like It*, for example, Jacques is partnered by the court jester Touchstone. In *Hamlet*, a court jester *does* appear, but he is present only in his skull as thrown up by the gravedigger's spade; thus Hamlet's living partner is the substitute or amateur jester represented by the gravedigger he meets, and between them they offer a dialogue of fools. Hamlet's jester-like jokes are often, significantly, based on biblical texts, so they appear to come with a certain weight of authority. The dust to which all return (Gen. 3:19) reappears, for example, in his graveyard joke that "Alexander died, Alexander was buried, Alexander returneth to dust, the dust is earth" and from that earth clay is made to mend a hole in a wall, or even used as a stopper for a beer-barrel:

> Imperious Caesar, dead and turned to clay
> Might stop a hole to keep the wind away. (5.1.202–3)

Three other "foolish" jokes which reuse biblical texts may be mentioned. Hamlet greets Polonius as "O Jephthah, judge of Israel" (2.2.30), quoting a snatch of a popular ballad about the biblical character (Judg. 11:30–40), to which Polonius replies "If you call me Jephthah, my lord, I have a daughter that I love passing well." Hamlet retorts, "Nay, that follows not," and when asked what *does* follow, answers with what follows his opening lines *literally*, a couple of further lines from the ballad. The joke is that he clearly implies something else does not follow which is unspoken and much more serious; it does not follow that because Polonius has a daughter, he loves her "passing well." There is a sharp poignancy in this accusation. The audience has observed Polonius advising his daughter to reject Hamlet's suit of love and to avoid him henceforth, on the grounds that Hamlet as a social superior cannot be serious in his wooing (1.3.95–134); Laertes, Ophelia's brother, had also just given the same advice (1.3.10–43). In the biblical story, in return for victory in war Jephthah rashly promises God to sacrifice the first person to greet him when he returns home, and this turns out to be his young daughter. Stress in the biblical story is laid on his daughter "bewailing her virginity," or sorrowing that she will not now find fulfilment in marriage, and the parallel with Ophelia's broken relationship with Hamlet is apparent. While Hamlet has not overheard the preceding conversations, he has suffered Ophelia's return of his letters and her denial of access to her, and may well have guessed the reason. The story of Jephthah was a popular one, and was presented as a key example of foolish swearing in the homily "Against Swearing and Perjury."[15]

Another instance of a fool's joke occurs when the king asks Hamlet where Polonius is, and he replies, "At supper" (4.3.16–20). To the further inquiry, "where?," Hamlet's answer is, "Not where he eats, but where 'a is eaten; a certain convocation of politic worms are e'en at him."[16] As well as a topical joke about the Diet of Worms, where Luther had been condemned at the instigation of the Holy Roman Emperor—"Your worm is your only emperor for diet"—the exchange evokes several biblical references about the human fate of being eaten by worms (Isa. 51:8; Job 24:20). One instance combines Hamlet's morbid interest in both dust and worms: "They shall sleep both in the dust, and the worms shall cover them" (Job 21:26). As fools do, Hamlet multiplies the jest; when the question "where" is repeated, he answers, "In heaven," a reference to the supper promised to the faithful in the Kingdom of God after death: "Blessed are they which are called unto the Lamb's supper" (Rev. 19:9; cf. Luke 14:15–16, and Matt. 22:2–4).[17] The humour is savage, and questions may certainly be raised about Hamlet's moral sensibility, but hardly about his sanity.

A different joke about flesh occurs when Hamlet makes his farewell on leaving for his enforced voyage to England immediately following this scandal. He exclaims, "Farewell, dear mother." When the king rebukingly adds, "Thy loving father, Hamlet," he replies:

> My mother. Father and mother is man and wife.
> Man and wife is one flesh. So—my mother. (4.3.49–50)

This riposte obviously echoes the scriptural affirmation that a man "shall cleave to his wife, and they shall be one flesh" (Gen. 2:24; Eph. 5:31; Mark

10:7–8), a phrase that forms part of the Marriage Service of the Book of Common Prayer.[18] But the meaning is dense: Hamlet could be simply saying that his mother and Claudius make one flesh, thereby neatly excusing his pointed act of ignoring Claudius, or he could be reminding his mother that she is still one flesh with his father. Archbishop Parker had drawn up a Table of Affinity in 1563 by which a man was forbidden to marry his brother's wife, and the marriage between Claudius and Gertrude might have been regarded as incestuous by the audience,[19] although the Table was not made legal until 1604 and was not added to the Prayer Book until 1681.

These four instances of fool-like quips, in addition to his expressions of melancholy, all based on scriptural texts, are some of the evidence that Hamlet is not characterized by mental instability, but is deliberately assuming the pose of a fool. More than this, a spirituality is beginning to emerge from this intertextuality about which I will have more to say: there is a facing of the reality of time and death (symbolized by dust and worms), and there is the centrality of relationships in this crisis, whether with a beloved or with parents (with the references to Jephthah and "one flesh"). There *is* something true about the picture of an indecisive and procrastinating Hamlet, but it is not rooted in a disturbed personality. Its cause brings us to a second possible answer to the question, "why does Hamlet delay"?

A CONFLICT OF ROLES

Hamlet appears in this play to be a man who is caught between two possible styles of life, two possible roles to play in society. On the one hand, there is the part of the intellectual, critical prince, and on the other, there is the role of the revenge hero. It is not that Hamlet is a psychological weakling who can never make up his mind: rather, he is caught between two ways of living which are in fact basically incompatible. The world being what it is, there are destructive tensions in trying to live on two levels at once.

In the first place, Hamlet is the Renaissance intellectual: it was an original stroke on Shakespeare's part to make Hamlet a university man, and someone who wanted to go back to Wittenberg University at what was then the advanced age of thirty. In the "source" materials of Saxo and Belleforest there is no mention of Wittenberg at all.[20] In this play, Hamlet's temperament is one of the professional scholar, proposing a thesis for debate like "To be or not to be,"[21] the man—in a medieval sense—"ordained" to learning. He has a vision of what a scholar-king might be (like Plato's Philosopher King in the Republic); he is highly critical of the artificiality of court life in Denmark. and he is brilliant at satirizing the conventional etiquette of the court as we see it in characters like Polonius and Osric. He has an attractive straightforwardness that cuts across the barriers of rank: conventional difference of status does not disrupt his affection for his friends, especially Horatio, and above all his love for Ophelia, who is below him in social status. Here Ophelia's father, Polonius, miscalculates badly, and finally, tragically, failing to perceive the visionary way in which Hamlet sees Ophelia. What kind of monarch Hamlet might have been is glimpsed in his praise of Horatio for neither flattering nor seeking to be flattered. Ever since, he assures Horatio, his soul was able to make its own "election" of friends, it had "sealed thee for herself" (3.2.59–61). In immediate succession we have two scriptural terms: "election" and "sealed."[22] It is biblical language that convinces us of Hamlet's basic integrity.

That is Hamlet the humanist prince. He has a vision of a particular style of life, and we must believe Fortinbras when he says at the end that he would have proved "most royal" if he had lived. But he cannot hold to this vision in a world that forces another role upon him, the conventional role of the avenger. The ghost requires him to take up a part that is not naturally his, and yet he believes he cannot escape it; a powerful conviction of duty compels him to engage in a battle for which he feels a natural repugnance. It is a convention that murders have to be avenged, and Hamlet feels he cannot escape from this role.

As I have already suggested, throughout his tragedies, Shakespeare shows us a protagonist caught between conflicting visions of life, the vision held by the hero and that held by the world around him—or her, in the case of Cleopatra. Several times Shakespeare shows a person hesitating and vacillating between two roles.[23] This is not because the person has a fatal flaw of indecisiveness, but because it is a fact of life that almost unavoidable tensions arise between conflicting worldviews. Any weaknesses of character that the hero has, or any unlucky accidents of fate (to take two powerful factors in classical and medieval tragedy), will only turn the tensions into unavoidable catastrophe—they do not create the tensions in the first place. Tragedy comes when a protagonist tries to have the best of two worlds, and each time we feel that we can scarcely blame him or her for it, since the pressures have been so great.

We are not surprised that Hamlet cannot play his role of avenger completely: we are only surprised that he plays it as well as he does. In drama of the time, the avenger was the scourge not just of his intended victim, but of the evil in the whole society; all the guilty were objects of his accusation, and so Hamlet adopts the role of the pursuer of all crime, reflecting: "The time is out of joint, O cursed spite / That ever I was born to set it right" (1.5.188). The scope of the role of the avenger may be at least part of the explanation of the second major mystery in this play, after why Hamlet delays—why Hamlet makes the verbal assaults on Ophelia that he does. It has often been

suggested that Hamlet's violent and insulting language is in reaction to Ophelia's own behavior in not only rejecting him, but consenting to being part of
a plot devised by her father, to enable him and the king to overhear Hamlet's
conversation with her and so come to a conclusion about his state of mind.[24]
However, the play offers no evidence that Hamlet is aware of this plan, beyond his question, "Are you honest?" (3.1.102). In any case, Harold Jenkins is
surely right that to consider Hamlet's attitude to Ophelia as a recompense
for her actions is "to make the mistake of Polonius, whose view the play specifically repudiates."[25] There remains, as a partial explanation, that Hamlet's
rants about lack of chastity in women and the falsity of cosmetics spring
from the role he has assumed as the scourge of *all* vices.

Ophelia then is being treated simply as an example of general guiltiness.
This raises irreconcilable tensions with Hamlet's actual love for Ophelia,
though she suffers even more than he does from the role he assumes: "I have
heard of your paintings well enough. God hath given you one face and you
make yourselves another. You jig, and amble and you lisp . . . and make your
wantonness your ignorance. Go to, I'll no more on't, it hath made me mad. I
say we will have no mo[re] marriage. Those that are married already—all but
one—shall live, the rest shall keep as they are. To a nunnery, go" (3.1.141–48).
The fact that Ophelia is a general target is underlined by the comparison
of this accusation with the homily "Against Excess of Apparell." That God
has "given one face" and women "Make yourselves another" has strong resonances with the homily's phraseology: "Who can paint her face . . . as though
shee coulde make herself more comely then God hath appointed." Hamlet's
charge that "you jig and amble" echoes the satire of Isaiah 6 that is quoted in
the homily: "they walked . . . mincing as they went, and nicely treading with
their feet." Repetition of the homily, as well as the recitation of St. Paul's
advice that the unmarried should "keep as they are,"[26] implies that Hamlet is
playing a role rather than venting his personal feelings. But for the audience,
as Jenkins maintains, the actions of Hamlet toward Ophelia remain as a dark
undercurrent.[27]

Now, the struggle between the role Hamlet *wants* to play (the lover, the
humanist prince), and the one he has been conscripted by the ghost to play
(the avenger of vices) is highlighted in this drama by a conflict between
Christian ethics and the ethics of revenge. I do not mean that Hamlet *himself*
has Christian moral scruples about killing Claudius: there is no open statement anywhere in the play that Hamlet delays because he finds it difficult to
reconcile his Christian conscience with the demands of revenge. It is simply
accepted by Hamlet and the other characters that revenge is right and proper.
Hamlet hesitates, as I have suggested, because the *style* of the revenger is not
his way of living and acting, not because he thinks it to be morally wrong. In

the Renaissance period two ethics existed side by side—the demand of personal revenge, and the Christian ethic that revenge belonged only to God, expressed in the biblical phrase, "vengeance is mine, I will repay says the Lord" (Rom. 12:19). People lived with the inconsistency; mostly the two moralities went their own way, but from time to time people felt there was a contradiction between them.[28] The play reflects the society around it in this. There is no *open* moral struggle in the play between Christian charity and forgiveness on the one hand and the revenge ethics on the other. But the conflict is still present in another way. Watching the play, *we* feel as though there *ought* to be some struggle. We, the audience, protest that there *must* be a conflict of ethics. The play makes us feel the contradiction.

There is nothing here *in the text* about the Christian conviction of leaving vengeance to God. It is never debated, yet we feel it *ought* to be. The question about the relation between a Christian worldview and the convention of revenge is always being thrown up—not overtly but in the silence between the lines. There is an underlying complexity here, an unresolved moral issue that troubles the situation. It adds depth to the conflict between Hamlet's two roles of philosopher prince and revenger. There is an uneasy tension which probably accurately reflects the tension in the society of Shakespeare's own day. The conflict is not at all resolved by Hamlet's passing claim that he is God's minister of vengeance: "Heaven hath pleased / To punish me with this, and this with me, / That I must be their scourge and minister" (3.4.4.171–73). The audience would probably have recognized the statement of St. Paul in Romans 13:14 that the monarch is "the minister of God to take vengeance on him that doeth evil," and this power is extended also to magistrates by the homily "Concerning Good Order, and Obedience to Rulers and Magistrates."[29] But the effect of reference to the scripture text would have been to make the audience respond that this could not apply to Hamlet, as he was neither ruler nor magistrate, and the homily stresses that no one should take it on themselves to judge, punish or kill "of his owne priuate authoritie."[30] Moreover, Hamlet has the fantasy view here that his call to be a "minister" is a means by which God is punishing him, which does not fit with the Pauline text at all. Earlier he has also disqualified himself from being a "minister" by claiming that he is "Prompted to my revenge by heaven *and* hell" (2.2.519). As Kastan perceives, the copulative "and" means that his revenge "cannot sustain the moral differentiation" that would make it heavenly justice.[31] Belleforest does call Hamlet a "minister of just vengeance,"[32] but if Shakespeare was inspired by these words to write the passage, he does so precisely in order to prompt the audience to *question* it. The tension between two orders of morality is thus not dispersed by Hamlet's appeal to Romans 13:14 for appointment as a "minister"; indeed, it appears to be intensified by it.

The main place where we get this complexity of moral feeling is in the scene where Hamlet fails to take his opportunity to kill Claudius because he is at prayer. Hamlet's reasoning is that while he is at prayer, Claudius is in a state of grace: if he killed him while praying, he would simply send him to heaven (3.3.77–78). Why should he do for Claudius what Claudius did not do for his own father, who was killed without opportunity to prepare for death? At this moment in the story Hamlet evidently accepts that the ghost is genuinely his father's spirit, which has been consigned to the flames of purgatory, dying "with all his crimes broad blown," or as the ghost himself laments (1.5.76–80), "Unhouseled, dis-appointed, unaneled"—that is, without benefit of communion, confession, and anointing. He complains that there was "No reck'ning made, but sent to my account," just as Hamlet comments that "how his audit stands who knows, save heaven" (3.3.82). The account and the audit presumably refer to the number of years to be spent in purgatory. As we shall see, Hamlet is not consistent in his identification of the ghost as a soul in purgatory, but he accepts it at this point of crisis when the praying Claudius is in front of him. Thus he refrains from killing Claudius in order to kill him another time when he is unprepared ("about some act / That has no relish of salvation in it") so Hamlet can damn his soul and send him to hell. This action, or nonaction, of Hamlet has shocked many critics: but we notice that it springs from Hamlet's own Christian beliefs. If he were a pagan, he would have revenged himself there and then. Only because he believes in life after death, heaven and hell, does he resolve upon the most vicious form of revenge possible.

This is, however, an extraordinary piece of theological drama. Hamlet's desired revenge on Claudius is motivated by the ghost's lament that he is suffering in purgatory, which is a Catholic view. But Hamlet appears to be manifesting a Protestant conviction that repentance and faith before death will ensure an *immediate* transit to heaven, since in the Protestant view there *is* no purgatory.[33] In Hamlet's words, Claudius by praying is here and now "*purging* his soul," a process of spiritual purgation commended and undertaken later by the Anglican John Donne, who thought the place of purgatory to be simply a "dream."[34] In Catholic moral theology, it is not *impossible* that God might decide, in the mystery of divine grace, to receive this murderer directly into heaven without last rites and absolution, but such an outcome seems highly unlikely. As Greenblatt points out, "one of the worst medieval nightmares [was] a sudden death."[35] The ghost speaks of his "imperfections," which means his sins were not mortal, and that he will eventually burn and purge away his crimes; but—as Greenblatt points out—"his inability to make a proper reckoning and his failure to receive the Catholic last rites weigh heavily against him."[36] Thomas Aquinas had dropped a heavy hint that speedy reception into heaven might be one of the compensations of the poor,[37] but this exemption hardly applied to King Hamlet. The point is that Hamlet's *confidence* that Claudius's repentance would ensure him immediate passage to heaven has a distinctly Protestant feel to it. In fact, he has misread the situation since Claudius admits he cannot repent, and knows that a mere attitude of prayer will achieve nothing: "My words fly up, my thoughts remain below. / Words without thoughts never to heaven go" (3.3.97–98). Hamlet's delay here seems to require a Catholic belief in purgatory and a Protestant belief in the efficacy of personal repentance simultaneously. The Protestant feel to Hamlet's reaction to the scene is underlined by his resolution to kill Claudius at a time when he could send Claudius to the alternative destination of "hell." While he believes his father, taken unprepared, was consigned to a midway state of purgatory, there seem to be only two options for Claudius. Here is a startling example of the evenhandedness of Shakespeare toward Catholic and Protestant convictions, of which I have already given multiple examples. Shakespeare is not committing himself to a particular dogma, either of purgatory as a nightmare to be guarded against or as a dream to be awoken from. The blurred borders between Catholicism and Protestantism in society find a location in this scene, and what matters is the spirituality that emerges.

And here we are faced with an extraordinary moral complexity. As the audience, do we actually *want* Hamlet to kill Claudius? If we are standing on the ground of Christian morals, then we cannot blame Hamlet for not killing Claudius. Measured by Christian charity, Hamlet appears to be doing the right thing, though for the wrong reason. Both in Hamlet's mind and in the audience, issues of morality are being raised in a highly subtle and complex way: there is no open debate, but the issues are there, giving depth to the action. It is this interweaving of moral values into the play, without any open discussion of them, that makes *Hamlet* the enigma it is. I do not mean that there are distinctive Catholic and Protestant sides to this question; those of both confessions would feel the moral struggle. But, *like* the Catholic-Protestant tension over purgatory in the play, this dilemma prompts us to develop our own spirituality. Shakespeare himself is using uncertainty in doctrine not only to drive the plot, but to develop a spirituality in which relationships between people are centrally important, perhaps *more* important than doctrine.

Theological Doubts about the Ghost

A conflict of roles, focused in a moral dilemma, is certainly a reason for Hamlet's delaying tactics where psychological instability is not. But we can discern another reason which is already implied in the "prayer scene" between Hamlet and Claudius. Hamlet delays in killing Claudius partly because he is not sure whether the ghost is "honest," as he puts it (1.5.138). That is, he is uncertain about whether the ghost is really the spirit of his dead father, or whether it is the devil assuming the shape of his father in order to trick him into an action—murder—that will damn him eternally:

> The Spirit that I have seen
> May be a de'il [devil], and the de'il hath power
> T'assume a pleasing shape. Yea, and perhaps
> Out of my weakness and my melancholy,
> As he is very potent with such spirits,
> Abuses me to damn me! I'll have grounds
> More relative than this. The play's the thing
> Wherein I'll catch the conscience of the King. (2.2.535–40)

Here Shakespeare is drawing upon a substantial theological dispute of the time about whether the souls of the dead could ever return to earth. Catholic theologians who held the doctrine of purgatory generally thought that they could, as souls in purgatory were in an intermediate state, not yet assumed into heaven.[38] Protestant theologians, dismissing purgatory, insisted that all ghosts were deceitful appearances of the devil or demons *pretending* to the spirits of the departed.[39] For a Catholic, an apparition *might*, of course, be demonic, and so a process of "discernment of spirits" (*discretio spirituum*) had to be employed; accounts exist in which (it is claimed) a ghost is forced to submit to a rigorous cross-examination, such as Horatio attempts unsuccessfully with the apparition on the battlements of Elsinore (1.1.128–38).[40] But in a Catholic view, a ghost *might* be what it claimed to be, a spirit of a dead person. Only a Catholic could (or at least should) entertain the view that the ghost was possibly Hamlet's father, released for a nightly walk from purgatory. The situation in Hamlet is neatly summed up by Greenblatt as "A young man from Wittenberg, with a distinctly Protestant temperament, is haunted by a distinctly Catholic ghost,"[41] although Hamlet's doubts about the ghost could *either* stem from a Protestant conviction about ghosts generally, or from a Catholic suspicion about a particular ghost. Even in the encounter with the supposed ghost, confessional boundaries are blurred.

For whatever reason, Hamlet is racked by uncertainty about whether the ghost genuinely is his father, claiming as he does to be "doomed for a certain term to walk the night / and for the day confined to fast in fires / Till the foul crimes done in my days of nature are burnt and purg'd away" (1.5.11–13).[42] From time to time Hamlet appears to believe him, calling the ghost "he," referring to his father. Confronted by the apparition, he quickly decides, "I'll call thee Hamlet, King, father, royal Dane" (1.4.44). But at other times Hamlet calls the ghost "it," addressing it disrespectfully as an "old mole" that "works in the earth" and "this fellow in the cellarage" (1.5.51, 161), more suitable terms for a demon who inhabits the underworld than for a beloved father in purgatory. It seems that Hamlet never actually overcomes his uncertainty about the ghost since—after appearing in a bedroom scene with Hamlet and Gertrude—it fades from the scene and from any mention. In Hamlet's final killing of Claudius he makes no appeal to revenge for his father; the killing happens in reaction to the confused events of the duel, and in explicit recompense for the death of his mother. This uncertainty, felt by the audience as well as embodied in Hamlet, is fostered by a series of scriptural and theological references, operating for and against the "honesty" of the ghost. There can be no direct scriptural reference to purgatory, a dogma of an intermediate state that arose in the latter part of the twelfth century, but Shakespeare's use of scripture works to arouse a sense of contradiction in the mind, as well as being the seedbed for an emerging spirituality.

On the side of persuading us toward an acceptance of the existence of purgatory, the ghost's appearance on the battlements is heralded by Barnado in a speech (1.1.114–24), ostensibly full of classical references to portents but actually larded with scriptural images of the dead coming out of their graves (Matt. 27:52) and the cosmic disturbances which will be the signs of the Last Times (Matt. 24:29; Luke 21:25–26; Acts 2:19–20).[43] All this lends the ghost when it does appear a certain credibility, as if predicted by scripture itself. The ghost then refers to its immersion in "sulph'rous and tormenting flames," evoking scriptural descriptions of the destiny of the wicked ("tormented in fire and brimstone [i.e., sulphur]," Rev. 14:10, cf. Rev. 20:10; and Luke 16:24). The effect is not diminished by the fact that scripture uses these images about hell, not purgatory, since the Catholic dogma held that the pains of hell and purgatory were identical, those of purgatory differentiated only by having a point of termination. When, further, Hamlet urges Horatio to consider "more things in heaven and earth," he bids him to give "the strange" a welcome (1.5.164), recalling instructions from scripture to offer a "stranger" welcome (Heb. 13:2; Matt. 25:35); the admonition appears to be applied to the ghost himself, whose appearance has just been referred to as "wondrous strange."

Other religious texts than scripture also nudge the viewer and reader toward accepting the ghost's story. Hamlet invokes the name of St. Patrick (1.5.135), associated strongly with purgatory through the medieval pilgrimage site of "St. Patrick's Purgatory" in Ireland, and he quotes from two prayers for the dead familiar to Catholics but which would be avoided by Protestants:

"Rest, rest, perturbed spirit" (*requiem*, 1.5.180) and *hic et ubique* ("here and everywhere," 1.5.156), which appears to be a phrase from a prayer for all the dead ("those souls here and everywhere who rest in Christ").[44]

On the other hand, other resonances with scripture and religious texts produce the opposite effect, fostering uncertainty. Hamlet's fear that the spirit he has seen "may be a devil, and the devil hath power, / T'assume a pleasing shape" echoes Paul's phrase in 2 Corinthians 11:14 that "Satan him self is transformed into an Angel of light." This text is associated with apparent apparitions of the dead in the gloss of the Geneva Bible at 1 Samuel 28:14, where Saul attempts to communicate with the dead prophet Samuel; the Geneva note states baldly that the figure who appeared to Saul was Samuel "to his imagination, albeit it was Satan," then quoting in support Paul's phrase about Satan appearing as an "Angel of light." When the ghost first appears to Hamlet, he exclaims, "Angels and ministers of grace, defend us!" (1.4.39), repeating the prayer "defend us," which appears in a collect in Evening Prayer— "Defend us from all perils and dangers of this night"—as well as in two collects in Morning Prayer. He goes on to address it as "a spirit of health *or* goblin damned," but his first reaction is negative. Later, Hamlet declares that death is "The undiscovered country, from whose bourn / No traveller returns" (3.1.78–79). If nobody returns, that includes the ghost, though Hamlet seems to miss the implication. The nonreturn has scriptural authority, since the assertion that one does not return from death is repeated three times in the book of Job: "Before I go and shall not return, even to the land of darkness and shadow of death" (10:21–22; cf. 16:22, 7:9–10; see also Wisdom 2:1).[45] The scriptural echo is strong here, with the image of the "country" (Job's "land") and the verb "return." At first death ("not to be") seems an attractive solution to all the problems of life, as a kind of sleep: "to die to sleep."

The image of sleep for death is a common one in theological and devotional writing of the period;[46] it is indeed taken from the Bible, derived from texts such as Daniel 12:2, "many of them that sleep in the dust of the earth, shall awake."[47] Such sleep is, reflects Hamlet, "a consummation / Devoutly to be wished," echoing the dying cry of Jesus in the Fourth Gospel, *consummatum est*—"it is finished."[48] But then a more dreadful thought strikes him. Suppose, he muses, there are *dreams* in that sleep:

> To sleep, perchance to dream—ay, there's the rub:
> For in that sleep of death what dreams may come
> When we have shuffled off this mortal coil
> Must give us pause. . . .
> . . . .
> . . . The dread of something after death

(The undiscovered country from whose bourn
No traveller returns) puzzles the will. (3.1.64–67, 77–79)

If in this life we have done damnable actions, those dreams will be nightmares. In this meditation Hamlet continues the mood of uncertainty aroused by the use of scripture in opposing ways: he does not commit himself to whether the feared dreams are hell or interminable purgatory; they are simply "dreams" and could be either or neither. They are, ambiguously, "the dread of *something*" after death. Nevertheless, the balance is tipped toward doubting the ghost: the phrase "no traveller returns" rules out return from purgatory, and the "dread" will evidently be worse if Hamlet has been incited to kill Claudius through a trick of the devil.

Shakespeare himself is not taking up either a Catholic or Protestant position about whether the dead return. We do not know whether *he* is as Catholic as the ghost claims to be. Uncertainty is further compounded by the ghost's being a curious mixture of a Senecan revenge ghost and a Catholic soul from purgatory, the one aspect conflicting with the other: a soul wishing finally to escape the fires of purgation seems to be multiplying its problems by calling not for prayers but for vengeance and murder.

Shakespeare thus uses uncertainty about a theological dispute, reinforced by scriptural and other religious texts, first to provide metaphors and to motivate the action. Hamlet's behavior in delaying his revenge and planning the "mousetrap" of the play is dictated by his Christian convictions about the devil and life after death. At the same time we can see the second aspect of Shakespeare's interest in religion that I have identified: the situation of uncertainty, both in the doctrine of the time and in Hamlet's own belief, becomes the ground for developing a spirituality. In contrast to unavailable certainty in dogma is a certainty of feeling, emotion, and imagination: relationships of love between people are centrally important. For instance, while Hamlet wavers in his theology, at times seemingly Catholic, at times seemingly Protestant, what really matters is his loving relationship to his father. Near the beginning of the play, Hamlet tells Horatio, "My father, methinks I see my father," and Horatio asks anxiously, "Where, my lord?," fearing that the ghost has appeared once more. But Hamlet replies, "In my *mind's* eye, Horatio" (1.2.183–85). It is in the mind and the memory that Hamlet sees his beloved father most clearly. As Kastan has pointed out, the ghost has to keep bidding Hamlet to remember *him*; Hamlet doesn't have to be told to remember his *father.*[49]

Having commissioned Hamlet with his task of revenge, the ghost leaves with the farewell words: "Adieu, adieu, adieu, remember me" (1.5.91). Hamlet responds:

> Remember thee?
> Ay, thou poor ghost, whiles memory holds a seat
> In this distracted globe. Remember thee?
> Yea, from the table of my memory
> I'll wipe away all trivial fond records,
> . . . .
> And thy commandment all alone shall live
> Within the book and volume of my brain (1.5.95–103)

Greenblatt has supplied a significant intertextual link for this appeal to "remember." The Catholic lord chancellor to Henry VIII, Sir Thomas More, had written a work called *The Supplication of Souls* as a riposte to a tract by Simon Fish called *The Supplication of Beggars* (1529), in which Fish had launched an attack on belief in purgatory; Fish's "supplication" had been a plea on behalf of the homeless "beggars" in the land of England to redistribute to the needs of the poor the vast amounts of money spent on maintaining the whole machinery of prayers, masses, and indulgences associated with fear of purgatory. More's reply was written as if it were a plea from souls in purgatory to "remember" them, to pay for prayers ("suffrages") in order to release them from their torments and suffering. More's *Supplication* was in effect an appeal from the dead to the living not to forget them, but to keep bonds of familial love and kinship alive. Alongside the ghost's command to Hamlet to "remember," Greenblatt sets the cry of More's souls: "Remember what kin ye and we be together," and "Remember how nature and Christendom bindeth you to remember us."[50] Fish's entire tract was reproduced at the place in Foxe's *Book of Martyrs* where Foxe gives an account of Fish's relations with Henry VIII,[51] together with a brief, hostile summary by Foxe of More's response, referring to "poor silly souls pewling out of Purgatory."[52] Through reading Foxe, Shakespeare would have been at least aware of both "Supplications," though he would have had to have read More's work if the ghost's command to "remember" is indeed an explicit echo of More's souls. Otherwise, Greenblatt makes a convincing case that the problem of how to "remember" the dead is a significant part of social textuality.

The plea by the dead to "remember" them is at the heart of Greenblatt's own study of Hamlet, which was prompted (he tells us) by his experience of saying the Jewish *kaddish* prayers for his own dead father. He diagnoses a cultural and religious problem arising in Shakespeare's time from the Protestant "abolition" of purgatory: how could people now satisfy their emotional and spiritual needs to "remember" dead loved ones, maintain their link with them, and feel that they had properly cared for them? He finds an answer in what he identifies as a shift "from vengeance to remembrance" in the actions of Hamlet.[53] The theater, he suggests, could "offer the viewer, in an unfor-gettably vivid dream of passion, many of the deep imaginative experiences, the tangled longing, guilt, pity, and rage, evoked by More." The theater thus possesses a "proximity to certain experiences that had been organized and exploited by religious institutions and rituals."[54] Shakespeare's theater in particular is "the cult of the dead": in it, the space of purgatory "becomes the space for the stage where old Hamlet's Ghost is doomed for a certain space to walk the earth." The contradictions in Hamlet's ghost do not matter, since this is not an attempt to depict a ghost satisfying certain dogmatic requirements, but a "stage ghost" satisfying emotional needs. Greenblatt indeed seems to extend this principle of the "cult of the dead" beyond Shakespeare's several ghosts to all dramatic characters: he asks, "Does he conceive of his charac-ters as something like ghosts, endowed with power to claim suffrages?"[55] The "suffrages" here would presumably be the applause and the payment of the audience.

Shortly, in considering the impact of Hamlet on theology "in front of the text," I want to take up again Greenblatt's proposition that with the demise of purgatory, "men and women had to be led to reimagine their own postmor-tem fate, as well as that of their loved ones."[56] Here I want only to stress that the uncertainty about the ghost in Hamlet's mind and that of the audience, reinforced by scriptural echoes, is the ground for a spirituality which meets emotional and imaginative needs by affirming the ultimate value of relation-ships. Bonds of love and kinship are exposed to the threat of being broken by death. Whether or not purgatory is only a dream, death is a reality, in the face of which the ghost's plea to "remember" can be separated from the demand to avenge. Hamlet appears to fail to remember the ghost as the play proceeds, but there is no evidence that he forgets the image of his father. "Look here upon this picture, and on this," he bids his mother (3.4.51), while he is *not* remembering to carry out the act of revenge. In this reproachful scene with his mother in her bedroom, we notice that only Hamlet sees the ghost, where before it was seen by all the watchers on the battlements. Perhaps it is al-ready fading into a projection of Hamlet's mind, or what Gertrude calls "the coinage of your brain"; since Shakespeare's ghosts are "stage ghosts," there is no reason why they should not be what we now call the result of a unique blend of veridical perception and psychological projection. If this is the case (in terms of the world of the play), it is significant that the ghost not only calls for the sharpening of Hamlet's "almost blunted purpose," but devotes the larger part of his speech to a touching concern for Gertrude's well-being:

> But look, amazement on thy mother sits!
> O step between her and her fighting soul.

> Conceit in weakest bodies strongest works.
> Speak to her, Hamlet. (3.4.108–10)

What matters is the loving relationship between old Hamlet, young Hamlet, and Gertrude; this is what Hamlet's mind appears to be dwelling upon. Relationship trumps uncertainty.

Similarly, while Hamlet's *dialogue* with Ophelia is full of riddles, game-playing, and ambiguous intentions, we do not doubt his love for her. We believe him when he declares at her graveside:

> I lov'd Ophelia—forty thousand brothers
> Could not with all their quantity of love
> Make up my sum. What wilt thou do for her?
> . . . .
> I'll do't. (5.1.258–60, 266)

The deliberate exaggeration of "forty thousand" (emended pedantically by Q1 to "twenty") makes clear that—as with Cordelia's love in *King Lear*—love cannot be computed, counted, and valued by mere quantity. The "sum" is of a different kind from mathematics. Hamlet, let it be admitted, has not treated Ophelia well in his pose as the avenger of all crimes, but like Lear at the last, he has a love that persists in the face of death. We are reminded of this extremity by Hamlet's offer to "drink up eisel" (vinegar), which recalls—without naming—the Christ who was given vinegar to drink on the cross (Matt. 28:48).[57] Hamlet's earlier accusations leveled at Ophelia would merely be insults directed at women if we did not feel that underneath it all, he loved her. This is what creates the pain and protest in our minds as we hear him telling her, "I did love you once," and when she replies, "Indeed, my lord, you made me believe so," to hear him say, "You should not have believed me" (3.1.113–16). This is subtle fencing with words as Hamlet attempts to hold together his conflicting roles under the guise of madness. Ophelia should not have believed him, he explains, because he is not believable, not trustworthy; even when virtue is grafted onto a fallen human nature, a trace of dishonesty will remain; perhaps echoing the image of grafting in Romans 11:17–18, he exclaims, "For virtue cannot so inoculate our old stock but we shall relish of it" (116–17).[58] In the light of this, when he therefore goes on to declare, "I loved you not," he could mean, "I never loved you at all, and was lying to you" or, "I didn't love you properly because I wasn't capable of it." She replies, "I was the more deceived," and when he responds, "Get thee to a nunnery!," the reason he gives is that she is better off without him: "I am very proud, revengeful, ambitious, with more offences at my beck than I have thoughts to put them in" (123–25). This is an extraordinary speech, in which he is not simply denying his love, but exploring what it means and putting it to the test with Ophelia. In the way that the conversation develops, though cruel to Ophelia, it does not contradict his later assertion, "I lov'd Ophelia."

HAMLET WAITS FAITHFULLY

Now we come to a fourth reason, a surprising one, that has been given for Hamlet's hesitation. As offered most eloquently by Helen Gardner, it admits Hamlet's delay, but excuses it as a necessary tactic. Here are we—Gardner suggests—urging that Hamlet should get on with the action, and we have missed the whole point of the revenge convention of the time: that is, the revenger is not an *agent* but an *instrument* of fate.[59] The revenge tradition, she asserts (citing, for example, Tourneur's *Revenger's Tragedy*), holds that the revenger must wait until the villains act to become the agents of their own destruction; *they* must make the first move and give the avenger his opportunity. Destruction must rebound on their own heads; *they* initiate the downhill movement toward destruction themselves, and the hero is committed to counteraction, to responding to events rather than initiating them.

So Hamlet must wait, like a soldier on guard,[60] until Claudius makes the fatal move himself which Hamlet can then capitalize upon. Thus, as Hamlet says of Rosencrantz and Guildenstern, they are destroyed "by their own insinuation" (5.2.58). Claudius had given Hamlet's old friends Rosencrantz and Guildenstern letters to the king of England requesting him to kill Hamlet as soon as he arrived there. These two companions are thus killed by their own letters they are carrying, once Hamlet has tampered with them, changing the names of the victims to themselves. Polonius too is killed by his own devices, though indirectly; lurking behind a curtain to eavesdrop on Hamlet once too often, he is killed by Hamlet as an intruder, or (more likely) by mistake for the king. Above all, Claudius and Laertes die from the machinations of their own evil devices, killed by the poisoned sword and the poisoned cup that they themselves have prepared for Hamlet. As Laertes comments of Claudius, "he is justly served. / It is a poison tempered by himself" (5.2.312). Horatio gives the final verdict, that the story they have lived through is of "purposes mistook / Fallen on th' inventors' heads" (5.2.368–69), and with this phrasing he adds a scriptural validation to the theme of waiting for an internal process of retribution: Psalm 7:17 (16, Geneva) reads, "His mischief shall return upon his own head, and his cruelty shall fall upon his own pate."[61]

Hamlet's role as avenger then—it may be argued—is a waiting one: he is the soldier on watch, which is the image with which the play begins and ends. The opening scene is that of a nightwatch. We are presented with

sentries, soldiers on watch at night on the battlements of the castle of Elsinore, and among them is a royal person who is "sick at heart," a kind of sen-
try himself. The play ends with the dead Hamlet being borne away in state
as a soldier who has faithfully done his duty: he has kept his watch. Helen
Gardner suggests that this arouses in our minds the Renaissance image of
the soul as a soldier on watch in this world, refusing easy ways out—either
of suicide or refusal to engage in conflict when it is demanded.[62]

I am not entirely persuaded myself that there is *no* element of procrastination in Hamlet's delay, and that it is *entirely* strategic. After all, he reproaches
himself with delay, referring to himself as "Like John-a-dreams, unpregnant
of my cause" (2.2.503) and looking for occasion to "spur my dull revenge"
(4.4.32). His hesitation arises, as I have been suggesting, from the situation
of conflicting roles in which he is placed and from his uncertainty about the
ghost. But I do think that Helen Gardner is right when she denies that Elizabethans watching this portrayal of a faithful soldier "on watch" would have
thought that they were witnessing a story of personal failure.[63] There is a
spirituality here of living life as responsibly as possible in face of death.

This revenge tradition of waiting qualifies what would otherwise be
a strongly Puritan expression of predestination by Hamlet late in the play, a
conviction which also encourages a stance of faithful waiting, though in this
case for God's sovereign purpose to be worked out:

> We defy augury. There is special providence in the fall of a sparrow. If it be,
> 'tis not to come. If it be not to come, it will be now. If it be not now, yet it
> will come. The readiness is all, since no man of aught he leaves knows what
> is't to leave betimes. Let be. (5.2.197–202)

Hamlet is apparently surrendering to divine providence as he faces the possibility of being defeated in the duel with Laertes to come; perhaps he shows
some premonition of a more serious danger that awaits him beyond death.
The Reformed theologian John Calvin had insisted on a "special providence"
manifested not just in the whole structure of creation (general providence) but
in particular events, and exemplified in the Gospel text about God's knowing
the fall of a sparrow (Matt. 10:29). There is a parallel with Hamlet's "special
providence in the fall of a sparrow" in Calvin's *Institutes of the Christian Religion*, 1.17.6:

> Therefore as a litle before we haue rightfully reflected their opinion which
> do imagine an vniuersall Prouidence of God, that stoupeth not specially
> to the care of euery creature: yet principally it shal be good to reknowledge
> the same speciall care toward our selues. Whereupon Christ after he had
> affirmed that not the sparow of least value, doth fall to the ground without

the will of the Father, doth byandby apply it to this ende, that we should consider that howe much we be more worth than sparrowes, with so much nyer care doth God prouide for vs.[64]

There is only a *near*-quotation from Calvin here, since, according to this translation by Thomas Norton of 1574, Calvin contrasts "universal providence" with "special care" rather than "special providence," and the French text bears this out (*spécialement soin*), although elsewhere Calvin does associate the Gospel case of the sparrow with particular providence.[65] Elizabethan divines often made a distinction between "general" and "special" providence,[66] and so it is likely that Shakespeare heard of "special providence" linked to the instance of the sparrow in a sermon, rather than directly from Calvin. In any case, Hamlet's speech contains reference to at least two scripture texts,[67] Matthew 10:29 on the sparrows ("one of them shall not fall on the ground without your Father") and Matthew 24:44 on "readiness" ("Therefore ye also ready: for in the hour that ye think not, will the Son of man come"). The latter allusion hints at death, which may also be the meaning of "leaves" in Hamlet's declaration, "no man of aught he leaves knows what is't to leave betimes." We are being warned that we all die: the question is whether we are ready. Earlier in the same scene Hamlet offers a similar submission to providence and makes a play on the word "ends"; they are first ends of a piece of wood in the metaphor, and second they are our "destinations"—including the end of life. "There's a divinity that shapes our ends, / Rough-hew them how we will" (5.2.10–11). Here Hamlet is reflecting on the circumstances by which he came to survive the plot to kill him on his voyage to England, though we may feel he goes too far in claiming heavenly providence—"why even in that was heaven ordinate"—in having the means to play his deadly trick on his former friends (5.2.48). Michael Witmore suggests that in act 5, "Hamlet finally manages a cooperation with divine providence which, paradoxically, enables him to fulfil the ghost's charge to revenge."[68] Yet this is not quite right: when Hamlet finally does kill the king, it is not from motivation to revenge his father at all, but a reflex movement reacting to Claudius's murder of himself (intentionally) and his mother (unintentionally). Shakespeare is invoking Christian doctrine, but without dogmatic purpose. The Puritan tone of submitting to "special providence" is immediately diffused by the presence of a different approach which could be purely secular—waiting for events to unfold, and for people to defeat themselves by their own actions. Once again we see Shakespeare making intertextual reference in order to support a general spirituality.

Dogma of the "divinity that shapes our ends" is also balanced by a different worldview altogether, that of chance. Horatio's summing up of Hamlet's life is as a series of accidents:

> Of accidental judgements, casual slaughters,
> Of deaths put on by cunning, and for no cause,
> And in this upshot purposes mistook
> Fallen on th'inventors' heads. (5.2.366–69)

Here he echoes Hamlet himself, who in dying addresses those "that look pale and tremble at this chance" (5.2.318). Brian Cummings argues that the idea of "chance" is not as incompatible with Puritan convictions about God's providence and predestination of events as has usually been supposed. He points out that, although the Geneva Bible excised the English word "luck" from the entire text of scripture, it left in references to "chance" and "fortune," though with stern warnings in the margin that "there is nothing done without Gods providence and decree."[69] Calvin himself points out in a passage following his comment about providence and the sparrow, that while events are governed by secret processes beyond chance, they still *look like* chance. To translate Calvin's phrase *quasi fortuites*, the English translator (Norton) came up with "chaunceable," giving us: "I say, therefore, howsoeuer al things are ordained by the purpose and certaine disposition of God, yet to vs they are chaunceable."[70] A modern translator offers "fortuitous."[71] Cummings concludes that "Shakespeare, in creating such a complex world of chance in Hamlet, was not reacting against this theological sensitivity, he was participating in it."[72] Cummings is convincing in showing there is no outright conflict between Horatio's "accidents" and Hamlet's "special providence," but Shakespeare's mode of "participating" in theology is nondogmatic. He appears deliberately to be moderating Puritan predestination by both the conventions of the revenge plot and the dramatic presentation of a world of contingency. He is refraining from taking up a theological position, so that a spirituality and not a dogma can emerge. The scriptural image of a sparrow falling to the ground gives room for "many things."

The spiritual stance of living one's life responsibly in expectation of death, and affirming relationships even where there seems to be no future in which they can be realized, is embodied in the end of the play. Gardner is right that Hamlet's life cannot be read simply as a failure. The play *does* end on an upbeat, and Hamlet *is* celebrated, and yet this is done in a manner typical of Shakespearean tragedy. If in his comedies Shakespeare never gives a simple happy ending, but leaves a shadow cast over the happy circle of the reconciled, then in his tragedies something is always rescued from the wreckage of mortality. Shakespeare's tragic heroes die well. We wish they did not have to die, or there would be no tragedy at all; but they die in a way that has *some* positive achievement in it.[73] This achievement is nothing so dogmatic, however, as a looking forward to life after death in the conventional Christian sense. Truly, Horatio's benediction following Hamlet's death follows closely the Latin Burial Service of the Sarum rite:[74] "Good night, sweet Prince, / And flights of angels sing thee to thy rest" (5.2.343–44). Shakespeare here truncates[75] the antiphon *In Paradisum*—"May angels lead you to paradise ... may the choir of angels receive you, and care for you in Abraham's bosom, and with Lazarus, who was once poor, may you have eternal rest." (In paradisum deducant te angeli ... Chorus angelorum te suscipiat, et in sinu Abrahae collecet, ut cum Lazaro quondam paupere aeternam habeas requiem)—in order to bring to prominence the word "rest" (*requiem*), so picking up immediately Hamlet's own dying pun: "the rest is silence." Hamlet has just given his "voice" (vote) to Fortinbras's succession to the kingdom; by "the rest is silence" he means that no more can be said, but we also hear the phrase as hinting that in the "rest" of death there is only silence. This lingers on in the mind as a qualification to Horatio's vision of singing angels; they conduct to a "rest" about which there can only be silence on our part, and which may in itself be nothing but silence. There is an echo here of Psalm 115:17, "The dead praise not thee, O Lord; neither all they that go down into the silence" (Coverdale),[76] and we should recall that this psalm was written at a time when the Hebrew faith had no concept of human flourishing in life after death.

Horatio's commendation may be understood in either a Protestant or Catholic way: either the angels lead the soul *immediately* at death to Paradise, or they are acting as they are depicted in many descriptions of purgatory,[77] assisting in the deliverance of suffering souls from punishment. There are also resonances of the Gospel text that Lazarus the beggar "died, and was carried by the Angels into Abrahams bosom" (Luke 16:22), and Lazarus is indeed mentioned in the bidding of the Sarum rite that Horatio is quoting (*cum Lazaro quondam paupere*). Catholic conceptions of purgatory, as we have noted, give special privileges of access to heaven to the poor. But whether this is a Catholic, Protestant, or indeed simply biblical hope that is being articulated here, any dogmatic certainty is undercut by Hamlet's words, "the rest is silence." When we come to consider the impact of the play "in front" of the text we shall need to pay special attention to Hamlet's pun.

There is no doctrine of eternal life here, but there is a *spirituality* of facing death. The achievement is in the dying itself: the hero in several Shakespeare plays uses the act of dying in order to fix his or her story in our minds—he or she makes out of death a monument of art. There is Othello dying upon a kiss and recalling his past glories; Cleopatra, looking "as she would catch another Anthony in her strong toil of grace"; Romeo and Juliet in each other's arms; Richard II dying with the name of the king upon his lips whom he had previously betrayed. They each make death serve them by using death itself to fix pliable life into solid art. If they went on living, then they could make other mistakes, betray their vision once again—but in the moment of death they can recall their story secure in the knowledge that they can never be contradicted, or cannot contradict it themselves.

Supporting this storytelling, the end of Hamlet is full of images of the theater. Death is made a stage, and Hamlet stops Horatio from drinking the cup of poison so that he will be alive to tell Hamlet's story there properly. He bids Horatio:

> Horatio, I am dead.
> Thou livest, report me and my cause aright
> To the unsatisfied. (5.2.322–24)

And:

> Absent thee from felicity awhile,
> And in this harsh world draw thy breath in pain
> To tell my story. (5.2.331–33)

The bodies are placed "high on a stage" (5.2.362, 380), and Fortinbras calls all the noblest to form "the audience" (371) as the story is to be told, or "presently performed" (377). It seems that art has conquered death. Hamlet has been made immortal through his story.[78] In his command to Horatio he shows, then, another mark of the spirituality I have identified—the concern to make a story out of our lives when life so often appears random and meaningless. Yet, as in other plays, Shakespeare adds his reservations and qualifications. Even art, even the story, he tells us elsewhere,[79] is threatened by time and death at the last. In the tragedy of Hamlet, the achievement of the story is a provisional one, only a penultimate success of art. Here, too, Shakespeare gives just a hint that the soldierly end of Hamlet, the story that is to stick in our minds ("Bear Hamlet like a soldier to the stage"), invites some doubt under the glance of eternity. Horatio himself finds problems with the story, as he struggles to tell it "aright"; we are not altogether sure that his reference to "carnal, bloody and unnatural acts" applies only to Claudius and Laertes, and that Hamlet is entirely exempt. Fortinbras, moreover, ends the play thus:

> Take up the bodies—such a sight as this
> Becomes the field, but here shows much amiss.

That is to say, a heap of bodies is fitting for a field of battle, but it is out of place in a domestic setting. "Amiss" is the last word of the play. In itself, then, a story may not be enough. But there is always love and forgiveness, which may shape the story and reinforce it against death. In the face of death, Hamlet and Laertes "exchange forgiveness"; Laertes expresses the wish that Hamlet's action in killing both his father and himself should not count as charges against Hamlet in any judgment—whether that of God or the audience ("come not upon thee")—and Hamlet asks heaven similarly to free Laertes from guilt (5.2.313–16). Earlier, Laertes had exclaimed, "The devil take thy soul!," and Hamlet had replied that, "Thou prayst not well" (5.1.259), probably alluding to the Gospel injunction that we should pray for those who hurt us (Matt. 5:44).[80] Laertes had also dissimulated in saying, "I did receive your offered love like love" (5.2.228) while planning Hamlet's death. But what matters at death, the point of human extremity, is that the loving brotherhood that has been lost between Laertes and Hamlet as they have both become avengers should be restored.[81]

SHAPING THEOLOGY: REIMAGINING BEING DEAD

Becoming exasperated by the many studies of Hamlet's character and psychology that contradict each other, C. S. Lewis declared in an address of 1942 that the real subject of the play was not the prince, but death: "I believe that we read Hamlet's speeches with interest chiefly because they describe so well a certain spiritual region through which most of us have passed . . . rather than because of our concern to understand why and how this particular man entered it."[82] That "spiritual region" he finds to be "fear of death; not . . . a physical fear of dying, but a fear of being dead."[83] The mystery is not in Hamlet's character but in "the darkness which enwraps Hamlet—dread, waste, dust, emptiness."[84] While criticism since Lewis has continued to show an interest in the question as to why Hamlet delays (as I have just done myself), it has also confirmed his diagnosis that the play brings us to consider how to think about being dead.[85] Indeed, Samuel Johnson had suggested, long ago, that the famous line "To be or not to be" was not directly a question about whether to live or die, but about the state of the afterlife. Hamlet's train of thought, as Johnson reconstructed it, was this: "Before I can form any rational scheme of action under this pressure of distress, it is necessary to decide, whether, *after our present state, we are to be or not to be. That is the question*, which, as it shall be answered, will determine, whether 'tis nobler, and more suitable to the dignity of reason, to suffer the outrages of fortune patiently, or to take arms against them, and by opposing end them, though perhaps with the loss of life."[86]

More recently, Greenblatt has given a new twist to the question. *Hamlet*, he proposes, shows that in the face of the loss of belief in purgatory in the English Reformation, a new way of "imagining" the afterlife and maintaining a relation to the dead needed to be created.[87] Here he echoes the lament of Eamon Duffy that in the world of the revised Book of Common Prayer of 1552, "the dead were no longer with us."[88] English culture was facing a crisis in which a centuries-old social practice of living with the dead through prayer had been lost. Greenblatt himself thinks that ("perhaps") Shakespeare's response was "one in which the theater offers a disenchanted version of what the cult of purgatory once offered."[89] The place of purgatory was replaced by the space of the stage, giving room for imaginative engagement with the dead and with one's own future state of being dead. In this final section of my chapter, I want to offer a less secularized account of such "reimagining" for the sake of making theology today. Shakespeare's intertextuality with Bible and theology in this play, I have wanted to show, provides him with material for plot and imagery, and is also the seedbed for a spirituality of facing death, making and restoring relations, and creating a story. As we now consider the impact of the play on the text of theology "in front" of the text of the play, we find that the theological task of reimagination needs to be shaped by the ghost's command, "remember me," and Hamlet's dying pun, "The rest is silence."

How shall we remember the dead in a way that maintains relations, and even a communion of prayer between the living and dead? How shall we speak about such things while respecting silence? The second question reminds us that all talk about life after death can only be conducted in metaphors which are more or less appropriate in hoping for a "new creation." The tools of language belonging to our present created state must have limited use in face of the reality of death; we must learn to "say" and "unsay"[90] at the same time, being both kataphatic and apophatic. As I have already maintained in reflecting on King Lear, the evident psychosomatic unity of the human being makes it impossible to use the dualistic language of the detachment of a soul from the body and its ongoing survival in a disembodied state.[91] I now want to add that such a scenario does not take full account of Hamlet's dictum, "The rest is silence," and the undogmatic uncertainty about "what dreams may come" with which Shakespeare suffuses the play; the language of an "immortal soul" is far too "talkative,"[92] too confident about the nature of a future state based, supposedly, in present experience. Hope in a "resurrection of the body," which is not a revival but a transformation of the present body, must by contrast remain a metaphor, but it does at least affirm a wholeness of the human person. It does, however, raise a question of identity which theologians must resolve.[93]

If a person goes out of existence at the point of death, and is later re-created by God ex nihilo, would this resurrected person be the same person? The philosopher John Hick argues that it would, if it were an exact replica of the living person.[94] This analogy between resurrection and a replica is not, however, completely convincing. The break between death and resurrection, however brief, seems to be a gulf in which identity will be swallowed up forever unless there is some kind of continuing link between the old person and the new. This leads some theologians to make the move of filling the gap with a modified kind of dualism, that is, with a *temporary* disembodiment of the soul. While insisting that the ultimate and proper destiny of the human being is the resurrection of the body, it is suggested that the continuing of a disembodied soul through death into an interim period would solve the problem of continued identity, as this soul would finally be reunited with a re-created body and link the new person to her older version. The combination of a disembodied soul with resurrection (a sort of eschatological cocktail) is a popular solution, and while it has very widespread precedent in classical Christian thought (for example, in Aquinas and Augustine), it has been recently argued most strongly by such philosophers as Stephen T. Davis,[95] Paul Badham,[96] Richard Swinburne,[97] and finally by John Hick himself in a later development of his thought.[98] Advocates of a temporarily disembodied soul maintain that it is logically possible for the soul to continue to exist without the brain. But they modify traditional dualism by arguing that the high degree of soul-brain interaction means that for the soul to remain in being without the body it must depend entirely on the act and power of God.[99] Yet a further, and fundamental, modification of dualism in this approach is the interim nature of the soul's disembodiment. The human person is diagnosed as being *incomplete* without a body, a "plugging" of soul into a new physical brain, which is granted in the resurrection from the dead.[100]

However, I believe this interim state to be a quite unsatisfactory idea. Philosophical objections can be leveled against a temporarily disembodied state in the same way as they are brought against a more thoroughgoing view of an immortal soul, and I briefly mention only two. A disembodied soul would have to rely upon memory alone for its own identity, and for recognizing the identity of others, and (as philosophers like Terence Penelhum have argued),[101] there are problems about the reliability of memory. Further, there is the problem of how souls without bodies could communicate with each other in such an existence, even if it were only temporary.[102] Here I do not wish to enter in any detail into these arguments, because they do not seem to me to be the decisive ones. The real objections to a continuation of the soul in a disembodied state are that it does not take death seriously, and that it attempts to give more detail than is possible. No less than the view of an immortal soul, it fails to reckon with the impact of death upon the whole human person that we cannot escape if we live in the world of such tragedies as Shakespeare's *King Lear* and *Hamlet*.[103] The cry, "O, thou'lt come no more, / Never, never, never, never, never!" (*King Lear*, 5.3.306–7) must be respected. Belief in an immortal soul cannot satisfy our desire for protest against death. Only an entering of the nothingness of death and a throwing of ourselves in trust upon God to justify us in the face of this utter destruction can accord with our experience of death's finality. As Hamlet tells us, "The rest is silence"—though, while keeping to the spirit of Hamlet's warning, I shall attempt to say a little more about a theology which is shaped by living in the world of *Hamlet*.

In the face of the impact of death, putting an end to the whole person as far as *our* capacity to survive is concerned, the only hope for continuing identity can be in God. As I have already described it, the symbol of the Trinity points to the divine life as being infinitely interpersonal in itself while simultaneously embracing relations between human personalities.[104] If our existence comes to an end at death, and if we hope in God to re-create us, the only possibility of our being the same person is in God, and not in ourselves. God alone is the link between the old person and the new. We can trust that "I" will be the same person with the same life story, not just because God *identifies* us, but because God has preserved our *identity* within God's own self. According to the Christian vision of the Trinity, we share already in an interpersonal life of God as Father, Son, and Holy Spirit; God makes room for us in the divine communion of relationships, and in re-creating us God will—as the Apostle Paul puts it—"conform us to the image of his Son, Jesus Christ"[105]—that is, our identity will be even more deeply bound up with the resurrection body of Christ than it is at present.

We may use an analogy and say that when we have died, God will "remember" us, and from this memory will re-create us.[106] But memory is hardly an adequate term; to be remembered by God is a quantum leap forward from being in the memory banks of a computer, or to be remembered by a fellow finite being. To be remembered by God would be nothing less than being alive in God. We can give no rational or literal description of this state since if we *could* conceptualize it, it would no longer challenge present reality and we would cease to depend on God alone for justification. In thinking about life after death we might, however, tentatively suggest that everything a person is—all her or his memories, habits, attitudes, hopes, fears, and loves—is preserved in God. What characterizes people and makes them lovable is taken into God, and God lives that life in their place, representing them, vicariously standing in for them. After all, we only exist *now* as a person because we exist in God. According to the Christian vision of the Trinity we share already in the interpersonal life of God as Father, Son, and Holy Spirit; we can trust that "I" will be the same person with the same life story after death because God preserves our *identity* within God's own self. Out of God's memory of us, God will re-create us as a whole person in the resurrection from the dead. Representatives in many areas of life stand in for a person until that person appears as him or herself;[107] God stands in for the dead until they appear in the resurrection.

This kind of theology of life after death is grappling with Hamlet's question of self-identity, "To be or not to be?," at least in the way that Samuel Johnson reads it. On this basis, we might then be able to develop a theology of relations with the dead which begins to do what—as Greenblatt maintains—*Hamlet* does imaginatively, offering a sense of community over the generations, answering the plea of the ghost and of the countless souls of More's *Supplication*, to "remember me." That is, we shall need to develop a modern approach to the traditional belief in a "Communion of Saints,"[108] while understanding the word "saints" to refer to all Christians who have led "holy" lives, as well as to named saints who appear in ecclesiastical calendars. But to develop a theology of intercession *for* and *by* all the saints, we need to answer a prior question: why are intercessory prayers needed at all? There is the moral problem of whether it is justice that God should help one person because we prayed to God for them, and should leave another in trouble because we failed to ask. Or, we ask, why do prayers often apparently go unanswered? There seem to be many situations where it is the very purposes of God disclosed in scripture and church tradition that do not seem to be fulfilled. I suggest that these problems are the more acute and baffling if we think of God's action as unilateral and coercive, and that there is an alternative model of God's relation to the world: that God acts only in a persuasive way, always calling for cooperation from created beings, and that God's "lure" toward the good is open to being rejected or modified within a complex network of influences.[109]

I suggest that if divine activity takes the form of symbiosis between God and the world, then as we pray we can add the persuasive power of human love to God's. That is, in praying for others we are expressing our love and concern for them, and God takes that desire into the divine desire for their well-being. This is not to suppose that our love is being added quantitatively to the divine love, as if to make an arithmetical sum; rather, we must conclude that it is the desire of God in creation to combine uncreated love with the love of created beings to effect change. God already wants to create a response within persons at every level (conscious and unconscious), to entice them into an openness to new possibilities that will promote healing, to woo them into cooperating with initiatives of grace. God does not have to be moved from reluctance to willingness to help. Our hopes, expectations, and longings for someone are assumed into God's own persuasion, augmenting and amplifying the urgings of God's Spirit, so that together God and the interceders begin to work transformation. Whether we want someone to act justly and generously, or to be comforted, or to be strong in the face of adversity, God is the means of communicating this desire to them, and of making it effective within God's own pressure of grace where on its own our wishes could achieve little. At the same time, of course, the one praying is becoming attuned to the desires of God, prompted to act appropriately, and where possible, to change the situation with practical deeds of help.

Thus in intercession we find that we are being pulled into a zone of interconnection. This kind of prayer is supremely social. We are being swept into a current in which nothing is separated from anything else, no one from anyone else. We find we are being urged by the Spirit of God to pray for those far away in the world, some of whom we have never met; we find that we can enter with empathy into the experience of the hungry and needy of the world, and that this opens up an awareness of the hungry and needy parts of ourselves. We who pray for others find that we too are being prayed for as we enter the community of prayer. In intercession we discover the hidden connections between persons and things which do not appear obviously on the surface of life and which we often fail to notice. Intercessory prayer is an experience of connectedness and mutuality, because it is praying "in God" who lives in relationships.

To this understanding of *praying* "in God" we can now add a belief in *existing* "in God" after death, in order to make sense of intercession for and by those who have died. We can think that the characteristic way that the saints who have died once glorified and praised God in their lives, their concerns for others, their particular ways of self-giving, their love which they expressed for those near to them and those far away, including those they never personally knew—all these aspects are kept alive in God as their prayers. The human love that they added to the uncreated love of God, and which had a powerful effect on the world, is still enriching the transforming love of God and making a difference. In this sense, the saints who have died are still praying for the world, though not within any structure of mediation between the living and God. Correspondingly, we can certainly go on praying for those who have died. Intercession is, as I have described it, a loving concern that enriches God's transformative actions, and there is no reason why death should put an end to this. The widespread loss of belief in purgatory, and the termination of a system of bought prayers and masses for the dead during the period of the English Reformation, as recalled by Greenblatt, ought not then to prevent Christians from praying for each other and so keeping contact between the generations alive.

My account of God's "standing in" for those who have died, and of their intercessions continuing through the love of the Trinity, depends on the hope that God will re-create those whom God holds vicariously alive at present. Divine representation of them requires, I suggest, the concreteness of the assurance that they will be re-created as whole persons who can again pray in new situations, though in a less individualistic, more corporate, and more communal life for which we only have metaphors: "The rest is silence." In this sense, there is authentic grief that "Thou'lt come no more / Never" (*Lear*); re-creation cannot mean a mere repetition of life as it is now, and so such hope involves the painful loss of the familiar. It does not seem impossible, scientifically, to conceive of the raising the physical universe, in which energy takes a whole variety of forms, through the creative spirit of God to a new level of complexity. This would not be the "replacing" of the universe but its transformation.[110] For the universe as we know it to be the creation of a good, just, and living God (i.e., for what theologians call "theodicy"), several factors call for those "remembered" to be remade as whole persons in this environment.

First, creation is about God's going out of God's self to create diversity, in which God takes pleasure; if all created things return only to the memory of God, this seems a denial of the extravagant generosity of God in creating multiple things of beauty that glorify the rich life of God. Second, and related to this, others have spent their love and care in enabling "me" to be myself; "my" survival with some unique identity, though in deeper community, is not because of my own worth (Derek Parfit rightly objects to such egotism),[111] but because "my" total loss would waste the love of others. Third, the fact of suffering calls for a consummation of all things; there are too many for whom we pray whose potential was stunted and never came to fulfilment, and whom justice requires should have the opportunity of growth, adventure, and greater completion. As the Protestant theologian John Macquarrie argues, the symbol of "purgatory" is "indispensable to any reasonable understanding of Christian eschatology" since—while we should abandon any view of externally inflicted punishment—it indicates a "dynamic" rather than "static" view of an eternal state in which "new possibilities" continually open up. Moreover, it can also be reimagined as a symbol of hope for salvation of the whole creation, rather than an intermediate state between two fixed destinies, indicating that "God's reconciliation can reach anywhere," while we must recognize that "this victory can only come when at last there is the free cooperation of every responsible creature."[112]

The impact of *Hamlet* "in front of the text" will thus come partly from allowing the spirituality actually expressed there to shape theology, and partly from finding theological solutions to the problem with which the play itself seems to be engaging—how to relate imaginatively to those who are loved, whether alive or dead. The eucharistic command, "Do this to remember me" (1 Cor. 11:25) resounds unspoken through the text. The "more things" to which

Hamlet urges Horatio to give attention thus open a horizon of uncertainty, sufficient to make Hamlet hesitate. But at the same time they open up the promise of "excess," of "surplus" in human existence, which a theologian *might* (as I have done) symbolize as the interactions of a vast web of personalities, held in the embrace of a triune God. But whatever theology emerges, the theologian who lives in the play-space of Hamlet is required to consider how to envisage a love between persons which transcends death, and which heals the broken relations between generations.

8

King Richard II, *King John*, and the Ambiguities of Power

Two of Shakespeare's English history plays, *King Richard II* and *King John*, give considerable scope to Shakespeare's strategy of avoiding partisanship amid the confessional clashes of his age. Though the first tells the story of a monarch of the late fourteenth century, and the second of the early thirteenth century, they reflect stresses and dangers experienced by the monarch contemporary to Shakespeare at the time of writing, Elizabeth I, offering parallels which would have been very well recognized by his audience. While threats to the supremacy of Elizabeth and to her establishment of the Church of England in the wake of the English Reformation arose from the very different quarters of Roman Catholic and Puritan dissidents, Shakespeare takes care to remain above the confessional fray, and handles the associated issue of divine-right kingship with a skilful ambiguity.

An intertextuality of biblical and other theological references both enables the development of image and plot, and provides the seedbed for the emerging of what I have been calling a "general spirituality," free from dogmatic commitments in considering the question of where power lies in the state. Probably written during the same two years as *A Midsummer Night's Dream* and *The Merchant of Venice* (1595–96), these historical plays reflect spiritual themes similar to those in the other two plays, but grounded in a very different ethos and genre. I also want to show how theologians who live in the world of the plays should be alert to their impact "in front of the text," affecting the way that they understand the tragedy of another person who was, and is, called "Lord" and "King" by his community—Jesus Christ.

THE WORD OF "KING"

When the play of *King Richard II* is over, we are likely to remember Richard as a beautiful voice, speaking ceremonial and lyrical words, constructing a world *by* words and making a world *of* words.[1] The play is suspended between two set-pieces of ceremony devised by Richard and dominated by his voice and rhetoric; in between, as Richard is absent on wars in Ireland, the kingdom slides away from him as Henry Bolingbroke exercises power politics.

The play begins with a trial by combat between Bolingbroke and Thomas Mowbray, presided over and then canceled by Richard with regal majesty; in the latter part of the play Richard makes a ceremonial theater out of the abdication forced on him by Bolingbroke, shortly to become King Henry IV. Richard is without doubt a maker of words, luxuriating in their power, often with successful effect, and yet at other times lapsing into an absurdity of word-spinning. Richard appears to be the poet of the play, the "artist" who caught the imagination of W. B. Yeats in a Stratford production;[2] but this is because self-conscious and elaborate poetry is Shakespeare's style of writing in his earlier period.[3] Although Richard tends to be inactive, and is chided for it, no simple contrast can be made between Richard as "poet" and Bolingbroke as "practical man"; Bolingbroke too can use words effectively. Rather, Shakespeare is employing his style of writing, and giving a double-share of it to Richard, in order to say something about Richard's state of mind: he is entangled in complexities about a *particular* word—namely the word of "king."

Richard is laying claim to the divine right of kings, in an extreme form of comparing himself with a greater "deputy" of God on earth, Christ. Several references to scripture make this clear. After he has deposed himself under duress, he complains:

> Though some of you, with Pilate, wash your hands,
> Showing an outward pity, yet you Pilates
> Have here deliver'd me to my sour cross,
> And water cannot wash away your sin. (4.1.239–42)

The reference is to Matthew's Gospel account, where Pilate "took water and washed his hands before the multitude, saying 'I am innocent of the blood of this just man'" (Matt. 27:24), an action shortly followed by the record that he "delivered him to be crucified" (26), echoed in Richard's words "deliver'd me to my sour cross." As Shaheen suggests,[4] Shakespeare may have found the comparison of Richard's passion with that of Jesus before Pilate in Jean Créton's *Histoire du Roy d'Angleterre Richard,* a manuscript consulted by

Holinshed for his *Chronicles* (1587), which were themselves the major source for Shakespeare's play. If this is so, Shakespeare has nevertheless added his own reading of scripture to the reference, by a more exact quotation of the Matthean text, and also by associating Pilate's washing of his hands with the biblical image of washing away sins, recalling Acts 22:16: "Be baptized, and wash away thy sins."

Richard continues his self-identification as Christ by adding accusation of betrayal by his own Judases. Mistakenly thinking that his three faithful followers, Green, Bushey, and the Earl of Wiltshire, have betrayed him to Bolingbroke, he exclaims, "Three Judases, each one thrice worse than Judas!" (3.2.132), and then later explicitly compares his betrayal to Christ's—indeed, he will out-Christ his predecessor in this respect:

> Did they not sometime cry "All hail" to me?
> So Judas did to Christ, but He in twelve
> Found truth in all but one; I, in twelve thousand, none. (4.1.170–72)

With "found truth in all but one" we may compare "Ye are cleane [guiltless], but not all" (John 13:10).[5] In Matthew 26:49, Judas greets Jesus in Gethsemane with "Haile master" (cf. also Mark 14:45), while the exact words "All hayll" only appear in the York Mystery Cycle.[6] There may also be a recollection here of the acclamation of Jesus by the fickle crowd when he entered Jerusalem (Luke 19:9), they who were soon to cry "crucify." The key word there is "Hosanna," but there may be an echo of the story as Richard has already made a reference to it in 3.2.24–26 (see below).

The comparison with Christ has its basis in the doctrine of the king's "two bodies," parallel to the two natures of Christ, human and divine.[7] One body is the physical one of flesh and blood, and the other is the sacred body which is identified with the body of the state, an eternal nature—or at least enduring in a nontemporal way beyond the transient epochs of particular monarchs' lives. When Richard sits on the ground to meditate on the common needs of his body and its vulnerability to death, he appears to refer to the abandonment of the sacred body: "Throw away respect, / Tradition, form and ceremonious duty." Without this nature, he asks, "How can you say to me I am a king?" (3.2.172–77). Later, having taken off his crown, he blames himself for having given consent "T'undeck the pompous body of a king" (4.1.250).

Scripture resonances draw attention to Richard's claim to be like Christ, and the analogy is not altogether absurd, since Bolingbroke twice compares himself to Pilate (3.1.5–6; 5.6.49–50), vowing that "I'll make a voyage to the Holy Land / To wash this blood off from my guilty hand." Yet at the same time the very scriptural references subtly undermine Richard's assertions; they reveal that Richard is not like Christ at all. They thus show that he has placed a false confidence in the word "king," unlike Christ, who consistently refuses to use it of himself. When asked, "are you the king of the Jews?" all four Gospels agree that he makes the response, "*you* have said so" (Mark 15:2; Matt. 27:11; Luke 23:3; John 18:27), while the Fourth Gospel adds, "my kingdom is not from this world." The way that Shakespeare draws on scripture texts thus enables him to take an equivocal approach to the idea of divine-right monarchy: while paying respect to the sacredness of the office, he constantly throws doubt on whether there can be any model example of an occupant of it, and thereby questions any demand for absolute allegiance to power in society.

Richard, for instance, exhibits a simplistic view of divine right of kings when he declares:

> Not all the water in the rough rude sea
> Can wash the balm off from an anointed king;
> The breath of worldly men cannot depose
> The deputy elected by the Lord.
> For every man that Bolingbroke hath pressed
> To lift shrewd steel against our golden crown,
> God for His Richard hath in heavenly pay
> A glorious angel. Then if angels fight,
> Weak men must fall, for heaven still guards the right. (3.2.54–62)

These lines begin with scriptural and theological resonances that appear to support Richard's viewpoint. The Hebrew Bible often uses the phrase "the Lord's anointed" of the Davidic kingship, and the office of David was transferred to the English king in Anglican theology of the period.[8] Like David, the ideology ran, the English king was the head[9] of both civil and religious institutions, not only the state but (replacing the pope) also the church. Romans 13:4 refers to the ruler as the "minister of God," a term used in parallel with "deputy" by John of Gaunt in 1.2.38–41, who articulates the typical Tudor doctrine of unconditional obedience to the sovereign. Even if the "deputy anointed in His sight" has done wrong, "Let heaven revenge, for I may never lift / An angry arm against his minister." As expressed in the homily "An Exhortation to Good Order and Obedience," even in the case of wicked rulers and magistrates "we may not in any wyse withstand violently, or rebel agaynst rulers, or make any insurrection . . . agaynst the anoynted of the Lorde . . . referring the iudgement of our cause onely to God."[10] The proof-text for the instruction is

Romans 13, "the powers that be, be ordeyned of God."[11] This dogma appears to be strengthened by Richard's appeal to the guardianship of the king by angels, recalling both Psalm 91:11, "he shall give his angels charge over thee: to keep thee in all thy ways," and Christ's own claim that if he prayed to God his Father, God would "cause to stand by me more than twelve legions of Angels" (Matt. 26:53). There, indeed, *it might seem*, was the supreme instance of the Lord's anointed, the Messiah, guarded by angels.

But it is Richard's implicit comparison of himself with Christ that undermines his case, and gives us the hint that the whole speech is a falsely based confidence. According to the Gospel text, Christ *refused* the aid of angels to keep him from harm. When Peter in the garden of Gethsemane draws a sword to defend Jesus, and Jesus asks, "Thinkest thou, that I can not now pray to my Father; and he will give me more then twelve legions of Angels?" (Matt. 26:53), the point is that he is *not* going to do so and so Peter also should not use violence on his behalf. The incident recapitulates a temptation in the wilderness, when Satan suggests that Jesus should make the dramatic gesture of throwing himself from a great height, citing the text from Psalm 91:11 to the effect that angels would take charge and lift him up (Matt. 4:6; also cf. Ps. 34:7). Jesus rejects the temptation, and refuses to "tempt the Lord thy God"—that is, put God to the test. Richard seems all too willing to test God, whom he believes has many "a glorious angel" in his "heavenly pay." Since there is also a pun here on the name of a golden coin of the realm, called an "angel," Richard is backing up his confidence that God will fight for him by envisaging angels as "wage-earning soldiers in God's army,"[12] a view of brute power entirely at odds with Jesus's behaviour. Other elements too, thinks Richard, can be conscripted to his cause:

> This earth shall have a feeling, and these stones
> Prove armed soldiers, ere her native king
> Shall falter under foul rebellion's arms. (3.2.24–26)

As Hamlin suggests,[13] Richard is here recalling the saying of Jesus when Pharisees rebuked his disciples for loudly acclaiming him as king and as the "one who comes in the name of the Lord" at his public entrance into Jerusalem. Jesus's response was: "if these should hold their peace, the stones would cry" (Luke 19:40). In what he says Richard implicitly compares himself with Christ, but at the same time the scripture text deconstructs his fantasy of stones becoming armed soldiers,[14] since Jesus's disciples are following a deputy of God whose kingdom is not of this world. The stones will bear witness, but will not become an army of followers, any more than Jesus made stones into bread during his temptations (Matt. 4:3–4).

Yet another comparison with Christ against the grain of the biblical text is Richard's endowing himself with the features of the sun; faced with Bolingbroke's rebellion, he claims that when Bolingbroke sees him "rising in his throne, the east / His treasons will sit blushing in his face" (3.2.50–51). Later, after the success of the revolt, staring into the mirror for which he has called, Richard grieves:

> Was this the face
> That like the sun did make beholders wink?
> . . . .
> a brittle glory shineth in this face—(4.1.283–85)

The text from Malachi 4:2, "unto you that fear my Name, shall the Sun of righteousness arise, and health shall be under his wings," has been traditionally ascribed by the church to Christ, as in the marginal gloss of the Geneva Bible: "Meaning, Christ, who with his wings or beams of grace should lighten, & comfort his Church." Seeing Christ, the "Son of Man," the visionary of Revelation 1:16, exclaims that "his face shone as the sun shineth in his strength," and the Evangelist writes of the transfiguration of Jesus that "his face did shine as the sun" (Matt. 17:2).[15] All these Christological echoes are in Richard's image, but he expects that his own sun-like glory will overwhelm his enemies, rather like the confidence that Israelite Psalmists had in the theophanies of Yahweh in Holy War, again using sun imagery: "cause your face to shine . . . they perish at the rebuke of thy countenance" (Psalm 80:3, 16). By contrast, Christ as the "sun of righteousness" brings only healing. The "sharp two-edged sword" that issues from the mouth of his shining face (Rev. 1:16) is the "Word of God" (Rev. 19:15). As one commentator puts it: "the only weapon the Rider needs, if he is to break the opposition of his enemies, and establish God's reign of justice and peace, is the proclamation of the gospel."[16] Bolingbroke only augments the effect of the biblical texts themselves when he offers a jaundiced view of Richard's solar claims:

> See, see, King Richard doth himself appear,
> As doth the blushing discontented sun
> . . . .
> When he perceives the envious clouds are bent
> To dim his glory. (3.3.62–66)

In these ways, Shakespeare uses biblical allusions to increase ambivalence toward the monarch's claim of divine right to rule, while not overtly denying it. At one crucial point, Richard—through his quibbling with words—is portrayed as failing to obey a command of Christ. His equivocal answer to Bolingbroke's question as to whether he is "contented to resign the crown" is:

> Ay, no. No, ay; for I must nothing be.
> Therefore, no "no," for I resign to thee.
> Now mark me how I will undo myself. (4.1.201–3)

The surface meaning is that he is hesitating between the answers of "yes" (ay) and "no" in the state he is in; he is swinging from one response to the other: "Yes, no. No, Yes" Finally he resolves the issue: he rejects the "no": "Therefore, no(t) 'no.'" He will resign the crown, lose his identity, and become "nothing." But his initial "Ay, no. No, ay" is a failure to follow Jesus's words (Matt. 5:37): "Let your communication be, Yea, yea: Nay, nay." It would have underlined to the audience that Richard's use of words has something deeply suspect about it. The text was evidently in Shakespeare's mind, as he reuses it in *King Lear*: "to say 'ay' and 'no' . . . was no good divinity."[17]

Richard's playing with words, and his increasing sense of loss of identity as he loses his grip on the word "king," is shown in this very passage by a double pun. "Ay" (yes) can be heard as "I" (the personal pronoun), and "no" can sound like "know." So he might also mean: "I know no 'I,' for I must nothing be. / Therefore [I must] know 'no,' for I resign to thee." The surface meaning and the quibbling meaning can further be heard both at once, such as: "Yes, No. No 'I,' for I must nothing be."

LOSS OF IDENTITY: SETTING THE WORD AGAINST THE WORD

Richard finds he is reduced to "nothing," since he is no longer able to use about himself the word in which he had invested so much confidence. On hearing of Bolingbroke's rebellion he had exulted, "Is not the King's name twenty thousand names? Arm, arm, my name" (3.2.85–86). Now, without this name of "king," he feels he has no name at all. Following his self-deposition before Henry, he laments:

> I have no name, no title—
> No, not that name was given me at the font—
> But 'tis usurp'd. Alack the heavy day
> That I have worn so many winters out,
> And know not now what name to call myself. (4.1.255–59)

He calls for a mirror, "that it may show me what a face I have, / Since it is bankrupt of his majesty." It marks a moment of profound loss of identity

when he shatters the mirror and bids the new king to see "how soon my sorrow hath destroyed my face" (291). Bolingbroke dismissively assures him that
it is only the "shadow" of his sorrow that has destroyed the "shadow"—
that is, mirror image—of his face, intending to say that his sorrows are unreal, only an illusion. Richard, as the superior wordsmith, ingeniously seizes
on the word "shadow" to produce the opposite meaning: his external sorrows are mere shadows because his true grief lies "all within": "there lies the
substance," he declares, and ironically thanks Henry not only for causing his
sorrow but teaching him the way to lament it. But the implication is that
the substance of grief is ungraspable and elusive, like a Platonic idea.[18] His
queen, too, had earlier been bidden by her courtiers to think that her sorrow
was an illusory shadow, and she complains that by their sophistry they have
deprived her of the word "sorrow" altogether, so that she is left only with what
she calls a "nameless woe" (2.2.34). This is even more apt for Richard, looking
for the inner "substance" of himself which has no name.

This is the situation in which Richard delivers himself of his last soliloquy in Pomfret castle, and in which he draws on scriptural references to express his sense of inner turmoil and lost identity. Alone, without company of
others, he imagines his prison as being a world which is populated only by
his own thoughts. But if this is so, the "people" will be as much at odds with
each other as his thoughts are, and to express this conflict he significantly
speaks internally some phrases of Christ as if they are his own; after all, he
has seen himself as Christ, the man of sorrows:[19]

> And these same thoughts people this little world,
> In humours like the people of this world,
> For no thought is contented. The better sort,
> As thoughts of things divine, are intermixed
> With scruples, and do set the word itself
> Against the word, as thus "Come, little ones";
> And then again:
> "It is as hard to come as for a camel
> To thread the postern of a small needle's eye." (5.5.9–17)

Here he sets against each other two scripture verses, both words of Jesus. In
the first, Matthew 19:13–14, Jesus bids children welcome: "forbid them not
to come to me for of such is the kingdom of heaven." In the second, arising
from the incident of the rich young man immediately following the story of
the children, Jesus declares that "It is easier for a camel to go through the eye
of a needle, than for a rich man to enter into the kingdom of God" (Matt. 19:
24). The exact words "it is as hard" reflect the Markan version of the saying,

beginning, "How hard is it for them who trust in riches, to enter the kingdom of God" (Mark 10:24–25). Thus, in the one saying about entering God's kingdom Jesus says, "Come," and in the other he warns, "it is hard to come." The two texts are in the same chapter in all three synoptic gospels. Richard's procedure of considering an apparent conflict of sense in different texts was, as Cummings points out,[20] a standard form of exegesis in the sixteenth century, a trope known as a *contradictio*: it was, as Richard puts it, "setting the word itself against the word." But as a mode of textual exegesis it was intended to lead to a resolution, unlike here. Richard has adopted the sayings as his own thoughts, and so now they typify conflict. Scandalously, the impression is now given that Jesus might be contradicting himself.

Shakespeare may indeed be employing a theological conundrum among Puritans in his own time to exemplify "setting the word against the word" (which in the Quarto is even more shocking, reading "faith" instead of "word"). As Alison Shell summarizes it: "The first text shows God inviting humankind to Himself, only to turn them away in the second text by making the conditions of salvation impossibly difficult. This has the effect of pointing to the painful contrast between the Protestant ideal of evangelism and the Protestant doctrine of predestination, in a manner which . . . was acutely topical at the time the play was first performed."[21] Cummings further points out that the "contentment" which Richard cannot find among his thoughts is a term used in the period for a "theological sense of fulfilment equivalent to an apprehension of God's grace or election as a subjective experience."[22] Shakespeare is not, however, indulging in Catholic polemic against Protestantism, but is impartially probing tensions within the Puritan scene of the time, for the sake of exposing Richard's uncertainties about words, not only the ambiguous "come," but the more pressing word "king."

Moreover, the second text contains internal questions of meaning of its own, regardless of its relation to the first. There is a long history of exegesis of this saying, of which Shakespeare appears to be aware. "Camel" and "needle" could both be taken in their literal senses, which creates the highly extravagant metaphor of pushing a very large animal through a minute hole, and which might thus be seen as an example of a Jewish joke—even of the humor of Jesus himself. Alternatively, "camel" (Greek *kamelos*) might be supposed to be a misreading of *kamilos*, a ship's cable, still expressing an impossibility—threading a thick cable through a needle—but presenting arguably a more coherent picture. Third, it has been observed that a "needle's eye" is a widely used metaphorical expression in the Middle East for a narrow gate in a city, intended not for animals but for pedestrians; there was one, for instance, in the Jerusalem of Jesus's day. Pushing a camel through a small gate is obviously difficult, and might be thought to be *almost* impossible. There is precedent in exegesis for all three of these options, portraying to various degrees of difficulty the entry of a rich man into the Kingdom of Heaven. The second can be found in the Tomson edition of the Geneva Bible (1576), which adopts it from notes in Theodore Beza's *Novum Testamentum*; the marginal note in the Geneva-Tomson edition, following Beza, also contains the first, more literal, reading as an alternative. As for the third, this can be found in the medieval *Glossa ordinaria*, and is mentioned by Aquinas.[23] Remarkably, Shakespeare has Richard allude to all three meanings at once in one brief phrase: "A camel [the literal animal] / to thread [evoking a cable] the postern [gate] of a small needle's eye."

Discussing these different kinds of exegesis, Cummings rightly associates the complexity of meaning with Richard's own attempt "to understand the limits of language," writing that "Each word of Jesus' saying implies a complex set of referents which, when the words are put in sequence in a sentence, engenders ever new metaphorical correspondences. The very conflict of meaning among the scriptural exegetes is an exemplary case of Richard's more general sense of a problem over meaning."[24] Though Cummings does not add this, the problem is in particular with the meaning of "king." In behaving the way that he has—sometimes self-motivated, often compelled by external necessity—Richard has been setting the word "king" against itself, introducing contradictions. There is a strong hint that "king" is the word in question, since Jesus's two sayings are about entering the kingdom. At the end of the speech Richard spells matters out:

> Thus play I in one person many people,
> And none contented. Sometimes am I king;
> Then treasons make me wish myself a beggar,
> and so I am. . . .
> . . . .
> Then am I kinged again, and by and by,
> Think that I am unkinged by Bolingbroke,
> And straight am nothing. But whate'er I be,
> Nor I nor any man that but man is
> With nothing shall be pleased till be eased
> With being nothing. (5.5.31–41)

The audience will no doubt remember that only minutes earlier, in another scene, the striking phrase, to "set the word itself against the word," has already been used, and there it was also associated with a saying of Jesus. On that occasion, however, there was a resolution which underlines Richard's lack of "contentment." The old Duke of York and his equally elderly wife vie to make words work for them after they have discovered their son, Aumerle, has been plotting with fellow conspirators, including the Bishop of Carlisle, to over-throw the new king, Henry, in support of the deposed Richard. In a some-what comic scene, York, the Duchess, and Aumerle rush to Henry—York to insist that Aumerle must be punished, Aumerle and his mother to plead for his life. The Duchess pleads, "Say 'pardon' king, let pity teach thee how," but York picks up and plays on the word "pardon": "Speak it in French, King, say 'pardonne moy'"—that is, "I'm sorry, no." The Duchess then responds:

> Dost thou teach pardon pardon to destroy?
> Ay, my sour husband, my hard-hearted lord,
> That sets the word itself against the word. (5.3.119–21)

Henry resolves the lexical conflict over "pardon" by referring to a Gospel text which Shakespeare also employs at about the same time in the courtroom scene of *The Merchant of Venice*, namely the petition in the Lord's Prayer, "And forgive us our sins: for even we forgive every man that is indetted to us."[25] Portia urges "that same prayer, doth teach us all to render / The deeds of mercy,"[26] and Henry responds, "I pardon him as God shall pardon me." Thereby he hints at the guilt he feels for usurping the throne; while the issue of forgiveness is settled in this instance, the question of whether it is ever right to rebel against "the Lord's anointed" seems to remain open, underlined by the Duchess's plaudit, "A god on earth thou art!" The ironic tone both af-firms and undermines the divine right of kings which has been a dogma for Richard.

Henry's forgiveness of Aumerle lingers in our mind as we listen to Rich-ard's last soliloquy, which belongs to the genre of a confessional prayer before death, or what Shell calls "the theatre of the scaffold."[27] She suggests that the audience is "anxiously waiting to see whether Richard will achieve a good death," but is constantly disappointed throughout the speech. A final frustra-tion occurs in Richard's exchange with the groom, which divides his soliloquy from the entry of his murderer Exton; bitterly reflecting on the news that his favorite horse has carried Henry in his coronation procession, he ex-claims, "Forgiveness! Horse, why do I rail on thee?" (5.5.90). Shell comments, "To an audience holding its breath for Richard to ask forgiveness of God," asking forgiveness only from a horse "would have had a grossly parodic feel."[28] Richard is all too clearly not following the injunction of Jesus to pray for forgiveness as we forgive others, which once again undermines his frequent claim to be like Christ. Whether Richard does in the end make a good death we must leave for a moment.

THE TWO ADAMS

In much of the play Richard indeed appears less like Christ than Adam, regarded as the first and archetypal sinner in the theology of the time. As has been noted by several commentators,[29] alongside the scriptural theme of the passion of Christ there runs the scriptural theme of the fall of humankind We have already reviewed passion imagery, including scriptural references to the cross, Pilate, and Judas. The play also draws on textual tradition about fallenness—the paradisal Garden of Eden, the sin of Adam (Gen. 2–3) and the "fall" of the city of Jerusalem to the invading Babylonians and punitive Romans during Israel's history.

Near the beginning of the play, Gaunt's lament over the state of England depicts it as "This other Eden, demi-Paradise" and grieves that it is now a paradise lost, spoilt by the mismanagement of Richard (2.1.42). The theme is recapitulated in the conversation of the gardeners, comparing the realm of England to a garden that has not been cultivated and cared for. Plants that have been allowed to grow wildly are described as "prodigal," recalling the parable of the wild son who fell away from his father, and:

> He that hath suffered this disordered spring
> Hath now himself met with the *fall* of leaf. (3.4.48–49; my italics)

The queen makes the Adamic theme explicit. While addressing the gardener as "Thou, old Adam's likeness, / Set to dress this garden," she chides him for speaking of Richard's downfall:

> What Eve, what serpent hath suggested thee
> To make a second fall of cursed man?
> Why dost thou say King Richard is deposed?

Although she accuses the gardener of having listened to tempting voices (Gen. 3:1–7, 17–19), the Adamic fall she grieves over is that of Richard, so great a catastrophe that it is like a second fall of humankind. Just as Adam's fall caused disruption in the created world, bringing a "curse" on the earth (Gen. 3:17) and making it produce thorns and thistles (18), so Richard's fall will result—as the Bishop of Carlisle predicts—in "the woefullest division . . . that ever fell upon this *cursed* earth" (4.1.148). Uniting the themes of the Fall and the passion, Carlisle predicts that "this land [will] be called / The field of Golgotha" (145). For the Tudor historian, the supplanting of Richard by Henry was the fatal act, the original sin, that in due time unleashed the Wars of the Roses; this savage civil war between followers of the royal houses of York and Lancaster was only to be brought to an end by the marriage

settlement of Henry Tudor, grandfather of Elizabeth. The fall of the kingdom *under* Richard was to be succeeded by the even greater disaster set in
motion by his own fall.

This theme of the fall of England is supplemented by reference to biblical laments over the fall of Jerusalem to the armies of Babylon. As Hamlin
has suggested, references to the tongues of Mowbray and Gaunt as string-
less instruments—the first in exile and the second dead—recall Psalm 137,
where musical instruments are hung up unused and the Psalmist refuses to
"sing the Lord's song in a strange land" because Jerusalem is fallen.[30] The
widowed Duchess of Gloucester, in the wake of the murder of her husband
and the misrule of Richard, finds everywhere to be "desolate, desolate"—with
"unfurnish'd walls, / Unpeopled offices, untrodden stones" (1.2.66–73). As
Hamlin further suggests:[31] "Desolate is the key word of the book of Lamentations, bewailing the destruction of Jerusalem: 'How doth the city remain
solitary that was once full of people? . . . All her gates are desolate'" (Lam.
1:1, 4). Hamlin aptly quotes Thomas Nashe, declaring "as great a desolation
as Ierusalem hath London deserued," asserting that "No image or likenes of
thy Ierusalem on earth is left, but London," he warns, "London, thy house . . .
shall be left desoluate vnto thee."[32] Hamlin does not mention that the word
"desolate" also appears in the Gospel story of Christ's weeping over Jerusalem,[33] foretelling the fall of Jerusalem to the Romans, on which Nashe is
basing his own work here (1593). Further, the "Homily Against Disobedience," written in the wake of the Catholic Uprising, had already compared an
England divided by rebellion with a Jerusalem fallen.[34]

Augmenting these biblical images of fallenness are other metaphors expressing a downward motion, such as the word "depose" itself, and Richard's
throwing of the mirror on the ground. Then there is Richard's analogy of the
two buckets which he offers to Henry at the beginning of the ceremony of his
uncrowning, skilfully taking hold of a scene where he is at the disadvantage:

> Here cousin, seize the crown. Here, cousin,
> on this side my hand, and on that side thine.
> Now is this golden crown like a deep well
> That owes two buckets, filling one another,
> The emptier still dancing in the air,
> The other down, unseen and full of water.
> That bucket down and full of tears am I,
> Drinking my griefs while you mount up on high. (4.1.181–89)

The image may seem overfanciful, Richard's bucket falling and Bolingbroke's
rising, but Richard has cleverly turned the admission that Bolingbroke has
now risen above him to advantage: his enemy rises because he is "emptier,"

while Richard falls because he has weight, full of *gravitas*. While recognizing his fall, Richard manages to imply that Bolingbroke is of less worth, unworthy of monarchy. Again we have the quandary as to where rightful power lies. Bolingbroke's response to Richard's analogy is the terse, "I thought you had been willing to resign," but Richard again seems to take the advantage by replying, "My crown I am, but still my griefs are mine." He remains, he asserts, still "king" of griefs, which appears to be a veiled allusion to Christ, crucified under the name of "king" (Matt. 27:37).

In fact, the double set of biblical analogies—on the one hand, the fall of Adam and on the other, the passion of Christ—are linked in the New Testament (specifically Pauline) idea of Christ as the Second Adam, reversing the disobedience of the first.[35] The typology, then, is complex: Richard shows elements of both Christ and Adam, where the "Old Adam" element undermines Richard's claim to be Christ and yet where the potential to be Christ-(New)Adam is always present. As J. A. Bryant has suggested (followed by Forker), the Christ-Adam identity is further complicated by another biblical theme linked to the fall of Adam in Genesis 4, the murder of Cain by Abel.[36] At the beginning of the play, Richard seems cast for the part of Cain, since Bolingbroke associates Thomas Mowbray with Cain in accusing him of the murder of Thomas, Duke of Gloucester, whose blood "like sacrificing Abel's, cries / Even from the tongueless caverns of the earth" (1.1.104–5; see Gen. 4:10). Richard is implicated in the murder, although we do not know this for certain until later, and so—ironically—it is Richard, the close kinsman of Gloucester, who is really the Cain who slew his brother out of jealousy. Yet at the end of the play Richard is identified with Abel, since Bolingbroke denounces Exton his murderer as Cain (5.6.43), who must "go wandering through the shades of night" (Gen. 4:12). In Patristic exegesis, J. A. Bryant points out, Abel is seen as a type of Christ, whose shed blood "speaks better" than that of Abel (Heb. 12:24), promising salvation rather than demanding retribution.

Shakespeare has thus employed an intertextuality with scripture and theology to produce this mixed picture of Richard as Christ-Adam-Cain-Abel, which presents an ambiguity partly about the character of Richard, but partly about the rights of kingship itself.

EVACUATING THE WORD "KING" OF MEANING

While Shakespeare seems to leave the question of *unconditional* obedience to rulers as an open question, unlike the plain injunctions in the books of Homilies to be obedient even to evil rulers, he does at least hint at one way of resolving the issue. Richard has "set the word itself against the word" because he has evacuated the word "king" of meaning. If Richard's passion story is the loss of his identity, then it is largely due to his having given his identity away in the first place. His great crime, according to John of Gaunt, is his leasing out of the land of England in order to raise money, mainly for his Irish wars: "This royal throne of kings, this sceptred isle" is "now leased out . . . like to a tenement or pelting farm" (2.1.40, 60). Richard himself has boasted, "We are enforced to farm our royal realm" (1.4.45). When the dying Gaunt declares to Richard, "Landlord of England art thou now, not king," Shakespeare is probably echoing Richard's words in the earlier anonymous play *Woodstock*, "And thou no king, but landlord now become."[37] But Shakespeare has radical- ized the images, emphasizing that Richard has un-kinged himself; Gaunt de- clares to Richard that if his grandfather Edward III had foreseen his actions, he would have "deposed" him before he could be "possessed of the realm," and in fact Richard is now "possessed" only to "depose thyself" (2.1.107–8).

The same point is made by York when Richard takes the opportunity of Bolingbroke's exile—imposed on him by Richard in order to avoid the em- barrassment of his trial by combat with Mowbray—to seize his lands after the death of his father, Gaunt:

> Take Hereford's rights away, and take from Time
> His charters, and his customary rights;
> ·
> Be not thyself. For how art thou a king
> But by fair sequence and succession? (2.1.195–99)

York's words that if Richard acts in this way he will "be not thyself" are to be repeated by Richard himself after his deposition: he does not know what to call himself, and has become "nothing." When he finally resigns to Henry, he speaks truly, not just of the ceremonial event but of his behavior while still king:

> Now mark me how I will undo myself:
> I give this heavy weight from off my head,
> ·
> With my own tears I wash away my balm
> With my own hands I give away my crown,
> With mine own tongue deny my sacred state. (4.1.203–9)

The actual moment of deposition has been forced on Richard by Boling- broke's having seized the power for all practical purposes. But Richard has already voluntarily "denied [his] sacred state." The point is not just that he has acted unjustly, or "evilly," as the Book of Homilies puts it.[38] In his case he has emptied the word "king" of its customary content. The sceptred isle is bound in a prison of other, false words: "with inky blots and rotten parchment bonds" (2.1.64), and thus the word itself is set against the word.

Here Shakespeare seems to have approximated to Calvin's exegesis of Romans 13 in the final section of the *Institutes*, where he argues that disobedience against rulers is allowed if they cease to act as God's minister. To that point Calvin had been proposing in a conventional way that in the case of bad rulers, the Bible prioritizes the sovereignty of God in placing and deposing them. But at the very end of the chapter, he takes a different, more radical direction: "But in that obedience which we have shown to be due the authority of rulers, we are always to make this exception, indeed, to observe it as primary, that such obedience is never to lead us away from obedience to him, to whose will the desires of all ought to yield, to whose majesty scepters ought to be submitted . . . next to him we are subject to those men who are in authority over us, but only in him."[39] Calvin cites the biblical example of Daniel, who denied that he had committed any offense against King Darius when he refused to obey his edicts; the king, asserts Calvin "had exceeded his limits," and by wrongdoing against his subjects and exalting himself against God he had "himself abrogated his power." He concludes resoundingly: "we should not enslave ourselves to the wicked desires of men."

Such sentiments were in accord with constitutional theorists of the late medieval period who argued that England was traditionally a limited monarchy, with the king "under God and under law";[40] this constitutional view enjoyed quite wide respect in Elizabeth's reign alongside more passive views of obedience,[41] probably given new impetus through such Reformed views as Calvin's. As the Anglican Richard Hooker put it, the commonwealth is like a melodious instrument "where the king doth guide the state and the law the king."[42] He regarded rule by "mere divine right" (without other legal sanction) as extraordinary and infrequent, and normal rule as being the monarch working together with Parliament.[43] Notably, he interpreted Romans 13:1–7 as referring to submission to public power as a *whole* in the making of laws, not solely to the monarch.[44] Shakespeare is, of course, writing poetry rather than dogma (like Calvin) or legal opinion (like Hooker). Calvin is concerned with the primary duty of obedience to God, while Shakespeare is fascinated by questions of human identity, but they arrive at a similar place. There can no longer be unquestioning obedience to a ruler instituted by God when he has lost the character and nature of the rule that God intended, having (in the words of Calvin) "himself abrogated his power" or (in Shakespeare's words) "deposed himself."

This, then, was a warning message to Elizabeth I, who once herself admitted, "I am Richard II, know ye not that?"[45] Those who took the more "limited" view of monarchy tended to be either Roman Catholic or Puritan. Both factions were antagonized by royal behavior that was compared to that of Richard—including susceptibility to flattery, levying of heavy taxes to finance Irish wars, exacting customs duties on merchandise, confiscations, and benevolences (forced loans). Shakespeare's use of the terms "new exactions" and "benevolences" (2.1.249–50) imposed by Richard seems to echo the words of a Romish tract, *A Declaration of the True Causes of the Great Troubles* (1592),[46] and similar accusations were made by Puritans behind the Marprelate pamphlets.[47] Radical Puritans added to financial grievances a resistance to the appointment of bishops by the monarch, and Elizabeth coupled Puritan "Separatists" from the Church of England together with Catholicism as a menace to the state. She and her divines were troubled by any sect, no less than Catholicism, that seemed to separate itself from the state in separating from the state church, and the term "Puritano-papismus" came into being. The Separatists Henry Barrow and John Greenwood were hanged under an act of 1581 against sedition, ignoring the intent of the measure against Papists.

There is no *direct* reference to the (soon suppressed) Catholic Uprising in the North of 1569 in any of Shakespeare's plays, but it casts a long shadow over several of them, including *Richard II* and *King John*, in which rebellions play a central role. It was in fact the 1569 Uprising that prompted, in 1571, the addition of the homily "Against Disobedience and Wilful Rebellion" to the twenty homilies already contained in the Second Book of Homilies, first issued under Elizabeth I in 1563. This repeated and emphasized the doctrine of passive obedience to rulers, urging that redress against their evil actions should be left to God, which had already been expressed in the homily "An Exhortation to Obedience" in the First Book. Memories of the Uprising, generally incompetent though it was, must have given substance to the mood of anxiety about disorder in the state of England that we can discern in the plays.

There is evidence that *Richard II* was considered to be a politically dangerous play. The scene depicting the deposition of an anointed monarch was omitted from the Quarto published in 1597.[48] Notoriously, however, on 7 February 1601, on the day before the Earl of Essex staged an unsuccessful rebellion against the Queen, a group of his supporters paid Shakespeare's company (the Chamberlain's Men) to revive *Richard II*, complete with deposition scene. They must have thought that this would encourage seditious feeling, but remarkably the company of players escaped any punishment and retained favor at court.

In these troubled times, Shakespeare was navigating a skilful passage between respect for the sacred office of kingship, and skepticism about a dogma of unconditional obedience. He keeps to his bearings by a subtle use of scriptural texts about Adam and Christ, and by diffusing the responsibility for Richard's loss of the "name" of king between his opponents and his own behavior. His is not the way of an ecclesiastical jurist like Hooker, or a dogmatic theologian like Calvin, looking for exact definitions. Given that critique of the Tudor political establishment came from both Catholic and Protestant, neither can Shakespeare be aligned with one party or another. Through a poetry drawing upon many resonances from other texts, he is hinting at "more things" than can be contained within any political "philosophy," as Hamlet urges. Through a web of intertextuality, space is being opened for something "more" than mere submission to power.

THE SPIRITUALITY OF THE PLAY

Shakespeare's intertextuality with scripture, the Anglican homilies, and the theology of his time shapes the plot and the characters, and it also forms the basis for the kind of spirituality that I have outlined earlier. The ambiguities of Richard's deposition prompt what I have called a "spirituality of authority,"[49] in which the health and well-being of the community take precedence over any doctrinal view of God-given rights of rulers, as is demonstrated by the allegory of the garden, "our commonwealth" (3.4.35). The gardener's lament that the land is "full of weeds, her fairest flowers choked up, / Her fruit trees all unpruned, her hedges ruined" (44–45), echoes the prophetic lament over the people of Israel as a ruined vineyard (Isa. 5:1–6). By contrast, Richard expects the same land (literally) to fight for his divine kingship with its most noxious flora and fauna (3.2.15–25). The garden episode features two Adams—the gardener who faithfully tends the commonwealth, and the Adam who has proudly asserted his right to power and whose fall is presaged (3.4.72–78). Shakespeare's concern for the survival and flourishing of the community means also, as we have seen already, that there is a need to exercise forgiveness in human relationships. Richard fails to rise to the challenge, but Mowbray at least makes a start with the pardoning of Aumerle, thereby preventing further conflict within the extended royal family at the beginning of his reign. The Bishop of Carlisle is not so fortunate, and on the brink of arrest he makes his prediction of wars that will "kin with kin and kind with kind confound" (4.1.142).

A spirituality which pays heed to the passing of time and the pressing boundary of death also emerges from the action. Here the image of pilgrimage is recurrent, evoking—as Forker puts it—"the sense of life as a spiritual quest."[50] Henry concludes the play with a vow to make a pilgrimage to the Holy Land "to wash this blood off from my guilty hand," but he is destined to make only a virtual pilgrimage in his daily life, dying in the "Jerusalem Chamber" at Westminster (2 Henry IV, 4.5.232–40). Gaunt, in facing the prospect of his imminent death, refers to life as the pilgrimage of time (1.3.20), and Richard dismisses his death with the careless comment, "His time is spent, our pilgrimage must be" (2.1.154). He is to learn that he must exchange his sceptre "for a palmer's [pilgrim's] walking staff" (3.3.151) and will admit that "I wasted time, and now doth Time waste me" (5.5.45–49). He must now, in prison, measure out his "minutes, times and hours" in "sighs, tears and groans" which he knows are leading toward the inevitability of death. He might well recall the earlier words of Salisbury, when Richard lost the support of twenty thousand Welsh soldiers by a late arrival back in England:

> O, call back yesterday, bid Time return.
> . . . .
> Today, today, unhappy day too late. (3.2.67–71)

Richard's soliloquy, in the genre of a meditative prayer in face of death, disappoints the audience which overhears it, as Alison Shell makes clear, but this irony is intended to prompt the hearers to make their own reflection on time, transience, and death. When Richard remits four years of Bolingbroke's ten-year exile, he exclaims with ironic admiration at Richard's power of words:

> How long a time lives in one little word!
> Four lagging winters and four wanton springs
> End in a word; such is the breath of kings. (1.3.213–15)

But his aged father, Gaunt, predicting that in these six years he will die without seeing his son again, knows that there is "not a minute, King, that thou canst give" (226).

It is a characteristic of the spiritual quest to create a story to make sense of life and impending death. Gaunt hopes that the solemn words he will speak on his deathbed about the course of affairs in England, "death's sad tale," will "undeaf" Richard's ear (2.1.16). Richard, too, wants his life to be told as a story, commanding his followers to sit on the ground and "tell sad stories of the death of kings," all of which carry the message for the hearers that "within the hollow crown / That rounds the mortal temples of a king / Keeps death his court" (3.2.160–62). Making his queen a last farewell, he bids her:

> In winter's tedious nights sit by the fire
> With good old folks, and let them tell thee tales
> Of woeful ages long ago betid.
> And ere thou bid goodnight, to quite their griefs,
> Tell thou the lamentable tale of me (5.1.40–44)

The point of the tale, and the way that he wants to be remembered, is: "the deposing of a *rightful* king" (50; my italics). He fails to sustain this story in most of the play, displaying all the ambiguities that we have explored. However, on the edge of death, he makes the "good end" that he has failed to achieve in his meditations, finally telling the story with conviction. He affirms at last his name and identity that he had lost, twice laying claim to the title of "king":

Exton, thy fierce hand
Hath with the King's blood stained the King's own land. (5.5.109–10)

Death in Shakespearean tragedy is always a waste of life, but—as we have seen already with *Lear* and *Hamlet*—it gives the opportunity for something of worth to be affirmed. There is some value that the tragic hero has tried unsuccessfully to live by, and failure to hold to it has been a partial cause of his downfall; this is now triumphantly articulated in his death. Richard has had some vision of what a true king might be, but has set the word against the word. We may protest that it is only the coming of death that has prevented Richard from un-kinging himself again, and that it is only death that is enabling him to use the name of "king" without contradiction. But this is the case with most of Shakespeare's heroes in the tragicomedies he writes for them. While even the breath of kings cannot hold time back, and can "stop no wrinkle in his pilgrimage" (1.3.230), the last enemy, death, can be conquered by using it to capture a lasting image, a monument that will outlast time.

A story is a monument of art, and can survive a particular death, but this on its own may not be resistant enough finally to hold back time's "swift foot" (Sonnet 65). At the heart of Shakespeare's spirituality is the persistence and resilience of love that in some way can defeat death. We have a witness to this in the love that Richard and his queen show for each other as they must part, Richard to take the path to his death. *Richard II* was written at about the same time as *Romeo and Juliet*, and Richard and his queen exchange kisses as do Shakespeare's younger lovers, with a similar quibble. When Romeo and Juliet meet, Romeo kisses a second time in order that his "sin" may be returned to him (1.5.107–10); in their parting, Richard kisses his queen for a second time in order that her "heart" might be returned to *her* (5.1.97–98).

Romeo first declares that by kissing Juliet, "Thus from my lips by thine my sin is purged," and she replies, "Then have my lips the sin that they have took." His response is to kiss her again, with the words, "Give me my sin again." Richard declares on kissing his queen for the first time in parting that they have thereby exchanged hearts: "Thus give I mine, and thus I take thy heart." She then responds that it would be no good exchange for her to take his heart, as she would kill it by her grief for his fate, and so they kiss again: "Give me mine own again; 'twere no good part / To take on me to keep and kill thy heart." The parallel is striking: "Give me my sin again" (Romeo); "Give me my own again" (the queen). The conceit that lovers give their hearts to each other through kissing, the heart passing through the open lips, was a "well-worn idea" in Elizabethan love poetry.[51] In these two cases Shakespeare alludes to the trope and modifies it: Romeo substitutes his sin for his heart, complimenting Juliet as a saint who can purge it; Richard's queen asks to return Richard's heart to him and retrieve her own for his own good.

The effect of employing this conceit is to make us believe in the reality of the love between Richard and his queen, just as we believe in the love between Romeo and Juliet. The queen, moreover, strengthens this impression with a scriptural allusion; when she appeals to Northumberland, "whither he goes, let me go," she echoes the fabled love of Ruth for Naomi: "whither thou goest, I will go also" (Ruth 1:16). Love of a different kind, but no less sincere, is also to be expressed on the very brink of Richard's murder, when the Groom expresses his loyal love for Richard: "What my tongue dares not, that my heart shall say" (5.5.97). *How*, we do not know with any certainty, but *that* love is not quenched by death is what our own hearts say.

KING JOHN AND CATHOLICISM

The implied challenge to Elizabeth's security as monarch in *Richard II* is not spelled out as either specifically Catholic or Protestant-Puritan in nature, but in Shakespeare's next English history play, written within a year, the Catholic threat is made clearer. Neither the rebellion against the pope's headship of the English Church under Henry VIII, nor the Roman Catholic rebellion against a Protestant monarch in 1569, finds *direct* portrayal in Shakespeare's plays, written within less than a century of both events. Indeed, although Shakespeare in his final years collaborates with another playwright, John Fletcher, to write *Henry VIII*, the play stops short of the break of England from Rome. The climax of the play is not Henry's excommunication by Rome, but the birth of Princess Elizabeth, later to be queen, accompanied by a suitable hymn of praise. Moreover, by a sleight of hand of the playwright, it is not immediately clear to the audience whether we are celebrating the birth of a child of the discarded Roman Catholic Catherine of Aragon, or of the Protestant Anne Boleyn. Shakespeare's reticent handling of this theme is part of his "general spirituality" of outlook, an attitude free of dogmatic commitments. We can detect, as we have already seen, a certain impartiality, a reluctance to take sides, a breadth of sympathy in Shakespeare toward the religious conflicts of his time. Thus, detachment from the ecclesial authority of the pope, and consequent threats to the order of the state, are dealt with under the cipher of King John's broken relations with Rome in the thirteenth century, and are colored by John's own character.

Certainly, King John makes a show of rejection of papal authority:

> Tell him this tale, and from the mouth of England
> Add thus much more, that no Italian priest
> Shall tithe or toil in our dominions;
> But as we, under God, are supreme head,
> So under him that great supremacy
> Where we do reign, we will alone uphold
> Without th'assistance of a mortal hand;
> So tell the Pope, all reverence set apart
> To him and to his usurp'd authority. (3.1.152–60)

We notice immediately the resonances with the assertions of the Act of Supremacy of 1534, and even more immediately with Article 37 of the Articles of Religion as adopted by the Church of England in 1563. The clause runs: "The Queenes Maiestie hath the chiefe power in this Realme of England, and other her dominions, . . . and is not, nor ought to be, subiect to any foraine iurisdiction. . . . The Bishoppe of Rome hath no iurisdiction in this Realme of England."[52] The phrase "usurp'd authority" in this Shakespearean speech also has echoes of the "usurped power" taken by the pope according to the homily "Concerning Good Order, and Obedience to Rulers and Magistrates": there we read a warning against "the pretended power of the bishop of Rome. For truely the Scripture of GOD, alloweth no suche vsurped power, full of enormities, abusions, and blasphemyes."[53]

Yet the distance of time from King John's reign allows Shakespeare to put a speech of defiance against Rome into the mouth of someone whom he plainly does not regard as a religious hero. Truly, King John is presented by others as heroic, and a chosen vessel of God in anticipating the sixteenth-century break with Rome. This is the picture of John in Foxe's Book of Martyrs,[54] and in the anonymous contemporary play The Troublesome Raigne of John King of England, both of which Shakespeare knew. Shakespeare would also have been familiar with the homily "Against Disobedience and Wilfull Rebellion," which was written and added to the Second Book of Homilies after the Catholic Uprising of 1569; this presents King John as being forced to submit as a vassal to "this forraigne & vnnaturall vsurper," and laments that Englishmen of the time had not "knowen their duetie to their prince set foorth in gods word."[55] Shakespeare, however, makes John into a dubious character in a way that he could not have done with Elizabeth or even Henry, her father. Though he has taken much of the speech of defiance from the play *The Troublesome Raigne*, his contextualizing of it in his own picture of John allows him ostensibly to support the Reformers of his time while at the same time introducing a note of ambiguity into any strict polarization of Protestantism and Rome into the pious and the blasphemers.

Shakespeare's play opens with a challenge to the legitimacy of John as king of England, shortly following the death of Richard I in 1199. Messengers come to the English court from the king of France, Philip, and from Philip's son Prince Lewis. They address John, somewhat untactfully, not as "your majesty," but as "borrowed majesty" (1.1.4). Their case is that John is not the rightful king of England, and so also not king of the territories that England owns in France—notably Poitiers, Anjou, Touraine, and Maine. The rightful and legal king, they maintain, is young Arthur, the son of John's older brother Geoffrey, now dead, and John's nephew. Of course, John replies defiantly to the French ambassadors: he will fight them to the death over his right to the throne.

The scene now changes to France, in front of the city of Angiers, which is the property of the king of England. Battle between English and French forces has resulted in a stalemate, and at this point the chief citizen of Angiers, Hubert, makes a proposal: suppose that the Lady Blanche, John's niece, marries Prince Lewis—then a new alliance could be forged between England and France in which everyone might be satisfied in terms of land and property, even tossing Arthur a consolation prize. Arthur's mother, Constance, is predictably furious, declaring herself and Arthur to be betrayed by this deal. But both John and Lewis secretly think, of course, that the alliance will give them a claim on taking more land in the future, and at this point the faithful follower of John nicknamed "the Bastard" delivers himself of the most important speech in the play, on the theme of "commodity," which means self-interest or gain. To this we shall return, though noting that "the Bastard," an illegitimate son of Richard I who has chosen to serve John and has been knighted as "Sir Richard," is one of the few characters in the play to be relatively free of the vice of commodity himself.[56]

It is at the ensuing marriage celebration of the Lady Blanche and Prince Lewis that the Church of Rome dramatically enters the scene, in the person of Pandulph, the pope's legate. John has refused to appoint the pope's nominee, an Italian priest named Stephen Langton, to be archbishop of Canterbury. He goes on refusing in the face of Pandulph's request, declaring that his will as the king anointed by God is superior to that of the pope. The audience in Shakespeare's time would have heard echoes of the English Reformation here, to come three centuries later, when Henry VIII denied that the pope's authority ran in the Church of England. John adds for good measure that he rejects the buying and selling of pardons as "this juggling witch-craft with revenue" (3.1.169), a central theme of the Reformation opposition to the Church of Rome. There would have been a frisson of recognition among the audience of 1591, for just the same challenge had been issued fifty years earlier.

But this is 1200, and the result is that Cardinal Pandulph excommunicates John, and commands France to break its newly agreed treaty with England and fight England in the pope's name. In this Pandulph practices commodity himself by urging the doctrine of equivocation, the righteousness of a broken oath that was often lampooned by Protestants at the time of the Reformation: to be faithful to God, Philip must break his faith to a fellow man. Philip fears the disorder that will come by the bloody breaking of their pledge, but Pandulph judges: "All form is formless, order orderless / Save what is opposite to England's love" (3.1.253–54). Philip and Lewis decide for war against John, and battle is joined once more between England and France.

John captures Arthur, and puts him into the safekeeping of Hubert, chief citizen of Angiers and John's right-hand man in France. John now proceeds to practice commodity in a major way. On the one hand he commissions the Bastard to confiscate huge sums of money from the monasteries and churches in England:

> see thou shake the bags
> Of hoarding abbots. . . .
> . . . .
> Imprison'd angels [i.e., gold coins] set at liberty. (3.3.7–8)

Even more ruthlessly, he drops very heavy hints to Hubert that he would like Arthur killed in prison, blinding him first. Pandulph, on behalf of the church, continues also to practice commodity, or self-interest. He tells Philip and Lewis not to worry that Arthur has been captured: John is bound to have him killed, and this will be to the advantage of France, since the English barons will be outraged by this action and will oppose John. Lewis asks, in the spirit of commodity, "But shall can I *gain* by young Arthur's fall?" (3.4.141), and Pandulph points out that he can then lay claim, on behalf of himself and Blanche, to all the lands that Arthur had claimed.

What Pandulph predicts more or less happens, as Shakespeare telescopes fifteen years of history into one year. First the scene shifts to a castle (unnamed) where Arthur is imprisoned. Arthur shames Hubert into letting him live after all, unblinded. Meanwhile John has been faced by a rebellion by his barons, who are outraged at a rumor that Arthur is dead. First he blames Hubert for zealously exceeding orders, but learning that Arthur is in fact still alive, he hastens to get the good news to the truculent barons. Unfortunately, the news is not so good after all. Arthur has tried to escape the castle and has killed himself in the process, falling from the battlements, and English barons happen at that moment to come upon his dead body. Convinced that this is the work of John, they make an alliance with Lewis and the French to overthrow him. John then takes a final step of commodity by making peace with Rome: he consents to the appointment of Stephen Langford as archbishop of Canterbury, and Cardinal Pandulph immediately commands Lewis and the French to cease their attack on John. Consulting their own commodity or self-interest, the French ignore Pandulph and continue their invasion.

Nevertheless, Lewis is forced to abandon his invasion of England when the largest part of the invading fleet of France is wrecked off the coast. John has little time to enjoy his escape. Just when the barons have returned to their allegiance and the French armada is wrecked (in 1216), John is carried off the battlefield in a high fever. He is taken to Swinstead Abbey, where he dies of three poisoned pears served to him by a Catholic monk, thereby earning his place in *Foxe's Book of Martyrs*.

The play is, we can readily see, full of resonances of tensions between the Protestant Elizabeth and the Catholic Church and its representatives. Shakespeare is telling the story of a king whose legitimate succession to the English throne is questioned, who has defied the authority of the pope, who has been excommunicated, who has imprisoned a rival claimant to the throne and arranged for him to be killed, who blames the person commissioned to carry out the task when it causes a bad reaction among his nobles, and who is only saved from an invasion by a foreign army when the armada is wrecked off the coast. All this is remarkably similar to the story of Elizabeth. *Her* succession to the English throne is questioned by Catholic authorities, who refuse to recognize Anne Boleyn as a legal wife of Henry VIII; she defies the pope and is excommunicated;[57] she imprisons her rival, Mary Queen of Scots, and sends a warrant for her to be executed; after Mary's death, when her enemies make propaganda out of it, she blames the overzealousness of the person who carried out the deed, Secretary Davison. She is only saved from foreign invasion by the destruction of the Spanish Armada in 1588. Pandulph promises canonization as a saint to anyone who murders John, and such canonization was promised by Rome to anyone who murdered Elizabeth. The audience would have been excited and perhaps horrified by the parallels, especially since John was depicted as suffering a rebellion.

There was a continual anxiety throughout Elizabeth's reign that a decisive rebellion would be fostered by dissident Catholics. The memory of the Northern Uprising, centered on the imprisonment of Mary Queen of Scots, was doubtless in mind. There is indeed a more visible, but still indirect, reference to the Uprising in *Henry IV Part 1*. The rebellion against Henry with which the play climaxes is organized by Harry Percy (Hotspur), his father and uncle Percy, together with the archbishop of York. The 1569 rising was hatched by descendants of Shakespeare's Percy, and the Catholic bishop of Ross played a part like that of Shakespeare's archbishop. In Shakespeare's play, the Percys' resentment is over Henry IV's refusal to ransom Mortimer, a pretender to the throne; in 1569 the case of the northern lords focuses on the demand that Mary, the Scots pretender to the throne, should be left in the keeping of an *Elizabethan* Percy, the Catholic Sir Thomas Percy, the Seventh Earl of Northumberland. Both rebellions, the rising against Elizabeth and that against Henry IV, reflect a schism within the kingdom between north and south, approximating to a division between Catholic and Protestant.

In the setting of the anxious 1590s it might be thought that Shakespeare would be absolutely opposed to any thought of rebellion, any disturbance of the order in the individual body, the body of the state, and the body of the cosmos that Elizabethans prized so highly. But as we have already seen in *Richard II*, Shakespeare cannot be categorized so easily. All the major players in *King John*—perhaps with the exception of the Bastard—practice commodity, or self-interest, kings, princes, and churchmen alike. This is neither a Protestant nor a Catholic play; its evenhandedness is characteristic of Shakespeare's spirituality.

King John, Sacral Kingship, and Spirituality

In *King John*, echoes of the Homilies and the Thirty-Nine Articles are used to develop the drama of a king who follows commodity and thinks there is a price for everything. There are also numerous biblical references in the play, employed at key moments. For example, about to break his sacred oath to King John, King Philip contemplates washing his hands of responsibility like Pilate (3.1.234, 239), and also like Bolingbroke in *Richard II*. Lady Faulconbridge, asking the Bastard not to blame her for the circumstances of his birth, echoes a prayer of the proto-martyr Stephen: "Heaven! Lay not my transgression to thy charge" (cf. Acts 7:60). Arthur, about to be blinded by Hubert, wishes there were a "mote" in Hubert's eye (4.1.90–91; cf. Matt. 7:3), and Pandulph gloats that John is set in a "slippery place," echoing Psalm 73:18–19 (3.4.137). Not so obvious, but highly significant, is the Bastard's scathing analysis of the commodity that drives everyone toward their own gain, where he refers to commodity as an "all-changing word"; here the term "word" reflects and reverses the activity of the divine word in creating the world according to John 1:

> Commodity, the bias of the world;
> The world, who of itself is peised well,
> Made to run even, upon even ground,
> Till this advantage, this vile-drawing bias,
> This sway of motion, this Commodity,
> Makes it take head from all indifferency,
> From all direction, purpose, course, intent.
> And this same bias, this Commodity,
> This bawd, this broker, this all-changing word. (2.1.574–81)

The image of Commodity as the bias or weight in a bowling ball, making it—and so, by analogy, the world—sway from a straight course is not scriptural. But when Commodity is described as a word that changes everything—the "direction, purpose, course, [and] intent" of the world, it is undoing the work of the divine word which changed chaos into order (John 1:3; cf. Gen. 1:1–3).

As in *Richard II*, the accumulation of biblical and theological references is the basis for a spirituality in which the divine right to rule of an anointed king can be challenged. Shakespeare's way of proceeding is, however, different from the previous play. There scripture is used both to illustrate and to deconstruct Richard's claim to be a sacral person in the image of Christ himself. Here it is used to support the transfer of sacral kingship from John to another claimant altogether—Arthur. Christological imagery is used to enhance the sympathetic portrayal of Arthur in a way which is fundamentally opposed to the application of such imagery to John by Shakespeare's own sources. In the scene where Hubert intends to blind Arthur, the boy refers to himself in the biblical language of a sacrificial lamb:

> I will not struggle, I will stand stone-still.
> For God's sake, Hubert, let me not be bound!
> Nay, hear me, Hubert! Drive these men away
> And I will sit as quiet as a lamb;
> I will not stir, nor wince, nor speak a word.
> Nor look upon the iron angrily.
> Thrust but these men away, and I'll forgive you (4.1.76–82)

Beatrice Groves has convincingly proposed that this scene has strong resonances of the mystery plays which depicted the sacrifice of Isaac;[58] these substituted a lamb for the "ram caught in a thicket" of Genesis 22:13, which took Isaac's place as a sacrifice. In the Genesis text Isaac in fact asks, "where is the lamb for the burnt offering?" (22:7). The use of a lamb in performance of the Mysteries underlined the typological reference from Isaac to Christ, the lamb of God, of whom the words of Isaiah 53:7 were seen as a prediction in the New Testament: "he was led as a sheep to the slaughter; and like a lamb dumb before his shearers, so opened he not his mouth" (Acts 8:32–35). Preaching of the period saw Isaac as a type of Christ precisely in his lack of resistance, as in Isaiah 53:7,[59] and similarly, Arthur-Isaac-Christ promises to "sit as quiet as a lamb."

Groves also shows that the binding of Arthur echoes the binding of Isaac in the Mysteries, typologically related to the binding of Christ (John 18:12), and designed to make the suffering of Isaac close to that of the passion. In the Mysteries, Isaac is also blindfolded to prefigure the suffering of Christ (Mark 14:65; Luke 24:62), which was expanded in the Towneley play of the buffeting into a near-blinding, comparable to the near-blinding of Arthur.[60] We may add other biblical echoes which associate Arthur with Christ. Arthur longs to be a shepherd (4.1.17–18), a Davidic image of kingship applied to Christ (John 10:11). He is identified with Abel, a type of Christ: when King John drops a heavy hint to Hubert about murdering Arthur, the words "Thou art his keeper" invite Hubert to play the part of Cain (Gen. 4:9). In his dying words, crying, "Heaven take my soul" (4.3.10), Arthur echoes the prayer of Christ, "Father, into thine hands I commend my spirit" (Luke 23:46). Shaheen suggests that this phrase is based on the language with which wills often opened, itself derived from Jesus's prayer: "I commend my soul into the hands of God my Creator."[61]

In *The Troublesome Raigne*, this kind of good parting from life given to Arthur in *King John*, is granted to John himself:

> But in the spirit I cry unto my God.
> As did the Kingly prophet David cry
> (Whose hands, as mine, with murder were attaint).[62]

As Groves suggests, with this reference to David's murderous actions, the author of *Troublesome Raigne* is able, subtly, to reconcile Protestant polemic about John as Davidic/Christly King with his "problematic character."[63] No such end is allowed to John in Shakespeare's *King John*. Although Shakespeare does follow Foxe in comparing the monk who poisons John with Judas, both of whose bowels burst out (5.6.29–30; cf. Acts 1:18), John's final words do not, as with Richard, reaffirm his vision of kingship with the claim "the king's own blood." Rather, John declares himself to be in a living hell, with poison working on blood which is "unreprievable, condemned." His final words are: "all this thou seest is but a clod / And module of confounded royalty" (5.7.58). As with Hamlet, later, a follower echoes the Sarum rite of burial at the moment of his passing; but where Horatio prays "choirs of angels sing thee to thy rest,"[64] Salisbury notes that the only one singing at John's death is himself: from his "organ-pipe of frailty," madly he "sings / His soul and body to their everlasting rest" (5.7.23–24).

A little earlier his most faithful follower, the Bastard, had recognized Arthur (now a dead body) as the true king. His moment of revelation is attributed by implication to the Word of Christ, since he begins by confessing himself to have previously "lost his way / Among the thorns and dangers of this world" (4.3, 140–41). As Shaheen suggests, this is probably borrowed from Jesus's parable of the sower, in which thorns "choke the word" (Matt. 13:22).[65] Now he hears the true Word, which is not that of Commodity.

Thus Shakespeare uses a constellation of textual echoes of scripture in order to transfer the sacredness of kingship from John to Arthur. In *Richard II* Shakespeare shows respect for the sacral office of kingship, but apparently believes that an anointed occupant of the office can nevertheless disqualify himself from holding it, losing his identity. Logically this must mean that the office can be transferred to another, but a cloud of ambiguity hangs over Henry's right to succession, and his action is to have fatal consequences in the future, so Shakespeare does not give him this kind of validation. With Arthur we do not know how he would have embodied the sacral heritage.[66]

This transfer of sacral identity does not mean that Shakespeare is taking sides in an ancient succession dispute, or even that there is a coded sympathy with Catholic doubts about Elizabeth in the present.[67] Shakespeare appears to be saying that if a monarch acts tyrannically, or in self-interest rather than in the interest of the commonwealth, then even anointing in the name of God cannot validate his rule. As Calvin perceived, the divine right of kings cannot save a monarch when he has ceased to act as a king should act in obedience to the laws of God, and so when he (or she) has effectively denied the true meaning of kingship. Facing each other before battle, both Philip of France and John claim to hold God's commission in the matter; John calls himself "God's wrathful agent" (2.1.87), and Philip asserts he has God's "warrant" (116). They might, without mutual contradiction, both claim generally to be God's "ministers" in line with Romans 13, or—as Pandulph hails them unctuously, "anointed deputies of God" (3.1.136)—though it shortly becomes clear that he really means deputies of Rome. However, they disqualify each other in identifying themselves as God's agents in the dispute, and Shakespeare thus introduces a note of skepticism into the royal theology.

In Shakespeare's spirituality of power, to follow commodity rather than justice places any monarch in a vulnerable position, and this must sound a warning note even to Elizabeth I. Hubert's vociferous mother, Constance,

cries for justice against "these perjured kings," appealing to the many scriptural statements about God's concern for widows and orphans: "A widow
cries; be husband to me, heavens!" (3.1.108). The curious syntax "a widow cries"
in speaking about herself looks like an allusion to the "cry" of the "widow
and fatherless child" in Exodus 22:23. The particular contribution of *King
John* to this kind of spirituality already presented in *Richard II* lies in the
transfer of sacredness to Arthur, a helpless child; this enables a generalization
about authority—it properly belongs to the weak and powerless. As Arthur
says to Philip, "I give you welcome with a powerless hand" (2.1.12), and as
Groves boldly concludes, "King John shares with the New Testament and
the mystery plays a radical social agenda in which true royalty belongs to the
dispossessed."[68]

Two other notes of Shakespeare's spiritual approach to life are also sounded,
though less strongly. In face of what seems to be his impending death at the
hands of Hubert, Arthur speaks of love: "I would to heaven / I were your son,
so you would love me, Hubert" (4.1.23–24). He reminds Hubert that when
his head ached, he would hold it, and try to cheer him up, saying, "What
lack you?" and, "What good love may I perform for you?" With sorrow, he
admits that Hubert "may think my love was crafty love," but poignantly declares that—blinded or not—his eyes "never did, nor never shall / So much
as frown on you" (57–58). There is nothing in either Holinshed's *Chronicles*
or *The Troublesome Raigne* which corresponds to this desire of a "fatherless
child" for bonds of fatherly affection. In Shakespeare's sources, Groves comments, "Arthur attempts to escape not through submissive love, but through
threats and violence."[69] Hubert's response, despite his original intention, is,
"His words do take possession of my bosom" (32), and Shakespeare portrays
a growing love of Hubert for Arthur: "I honoured him, I loved him, and will
weep" (4.3.105). In this play, love is set over against commodity as love is set
over against commerce in *The Merchant of Venice*. Along with love there
is forgiveness, as so often in Shakespeare: "I'll forgive you," Arthur assures his
intending killer, "Whatever torment you do put me to" (4.1.83), echoing the
words of Jesus on the cross, "Father, forgive them" (Luke 23:34).

A THEOLOGY OF RESISTANCE AND TRAGEDY

Living in the space of these two history plays, the theologian can allow them
to make an impact "in front" of the text, shaping her own making of
theology. Two interlinked areas emerge as open to the impact of Shakespeare's own texts: the question of obedience to the powers of the state, and
the question as to whether Christ can be understood as a tragic hero, brought
low by the powers of his time. The second issue extends the discussion of

a previous chapter on whether the Christian Gospel must spell an end to tragedy,[70] but here we will focus on the figure of Christ himself.

In *King John* the monarch claims to be head of both civil and religious institutions, until he finally capitulates to Rome. At the time of the English Reformation this double headship, now actually established through the settlement of the Church of England, was being validated by associating the monarch with King David. This designation, however, was being resisted by Protestant-Separatist groups in Shakespeare's time, and then by early Baptists from their beginnings in 1609 onward. Their slogan was, "Only Christ sits on David's throne." While the Dissenters believed that rulers, whether monarchs, magistrates, or parliaments, had a God-given commission to keep justice, inhibit evil, and punish wrongdoing in the civil realm, they thought that only Christ exercised rule in the church. It was the prerogative of Christ to require true belief in God, to appoint leaders in the congregation, and to order worship. It was the privilege of Christian congregations, sharing in the rule of Christ as "prophet, priest and king,"[71] to discern what the mind of Christ might be in these matters. Only Christ exercised the dual rule in state and church which the Hebrew scriptures ascribe to David, and which Elizabethan jurists and ecclesiologists understood to have been inherited by the English monarch. In Anglican ideology, the authority of the pope to rule in the church, no less resisted by Separatists, had been transferred to the one who already held the headship in the state, the monarch. Richard Hooker, maintaining this supposed inheritance from David, writes against Henry Barrow, pastor of the London Separatist congregation, who was executed in 1593; Hooker writes ironically: "Tell the Barrowists what sway David and others the kings of Israel did bear in the ordering of spiritual affairs, the same answer [i.e., by the followers of Barrow] again serveth, namely, 'That David and the rest of the kings of Israel prefigured Christ.'"[72]

A little later, in 1612, the General Baptist Thomas Helwys was affirming this resistance to the monarch, writing that God has given to the king an "earthly kingdome with all earthly power against the which, none may resist," but "Christ alone is K[ing] of Israell, and sitts vpon Davids Throne, & ... the K[ing] ought to be a subiect of his Kingdome." The king simply "can have no power to rule in this spiritual Kingdome of Christ."[73] The conclusion followed that neither monarch nor magistrate had responsibility for "the maintenance of Gods true Religion" as the Prayer Book affirmed of Elizabeth and James I.[74] Instead, in a plea for general religious liberty, Helwys insisted that "mens religion to God, is betwixt God and themselves; the King shall not answere for it, neither may the King be jugd betwene God and man. Let them be heretikes, Turcks [i.e., Muslims], Jewes, or whatsoever, it apperteynes not to the earthly power to punish them in the least measure."[75]

In her book on "The hidden beliefs and coded politics" of Shakespeare, Clare Asquith rightly notes that, in conscience, "radical Puritans" (Dissenters) along with Roman Catholics could not assent to the Oath of Supremacy,[76] first introduced under Henry VIII (1534) and restored by Elizabeth (1559), since this acknowledges the monarch as "the onely Supreame Governour of this Realme, as well *in all Spirituall or Ecclesiasticall things* or causes, as Temporall."[77] This oath was required of all those holding public office, from which Dissenters as well as Catholics were excluded. She does not notice that Dissenters *could*, and did, swear the Oath of *Allegiance*, including the expanded form created by James I, importing antipapal elements from the Oath of Supremacy.[78] Asquith makes the interesting suggestion that Shakespeare intended a parallel between Cordelia's refusal in *King Lear* to make a public profession of unquestioning love and the refusal of Catholics and radical Puritans to take the Oath of Supremacy.[79] If so, then this is hardly evidence (as Asquith supposes) for Shakespeare's coded Catholicism, but it does show Shakespeare drawing together the threads of a resistance to the demands of absolute power with a nonlegalistic approach to love. If Asquith is right that *wherever* the oath sworn to the monarch is written about by Shakespeare "the word invariably conjured up the dilemma of divided loyalty involved in taking the oath of supremacy,"[80] then behind King Richard II's insistence on the validity of the oath made to him, relying on a damning by heaven of those who "crack" it (4.1.235), can be read a claim to dual headship in the state as much as in King John's tirades.

While Shakespeare appears to allow that a king can be resisted if he ceases to act justly and so no longer fulfills God's commission, in the view of Separatists and their dissenting successors, even a "godly ruler" could be disobeyed in the matter of freedom to worship since she or he was *not* "governor of all spiritual or ecclesiastical things of causes." In the eighteenth century the same logic of limiting the rights of rulers was to be applied to what were being called "the rights of man." Dissenters such as Baptists found the right of religious liberty to be only the foremost in a number of "rights" which God had granted to human beings, and infringement of them by the ruling powers was a justification for civil disobedience.[81] For this reason, considerable numbers of Dissenters were sympathetic to the rebellion of the American colonists.[82]

Living in the space of Shakespeare's plays in fact opens up the possibility of disobedience to the authorities in the name of obedience to God in a way that escapes exact definition. Disobedience becomes a matter of conscience, with all the risks attached to this appeal.[83] For the early Dissenters, conscience was not simply an individualistic matter, but the mind of an oppressed community. Nor was it simply subjective opinion, as the Reformers understood conscience to be an awareness of "things that are right, just and honourable, which are hidden to the bodily senses" (Calvin), and above all a recognition of being under the judgment of God.[84] Nevertheless, it was—and is—impossible to legislate for conscience. This is the kind of exegesis that New Testament scholars are increasingly giving to the saying of Jesus recorded in the Gospels: "Give to Caesar the things that are Caesar's, and to God the things that are God's" (Mark 12:17). Jesus's words leave open what things belong to Caesar and to God. As one recent commentator, Craig Evans, has written, Jesus's answer "thrusts the problem of whether Jews should pay their taxes back upon the interlocutor. Can they justify their views? . . . Perhaps something is owed Caesar, but what is it? There is much also that is owed God, but what is it?"[85] Karl Barth offers a similar interpretation of the contested passage, Romans 13:1–7, which was understood by some Elizabethan jurists as being a demand for unconditional obedience to a ruler ordained by God. He notes this passage is followed immediately by the injunction, "Owe no one anything, except to love one another," and suggests that the demand of love relativizes everything that has gone before. "Love of one another ought to be taken as the protest against the course of this world. . . . Inasmuch as we love one another we cannot wish to uphold the present order as such."[86] Readers of Paul are thus left asking themselves what is the loving thing to do, faced by unjust rule.

These two plays of Shakespeare about power leave the reader or viewer with the same question. There is no neat "philosophy" but only an openness to "more things." Allowing the plays to make an impact on theology means putting the readers of this theology in a position to make their own informed decisions in particular circumstances. Evans suggests that this question is already nestled in the saying of Jesus about what is owed to Caesar and to God: "Can the Pharisees justify a provocative policy of civil disobedience, which could, and on occasion did, lead to violence?"[87] In the Gospel story of the passion of Christ there is in fact a clue to the way that disciples of Christ might engage in confronting and breaking powers in the state when they have ceased to work for human welfare and seek to usurp the place of God, or have—in the language of Paul Tillich—become "demonic."[88] There is a dialectic that we can identify as "resistance" and "submission," active protest and passive obedience bound together, each element giving meaning to the other, and being necessary for the other. Observing this dialectic can give a framework for making decisions in a concrete situation.

This duality is focused in the silence which Jesus assumes in the trial before Pilate, according to all four of the Gospels. Three of the gospel-writers record that at some point in his trial Jesus refuses to answer when questions are put to him. The evangelists do not present the same details about what Jesus *does* say, or *when* he is silent, but they all testify that the moment comes when

Jesus submissively confronts his judges with silence. Matthew underlines this fact, writing that "he gave them no answer, not even to a single charge, so that the governor wondered greatly" (Matt. 27:14). The fourth evangelist relates that at a later stage of the interrogation "Jesus gave him no answer," and it is this evangelist who has previously portrayed Pilate as asking, "What is truth?" (John 18:38, 19:8). The story is presenting an irony; the truth is in fact emerging through the reaction of the Roman and Jewish powers to the silence of Jesus. "Silence makes room," as the ethicist Paul Lehmann puts it, for the "shock of recognition."[89] Apparent submission is also resistance. It is this extraordinary dialectic that is portrayed in *King John*, in the scene of Arthur facing the torture and death that Hubert intends to inflict, in which his submission "as quiet as a lamb" is blended with protest at what is happening. Both sides of the same dialectic are set out in Romans 13:1–8, as we have seen. Barth points out that the merely "negative" instruction to "submit" is set in the context of the "great positive possibility," which is the command to "owe one nothing except love . . . for by love we do the 'new' by which the 'old' is overthrown."[90] Yet the command to submit is not altogether replaced by the command to love; as Christian reformers confront the government not only with protest but with submission to the consequences of their actions. Such a submission is no merely passive acceptance of the status quo, but an obedient waiting for the new order. As Lehmann sums up this stance, "submission and silence become code words of revolutionary freedom"; they are "signs of a politics of confrontation that has arrived at the moment of truth and life."[91]

Here I am offering one suggestion about what might happen if we bring Shakespeare's spirituality of power, which refuses to be constrained within a tight "philosophy," into interaction with a modern theology of power. It could prompt political action marked by a continual pattern of resistance and submission. Living in the spirit of Shakespeare's "more things" means that this may result in a variety of forms of action, and a call to the decision of conscience about which to take. At the first level there is the action of protest within existing law, although that same law may take a violent revenge on those who question it and who submit to the consequences. The liberation theologian Leonardo Boff maintains that when the sufferer for a just cause joyfully maintains faith and hope in the coming Kingdom of God, this attitude of freedom "exasperates the agents of the system. . . . [I]t destroys their morale."[92] At the same time this has often meant the overcoming of a sense of fatalism. Through reflection on their situation with the aid of study of scripture within "basic Christian communities," peasants and workers have been "conscientized," coming to see that it is not the iron will of God that some people should be rich and others poor, but that this situation is a result of structural sin.[93] When the state reacts unjustly to consequent Christian resistance and agitation for justice, it only sows the seeds of its own down-fall. Closed systems grow more violent as they approach their end. Amid the silence of those who were once protesting and are now suffering, they hasten to their destruction.[94]

A still further step beyond direct action of protest is the method of "civil disobedience," which Martin Luther King made famous in recent times in his struggle against race laws in the United States. Following the example set by Mahatma Gandhi in his struggle for independence from British Rule in India, this kind of action refuses to use violence but is otherwise willing to break the laws of the state for the sake of a just cause.[95] In the context of demon-stration, this will mean a deliberate breaking of laws about public order, and where protests involve the symbolic cutting of security fences or "sit-ins" in public buildings, it may even involve charges of criminal damage. At another level it may take the form of refusing to pay taxes, or to cooperate with gov-ernment agencies in filling in official forms. It may mean promoting strikes as a political protest rather than simply as part of a legitimate industrial dispute. Within the biblical perspective the Christian owes normal obedience to gov-ernment as to Christ. In some circumstances, however, the claims of justice and love may outweigh all other prior claims, and Christians may find that obedience to Christ brings them into conflict with the law of their society. If so, they must submit to the consequences because it is through the process of resistance and submission that the truth emerges. It emerges for the protes-tors, who are not so arrogant as to think that they know the whole truth of the situation, and it emerges to mobilize public opinion.

Christians who are not pacifists will differ about a third level of resistance, where some believe that a measure of force is justified as a very last resort. It may be argued that the oppressor is already using institutional violence, and that love for the weak and powerless demands that all available means be used, as long as it is proportionate to a just end;[96] to leave the defenseless at the mercy of the oppressive powers would, it is said, be *lack* of love. In his critical situation in Nazi Germany, Dietrich Bonhoeffer understood that he was following such a path, in joining the plot to kill Hitler. In a letter of 21 February 1944, he writes: "We must confront fate . . . as resolutely as we sub-mit to it at the right time. One can speak of 'guidance' only on the other side of that twofold process. . . . It's therefore impossible to define the boundary between resistance and submission on abstract principles; but *both of them exist and both must be practised*."[97] If such a way of confrontation is taken, submission may take the form of accepting the consequences in failure, as with Bonhoeffer, or of offering forgiveness in the moment of victory. Recon-ciliation will only come about when the one who has gained the advantage through action does not press it in such a way as to repress the opponent.

The Tragedy of the Christ

Christ himself exemplifies this pattern of submission and resistance. His subjection to the powers in death on a cross only makes sense in context of his previous challenge to them through his disturbing—though nonviolent—proclamation of the kingdom of God. But this then brings us to a second way in which these plays have an impact on theology "in front" of the text. If some aspects of Christ can be seen in tragic figures (Richard, Arthur), conversely can Christ be a tragic hero? I have previously defended the view that Christianity is a tragedy, or a tragicomedy. This depends on the story of Christ himself, and I have argued that just as the resurrection of Jesus does not cancel out the cross, so the hope for general resurrection of human beings does not undermine the intolerable situation of their suffering in this life.[98] Does this therefore mean that the life and death of Christ takes the form of a tragedy? Unless it does, it seems impossible to maintain the tragic nature of Christian faith as a whole, and so take human suffering seriously.

David Bentley Hart is one theologian who denies firmly that Christ is a tragic figure. He points out that tragedies arise within a civic order of injustice, and Greek tragedy finds the origin of this earthly order in a cosmic conflict of irreconcilable forces embraced within an overarching violence of fate.[99] The destiny of the Greek tragic hero is to be a sacrificial victim, a scapegoat whose death, as René Girard has demonstrated, is intended to restore harmony within a society which has fallen apart.[100] Tragedy, pronounces Hart, is "an opiate of the tragic consciousness . . . in a sacrificial economy." Within Greek society, tragedy represents "that mystification of violence that sustains the sacred order of pagan society."[101] Conflict in the cosmic realm is reflected in the civic realm and is to be resolved, at least temporarily, by sacrifice. Greek tragedy, it may be said, does not ask us to look at the particular person who suffers but at the sublime backdrop against which the drama is being played out. It assures the audience that this is how things are, that justice can only be established through conflict. The wisdom that tragedy imparts is simply resignation and consent to this situation, the kind of serene consciousness that Schopenhauer commends in face of the tragedies of existence.[102] Relating to our previous discussion, it is simply submission without resistance.

The Christian story, it is rightly said, offers an alternative to this kind of tragic reading. As Girard maintains, the death of Christ deconstructs and debunks the myth that civic order has to be maintained by sacrifice. Told from the viewpoint of the victim, it makes clear that it is the society as a whole which is guilty, and which has been justifying its power by identifying and excluding persons and groups as scapegoats on whom the blame for disorder has been laid. The myth of redemptive violence is finally exposed and can be abandoned.[103] Christ dies in *protest* against the organized structures of the *polis,* whose violence presumes and reflects a cosmic violence.[104] This protest is vindicated by the resurrection, which forever associates the divine with the excluded rather than the excluders.

We can certainly agree with Hart's objection to reading the cross as an instance of tragedy which is centered on the place of sacrifice in Greek religion and society. But it does not mean that *other* modes of tragedy cannot be illuminating of the passion story. The story of *Richard II,* as with *Hamlet* and *Lear,* is of a person in conflict with his society. At the root of the conflict is a clash of values or vision, and tragedy comes when the protagonist fails to hold to the truth that he has glimpsed, and is crushed by the forces of society which he has been contradicting. Some tragic heroes may have had quite a clear view originally of a value or virtue they have wanted to foster; others have been uncertain and muddled, but still had some intuitive feeling about it. Richard has a sense of a vocation which is worthwhile—fulfilling the commission of being called by God to keep order and justice in human society. The audience of Shakespeare's day, having texts like Romans 13:1–7 and the biblical story of King David in mind, would also have considered this an authentic role, indeed necessary for the health of society. This image of a "godly prince" runs counter to other trends in society, notably the pragmatic approach to power politics, exemplified by Henry and the kingmakers with whom he allies. But Richard squanders his intuition (often expressed in poetic terms), through self-interest and dogmatic confidence in divine right; in losing the vision he opens himself to loss of everything. We cannot find the same pattern in the life of King John, who succumbs to "commodity" in the same way as his society as a whole, but then the play is not called a tragedy, but *The Life and Death of King John.* Arthur has the potential to be a tragic hero but is hardly given enough time and space to develop into one.

Living in these play-spaces, we see how the story of Christ fits to some extent into the pattern of a Shakespearean tragic hero, in conflict with his society. Christ has a vision of the kingdom of God, of justice, peace, acceptance of the outcasts, and unlimited forgiveness, running against the conventions of the society around him, both Jewish and Roman. His career is a failure in the sense that the society does not accept his vision and rejects him, and he ends in utter forsakenness and alienation. Christ does not, however, conform to the typical Shakespearean tragic hero in any *failure* to hold to his vision of transformative values under the pressures of life. According to the story of the Gospels, he remains obedient to God's purpose to the very end, but still suffers the complete loss that characterizes the tragic figure.

His vision is not that of being a king, since the "rule" of God has no need for an office which is anything like human kingship. At root, Richard's correspondence of his kingship with Christ fails. The title which Jesus owns is that of "son"; in his story, the words of anointing he hears from his heavenly Father are, "You are my son, the Beloved; with you I am well pleased" (Mark 1:11). While this echoes what seems to have been the coronation ritual of kings of Israel (Psalm 2:7), it is the sense of being a son of God that seems to have meant most to Christ. The notion of being a "son" of God was quite widely present in the Jewish world, but Jesus seems to have felt that he occupied the role in a peculiarly intense way,[105] to such a degree that he could open the kingdom of God to other sons and daughters whom he taught to pray "our Father." He did not fail in being this "son," and yet is brought to a point of nothingness which exceeded even that which Shakespeare portrays in *King Lear*. This is the particular nature of his own self-sacrifice; it points us to an experience of alienation undertaken in willing identification with human life at zero-point.

We notice that, unlike a Shakespearean hero, in dying Christ can make no comforting affirmation of human values. He can only (according to the tradition as recorded in Mark 15:37) make a desolate cry. In a Shakespearean tragedy, at the very moment when conflicting values run together into death, the vision can be affirmed, as Richard—for example—claims once again his identity as king. Death which seems to triumph has overreached itself and lost its prey. But even as Christ does not fail in holding to the vision given him, so his death does not embody and preserve any values that have been lost. The uniqueness of this tragic figure is that loss is total, the desolation ultimate. Thus the tragic pattern is still recognizable in the story of the cross, but it has been transformed. Christ *is* a tragic hero insofar as he has upheld a vision and values which are in conflict with his society, and this has brought him to utter disaster in the end. On the other hand, he is *not* a tragic hero since he neither has failed in holding to the vision, nor experiences any consolation in the face of death. He simultaneously fulfills and surpasses the genre of tragedy. In other words, to speak of his story as tragedy is a shorthand way of saying that it has an *analogy* to tragedy. This has the advantage of pointing to a continuity between the story of Jesus and all other stories. All stories, all tragedies (as well as comedies) can be a means of the self-revelation of God, a means of encountering the God who is acting to unveil God's self freely through worldly forms. For Christians, the story of Jesus is unique in the extent and focus with which it discloses the nature and purpose of God, but need not be different in principle from the whole world-archive of stories.

On the other hand, the disanalogy points us to the element of the story which is not contained in the literary tragedy (except on occasion in symbol). The proper consolations of a literary tragedy are absent from the cross, because vindication of the faithfulness of Christ in his vocation of being a "son" of God can only be found in resurrection. As I have already maintained, this is not a reversal of the tragedy of the cross because it is an event of a completely different order. It is just because death is final within the old order of creation, and Christ meets its finality head-on, that God has to do something new in the face of death. What has no meaning in itself acquires meaning. Hart rightly affirms that in the resurrection God "disrupts the analogy between cosmic and civil violence," untelling the tale by which power sustains itself.[106] Because of the resurrection it is, he urges, impossible to be reconciled to violence in society, by ascribing its origins either to fate or cosmic order. This leads Hart to deny that the death of Christ is a tragedy. However, if we understand tragedy in a Shakespearean rather than a Greek mode, we can affirm this "disorientating rhetoric of the empty tomb" and still understand the passion of Christ as a kind of tragedy.

Christian theology has affirmed, since earliest times, that Christ participated more completely in the sufferings of human life than others, that he was uniquely immersed into the "nothing" to which Lear is brought. This, according to theology, has been vicarious ("for all"), bringing hope to all those who suffer that they can share in a life characterized by resurrection. Living in the world of Shakespeare's tragedies, such as *Richard II*, gives theology a vocabulary for expressing this unique desolation of Christ. He suffers infinite loss precisely *in* faithfully holding to the vision of the "kingdom" of God. He alone suffers a death in which no opportunity can be found to affirm a transforming vision, yet "God raised him up, having loosed the pangs of death, because it was not possible for him to be held by it. For David says concerning him: 'I saw the Lord always before me'" (Acts 2:24–25, RSV). The claim is that because Christ alone sustained that vision throughout life ("I saw the Lord always before me"), death cannot hold him: From the other side of Easter, the meaningless cross can acquire meaning. Indeed, from the viewpoint of a Christian poetics,[107] the consolations of a literary tragedy are only possible *because* of that resurrection. Christ has brought into the textuality of human life the possibility of being lifted from death to life, and since this text is held and shaped by the life of the triune God,[108] the Christic pattern is embodied henceforth in all written texts that deal with human suffering. There is excess in human existence, the hope of "more things" because of the tragicomedy of Christ.

9

The Winter's Tale and the Renewal of Life

*

IN THE past, Shakespeare's last plays have not always been valued. *Pericles, Cymbeline, The Winter's Tale, The Tempest*—this group of final Romances which Shakespeare wrote toward the end of his life (1608–12) came after the great harvest of the tragedies, and some critics have suggested that they come as a distinct anticlimax. Among the strongest reactions was that of Lytton Strachey, who denounced the plays as the work of a Shakespeare "bored with himself, bored with people, bored with real life, bored with drama, bored, in fact with everything except poetry and poetical dreams."[1]

These plays do indeed have a strange landscape of fantasy—shipwrecks, wicked stepmothers, magic and marvels, supernatural interventions, monsters, riddle and quests, the strange loss of children and their even stranger recovery. One of the characters in *The Winter's Tale* admits that the play in which he is living is an improbable fantasy, "monstrous to our human reason" (5.1.41). Another tells us that the events are "so like an old tale that the verity [truth] of it is in strong suspicion" (5.2.28). It is perhaps in our own modern times that these plays have come into their own. It may be that the decline of imagination in an industrial and commercial world has given us an appreciation for fantasy. Novels and films of fantasy can give a powerful shock treatment to the imagination. There is, however, always the danger of escapism in fantasy, a retreat from the reality of the actual world. I want to claim in this chapter that the final fantastic plays of Shakespeare are never escapism, that (despite Strachey's view) they bring us face to face with reality, and that this is especially true of *The Winter's Tale*.[2] The play is characterized by a rich intertextuality: reference to scripture and other theological texts facilitate Shakespeare's project, fill out a spirituality, and must have a powerful effect on theology written "in front" of the text of the play.

COMEDY AND ROMANCE

The peculiar feel of these plays comes from a unique blend of two elements, two streams of European art: comedy and romance. For this reason, these last plays are sometimes classified as "Romantic Comedies"; but they are scarcely an Elizabethan version of the Hollywood "Romcom," whose classic expression is perhaps *When Harry Met Sally*.[3] The modern Romcom is simply a love-comedy, while the "romance" part of the last comedies is far wider than the theme of true love. The earlier comedies can also be called "romantic comedies," but in these last plays the element of romance becomes more prominent, and is integrated with comedy in a fresh way within Shakespeare's art.

The form that Shakespeare inherits from the classical world and from Italy is a comedy of confusion. It relies on people disguising themselves, people being mistaken for others, people wrongly thought to be dead, people playing tricks on others like sending them forged letters or telling them that A is in love with B when this is not true, and so on. It is a comedy that turns situations upside down. It brings disorder: the Lord of Misrule in his dance scatters errors, tangles relationships, upsets calm, and weaves a web of mistaken identities. Comedy sows confusion, and this is just what delights and amuses us. But the spirit of comedy also brings order out of disorder; the confusion is a healing process. In fact, as we have already seen with *A Midsummer Night's Dream* and *The Merchant of Venice*, the disorder is already there before the play begins and before the comic spirit enters on the scene. There are already broken relationships, or relations under strain, or disturbed personalities, or families divided, or wars threatening. The typical pattern of a Shakespearean comedy is to begin with something out of joint in human life, something amiss: then comic confusion creates *further* disorder in order to bring about restoration and harmony.

The chief comic spirit in *The Winter's Tale* is Autolycus, called "a rogue" in the cast-list. He is a beggar, pickpocket, cheat, and general merry fellow, whose philosophy is to look out for number one. He describes himself memorably as a "snapper-up of unconsidered trifles" (4.3.25–26). In stage productions he tends to steal the show, always playing tricks and working deceptions. But these shake up the situation—which as we shall see could not be in more of a mess already—confusing it just enough to enable the truth to emerge. Toward the middle of the play a prince falls in love with a shepherdess. Florizel, the young prince, loses his heart to Perdita, who is *supposedly* the daughter of a simple shepherd. Under severe displeasure from his father, King Polixenes, he elopes with her from his native Bohemia to seek refuge with the king of Sicily. It is Autolycus the rogue, through his trickery, who gets the girl's supposed father, the old shepherd, and her supposed brother (described as "a clown") on board ship for Sicily; there they will show the proofs of her real identity (clothes, jewel, and letters) to the king of Sicily, Leontes, and so a whole story of cruelty, broken relationships, guilt, and remorse involving Leontes will be exposed. Autolycus is not only the Lord of Misrule: he is the Lord of Revelation. Comedy plays tricks, but game-playing can expose the truth.

This revelation likewise requires Perdita and Florizel to adopt disguises as they flee from Bohemia, and Perdita to pretend to be a princess (which in fact she is) in Sicily, although Perdita herself is uncomfortable with this play-acting. Unlike Rosalind, who likes "to prove a busy actor" (As You Like It, 3.4.55), she reluctantly concedes that "I see the play so lies that I must bear a part" (4.4.658). Like Viola earlier ("disguise, I see thou art a wickedness"), she seems aware that damage can be caused on the way to a resolution through deceit, although, as Camillo assures her, there is "No remedy" but that (660). It is Camillo, former counsellor to Leontes and now in the same office to Polixenes, who sums up the healing mechanism of comedy by urging Perdita to "disliken / The truth of your own seeming." The phrase is packed with irony: there is a truth in the "seeming" which is being denied by the disguise, or the "dislikening," and yet Shakespeare is aiming by way of making confusion to get from "seeming," or mere appearance, to reality. In Perdita's case, the "seeming" is also a complicated mixture of shepherdess and the nobility which cannot be suppressed, as becomes clear when she dons the play-costume of a queen for a country festival and Polixenes grudgingly observes, "Nothing she does or seems / But smacks of something greater than herself" (4.4.157–58). In comedy, people are sometimes what they seem, and sometimes not what they seem, and sometimes partly both. In Much Ado about Nothing, for instance, Claudio exclaims of Hero, "Out on thee, seeming! I will write against it" (4.1.55), while she is as innocent as she seems. In Measure for Measure, Isabella is rightly outraged at Angelo's "Seeming, seeming" (2.4.150). The point is that only a good shaking up of the situation will show the truth.

Still in the spirit of comedy, Shakespeare can play more serious games too. A repeated device is to declare the heroine to be dead when she is still very much alive. This is how Hero in Much Ado wins the repentance of her lover who has falsely accused her of fornication: after he spurns her cruelly at the altar she pretends to have been killed by his unkindness, and he spends an uncomfortable night at her supposed grave. The same trick is to be played in The Winter's Tale, but for sixteen years instead of eight hours. Juliet tries a similar deception on her family without the same success, but then Romeo and Juliet begins as a comedy and turns into a tragedy, where The Winter's Tale begins as a tragedy and becomes a comedy. We have already seen that tragedy and comedy for Shakespeare are but a hair's breadth apart, two converging views of the same universe.[4]

Romance is the second great tradition of European art that Shakespeare inherited. Interwoven with the comic strategy there is a romance story. Romance is not just concerned with "true love," though this plays a part in it. Romances were fantastic stories of love and adventure—what would now be called fairy stories, or folktales, or even myths. They were especially about a quest for something lost—lost treasure, lost children, lost lovers, lost parents. Working to a sort of mythical formula, they stressed certain hopeful patterns of life: the lost will be found, the wicked will be punished, the good will be rewarded, what is broken will be healed. They had the kind of inevitable outcome that belongs to myth: life will follow death as spring follows winter; good will defeat evil in the end. These ritual patterns, expressed in romance, have the power of symbol to touch us at the deepest level.

Shakespeare was always, from his earliest comedies, weaving together comedy and romance.[5] A comedy that moves from disorder to order, and so often from loss to reconciliation bears a romance pattern superimposed over the comedy of confusion. But in these late comedies the romance element becomes still more powerful, the theme of loss and reconciliation ever more insistent. These plays stress that there has been a terrible fracturing of relationships, and restoration is at last achieved through various improbable adventures and journeys. There is a voyage from loss to finding. This is the comedy of reconciliation, celebrated in a Eucharist of harmony. But, as we will see, there are certain harsh realities of life which cannot be avoided, since Shakespeare the romantic is also the realist.

Loss

In these last plays the theme of loss and reconciliation is presented with the power of myths of rebirth and renewal of life. Let us recall the shape of the myth. As the play opens, Leontes, the king of Sicily, is enjoying an extended visit from his childhood friend Polixenes, king of Bohemia. But he suddenly becomes wildly jealous, suspecting that his wife, Hermione, is having an affair with his friend. He seizes, irrationally, on the fact that Polixenes has been staying for nine months and Hermione is nine months pregnant, and he is tipped over the edge of sanity when Hermione succeeds in persuading Polixenes to stay an extra couple of days, even though he had asked her do this himself. The now frantic Leontes instructs his most trusted counsellor, Camillo, to poison Polixenes, but Camillo warns him of the plot and escapes with him back to Bohemia. Deprived of his revenge, Leontes proceeds to bring his wife to trial for adultery and treason.

Anticipating the verdict, and convinced in his own mind that the baby girl to whom Hermione has just given birth is a bastard, the daughter of Polixenes, Leontes orders one of his lords, Antigonus, to take the baby and expose her to the elements and wild animals in some desert place. To avoid the appearance of being a tyrant, he sends messengers to the oracle at Delphos, for a verdict from the god Apollo as to whether Hermione is innocent or guilty. When the oracle is read out in court, declaring Hermione to be innocent and the newly born child to be Leontes's true issue, he rejects it as false and is immediately punished for his impiety. A servant rushes in with the news that Leontes's only other child, his son Mamillius, has just died of grief and fear at what is happening to his mother. Hermione faints at this and is carried out of the court, her attendant then returning with the dreadful news that she too has died. Too late, Leontes repents, and is left only with the tenuous hope held out by the oracle, with its message: "The King shall live without an heir if that which is lost be not found" (3.2.133). In the end, all *is* found, and Leontes receives an almost miraculous restoration of nearly all he has lost.

Any playwright faces a severe problem in depicting a myth like this on a stage. Mythical events lack human motivation, occurring with the authority of traditional patterns. Drama, on the other hand, requires a realism of character, and this is true both of tragedy and of comedy, at least when it is social comedy, dealing with human manners and relations. *The Winter's Tale* contains tragedy in the first part, and comedy in the second; both are in tension with romance. Leontes, in the more tragic phase of the play, is depicted with extreme psychological realism.[6] We can follow the progress of his destructive jealousy with an almost clinical precision, and finally we see him projecting onto Hermione the role of his own sexual fantasies, and even perhaps his guilt about his own behavior.[7] When his courtiers protest that there is nothing in his suspicions, he demands:

> Is whispering nothing?
> Is leaning cheek to cheek? Is meeting noses?
> Kissing with inside lip? Stopping the career
> Of laughter with a sigh? ...
> . . . .
> Skulking in corners? Wishing clocks more swift?
> Hours, minutes, noon, midnight? ...
> . . . .
> Why then the world all that's in't is nothing. (1.2.283–91)

Of course, he has observed none of this with Hermione and Polixenes—it is indeed "nothing,"[8] a word made ominous by King Lear—and so he may be recalling his own sexual unfaithfulness. We learn that he has often asked Camillo, his counsellor and confidant, to open the gates of the city so that he can go in and out easily at night, for undefined purposes (2.1.53–55). There is an almost pathological accuracy about the portrayal of Leontes's state of mind, yet Shakespeare is peopling a mythical landscape, devoid of human motivation, with characters like this. Here is the challenge Shakespeare faces: how to bring myth and real people together in a convincing way. He wants to draw on the power of myth, and also wants to present it onstage in a way that we can see before our eyes and believe.

J. R. R Tolkien, in his influential essay "On Fairy-Stories," writes bluntly that "Drama is naturally hostile to Fantasy. Fantasy, even of the simplest kind, hardly ever succeeds in Drama, when that is presented as it should be, visibly and audibly acted."[9] Tolkien finds the witches in *Macbeth* "almost intolerable" when acted on the stage, though "tolerable" when the play is read, but he passes no judgment on the sight and speech of fairies in *A Midsummer Night's Dream*, or of the message from the oracle in *The Winter's Tale*. I suggest that Shakespeare has, *pace* Tolkien, succeeded in bringing myth and "stage reality" (itself a work of imagination and illusion) together, partly because intertextuality with the Bible supports both the psychological realism of characters and the mythical events. In *The Winter's Tale* the familiarity of the scriptural text holds the whole action together—tragedy, comedy, and romance, in both the phases of loss and reconciliation. Moreover, there are distinct scriptural themes linking the parts, in particular those of the Garden of Eden in Genesis 1–3, and new birth. This does not make the play into an allegory of Christian doctrine; as in all his work, Shakespeare is using intertextuality to drive the plot, shape characters, and promote a general kind of spirituality.

Polixenes introduces the theme of "Paradise lost" in recollecting his shared boyhood with Leontes, and remembering an Edenic period, as if before the fall of humanity:

> We were as twinned lambs that did frisk i'th' sun,
> And bleat the one at th'other; what we changed
> Was innocence for innocence—we knew not
> The doctrine of ill-doing, nor dreamed
> That any did. Had we pursued that life,
> And our weak spirits ne'er been higher reared
> With stronger blood, we should have answered heaven
> Boldly, "not guilty," the imposition cleared
> Hereditary ours. (1.2.66–74)

"The doctrine of ill-doing" is the doctrine of original sin, developed by the Christian church from the story in Genesis 3, and interpreting St. Paul in Romans 5:12 to mean that Adam's sin was transmitted down through the succession of human generations.[10] In saying that "we knew [it] not," Polixenes may be claiming that that, in their innocence, they were actually free from original sin or that they simply did not know about it. The difficult last two lines appear to mean that that if they had continued in that state, then they could have claimed before heaven to be free of inherited guilt: "the imposition [of guilt] cleared from being ours by heredity." In the passage as a whole, then, Polixenes is either claiming that they were free from both original sin *and* from guilt, or—more likely—that they were free of guilt but not of original sin.[11] While this may simply be intended to be an exaggeration by Polixenes (and perhaps a piece of male chauvinism),[12] it could reflect a theological opinion about the state of infants.

Augustine had distinguished original sin, inherited from Adam, from original guilt (i.e., guilt for the sin of Adam), but found both to be endemic to human life.[13] Anselm, however, had implied that infants were free from original guilt, and Abelard had explicitly stated this.[14] Some Reformed theologians, especially those who rejected the baptism of infants—first Anabaptists and then Baptists in England—also denied original guilt. They thought that all, including infants, were contaminated by sin, but guilt before God only arose when a person committed sin for himself or herself.[15] Although Article IX of the Articles of Religion of the Church of England followed the Augustinian tradition in ascribing both original sin and original guilt to infants, Shakespeare in this passage seems to show an awareness of a greater diversity of theological approaches.

Such a state of innocence only existed, according to Polixenes, before the onset in puberty of what he calls "stronger blood," as manifest in erection of the penis ("higher reared"), and this leads on to an elaboration of the Eden theme: Polixenes and Hermione play in conversation with the idea that Polixenes and Leontes committed their "first sin"—regarded as sexual—because of the temptation of their queens, as Adam was tempted by Eve.[16] On this somewhat jarring note, Leontes enters the exchange with the inquiry to Hermione, "is he won yet?," which contains an ambiguity between "is he persuaded to stay?" and "is his heart completely yours?" (1.1.87).[17]

In an aside, Leontes quotes and reverses Psalm 28:8, which reads "my heart danceth for joy" in the Coverdale Psalter;[18] Leontes complains that "My heart dances / But not for joy; not joy" (1.2.110–11). For he now pitches himself into feverish imagination of a sexual affair between Hermione and Polixenes, in which he momentarily doubts the parentage of his son Mamillius and makes his own recollection of his boyhood stay in Eden:

> Looking on the lines
> Of my boy's face, methoughts I did recoil

> Twenty-three years, and saw myself unbreeched,
> In my green velvet coat; my dagger muzzled,
> Lest it should bite its master. (1.2.153–58)

While "unbreeched" means too young to wear a man's breeches, Hamlin suggests that the word is also a subtle allusion to Genesis 3:7; in the translation of the Geneva Bible, when Adam and Eve realize they are naked after their primal sin against God, they "made themselves breeches." Leontes is imitating Polixenes in recalling a prelapsarian state, before "breeches" were necessary, and perhaps then the reference to a "muzzled dagger" is a phallic euphemism corresponding to Polixenes's "higher reared / With stronger blood."[19] Both Polixenes and Leontes appear to be repeating the Augustinian idea that original sin is connected with concupiscence, aroused in the sexual act.[20] There is no evidence that Shakespeare either approved or disapproved of this dogmatic idea; he is simply using the association to relate the Edenic imagery to Leontes's destructive sexual jealousy, as it will later be related to reconciliation.

The reference to Eden remains an undercurrent in Leontes's complex and increasingly incoherent speech. When Leontes exclaims, "Inch-thick, knee-deep, o'er head and ears a forked one!" (1.2.185), the person he imagines sinking into the mire could be either himself (a cuckold, wearing the traditional horns) or Hermione. But if he has Hermione in mind, then he probably means that "Hermione is an equivocator, a fork-tongued serpent or she-devil with horns,"[21] continuing the imagery of the Garden of Eden. The women have already been defamed, jokingly, by Polixenes as being the tempting serpent in the garden, and Hermione had protested that he should stop before actually saying, "Your queen and I are devils" (1.2.82). When Hermione tells Leontes, lightheartedly, that he can find her and Polixenes "i'th' garden," he appears to associate this garden with Eden, replying, "You'll be found, / Be you beneath the sky" (178–79), as if he were "like God in Eden discovering sin."[22] Insisting that Camillo should also accuse Hermione, Leontes complains that he needs to use his eyes to see the difference between good and evil (1.2.303), recalling the serpent's words to Adam that "Your eyes shall be opened . . . knowing good and evil" (Gen. 3:5). Later, he regrets his acquired knowledge about what he supposes is Hermione's faithlessness, wishing to regress to the innocent stage before his eyes were opened: "Alack, for lesser knowledge—how accursed / In being so blest" (2.1.37).[23]

The trial of Hermione recapitulates Polixenes's appeal to heaven in his Edenic state, "not guilty," but this time the appellant is Hermione. Indicted for treason and adultery, she invokes "powers divine" to support her cry "not guilty" (3.2.25). The verdict of higher powers than Leontes comes by way of

the oracle of Apollo at Delphos, and even before the trial begins we are heart-
ened to think it will be favorable to Hermione since the messengers report
on its origin from a temple which stands in a kind of Eden: "The climate's
delicate, the air most sweet, / Fertile the isle."[24] The imagery of the primal
fruitful garden ("We eat of the fruit of the trees of the garden," Gen. 3:2) is
also recalled when Hermione refers to Mamillius as the "first-fruits of my
body" (3.2.95).[25] This is a complex biblical image, recalling the Hebrew idiom
"the fruit of the womb" (Gen. 30:2), and the "first-fruits" of the harvest to be
offered as a sacrificial gift to God (Lev. 2:12); in particular it recalls the "obla-
tion of the fruit of the ground" and the "first fruit of his sheep" that Cain and
Abel brought to God after the expulsion of their parents from Eden (Gen.
4:2–4). Leontes indeed has tried, and failed, to be Cain in killing his brother-
king. As in *Richard II*, the story of Cain and Abel is linked with the story of
Eden.[26] The sequence of biblical quotations and allusions thus keeps the idea
of the loss of Eden in our minds, as well as reminding us of the life-giving
natural forces it represents.

This imagery, in fact, helps to solve the problem Shakespeare confronts
of combining myth, with its unmotivated and inevitable patterns of life and
death, with the realistic characters of comedy and tragedy. In a previous romantic comedy, *Cymbeline*, he had attempted a solution by the use of a *deus
ex machina*: Jove descends from heaven on an eagle and claims responsibility
for what has happened in people's lives, declaring: "Those whom I best love /
I cross." In this play, Shakespeare finds a better solution: the power behind
the events which confront Leontes is what Perdita later calls "great creating
Nature," and what Paulina in this part of the play calls "great Nature." By this
power, she declares, Hermione's new baby is "freed and enfranchised" from
the womb (2.2.59–60). This is the power which shows itself in Leontes's son,
Mamillius, who brings the springtime of new life to the court, who "physics
the subject, makes old hearts fresh," who is a "kernel, a squash [pea-pod],"
who, as Leontes confesses, "makes a July's day short as December / and with
his varying childishness cures in me / thoughts that would thick my blood."
The vital power of this new-creating nature abandons the court with the
death of Mamillius, and only returns with Perdita, of whom Florizel declares:

> When you do dance, I wish you
> A wave o' the sea, that you might ever do
> Nothing but that. (4.4.140)

This is the counterpart to Leontes's finding that, crippled by jealousy, "my
heart dances, but not for joy." His servant, Antigonus, anticipating his ex-
posure in the wild of the newborn and rejected child of Leontes, prays to

what seems to be a spirit of nature: "Some powerful spirit instruct the kites and ravens / To be thy nurses!" (2.3.186–87). This has undertones, as Shaheen points out,[27] of the scriptural story of the ravens that fed Elijah at God's command (1 Kings 17:4–6), and which brings "great creating Nature" into the orbit of the Christian creator God.

For all this does not mean that Shakespeare is commending nature-worship, or an unconditional allegiance to nature; how badly wrong that went with Edmund—"Thou, Nature, art my goddess" (*Lear*, 1.2.1)—is clear from *King Lear*. There is a kind of spirituality here of "going with the grain of the universe," working in harmony with life-giving energies, that *could* be interpreted in a Christian way, or through a number of theologies, but need not be. It is a similar strategy to Hamlet's appeal to "special providence," which Shakespeare has qualified into a general spirituality of living responsibly in the face of death.[28]

One of the possible theological interpretations is offered by Alison Shell. She proposes that the fate and destiny portrayed in this play and others had a "disturbing analogue" in high Calvinism, and that we can detect a Shakespeare who "apprehended and aestheticized the sorrows of predestination."[29] The horribly amusing end of Autolycus, exiting "pursued by a bear" which is shortly to maul him to death, tells us that, unlike Leontes, "not every sinner gets a second chance." Antigonus's fate, she asserts, would have "played on topical theological sensitivities about the exceptional nature of grace."[30] Antigonus, in the course of faithfully carrying out the command of Leontes to expose the newborn child in a wild place, tells the audience that he has had a dream in which a figure "in pure white robes" had appeared to him and instructed him to lay the child on the coast of Bohemia. Hermione—for he believes it to be her—commiserates with him, as one whom "fate, against thy better disposition, / Hath made . . . the thrower-out" of her child (3.3.28–29), even though he has willingly consented to obey Leontes, and has not looked for a way to evade an unjust command, as had Camillo. Laying the child on the ground in a growing storm, he judges, "most accursed am I / To be by oath enjoin'd to this." He makes, as Shell judges, "a bad death," despairing that "I am gone for ever!"

Though this scene is presented in the context of a pre-Christian set of beliefs, Shell judges that for Calvinist believers of Shakespeare's time, Antigonus and Leontes represent two possible outcomes of divine providence. The clue is given us by a scriptural reference, Antigonus's own version of the prayer of Jesus, "Thy will be done" (Matt. 6:10), as he exclaims to the mariner, "Their sacred wills be done." If one believes that God's will is remorselessly worked out in history, Shell pronounces, "Antigonus's fate is what every sinner has the right to expect. Leontes's displays a marvellous and exceptional instance of grace."[31] Repentance is granted to the one by divine grace, but not to the other. Leontes's destiny is tragicomedy, where Antigonus's is simply tragedy. If the play is to be read, as it often is, as a parable of grace, she advises us to respond to "the full tragi-comical implications of grace in post-Reformation England."[32] The theater was a place where rigid Calvinist views of divine will could be questioned, and more Arminian views—giving more space to human freedom—could be fostered.[33] The response of the audience might then be not only to "rejoice at exceptional grace" but also to "deplore the fact that grace is exceptional."[34] The loss suffered by Paulina, Autolycus's wife, is dwelt upon at the end of the play, making clear that grace has its tragedies to be properly grieved over.

Such a proposal certainly accords with Shakespeare's habit of not "taking sides" in doctrinal disputes, and leaving decisions to the audience; viewers are being called on to ask themselves whether a strong doctrine of Providence is tolerable in light of the losses in the play that are never made up. Can "great creating Nature" really be understood as a Creator's absolute determination of events and allotment of destinies to persons? But posing this open question is, I suggest, only one result of alluding to this mysterious force with the help of intertextual clues, and I intend to sketch another shortly.

RECONCILIATION

"The King shall live without an heir if that which is lost be not found," runs the oracle. What is lost is of course the baby girl (Perdita, meaning "lost"), but finding her proves impossible, since Antigonus has been killed, and the ship which has brought him to Bohemia has been sunk in a sudden storm, together with all hands. That, as with Antigonus's fate, should also have proved a problem to those members of the audience who held rigid views of divine Providence. Leontes has no way of tracing his daughter. She has, however, been found by a local shepherd, together with some gold pieces, a jewel, some clothes, and letters, important pieces of identification later on. Now, in the play, the scene changes from the darkness and gloomy atmosphere of the court to the light and the sun of a pastoral life. The shepherd's simple son, named only "the Clown," exclaims: "I have not winked since I saw these sights: the men are not yet cold under water, nor the bear half dined on the gentleman—he's at it now" (3.3.101–3), and the shepherd replies: "Heavy matters, Heavy matters. But look thee here, boy, now bless thyself: thou met'st with things dying, I with things new born."[35]

Scriptural quotations evoke the sense that rebirth, and so some kind of new Eden, is possible. The shepherd's comment about "things new born" refers in the first place to the literal "new birth" of the baby, but it seems to indicate a general renewal of life that is at hand. The image of "new birth" occurs several times in the New Testament, especially in the Johannine literature.[36] The Clown reacts to the discovery of gold coins with the exclamation that the shepherd has a new lease of life; citing Psalm 25:7, "Remember not the sins of my youth," he assures him, "You're a made old man. If the sins of your youth are forgiven you, you're well to live" (3.1.116–17). The contrast between "things dying" and "things new born" is repeated sixteen years later when Perdita's identity is discovered on her arrival in Sicily, and a garrulous Gentleman reports, "They looked as they had heard of a world ransomed, or one destroyed" (5.2.15); Pitcher aptly directs us to Mark 10:45, where Christ is said to die "for the ransom of many."[37] The new world has only come into being through sacrifice, such as that of Mamillius, Antigonus, and—all suppose—Hermione. There are also resonances here of 2 Corinthians 5:17: "if any man be in Christ, let him be a new creature. Old things are passed away: behold all things are become new." The Clown supplies a humorous parody of these New Testament texts when he crows to Autolycus that he is now "a Gentleman born":

> CLOWN. Give me the lie, do. And try whether I am not now a gentleman born.
>
> AUTOLYCUS. I know you are now, sir, a gentleman born.
>
> CLOWN. Ay, and have been so any time these four hours.
>
> SHEPHERD. And so have I, boy.
>
> CLOWN. So you have; but I was a gentleman born before my father, for the king's son took me by the hand and called me brother. (5.2.131–37)

This exquisite exchange recalls the conversation between Christ and Nicodemus in John 3:1–16, which is the key text about new birth, containing the question, "How can a man be born when he is old?": "Jesus answered, and said unto him, Verily, Verily I say unto thee, except a man be born again, he can not see the kingdom of God. Nicodemus said unto him, How can a man be born which is old? Can he enter into his mothers womb again, and be born? Jesus answered, Verily, verily I say unto thee, except a man be born of water and of the Spirit, he cannot see the kingdom of God."

We have, incidentally, already been alerted to scriptural references from the Gospel of John in the play generally by the exchange between Hermione and Polixenes early on, where (as Shaheen points out)[38] the word "verily" is repeated between them:

> POLIXENES.   I may not, verily.
>
> HERMIONE.   Verily? (1.2.45–46)

Throughout John's Gospel (from John 1:51 to 21:18) this double use is a favorite idiom of Jesus, where in the Synoptic Gospels he uses a single "verily." The sense of a new world dawning is also given us by the chorus of "Time," who bridges the gap of sixteen years between the finding of the baby Perdita and her development into a young woman. Brought up by the shepherd as his own daughter, she is showing most uncommon qualities for a shepherdess. Time is eager "To speak of Perdita, now grown in grace" (4.1.24), which echoes the injunction of 2 Peter 3:18, "But grow in grace." While we might consider the Clown's claim to be "a gentleman born" to be an "exuberant falsehood," as does Richard McCoy,[39] we can also be glad for him and recognize the sense of miraculous renewal that the Johannine text evokes.

The point of this string of scriptural allusions about new life and a new world, taking up the Edenic imagery from the first half of the play, is not that Shakespeare is making an allegory about rebirth. It is to create a sense of unity and continuity between a mythical plot and a "realistic" depiction of character and personality, melding romance with comedy and tragedy. The constant scripture echoes about Eden and a new birth, within the general idea of "great creating Nature," hold the whole piece together. Nor am I suggesting that the rural life of Bohemia is being portrayed as a return to *prelapsarian* Eden. This is a place which contains rogues and fools, and which is presided over by a king who tends toward the tyrannical manner in which Leontes had behaved in the first part of the play. But it is a place where it is appropriate to perform Christ's parable of the Prodigal Son (Luke 15:11–31), who was given the opportunity of new life after his fall from grace, since any new Eden can only take seriously the weakness and failings of human beings. Autolycus tells us that "he compassed a motion of the Prodigal Son" (4.3.97), or obtained and took on tour a puppet-show ("motion") of the parable, a popular pasttime in Shakespeare's time. The words of the father in the parable, that "this thy brother . . . was lost and he is found" (v. 31), correspond remarkably to the words of the oracle, "if that which is lost be not found." Shakespeare appears to have followed his source, Robert Greene's *Pandosto*, exactly in reporting the oracle ("If that which is lost be not found"),[40] but there is no reason why he could not also have associated the phrase with the parable of the Prodigal Son, especially since the father's expression of joy also contains the words, "this thy brother was dead and is alive again," continuing the theme of new birth.

The allusion to Eden, which is strong in the conversation between Hermione and Polixenes in the first part, is now picked up in the conversation between Hermione's daughter and Polixenes in the second. Perdita, thought to be a shepherdess, is being wooed by no less than Florizel, the son of the king. At a sheep-shearing festival, where Perdita is taking the role of Queen of the Feast, and so playing at what she actually is (a theme familiar from previous comedies),[41] Florizel's father Polixenes visits her in disguise, accompanied by Camillo, who is now his trusted counsellor. There follows a discussion between them about the care of gardens and the growth of flowers. Perdita insists that she will have no *cultivated* flowers, flowers bred by the human intervention of grafting, in her garden. She has heard it said that "there is an art which in their piedness shares / With great creating Nature," but for her part she rejects any such sophistication; she disdains such flowers as carnations and gillyvors as "nature's bastards" (4.4.79–88). Polixenes, from the standpoint of civilization, opposes her: he argues that such breeding is not against nature, but is in fact nature's own activity through the human arts:

> You see, sweet maid, we marry
> A gentler scion to the wildest stock,
> And make conceive a bark of baser kind
> By bud of noble race. This is an art
> Which does mend Nature—change it rather—but
> The art itself is Nature. (92–97)

Perdita has the worst of the argument, though we sympathize with her desire to avoid any artificiality, which she compares to using face paint to attract Florizel's "desire to breed" (101–3). The irony, however, is that Polixenes is about to act against his own philosophy; having just argued that "we marry a gentler scion [i.e., offspring] to the wildest stock," he is about to break up the impending marriage between his son and Perdita on the grounds that—being a shepherdess—she is too common for him. In the end, however, the wilder stock of the country is to be married to the gentility of the court. Nature and art are to be wedded together.

The conversation is set in the convention of the Elizabethan pastoral, which has already appeared in our discussion of *A Midsummer Night's Dream*. In it there are echoes of Eden; as Pitcher comments, "The mythologies of Eden and the [classical] Golden World merged long before Shakespeare."[42] The action of pastoral was set in the countryside, among brooks

and hills, nymphs and shepherds, in order to criticize the civilized life of the
city and the royal court. The setting was among the simple and uneducated
folk of the countryside, in order to satirize the educated and sophisticated.
So a contrast was drawn between nature and nurture, nature and education,
nature and art. In *As You Like It*, people from the royal court go to live in the
countryside of Arden, whereas in *The Winter's Tale*, King Polixenes and Camillo turn up in disguise at a sheep-shearing festival. Court comes to country,
and the result is a criticism of the sophisticated life which has been momentarily left behind. That the noble class will return to the court in the end is
taken for granted; they are only on holiday on the countryside, and the true
virtues of the natural life will fertilize and revivify the weary life of the court
with its stale arts and graces. In *The Winter's Tale* this will happen when the
reverse journey takes place, when Bohemian country turns up at the court of
Sicily.

We must not forget that in this knitting together of nature and art, Perdita
is really a princess all the time. The mechanism of the plot is a romance, and
a major theme in romance stories is the emergence of "noble seed" in humble
surroundings. The weaving together of nature and nurture is a complex one;
a princess nurtured among shepherds could aptly symbolize a blend between
art and nature, each qualifying and correcting the other. There is real virtue
in the countryside, such as the old shepherd displays with a natural dignity,
and yet the gullibility and naivety of country people are also exposed, letting
themselves be cheated by Autolycus with his improbable ballads, his cheap
ribbons, and his skill in picking pockets. Art must not be allowed to become
artificial, but at the same time it cannot be reduced to a mere copy, or *mimesis*, of nature. It adds something to nature, being co-creative; in Perdita's
words, "there is art that *shares* with great creating Nature."

If there is to be a new Eden, it cannot simply be a return to the old Eden,
overturning all the arts of civilization. The conversation about the garden,
where "the art itself is nature," evokes the primordial garden, as it does in the
conversation of the gardeners in *Richard II*. There, where England is imagined as a new Eden, the theme is used to portray Richard as the old, fallen
Adam. Here the image is used to develop the idea that new life is not simply a reversal or cancellation of the old. Hamlin is surely correct to alert us
to analogies made in gardening books and herbals of the Elizabethan period between earthly gardens and the original Garden. He also aptly quotes
Rebecca Bushnell to the effect that it was a commonplace of early modern
gardeners that "through gardening we could restore some part of that paradise
we lost with the Fall, which condemned us to sweat for our food."[43] But Hamlin, I suggest, misses the point of the whole discussion of art and nature when
he concludes that *The Winter's Tale* "contemplates the possibility of *reversing*

the Fall."[44] Restoring "some part" of Eden (Bushnell) is not the same as a total return.

When Polixenes breaks up the festival and threatens Perdita with terrible punishments if she and Florizel do not break off this unsuitable match, the nobility of her nature gives her courage:

> I was not much afeard: for once or twice
> I was about to speak and tell him plainly,
> The selfsame sun that shines upon his court
> Hides not his visage from our cottage, but
> Looks on alike. (4.4.447–51)

Again there are resonances with scripture. In wording, the closest resonance is Ecclesiasticus 42:16, "The sun that shineth, looketh upon all things,"[45] but the text goes on significantly, "and all the work thereof is full of the glory of the Lord." *God* is involved in the shining, and in what is shone upon. Another close resonance therefore is Matthew 5:44–45:[46] "Love your enemies: bless them that curse you: do good to those who hate you, and pray for them which hurt you, and persecute you, That ye may be the children of your Father that is in heaven: for *he maketh his sun to arise on the evil, and the good*, and sendeth rain on the just, & unjust." Shakespeare seems to have had the final line of this text in mind, as we have seen, in writing Portia's lines in *The Merchant of Venice* as Shylock faces the "enemies" referred to in the text: "The quality of mercy is not strain'd, / It droppeth as the gentle rain from heaven / Upon the place beneath." In this context now, we are assured that the grace of God, in general providence, is bestowed upon every combination of nature and nurture, whether court or cottage, bringing renewal of life.

The same integration, or shifting boundary, between art and nature plays a key role in the final scene of reconciliation in the play. The couple elope for sanctuary to Sicilia, where they hope that King Leontes will help them, by now having a reputation for saintliness through his repentance. It is thus discovered, to everyone's joy, that Perdita is the long-lost daughter of Leontes—which is just as well, because when he lays eyes on her he has half a mind to marry her himself (5.1.222). Polixenes and Camillo turn up in pursuit of the couple and share in the wonder of the revelation. The play then ends with everyone viewing what is said by Paulina to be a newly made statue of the long-dead Hermione, a piece of art which is amazingly natural:

> LEONTES.   Her natural posture.
>   Chide me, dear stone, that I may say indeed
>   Thou art Hermione—or rather, thou art she

In thy not chiding; for she was tender
As infancy and grace. But yet, Paulina,
Hermione was not so much wrinkled, nothing
So aged as this seems.

. . . .

PAULINA.   So much more our carver's excellence,
            Which lets go by some sixteen years and makes her
            As she lived now. (5.3.23–32)

This wonder of art turns out, of course, to be nothing other than the living
Hermione herself, who has only pretended to be dead and has hidden herself
for sixteen years in hope of one day being restored to her daughter, as the
oracle had promised. The poignancy of the scene is largely due to the shifting
of perception backward and forward between what is viewed as art and what
is felt to be a natural body:[47]

POLIXENES.   The very life seems warm upon her lip.

LEONTES.   The fixture of her eye hath motion in't,
            As we are mocked with art.

. . . .

            There is an air that comes from her. What fine chisel
            Could ever yet cut breath? (66–68, 78–80)

Leontes exclaims: "Doth not the stone rebuke me / For being more stone
than it?" (37–38), echoing the response of Jesus to the "rebuke" of the Pharisees, that "If these should hold their peace, the stones would cry,"[48] a text to
which Shakespeare had previously alluded in *Richard II*.[49]

The effect is for the viewer to feel that art and nature cannot be polarized,
any more than can the experience of the theater (art) and life outside the
performance, a shifting boundary that Shakespeare will explore more fully
in *The Tempest*. Commentators insist on calling this scene the "resurrection"
of Hermione, but the term is misleading;[50] even as a symbol for the event,
"resurrection" does not fit well, since resurrection in Christian thinking is not
the revival of a dead body but transformation into some new reality that can
only be called a "spiritual body" (1 Cor. 15:44).[51] The imagery of the scene is
closer to the myth of Pygmalion, in which the statue of a woman comes to
life, and which Shakespeare may well have read in Ovid's *Metamorphoses*.[52]
What we are presented with is a renewal of life, in continuity with the images of new birth and a new Eden in which art and nature blend together.

Such a new world does require faith, as Paulina bids her audience: "It is required / You do awake your faith" (5.3.95). In the first place this is faith in her own performance, and beyond that, a "poetic faith" in Shakespeare's own art as a playwright. Richard McCoy has rightly stressed this, in his study entitled with a play on words, *Faith in Shakespeare*.[53] But, as a faith which is awoken by a blend of art and nature, we are taken into a wider area of faith, which for Shakespeare's audience surely could not be separated from faith in the God who renews all life.[54] It is almost unnecessary to cite any particular text from the very many in the New Testament which call for faith, or commend faith, but perhaps apt for this occasion are the repeated words of Jesus: "Thy faith hath made thee whole."[55] Shakespeare, typically, is leaving meaning open.

It may be the case, as Hamlin argues, that Hermione's earlier reference to the "first-fruits" of her body has resonance with St. Paul's celebration of the resurrection of Jesus as "the first fruits of them that slept" (1 Cor. 15:20), and so has a forward reference to the last scene of the play.[56] But if this is so, her own return to the life of her husband and the court is not an *analogy* of Christ's resurrection, but a new state of life which in Christian thinking is made *possible* by his resurrection. Too much stress has been laid on Paulina's words, "I'll fill your grave up," which may be interpreted as an image of resurrection, but which is only one of a number of injunctions, including "descend, be stone no more." Significantly, Paulina claims, "Dear life redeems you" (5.3.103), and it is a *redemption* of life that the scene presents, and with which it challenges all present. The Clown had already posed the question to the now groveling Autolycus, "Wilt thou amend thy life?," thus quoting from the opening sentences of the service for Morning Prayer, "Amend your liues, for the kingdome of God is at hand." While Sarah Beckwith finds the resurrection narratives of the Gospels to be paradigms for the "re-appearance" of Shakespeare's supposedly dead characters, she understands their "resurrection" in the specific sense of bursting into the present "as reminders of an ineradicable past that must be confronted in the lives and thoughts—in the self-recognition—of those to whom they so hauntingly return."[57] This "redemption of memory" plays a key part in the renewal of life which the scenes embody.

Leontes is being given even more cause to "leap out of himself for joy," as he was reported to be ready to do on the discovery that Perdita was "found." At that moment he hesitated in thinking of Hermione: "as if that joy were now become a loss, cries 'O thy mother, thy mother!'" (5.2.48–50). That loss too is now redeemed. The expression "leap for joy" appears to echo Luke 6:23, "Rejoice ye in that day, and leap ye for joy," according the Bishops' Bible translation.[58] The phrase makes a matching couple to Leontes's complaint in the dark time of his jealousy, again based on a scripture text, "My heart dances, but not for joy."

THE PATTERN OF MYTH

Though not a resurrection, the return, or "redemption," of Hermione to daily life from self-imprisonment appears as a miraculous act. The explanation given is hardly adequate, and we are discouraged from seeking further information as to how the trick was worked. Paulina hastily moves the topic on: "There's time enough for that." But Leontes persists in his bewildered protest: "How, is to be question'd, for I saw her / As I thought, dead" (5.3.139–40). Logically, there can be no convincing explanation, for Paulina herself had invited Leontes to examine her at the time of the tragedy, crying:

> . . . go and see. If you can bring
> Tincture, or lustre in her lip, her eye,
> Heat outwardly, or breath within, I'll serve you
> As I would the gods. (3.2.201–4)

Nothing is said, as in *Romeo and Juliet*, about drugs that might give the appearance of death to the examiners. Moreover, Leontes had determined to bury her in the same tomb as Mamillius, and for sixteen years he has visited the chapel once a day where she lies, making penance. Nothing is said, as in *Romeo and Juliet*, about a plan to rescue the living heroine from her tomb before it is too late. Paulina herself admits:

> That she is living,
> Were it but told you, should be hooted at
> Like an old tale; but *it appears* she lives. (5.3.115–17)

It "appears" because the mythical pattern of life brought from death *demands* it. As Paulina manipulates the revelation scene, the action "strikes" us like a physical blow. We feel the impact of a myth incarnated in flesh:

> Music awake her, strike!
> 'Tis time; descend; be stone no more; approach;
> Strike all that look upon with marvel. Come!
> I'll fill your grave up; stir, nay come away:
> Bequeath to death your numbness: for from him
> Dear life redeems you. You perceive she stirs.

... Do not shun her
Until you see her die again. (5.3.98–106)

The romance structure of this play is obvious: it is a story of loss and find-ing, estrangement and reconciliation. The mythical character of this narrative means that there is no clear human motivation or even explanation behind the events: we are simply "struck" by the supernatural oracle at Delphos, the sudden death of Mamillius, the dream which Antigonus has about taking the child to Bohemia, the chance meeting of Florizel and Perdita, and the return of Hermione to life. These are accident, coincidence, improbability. Putting it another way, they have the inevitability of myth. The logic of cause and effect is replaced by a mere necessity: things happen. Shakespeare has, indeed, intensified the element of romance by allowing Hermione to "pre-serve" herself. In his source, *Pandosto*, the slandered queen (Bellaria) actually dies, while Pandosto (the parallel character to Leontes) commits suicide.[59] The mythical rhythm of the play is exemplified by a detail that Shakespeare *has* copied from *Pandosto*—this Bohemia has a seacoast; it needs one for An-tigonus to land on it, deposit the child there, and be eaten by a bear, as well as for his crew to be shipwrecked off it. Shakespeare has often been mocked for geographical ignorance of a landlocked country, but he is giving us a knowing wink. We are alerted to the fact that we are in the middle of a make-believe, a child's world of "fairy-tale logic."[60]

I have suggested that the myth of romance and the social realism of comedy and tragedy are at least partly brought together by the power of "great creating Nature" (4.4.88), which is implied to be directing the action. It appears, be-tween the lines, as a transcendent force which is working to bring things and people from death to life. The oracle of Apollo is in some way identified with this power.[61] Perdita herself personifies it, unconsciously identifying herself with Proserpina (4.4.116–18), a fertility goddess whose story symbolized the natural cycle of life, death, and rebirth. A lost daughter of the goddess Ceres, just as Perdita is lost by Hermione, Proserpina is released from the land of death (Hades) each year to preside over spring and summer. With the appeal to "great Nature" (2.2.59),[62] we have some assurance that there is a pattern in life, and it is open to the audience to interpret this as divine providence and even election—along the lines proposed by Alison Shell[63]—if they wish. But the result is also to underline the vulnerability of the real characters in the drama. They are exposed to a universe that is not amenable to human con-trol. Human persons will feel weak in the face of myth.

The audience too, in these last Romances, shares the characters' sense of being involved in an unpredictable world. The audience is not given the ad-vantage over the characters that it is has had in the earlier comedies, where we overlook the action from a superior viewpoint, and know who is deceiving whom. In *Romeo and Juliet* and in *Much Ado about Nothing*, we know that the heroine is not dead as others in the play are manipulated into believing. But here Shakespeare not only withholds information from us: he goes out of his way to deceive us, his audience.[64] For in this matter of Hermione's supposed death, we do not only hear Paulina swearing that she is dead—which we might discount as direct evidence. More than this, Antigonus is directed to lay Perdita on the shore of Bohemia in a dream, in which Hermione appears to him as only ghosts are supposed to appear:

> I have heard, but not believed, the spirits o'th' dead
> May walk again . . .
> . . . .
> To me comes a creature
> . . . .
> in pure white robes,
> Like very sanctity she did approach
> My cabin where I lay. (3.3.15–23)

After she has given instructions to Antigonus, he continues:

> And so, with shrieks,
> She melted into air. . . .
> . . . .
> I do believe
> Hermione hath suffered death. (3.3.35–36, 40–41)

Since the instruction to lay the child on the ground of Bohemia is essential for the plot, and the spirit also gives the child her name, we are likely to believe, with Antigonus, that this is indeed Hermione and that she has died. Such a conviction will only grow as the plot develops and Perdita meets Florizel; she has to be in Bohemia to meet him sixteen years later, and this has been the doing of the apparition. People who are only pretending to be dead ought not to have the ability to appear to people hundreds of miles distant; such facility requires a death and a doctrine of purgatory, to which we shall return. Shakespeare does drop a small clue in our way: since as a result of the vision Antigonus believes Hermione to be guilty, and we know she is not, some doubt about the apparition might be raised in our minds. But Shakespeare deceives us as much as Paulina does the court, and so springs the surprise of her return on us too.[65] Romance, like myth, assures us that there is a pattern in things, and that this can even at times be working for life and good (especially when guided by the force of Nature); but it also

reminds us that the world can be an alien and hostile place with a capacity
to shock us.

SPIRITUALITY: THE FREEDOM OF FORGIVENESS

Romance, then, in these last plays, offers the paradox that life has patterns
of order and harmony within it, and yet that we are also vulnerable in the
face of powers greater than ourselves, whether of good or evil. The continual
intertextuality with scriptural themes of Eden and new life, linked to invocation of "great creating Nature," assures us, on the one hand, that it is possible
for damaged life to be renewed and "redeemed." On the other hand, it leaves
us feeling fragile in the face of mysterious forces we cannot control. In this
context Shakespeare offers a "general spirituality." Such an exposed condition
of humanity calls for the exercise of constant forgiveness. On the one hand,
it is forgiveness that brings order to disorder; and on the other, the power to
forgive is committed to weak human beings. To forgive another is a free act.
No force at work within the universe can compel or arrange a forgiveness or
the repentance it requires. At the end of *The Winter's Tale*, "great creating Nature" has restored his wife and his daughter to Leontes, but his repentance is
all his own, and forgiveness must be Hermione's own. A gap of sixteen years
has been needed for repentance to grow into something real, and when the
statue is unveiled and revealed for who it is, more time has to be given for a
relationship to be remade. Slowly, very slowly the statue stirs to life as Paulina
speaks, and only slowly do the two turn toward each other. Deep emotions
have been stirred in the earlier part of the action that will not be satisfied by a
conventional vision of union. There is no dance or feast as a symbol of reconciliation, as we have it in the early comedies: stress is laid on the individuals
whose lives we have been closely following.

There is an elegiac sobriety as Leontes in the closing lines suggests
that they should retire to a convenient place where they can, at leisure, exchange their experiences "Performed in this wide gap of time, since first / We
were dissever'd" (5.3.144–45). The characters must salvage what they can in
the time left to them. When Hermione moves, we notice that it is only when
Perdita kneels to her that she speaks; within the play she does not actually
speak to Leontes at all, though she embraces him. They will have to learn to
relate to each other again, and time presses in. The mythical pattern of the
romance plot is from loss to reconciliation, but for Shakespeare this is not a
mechanical progression. It requires the human act of forgiveness, and this is
a painful process, not a single act.

Before all the revelations of the last scene happen, Leontes's courtiers do in
fact urge Leontes to complete his penitence and accept the forgiveness which
they think he has surely earned:

Sir, you have done enough, and have performed
A saint-like sorrow. No fault could you make
Which you have not redeemed; indeed paid down
More penitence than done trespass. At the last
Do as the heavens have done, forget your evil;
With them, forgive yourself. (5.1.1–6)

This, however, is an easy appeal to both Prayer Book and scripture, of which
there are several resonances here in the words "penitence," "forget," and the
forgiveness of heaven.[66] The Absolution in Morning Prayer gives the minister the authority "To declare and pronounce to his people being *penitent,* the
absolution and remission of their sinnes," and the first opening sentence of
the service offers the promise, "At what time soeuer a sinner doth repent him
of his sinne from the bottome of his heart; I will put all his wickednesse
out of my *remembrance,* saith the Lord." This is a quotation from Ezekiel
18:21–23, and similar is Jeremiah 31:34, "I will forgive their inequity, and will
remember their sins no more." However, Leontes is not satisfied with these
assurances, and cannot simply "forget" (8). In this, as I intend to show in the
next section, Leontes is truer to the intent of scripture than those who simply
quote it to him. Forgiveness cannot be an easy matter of forgetting, and for
Shakespeare it does not have the nature of a transaction ("paid down")—so
much forgiveness for so much repentance—as his courtiers suppose. Love, as
we have learned from *The Merchant of Venice* and *King Lear,* is not a matter
of commerce.

Leontes explicitly asks forgiveness of both Polixenes and Hermione (5.2.51,
5.3.147), and implicitly, of Perdita, to whom he tells the story of Hermione's
death. The account of this moment by the Steward, when Leontes "bravely
confessed and lamented" (5.2.84), gives some hint of the pain involved in
forgiveness, both asking for it and in granting it, giving and receiving. The
Steward reports that Perdita "did . . . I would fain say bleed tears," and his
own "heart wept blood." Shaheen points to a resonance with the petition
in the Litany, "by thine agony and bloody sweat,"[67] which he notes is itself
based on the account of Jesus's praying in the Garden of Gethsemane: "his
sweat was like drops of blood" (Luke 22:44). The image of bloody tears is
probably, however, a convergence between the Lukan text and the account
of Gethsemane by the author of Hebrews: "[Jesus] did offer up prayers and
supplications, with strong crying and tears" (Heb. 5:7). The margin in the
Geneva Bible at the verse in Hebrews makes this connection, and so brings
together blood and tears: "Christ prayed in the garden where he swet droppes
of blood." In any case, the effect of resonance with these texts is to make clear
that repentance and forgiveness is no kind of merely commercial transaction,
but is deeply and painfully relational.

Shakespeare's working in the blurred area between religious confessions, to which I have many times alluded, means that a spirituality of forgiveness can be developed without being trapped in any particular doctrinal system of penitence and absolution. It has certainly been argued by Richard Wilson that the final scene is strongly colored by Catholic devotional practice, with its veneration of the statue of Hermione like the image of Mary, a saint, or a martyr. He claims that the performance of *The Winter's Tale* in the indoor Blackfriars Theatre had to mean a Catholic context, since the building was a conversion of the former chapter-house of a medieval Dominican priory, and the Gatehouse that led to it was being used in Shakespeare's time as a "command post" of London Catholics. He proposes that Shakespeare thus owned "a notorious centre of Catholic resistance,"[68] and claims that the audience of *The Winter's Tale* would have been largely Catholic in sympathy, welcoming the presentation on stage of forbidden Catholic image veneration.[69] Wilson further finds it significant that the sculptor specifically named in the play, Giulio Romano, was a servant of the Roman Church and had sculpted a famous altar piece of the Virgin Mary in the Santa Maria dell'Anima in Rome.[70] But any Catholic ethos in the scene is being deconstructed by the fact that the statue is not an image at all, but a living person. So Julia Lupton agrees that "Hermione as statue has become a kind of Madonna who bestows her gifts on those who pray in her Roman chapel," but she draws an opposite conclusion from Wilson. The point of the statue scene is that it "stages the visual condition of Catholic image worship, but only as cancelled." Catholic iconography is undercut and "recuperated into art."[71]

Shakespeare is thus providing his audience (of many different sympathies) with the thrill of watching a banned religious ritual,[72] while at the same time having no commitment to it, and defusing it of offense. It is, as Leontes exclaims, "An art / Lawful as eating" (5.3.110–11). I might add that we can find the same deconstruction in the matching piece to Leontes's vision of Hermione, namely Antigonus's dream of Hermione. As with the ghost in *Hamlet*, it can only be authentic if it is a spirit visiting from purgatory. While we believe the apparition to be Hermione, then the play seems to be offering some support for the doctrine, but we discover Hermione is no more a postmortem spirit than Hermione is a statue. While the question of the identity of the ghost is left open in *Hamlet*, it is resolved at the end in *The Winter's Tale*. Nevertheless, purgatory is not being absolutely rejected, since—unlike Hamlet's experience—this is only a dream.

If Catholic features assigned to Sicily are being undermined there, this is also true of Protestant details elsewhere. Knapp argues that these are located in Bohemia, and that Bohemia—as the home of the early Reformer Jan Hus, with its Protestant Reformation dealt with at length by Foxe,[73] and known to be "a centre of Protestant activism at the time"[74]—is placed in opposition to

Sicily. Between them there is "great difference" (1.1.3–4), as Archidamus mysteriously remarks in the opening lines. We can certainly find examples of a Protestant ethos connected with Bohemia: Polixenes is aware of radical Protestant unease about original guilt;[75] there is a psalm-singing Puritan among the sheep-shearers (4.3.44); and Autolycus mocks those who "superstitiously" covet his wares as if they are Catholic religious relics: "as if they had been hallow'd and brought a benediction to the buyer" (4.4.605–7). But Autolycus is a rogue and deceiver himself, and the country is presided over by a king who threatens cruel punishment, unjustly, and determines to suppress love (4.4.430–46). Once again, as in other plays, Shakespeare is taking no sides in the confessional conflict of his time. He is thus not committed to the particular penitential system of any church, to any dogma of how repentance, penance, and pardon connect, or to who has authority to pronounce absolution, all of which were key issues in an age when people lived under fear of final judgment.

Interwoven with a general spirituality of forgiveness is the need for faith, which can be similarly generalized. As we have seen, Paulina calls for faith in her abilities to give the statue life, and behind this appeal is a trace of faith in a more religious sense. But forgiveness also requires a renewal of characters' personal faith in each other, or, as McCoy puts it, the statue scene is "a transition from bad faith to good faith,"[76] from the delusional faith of Leontes in his wife's guilt to his reclaiming of his wife "and the good faith that she embodies."[77] Faith is "the evidence of things which are not seen" (Heb. 11:1), and in the first part of the play Leontes was demanding from everyone a faith in an invisible world that he alone had constructed like God "from nothing" (ex nihilo) and in which he alone could see the guilty actions of the players (1.2.294–312). Now the movement to true sight requires "not divine intervention but only the change of heart that comes with true repentance and renewed love." Seeing clearly what is visible, as in A Midsummer Night's Dream, requires eyes of love. As in that play, the result is also wonder. John Joughin writes of "a spirit that transfigures sense" in the last scene of the play, a sense of the visionary exactly in what belongs to the everyday. The revelation of the "secret" (to use Derrida's word, to which Joughin appeals)[78] lies in "learning to live in the instant," in "stillness and faith and growing in love."[79]

But forgiveness and recovered faith has a tragic dimension to it, and this too is part of Shakespeare's spirituality—the awareness of the encroaching border of death. Reconciliation is not for Shakespeare a stereotyped event, a mere stock-in-trade of myth. Shakespeare is a realist and does not present us with idealized scenes of harmony at the end of his comedies. The charmed circle of the reconciled is usually broken by someone's being excluded and left out in the cold. They remain as a threat to the reconciled, showing that restoration is always incomplete. Alongside them is another, even more fundamental threat: that of passing time and the advent of death. In *As You Like It* the threat of passing time is invoked even in the golden interlude of life in the Forest of Arden: there is, we hear, "no clock in the forest" (3.2.292), but in the end all must succumb to the remorseless pressure of time, which moves us on from role to role on the stage of life until the

> Last scene of all.
> That ends this strange eventful history,
> Is second childishness and mere oblivion,
> *Sans* teeth, *sans* eyes, *sans* taste, *sans* everything (2.7.174–78)

Death is the last enemy, and time leads into his hands. The losses suffered through time can never be compensated for. So it is at the end of *The Winter's Tale*. While Leontes thinks he is still viewing a statue of Hermione, he is disappointed with it in one respect. He exclaims:

> Hermione was not so much wrinkled, nothing
> So aged as this seems. (5.3.27–29)

When Hermione is revealed, Paulina cries, "Go together / You precious winners all," but we are all too aware that it is not exactly a "win-win situation." There has been a sixteen-year companionship of love lost which nothing can replace. New life has now returned to the court and Spring has come again, but sixteen years is a long winter's tale. As she speaks the statue into life, Paulina ominously advises Leontes:

> Do not shun her
> Until you see her die again, for then
> You kill her double. . . .
> When she was young, you wooed her; now in age
> Is she become the suitor? (105–9)

"Until you see her die again" could simply mean "while she is alive," but the phrase reminds us that she *will* inevitably die. This is no resurrection. Paulina herself is certainly not a "winner," since Antigonus, who never returned from his encounter with the bear, was her husband. Leontes urges her now to accept Camillo as a new spouse, but they will have little time left for happiness together; realistically, she calls herself an "old turtle" (dove). The mood of this final scene, for all its joy, is that of Prospero at the end of his drama: "Every third thought shall be my grave."

"Time" appears between the two parts of the play as an emblematic figure from traditional pageant and from new masques presented at court by Ben Jonson and Inigo Jones, the influence of which is apparent in Shakespeare's final romantic comedies.[80] This figure claims that he can leap sixteen years because:

> it is in my power
> To o'erthrow law, and in one self-born hour
> To plant and o'erwhelm custom. (4.1.7–9)

Thus he presents himself as, like the spirit of comedy, overturning the present order. This disturbance and confusion of things, as I have stressed,[81] brings truth to light, and Truth is conventionally the daughter of Time, reflected in his claim here to "unfold error" (2).[82] But this power to "o'erwhelm custom" also refers to the destructive nature of time; with wings fiercely beating, "cormorant, devouring time" (*Love's Labour's Lost*, 1.1.4) overturns not only institutions but life itself. The subtitle of Greene's *Pandosto*, in which Pandosto (Leontes) takes his own life is, aptly, "The Triumph of Time."

Shakespeare then is not presenting an escapist comedy of reconciliation. He knows about the enemy of time; values have been lost due to broken relationships that cannot simply be recovered. Experiences have been spoilt in the past, and in the future time and death press in. When Autolycus quotes the phrase "the life [of the world] to come" from the Nicene Creed, we may admire his insouciant attitude—unlike Hamlet—that he will just "sleep out the thought of it" (4.3.30), but he has nevertheless named the horizon of this earthly life, and we will also be reminded of the religious and poetic convention that daily sleep is an image of a greater unknown. While Autolycus chooses to forget it, the Shepherd is only too aware of the moment when the "priest shovels in dust" (4.4.458), or, according to a rubric in the Burial Service, "earth shall be cavst vpon the body by some standing by."[83]

In several plays we have seen embodied the hope that art might outlast death, but we have also seen that for there to be any confidence in this, love must also be present. Devouring time and even death might be conquered by a human art that truly embodies love. Such a love we see fleshed out in the tableau, or masque, of Hermione passionately embracing Leontes ("she hangs about his neck"), and then laying hands in blessing on the head of her kneeling daughter. This is a parallel to Lear with Cordelia in his arms at the end of *his* play: although Lear is utterly reduced to the "nothing" from which Leontes has been saved, both bear witness to the possibility that love and forgiveness, though weak and vulnerable, can still overcome death when they are fixed in art—in poetry, plays, and pictures. The image and the story will go on as a witness among the living. Whether love can do yet more than this in overturning death is neither affirmed nor denied. It remains a hope on which it is not necessary to pronounce explicitly within Shakespeare's spirituality.

Elsewhere, too, there is the anticipation that time and death can be defeated, in some way, by love. King Lear had demanded in the storm that the thunder should bring apocalypse now on ungrateful man: "Strike flat the thick rotundity o' the world / Crack Nature's mould, all germens spill at once" (3.2.7–8).[84] Using similar language, but in contrast to Lear, Florizel envisages that such an event would only come *in the case of* "the violation of my faith," that is, his faithfulness in love: only then "Let Nature crush the sides o'th' earth together, / And mar the seeds within" (4.4.484–85). Citing Jeremiah 6.22, where the destroyer (Babylon) comes from "the sides of the earth," it is as if Florizel's love is holding the apocalypse back, or perhaps (as Shaheen suggests) that Florizel will persist in his love "even if the earth and the seeds within it (all hope of future life) are destroyed."[85] Perdita offers a matching reflection, asserting that while the ravages of time might take the color from her complexion, it cannot untie "the bond of love" (4.4.579): "I think affliction may subdue the cheek, / But not take in the mind" (582). Here she offers a riposte not only to Camillo in context, but to all like the Duke Orsino who lament in conventional terms, "For women are like roses, whose fair flower / Being once displayed doth fall that very hour."[86] She also shows more hope in face of the ultimate threat of death than Viola, who replies to the Duke: "And so they are. Alas that they are so, / To die even when they to perfection grow."

When we have found the patterns of "great creating Nature," often expressed in myth, we may feel helpless and unable to cope with the powerful forces that confront us. That, Shakespeare shows us, is when we can find our freedom in exercising forgiveness toward each other. When even forgiveness seems to be undermined by loss of time and the threat of death, then our experience of love can be captured in art itself, to make a story that death cannot destroy—such a story as this tale made for winter.

A Theology of Forgiveness and Memory

Living through the space and time of this play, with a sixteen-year gap between an offense which breaks relationships and an event which restores them, the theologian must be impressed by its portrayal of a long process of forgiveness. The play will surely make its impact upon theological texts, "in front" of Shakespeare's own text, by helping to form a theology in which forgiveness is not a transaction ("paid down . . . penitence"), but a journey which requires empathy and pain.[87] This, I suggest, will consequently have an effect upon doctrines of the atonement, which attempt to explore conceptually the forgiveness of human persons by God. I do not mean that the play should be read as an allegory of atonement, but that living in its space will *shape* the doctrine, and that this in turn should have an impact on the human practices of forgiveness.

First, then, the journey of forgiveness. The play represents Leontes as having made a long progress in repentance and penitence; he had vowed every day to visit the chapel where Mamillius and Hermione lie "and tears shed there shall be my recreation" (3.2.237), and it appears he had fulfilled his vow without fail, performing "a saint-like sorrow" (5.1.1–2). What the viewer of the play realizes, at the wondrous moment of disclosure, is that Hermione must have been making a matching journey of emotions over the sixteen years, but on her part of forgiveness. Only this makes sense of her action, tersely reported by Polixenes, that "she embraces him." Living in the play, the theologians will immediately see the point of a phrase about forgiveness, which comes from a book written on the theme by H. R. Mackintosh: "How true it is that in heart and mind the forgiver must set out on voyages of anguish! It is an experience of sacrificial pain, of vicarious suffering."[88]

Forgiveness, writes Mackintosh, is a "shattering experience" for the one who forgives as well as for the one who is forgiven.[89] This is because forgiveness, unlike a mere pardon, seeks to *win the offender back* into relationship. And reconciliation is a costly process because there are resistances to it in the attitude of the person who has offended; the one who sets out to forgive must aim to remove those blockages and restore the relationship. Forgiveness then involves an acceptance which is costly. Forgiveness as an act creating response is bound to be expensive in time and effort, requiring mental and physical anguish. But only if the one to be forgiven experiences the one forgiving as a certain kind of person—empathetic and not judgmental—will he or she be won into reconciliation.

There are likely to be several kinds of resistance to receiving forgiveness in an offender. For the text of *The Winter's Tale* to shape a theology of forgiveness, it is not of course necessary that Leontes should fit into any particular psychological profile, since what has impact is the general experience in the play of the journey involved in forgiveness. But one kind of blockage to forgiveness *might* be seen as exemplified in Leontes's own state of mind, that is anxiety. Paul Tillich explores the sense of not being acceptable, given what has happened; in his fine phrase, we need to gain "the courage to accept that we are accepted." Human life, as a state of anxiety in face of the tensions of our freedom and our conditioning, calls for "the courage to be."[90] These feelings of anxiety may sometimes be due to the experience of a dominating parent; especially, they may have their roots in an implacable and demanding father for whom the child was never good enough, and who has now been internalized as a constant critic, whether or not we give this inner voice the Freudian name of the superego.[91] This fear that we are unacceptable is often directed toward God, created in the image of the Super-Father. The continual ritual of confession may, if we are not careful, simply become a framework for keeping someone in a state of anxiety like this. Confession can be a point of development, but it can also simply be a reinforcement of the harsh feelings that people have toward themselves. Perhaps we can see this syndrome being played out at the beginning of act 5, with the courtiers' unease about Leontes's practices of repentance. Pitcher, in his edition of the play, traces Leontes's apparently arbitrary jealousy in the first part to a regression to childhood in an attempt to deal with anxiety; Leontes, he suggests, "objectifies his fears and frustrations, making a false man-boy of them (the Elizabethans called such images idols)."[92] A similar approach was taken by Trevor Nunn in his "Freudian" production of the play at Stratford in 1969, with opening scene set in a nursery.[93]

But anxiety about being acceptable is only one kind of resistance to accepting forgiveness. Feelings of hostility can also block forgiveness; in what psychotherapists call "split feelings" we locate our own "nasty" feelings in the other, and this makes us even more angry with them.[94] Offenders are resentful at having the offense recalled; they fear blame and so want to justify themselves by blaming the other. They are angry with the one who offers forgiveness, saying (or at least feeling): "How dare you say that you forgive me! What presumption! It's as much your fault as mine." In many people's response to a situation in which forgiveness is offered, there is likely to be a mixture of feelings of anxiety and hostility. This is why forgiveness is a humbling and disturbing gift, requiring a journey of empathy, and it is not at all surprising if it is declined. The offender will only be enticed and enabled to accept forgiveness if he experiences the forgiver as someone who has truly drawn alongside him and feels with him. Forgiveness is a creative act, "calling a fresh situation into being" (Mackintosh).[95]

We notice that traveling the path of forgiveness means that a change takes place in *both* the participants, in the forgiver as much as in the one who is forgiven. For true reconciliation there must be a movement from both sides. Naturally, the offender has to move in sorrow and repentance toward the person he has hurt, but the forgiver also needs to move and experience change within herself, even when she is totally willing to forgive. In human acts of forgiveness this movement is often partly a matter of the one who wants to forgive recognizing that she herself has contributed something to the breach. In situations where an established relationship has been broken—in the family, between friends or colleagues—the forgiver may have been the one mainly injured, but in human relationships no one is an entirely "innocent party." So the forgiver also needs to be forgiven, and must move in her attitude to accept this. However, there is another kind of "change" in approach to the other, which belongs to the act of empathy itself. Forestalling our discussion to come, we may find this is also appropriate for God, who is perfect in relationships, as we are not. Borrowing Mackintosh's phrase, we can say that the forgiver must "set out on voyages of anguish"; she must make an agonizing and costly journey in experience, absorbing the anger and hostility of the other.

Through this process the forgiver is actually discovering how to prompt the offender to make his or her own painful journey of awareness, and so to win the offender back into relationship. Through identification with the feelings of the other, she is learning how to enable the other to accept her forgiveness. The inner "change" the forgiver undergoes is thus an empathetic entering into the other's life, and her approach to him is shaped by this experience. Participation in the other has a transformative effect, empowering him to overcome obstructions that lie in the path toward restoration. Returning to the statue scene of *The Winter's Tale*, Stanley Cavell has suggested that its impact depends on the participation both by Leontes onstage and by the audience offstage. Paulina's injunction, "it is required you do awake your faith," can be understood as asking the members of this audience to become actively engaged in this moment of reconciliation: "a transformation is being asked of the audience of a play, perhaps a claim that we are no longer spectators, but . . . participants."[96]

For the theologian, the experience of the journey of forgiveness in this play does not only alert us to the dynamics of forgiveness in everyday life, but will have an effect on the doctrine that lies at the heart of Christian faith—the atonement, or the reconciliation of human beings with God and each other through the death and resurrection of Christ, to which Shakespeare alludes at two points.[97] Other plays may enable the theologian to understand the passion of Christ as a tragicomedy; this one directs our attention to the purpose of the drama. The experience of forgiveness in human relationships helps us to interpret God's great offer of forgiveness to human beings, creating a new situation universally. This is not simply because human forgiveness is an appropriate *analogy* for divine forgiveness; in accord with the theology of participation in the triune God I have developed earlier, the forgiveness of God through Christ is actually *known* through human relations. The rhythm of human forgiving is embraced within the rhythm of God's forgiveness, and the two are inseparable. Once alerted to the human "journey" of forgiveness, by—for instance—living in the world of *The Winter's Tale*, the theologian must reject theories of atonement which are based on any kind of transaction, or which take the form of a merely legal pardon without the transforming dynamic of relations.

In differing ways, theology of atonement in the Western church has often taken the form of a legal transaction or even commercial arrangement. Anselm in the Middle Ages understood the death of Christ as settling a debt; by submission to death, Christ makes an infinite payment to God of the honor which humankind owes to God but had failed to pay. While transactional, this had the potential for a more relational understanding since it arose in the context of a monastic life of prayer and devotion. However, Calvin understood the atonement not as a satisfaction of the "honor" of God, but as the satisfaction of the law of God. What was "paid" down (*Winter's Tale*, 5.1.4) by Christ was not only honor, but punishment in place of human condemnation.[98] While both theories picked up language from the New Testament, Anselm and Calvin produced a whole mechanism from fragmentary parts.[99] The early church did not, in fact, regard the cross of Christ as either vicarious payment of honor or substitutionary punishment, while very early on the idea of God's forgiveness of sins *did* appear as an explanation for the puzzling and shocking event which befell Christ (Acts 2:38).

The impact of *The Winter's Tale* and other plays on the texts of theology should be to prompt theologians to discard transactional theories and to unfold the implications of the assertion that the life, death, and resurrection of Christ focuses God's long journey of forgiveness. It may be suggested that while God has always been voyaging into the world to share human life, nowhere is God seen as penetrating more deeply into creation than here. The story of the tragic hero,[100] Christ, is of one who, though himself living in tune with God's mind, consents to participate in the alienation which is the lot of a humankind which has lost communion with God. This pattern of identification is characteristic of the whole ministry of Jesus, as he offers God's forgiveness of sins and acceptance into the coming kingdom of God.[101] Then in death Christ identifies himself with human beings at the lowest point of their existence, immersed into utter forsakenness. The various words of Christ from the cross which the Evangelists place in their narratives interpret the event: the plea for forgiveness of others ("Father forgive them") brings out the meaning of the cry "My God why have you forsaken me?"[102] since forgiveness is nothing less than a voyage into the dark void of another's guilty life.

So the Apostle Paul affirms that Christ shares human death so that we might rise to new life with him (Rom. 6:1–11). When we analyze the act of forgiveness, we find the *power* of this participation; the forgiver enters the experience of the guilty, identifying with their predicament, in order to create change in them and draw them into reconciliation. Tillich rightly sees this journey of empathy as lying at the heart of atonement, when he writes: "The suffering of God, *universally and in the Christ*, is the power which overcomes creaturely self-destruction by participation and transformation."[103] So the cross brings all humankind into a journey of awareness of its condition, bringing clearly out into the open the vicious nature of human evil, and the end to which it leads. As Hegel put it, "God has died, God is dead: this is the most frightful of all thoughts . . . that negation itself is found in God . . . the human, the finite, the fragile, the weak, the negative, are moments of the divine."[104] This is what it looks like for people to sin against their neighbors, to crucify love. The initiative Christ takes in identifying with them in his life and death calls for a response; empathy becomes judgment. The life and death of Jesus thus reveals and focuses in one historical moment the journey of creative suffering in forgiveness, the process that always characterizes God's engagement with the world.

Atonement is about a change in God making change in us, but the divine change is not from wrath to redemption (as in transactional theories) but is a continual newness of experience in the life of the triune God.[105] We experience God as the one who empathizes with us, and so we are enabled both to face up to judgment and to acceptance. The conditioning of God by the world creates a new condition for human response, and opens up the future. As Karl Barth perceives, celebrating the radical freedom of God as Lord: "According to the biblical testimony, God has the prerogative to be free without being limited by His freedom from external conditioning, free also with regard to His freedom. . . . God must not only be unconditioned but, in the absoluteness in which He sets up this fellowship [with humankind], *He can and will also be conditioned*."[106] Such an understanding of the freedom of God makes it quite coherent to say that God is changed through suffering with the world, and that this contributes to the glory and completeness of God's own being.

This portrayal of the divine forgiveness envisages what Edward Farley calls a "merger of empathies,"[107] an interaction of journeys of experience: those taken by God, by Jesus of Nazareth, and by ourselves. Only a doctrine of God which is participatory, and thus—I suggest—triune, can properly express this. The perichoresis, or interweaving of relations in God, is like inner journeyings of love; these take the form of voyages of forgiveness, not because there needs to be forgiveness within God's own self, but because they are always generously open to include human relationships, and are open to being conditioned and even hurt by them. Thus they are journeys of forgiveness into the world which is in God. This means that wherever there are movements of empathy between human persons, these are leaning upon perfect empathetic movements which are there already before them. Using trinitarian symbols, we may describe these movements as being like the entering of a father into the feelings of a son, or of a daughter into the feelings of a mother, and a continual expanding of this shared experience through a spirit of empathy which is always provoking new depths of fellow-feeling. Unlike our faltering steps into the life of another, the Christian claim is that the journey of forgiveness of Jesus which was his life's journey can be *exactly* mapped onto the journeys of God. In consequence, we are as dependent upon his journey at one particular moment in history as we are upon the eternal currents of love in God.

Such an understanding of forgiveness, both human and divine, is not an act of forgetting. Forgiveness must be a voyage of memory, a calling to mind. Memory is subversive, calling the present situation into question. This theme has been taken up by a number of feminist theologians, including Mary Grey.[108] As a woman theologian, she feels keenly that women have always been expected to be the forgivers in family and society, and that this has been taken to mean a passive function, a self-denying victim role. But there can never be a restoring of relations, she believes, unless women take an active role of self-affirmation. Central to this movement for reconciliation is memory; this is "dangerous memory" (in the phrase of Jean-Baptist Metz),[109] a memory which brings judgment and awakens us to the truth, particularly when it is memory of the suffering, exclusion, oppression, and degradation of women.

Paulina in *The Winter's Tale* stands for this kind of remembering, when others around Leontes urge him to moderate his endless repentance by forgetting (5.1.5–6).[110] When Leontes has the fantastic thought that the "sainted spirit" of Hermione might animate her corpse in order to rebuke him, Paulina retorts:

> Were I the ghost that walked, I'd bid you mark
> Her eye, and tell me for what dull part in't
> You chose her. Then I'd shriek that even your ears
> Should rift to hear me, and the words that followed
> Should be: "Remember mine." (63–67)

In *Hamlet* the ghost commands, "remember me," and here Hermione in the *persona* of a ghost as mediated by Paulina bids, "remember my eyes [mine]." In the case of *Hamlet*, the stage-ghost is provoking the audience to ask themselves how they can maintain loving relations across the generations, in face of the collapse of belief in purgatory;[111] here the imagined ghost of Hermione also raises an emotional question for an audience which is being called to participate and not just to observe—is there a need to remember offenses which they have committed against love, or in which they have been the victims, where forgetfulness is hindering forgiveness? Although

Paulina has particular reasons for not wanting Leontes to forget Hermione, namely to prevent thoughts of remarriage, the principle stands out of holding "memory ... in honour" (49–50).

The theologian Miroslav Volf argues that there is nevertheless a place for forgetting in forgiveness. In his book *The End of Memory* he urges that if we are to remember in order to forgive, rather than to increase a cycle of violence, then we must remember truthfully,[112] but after that to forget. After right remembering, repentance of the offender and the achievement of reconciliation between offender and victim, then (and only then) the wrong can be allowed to slip from mind. Here Volf refers to Kierkegaard's reflection in his *Works of Love* on biblical metaphors for the forgiveness God offers, to be taken as a model for human forgiving: these are the images of "hiding" sin,[113] "blotting out" sin[114] or erasing it, and "putting it behind one's back."[115] We have seen that Leontes's courtiers allude implicitly to such texts in urging Leontes to forget: "Do as the heavens have done, forget" (5.1.5–6). Volf's reading of Kierkegaard is that the forgetting involved in forgiving is equivalent to a "not-coming-to mind," or a "non-remembrance." The forgiver has *known* the offense but allows it not to rise to consciousness, or permits it to fall back into nothing.[116] There is a clear sequence: truthful remembering, followed by an eternal slipping from memory. Indeed, Volf's proposal is that the forgetting of the wrong happens essentially in eternity; it takes place in a world of perfect love in a future new creation to be brought by God alone. He emphasizes that the forgetting which he commends is a "not-coming-to-mind of wrongs suffered *after* justice has been served and *after* entrance into a secure world of perfect love."[117]

Volf's strict binding together of remembering and forgetting in forgiveness, at least in an eschatological hope, is underlined by two theological reasons he offers for forgetting (in addition to pastoral concerns about dependence and humiliation). First, he asserts that forgetting is a necessary alternative to redeeming the past.[118] There are at least *parts* of the past that cannot be redeemed, and so must be forgotten. There are experiences of trauma that "stubbornly refuse to be integrated into a meaningful whole"; our whole past does not need to be rendered meaningful in order to be redeemed, and so aspects of it that are dissonant simply need to be forgotten.[119] Second, the forgetting of wrongdoing is God's consigning of evil to its proper place—nothingness. Echoing the words of Kierkegaard that "to forget is to take back into nothingness," and Karl Barth's insistence that God's word consigns *das Nichtige* "to the past and to oblivion,"[120] Volf proposes that evil would be triumphant if it remained in the memory for eternity, "casting its dark shadow over the world to come."[121] Both arguments require that God, as well as created persons, must forget.

However, as Stanley Hauerwas points out in opposing Volf's first argument, a denial that the past (or parts of it) can be redeemed implies an understanding of consummation that that replaces time with a nontemporal eternity, and this is not unquestionable:[122]

> God remembers because if God does not remember then God is not the timeful God we find in Israel and the cross and the resurrection of Christ. . . . The problem with Volf's non-remembering is . . . what it implies about God's life. God's eternity is . . . not the simple contradiction of time. . . . God makes possible all the time in the world to make our time, our memories, redeemed. Our time can be redeemed because time has been redeemed by Christ. That is why we do not need to deny our memories, shaped as they are by sin, but rather why we can trust memories to be transformed by forgiveness and reconciliation.[123]

To this affirmation that, given the "duration" of eternity (a term of Karl Barth's),[124] all memories can be redeemed, we should add the observation that for events to be redeemed is not necessarily equivalent to their becoming "meaningful," at least in the sense of "finding some good that has come out of them" or contributing to an "overall harmony," as Volf assumes.[125] There is room for dissonance and disharmonious notes within a redeemed existence, as there is a place for discord within music.[126] We discover this from living through the tragicomedies of Shakespeare, in which the ending is never a simplistic harmony. Forgetting is not the only way of dealing with disturbance, and we may suppose that it is a mark of the humility of God to allow for unassimilated elements within the whole; in God's redemption, they will however cease to injure us or undermine our joy.

The second argument, that any memory of wrongdoing must yield the final victory to evil, is reminiscent of the argument that God cannot suffer as this would mean an eternal suffering and so an everlasting persistence of evil. We may venture to say again that it is the humility of God, in the divine tragicomedy, to allow the co-creative freedom of the universe to leave its marks on God's blissful life;[127] poetically, as the Seer of the Apocalypse envisions it, the Lamb slain before the foundation of the world carries wounds while enthroned at the right hand of God (Rev. 5:6). The question is not whether there is a memory of evil but whether this has been overcome and transformed. If so, then the power of evil, *das Nichtige*, has indeed been consigned to oblivion.

But what of the biblical texts in which God promises not to "remember" sin?[128] They do not, in fact, carry the weight in favor of mere forgetting that Leontes's courtiers, Kierkegaard and Volf suppose they do. The Hebrew word for "remember" (*zakar*) can also mean "to act," so that God is promising not to act as the sin deserves. The point is that God does not "remember" in the sense of holding sin against human beings, bringing it up against them, or carrying out penalties. This is indeed the effect of the metaphors of "hiding," "blotting," and "putting behind one's back." It is consonant with reading scripture as a whole to think of forgiveness as a mutual journey which never entirely ends, and so always includes remembering; this is also the impression we gain when we hear the ending of *The Winter's Tale*, where Leontes commands:

> Lead us from hence, where we may leisurely
> Each one demand and answer to his part
> Performed in this wide gap of time since first
> We were dissevered.

If the "dissevering" is to be overcome in forgiveness, there must be a "leisurely" process of retrieving, with mutual sympathy, what has been done during the passing of long time. Truly. Shakespeare's spirituality is explicitly directed to this life, while I have been prompted by Volf to think about the place of remembering in a life beyond death, which can only be hoped for in imaginative images. However, Shakespeare's spirituality is also open-ended, allowing the reader-viewer to imagine other future possibilities, "more things"; what matters is that such imaginings are consistent with what we experience in this present life, and this includes the appeal "Remember mine!"

A discussion about forgiveness, called "Difficult Forgiveness," takes place as an epilogue—of some fifty pages—to Ricoeur's massive study *Memory, History and Forgetting*. Ricoeur's theme in his main text is the presence of the past, in a mode where the event is both absent and present in the consciousness, building the narrative identity of persons or their continuity within a story. In all this, he maintains, "forgetting and forgiveness, separately and together, designate the horizon of our entire investigation."[129] In his epilogue he finds that forgiveness requires the act of memory, which is so often "blocked" and "manipulated" but which can be healed through the invoking and sharing of memories with others.[130] In his main text, "forgetting" nevertheless occupies a third of the discussion, and he finds it to be of two kinds that we might identify as active and passive. Actively, forgetting is a deliberate erasing of the traces of the past. Passively, it is a "forgetting held in reserve," where impressions of the past remain in the mind but are normally inaccessible and unavailable.[131] They can, however, be recovered through a process of recognition, and relived, wrestled away from oblivion. This passive kind provides us with a motivation to create history as a struggle *against* forgetting; the sense that there are gaps in the account, aspects omitted or lost to sight, drives us to uncover what has been hidden and forgotten. On the other hand, active erasure of memory can be an abuse, imposing a favored view of history; after all, there is a "duty to remember," to keep alive the memory of the suffering of victims, and active forgetting—even in the form of an amnesty—can suppress this.

But Ricoeur wants to find a valid place for active forgetting. While forgiveness involves remembering, active forgetting can be the "education of memory." The best use of this kind of forgetting, he suggests, is in the construction of plots for imaginative narratives (as distinct from the writing of history) which shape our personal or social identity.[132] We cannot tell a story without eliminating or dropping some important events, although we must always be open to the way that other people recount their own stories, "telling otherwise." Forgetting for the sake of making a story can also overcome two dangerous psychological tendencies to which Freud alerts us—an obsessive repetition or commemoration of the past which blocks a movement into the future, and a melancholia which paralyzes us and prevents a proper "work of mourning" what is lost.[133]

We might see *The Winter's Tale* as such a story, in which Shakespeare is telling a tale which emerges from the cultural experience of his England, a place of diverse religious confessions. It is a tale where there is a memory of images, saints, and communion with the dead, but in which much is "forgotten" and omitted within the framework of the myth. The story bears witness, however, to the *need* to remember ("remember mine!") in everyday life if forgiveness is truly to be a mutual journey of empathy, and this is the impact that the play can still make on the writing of theology today. Ricoeur ends his book rather as Shakespeare ends his play, Leontes appealing to a "leisurely" telling and retelling of their stories, and Ricoeur remarking that "writing a life is another story. Incompletion." Both thus look forward to "more things in heaven and earth." There is an excess in human life that has been evoked in this play through a complex intertextuality which portrays mysterious power, not only disturbing us but promising renewal.

10

The Tempest and the Risks of Forgiveness

*

IN PETER Greenaway's film version of *The Tempest*, named *Prospero's Books* (1991),[1] for most of the drama Prospero himself speaks the lines of *all* the characters, at the same time as writing them in a "Book of Dialogues" which is to become the text of the play. Thus he summons the characters into being. While Shakespeare's Prospero produces only the storm and other illusions that befall the inhabitants and travelers on the island, Greenaway more evidently merges the roles of magus *in* the text and writer *of* the text: with the possible exceptions of Ariel and Caliban, the world of the island and its people is actually created by Prospero. As Greenaway explains his intention: "Prospero plans a drama to right the wrongs done to him. He invents characters to flesh out his imaginary fantasy to steer his enemies into his power, writes their dialogue, and having written it, he speaks the lines aloud, shaping the characters so powerfully through the words that they are conjured before us."[2]

Greenaway's portrayal of Prospero as "prime originator"[3] seems suitable for a late-modern world aware of logocentrism,[4] and is an exaggerated version of Shakespeare's Prospero, who controls and manipulates his small world through his magic arts. Shakespeare's own picture of Prospero is his ingenious solution, as a dramatist, to the theatrical problem of the final Romances to which I drew attention in the previous chapter. The question is how to combine the remorseless and inevitable patterns of myth that characterize romance, with the psychological realism of tragicomedy.[5] It is simply the case that lost children will be found, that shipwrecks will prove a blessing in the end, that lovers will be reunited, that riddles will be solved, and the wicked will either be punished or restored. Yet these events are being endured and promoted by people who are recognizable to the audience as being like themselves, living the kind of daily lives they live. So behind the theatrical and artistic problem, there is a spiritual issue: how are the members of the audience, living through their own tragicomedy, to face the hostile forces of existence before which they feel vulnerable?

In *The Winter's Tale*, as we have seen, Shakespeare resolves the technical, dramatic issue by invoking the guiding hand of "great creating Nature," which can be embodied in human persons (like Perdita and Paulina), and which is integrated in some way with human art and culture. An intertextuality with scriptural and theology builds up belief in "great Nature" through a series of biblical images about Eden and new birth, holding myth and domestic realism together, and offering the basis for a spirituality in which forgiveness is central. In *The Tempest* Shakespeare offers a different, and altogether neater, resolution to the technical problem: the romantic and tragicomic aspects are held together by one person, a magician who is in total control of the world of the play, at least as regards physical and external realities. This appears even more convincing as a solution since the play exhibits the classical unities[6] of action, place, and time—one story happening within the space of six hours of one day in one scene, a small island—unlike Shakespeare's wilful abandonment of any pretense at the unities in the sixteen-year span of *The Winter's Tale*. Intertextual resonances with scripture and theology, we shall see, are used in this play to build up a tension between the elemental forces which inhabit myth on the one hand and, on the other, a human method of coping with them, in the person of Prospero with his arts. The play makes clear, however, that the answer to the spiritual question of vulnerability is not the practice of theurgy, and in a surprising way Shakespeare finally concludes that even the theatrical solution is to be found wanting under the perspective of eternity. All this can have an impact on theology "in front of the text," and like *The Winter's Tale*, this is a fantasy which is far from mere escapism.

A Tempest under Control

True to its title, the play opens with a tempest—a storm at sea, reminiscent of accounts from a voyage of settlers to Virginia, when their flagship was wrecked off the coast of one of the islands of Bermuda in July 1609.[7] Several accounts of the wreck, and the eventual completion of the journey by the company in two new boats they had built, led by the new governor of the Virginia Plantation, Sir Thomas Gates, appeared in England in 1610. It seems that Shakespeare read at least some of the reports, and that they were the key momentum for the writing of *The Tempest*.[8] Here, a ship is being wrecked on the rocky shore of an island. The ship carries a list of royal passengers: there are Alonso, the king of Naples, his brother Sebastian and his son Ferdinand; there is also Antonio, the Duke of Milan, and various assorted nobles. We watch the ship break up under the force of the wind and the pounding of the waves, and the scene ends with the cry, "we split, we split," as the ship drifts onto the rocks. But as the scene shifts to a cave on the island, we discover that we as the audience have been sharing in an illusion with the characters onstage; meeting Prospero and his daughter, Miranda, we discover that the storm has in fact been created Prospero's magic arts, as he reassures his anxious daughter, "tell your piteous heart / There's no harm done" (1.2.12–13).

The magician explains that he has made this storm in order to bring his enemies into his power. He invites Miranda for the first time to look into "the dark backward and abysm of time" (1.2.50). Twelve years before he had been the rightful Duke of Milan but had been overthrown by his brother Antonio, in a plot assisted by Alonso, the king of Naples—the same Alonso and Antonio who are now caught in his storm. He and his young daughter, Miranda, had been forced into a small and leaky boat ("a rotten carcass . . . the very rats / Instinctively [had] quit it" [1.2.146–48]) and cast onto the open sea to drown. A faithful lord, Gonzalo, had covertly provided the boat with necessary supplies and—most significantly—Prospero's books of magic, which had enabled him to exercise his magical skills when washed ashore on this small island, and thus to become its lord and master. The only inhabitants on the island had been Caliban and Ariel—the first a savage, partly human monster, son of a cruel witch, Sycorax, who had previously ruled the island, and the second a spirit of the air who had displeased her and whom she had left imprisoned by magic in a pine tree when she died. Prospero had freed Ariel, who now serves him, and he has made Caliban his unwilling slave after Caliban tried to rape Miranda and "people the island with Calibans" (1.2.351–52).[9]

Such is the story so far, as Prospero tells it to Miranda and to us. By his magic Prospero has kept every sailor and passenger safe in the storm, and the ship too. But they are all scattered in different places about the island. Ferdinand, the son of King Alonso, thinks he is the only survivor and is shortly to turn up at Prospero's cave to meet him and—more importantly—to meet Miranda. The party of royals and nobles has been wrecked elsewhere on the island, and Alonso is full of grief, thinking that Ferdinand is drowned. By his magic Prospero has complete control of this island and its visitors. They can do him no harm, as once they could in Milan. Through his magic arts, during the next six hours Prospero leads his enemies a merry dance all over the island; he exhausts them, bewilders them, haunts them, and enchants them. Like all the last Romances that Shakespeare wrote, this play is about loss and reconciliation. It begins with loss—Prospero's loss of his kingdom; Milan's loss of Miranda, the royal child and heir; Alonso's apparent loss of Ferdinand; and Ferdinand's loss of his father. It ends, like the other plays, in reconciliation: Prospero is to forgive his enemies, get his dukedom back, and leave the island to return to Milan; Alonso and Ferdinand are to be reunited; Ferdinand is to marry Miranda, uniting Milan to Naples in a stronger bond than treachery.

Now, we know from the very beginning that nothing is going to go wrong with Prospero's plans to get his dukedom back. He is absolute lord of this island; he is in control, and no power can withstand him in the space of the island. We, the observers, are certain of this because we have seen a fearsome tempest in the very first scene, and then discovered immediately that it has been stage-managed by Prospero; Ariel was his stage manager, moving the scenery about in a theater of cruelty. Shakespeare employs a series of biblical references throughout the play to assure us of Prospero's mastery of the situation, centering on an association of Prospero with the story of Christ. This must not be taken to mean that Prospero is portrayed as a "Christ-figure," but that he is endowed with powers that the audience would recognize as being attributed to Christ in scripture; in fact, there is a distinct ambiguity about whether Prospero's assumption of these powers through magic is admirable or presumptuous, although he is presented as at least relatively virtuous, compared with his enemies. He shares, for instance, a power over the natural elements with the Christ of the Gospels. We have the first hint of this in the middle of the storm, when the Boatswain sarcastically bids the good, though garrulous, Gonzalo: "If you can command these elements to silence and work the peace of the present, we will not handle a rope more. Use your authority!" (1.1.21–23). He is being asked if he has the authority of Christ, who "rebuked the wind, and said unto the sea, Peace, and be still" (Mark 4:39; cf. Luke 8:24). Clearly, Gonzalo does not have this power, but we are shortly to move our gaze to see Prospero, who does. He assures Miranda that all are safe, with the words:

> there is no soul
> No, not so much perdition as an hair,
> Betid to any creature in the vessel (1.2.29–31)

Ariel in turn assures Prospero that he has carried out his instructions precisely, and so:

> Not a hair perish'd;
> On their sustaining garments not a blemish,
> But fresher than before. (1.2.217–19)

There is a catena of allusions to scripture in these two passages, clustering around the word "hair."[10] In the first place there are the words of Jesus to

his disciples, which Prospero is taking on his own lips, that at a time of severe persecution: "there shall not one hair of your heads perish. By your patience possess your souls" (Luke 21:18). Perhaps the story of the storm on the
sea of Galilee is still resonating here as well, when the disciples ask, "carest
thou not that we perish?" (Mark 4:38; cf. Luke 8:24). Then there is the reference to "hair" in Paul's reassuring words during the shipwreck recorded in
Acts 27:34: "There shall not an hair fall from the head of any of you." Luke
is the author of this passage, as well as the references to "perishing" in
Luke 8:24 and 21:18, and it may well be that he is modeling Paul's behavior
in the shipwreck on the story of Jesus on the stormy sea in his Gospel. Both
Luke 21:18 and Acts 27:34 are in passages set in the Prayer Book for Advent,[11]
at about the time when Shakespeare must have been beginning his writing of
The Tempest in 1610. A final allusion in the "hair" cluster is from the story
of Shadrach, Meshach, and Abednego, who were thrown into a fiery furnace
by King Nebuchadnezzar; according to Daniel 3:27, "Not an hair of their
head was burnt, neither was their coats changed, nor any smell of fire came
upon them." Ariel's words are "on their sustaining garments not a blemish,"
and the expected "blemishing" is most likely to be by fire, as in the Daniel
story. Ariel had produced "St. Elmo's fire," or discharges of static electricity
during the shipwreck ("in every cabin / I flamed amazement. Sometimes I'd
divide / And burn in many places," 1.2.197–99), and Shakespeare seems to
have culled this detail of the "sea-fire" from William Strachey's report of the
wreck off Bermuda.[12] The story of the fiery furnace also had a Christological
reference for exegetes from the Patristic period onward, since the account
portrays Nebuchadnezzar as being astonished to see a fourth figure in the
furnace, "and the form of the fourth was like the son of God" (Dan. 3:25), this
figure sometimes being taken to refer to Christ.[13]

　　While Shakespeare's busy imagination no doubt produced this catena of
allusions, triggered by the term "hair" in one or other of these passages that
he recalled or had recently heard read, there is also a Christological connection between them, as I have suggested. It is not surprising that Ariel thus
greets Prospero with, "All hail, great master," as Judas greeted Christ ("Hail
master": Bishops' Bible, Matt. 26:49). The exact phrase "all hail" is not in any
English versions of the Bible, but as Shaheen notes, it has resonances with
Judas's greeting of Christ with "All Hayll" in a York mystery play.[14] Ariel's
greeting of Prospero thus has an ominous ring to it, with a warning that he
too might be a betrayer, given half a chance; this is a hint I intend to expand
on later. Toward the end of the play, when Prospero reveals that he knows
about the plot between Antonio and Sebastian to kill Alonso, Sebastian associates Prospero with Christ when he exclaims, "The devil speaks in him"
(5.1.128), recalling the Pharisees' accusation that Jesus "has a demon,"[15] as

well as echoing the Gospel presentations of the demons speaking the truth through those they possess (Mark 1:34). In Prospero's valedictory speech he makes the association with Christ himself when recalling his past powers over the natural order, claiming that:

> graves at my command
> Have waked their sleepers, ope'd, and let 'em forth
> By my so potent art. (5.1.48–50)

The major influence on this whole speech seems to be Medea's invocation of Hecate in Ovid's *Metamorphoses*, book 7, and for these particular words the parallel phrase is often noted, "I call up dead men from their graves" (*manesque exire sepulcris*), which would imply what Renaissance thinkers regarded as black magic.[16] However, there is a closer parallel with words of the Gospel about Jesus's power over the state of death. Shaheen thinks there may be echoes of Matthew 27:52–53, "And the graves did open themselves, and many bodies of the Saints which slept, arose, and came out of the graves," especially since Shakespeare refers to that passage elsewhere.[17] This could be understood as the power of Christ over nature, insofar as the evangelist seems to think that it is the event of his death, disturbing the whole cosmos, that causes the graves to open. This would be in accord with Gospel stories of Jesus's restoring individuals from death,[18] and the notable episode of the raising of Lazarus in the Fourth Gospel, when Jesus commanded "Come forth!" (John 11:43)—compare here, "let 'em forth." I suggest that another relevant Gospel passage, therefore, and one in which Jesus like Prospero actually claims authority over death, is John 5:25–29:

> Verily, verily, I say unto you, the hour shall come, and now is, when the dead shall hear the voice of the Son of God: and they that hear it, shall live. For the Father . . . hath given him power also to execute judgement, in that he is the Son of Man. Marvel not at this: for the hour shall come in the which all that are in the graves, shall hear his voice. And they shall come forth, that have done good, unto the resurrection of life: but they that have done evil, unto the resurrection of condemnation.

This Johannine passage also strikes the notes of "the hour" and "judgement," which indicate another characteristic of Christ transferred to Prospero: he is the judge, and his hour for judgment has come. "At this hour," exults Prospero, "lies at my mercy all my enemies" (4.1.262), and Ariel reminds him that "On the sixth hour . . . / You said our work should cease." While this relates to the keeping of the unity of time in a drama, it also evokes God's ending of the original work of creation on the sixth day, and so alludes to the judgment that comes at the end of the present eon of time during which God is still continuously at work:

> And therefore the Jews did persecute Jesus, & sought to slay him, because he had done these things on the Sabbath day. But Jesus answered them, My Father worketh hitherto, and I work. (John 5:17)

> I must work the works of him that sent me, while it is day: the night cometh, when no man can work. (John 9:4)

Christ is presented in the Fourth Gospel as awaiting his "hour" for passion and for glorification,[19] when the end-of-the-world judgment would erupt into this present life in a "realized eschatology."[20] So Prospero acts as the judge in his little world, bringing his enemies to face the truth of their actions in a kind of last judgment, even though a final judgment still awaits in the future (4.1.153–55; see further below). Prospero's judgment of the wrongdoers is to be moderated by "a touch, a feeling / Of their afflictions" (5.1.21–22), alluding to the way that Christ is "touched by the feeling of our infirmities" (Heb. 4:15).

The derivation of Prospero's whole speech of farewell, and especially the lines beginning "Graves at my command," from Medea's invocation, gives the signal that no clear distinction can be drawn between theurgy and goety, between attempting to enlist the energies and relations of nature sympathetically, and the attempt to disorder them for wicked purposes.[21] If Prospero is to have any future as a ruling Duke of Milan—and perhaps if Shakespeare is to remain in favor with James I[22]—then both must be renounced. However, this renunciation of magic does not mean there can be no allusions to the words and actions of Christ in Prospero's claims and behavior. Further, his eventual renunciation could be seen as the abandoning of pretensions to be like Christ, and an end to any usurping what properly belongs to Christ.

THE POWER OF JUDGMENT

The picture of Prospero as final judge in his own "hour" is supported by several allusions to an Old Testament text about the judgment of God on "the *day* of the Lord." This too is Christological, to the extent that Christ is presented as executing God's judgment assigned to him by his Father (John 5:27). The text in question, Isaiah 29, is one appropriately set by the Prayer Book to be read in Advent, along with the other texts mentioned above. Ann Pasternak Slater is probably too exact in calculating that Shakespeare heard it read during the morning service of 8 December 1610, shortly after he had read the tracts on the recent voyage to Bermuda,[23] but there are verbal similarities between *The Tempest* and this passage which describes a "tempest" sent by God (Isaiah 29:6). The most obvious allusion is to the word "Ariel" in Isaiah 29:1–7, where it stands as a name for the city of Jerusalem. Shaheen judges that "the context in which Ariel appears in Isaiah 29 hardly suits the Ariel of the play," but he does not notice that there is an important difference between the place of "Ariel" in verses 1–4 of Isaiah 29, which admittedly does not fit well, and in verses 5–10, where it *does* fit into the spirit Ariel's role of bringing judgment on the wicked in the play itself. Much depends on the impression that hearers or readers of the passage take away with them.

The name "Ariel" does not actually appear in the main text of the Geneva Bible, where the relevant word is "altar": "Ah altar, altar of the city that David dwelt in: add year unto year: let them kill lambs, but I will bring the altar into distress, and there shall be heaviness and sorrow, and it shall be unto me like an altar" (Isaiah 29:1–2). However, the Bishops' Bible, which Shakespeare would have heard read in church, *does* contain the name "Ariel" in the main text: "Wo unto thee O Ariel Ariel, thou city that David dwelt in: Go on from year to year, and let the lambs be slain. I will lay siege unto Ariel, so that there shall be heaviness and sorrow in it: and it shall be unto me even an altar of slaughter." The name "Ariel" also appears in the marginal note in the Geneva Bible, explaining that "the Ebrew word, Ariel, signifieth the lyon of God, & figureth the altar because the altar served to deuoure the sacrifice which was offered to God." The Geneva translators thus understand "Ariel" to mean "lion of God," used metaphorically of an altar because the sacrifice was consumed by fire, as prey is consumed by a lion. Modern philology now tends to discount the meaning "lion of God" altogether and simply finds the meaning to be "altar hearth."[24] But in any case, the altar in Jerusalem, and so by extension the whole city, lies under the judgment of God, and the prophet warns that God will conduct a theophanic holy war against the city to punish it, making it an altar upon which the population will be immolated. However much they sacrifice to God ("let the lambs be slain"), God will "lay siege" to Jerusalem by aiding the besieging foreign army, which at this time in the early eighth century BC probably refers to a threatened attack by Assyria.

But in verse 5 there is a dramatic change in tone: the "multitude of strangers" and "multitude of strong men" who are attacking the city "shall be like small dust" and shall be driven away like chaff, because now God will fight against them on behalf of Jerusalem (Ariel): "Thou shalt be visited of the Lord of hosts with thunder, and shaking, and a great noise, a whirlwind, and a tempest, and a flame of devouring fire. And the multitude of all the nations that fight against the altar [Bishops' Bible: "that fight against Ariel"] shall be as a dream or vision by night." Those who fight against Ariel now suffer the judgment of God, in tempest and fire, just as the "strangers" in the ship suffer when they try to resist the actions of Shakespeare's Ariel. It is true that Ariel is presented in the play as a more active scourge of judgment than in Isaiah 29, but the picture in Isaiah is also that of the city itself becoming an agent of God's judgment against the foreign armies, in line with the royal ideology of Zion. In terms of the composition of the Isaianic text, an oracle of judgment against Jerusalem has been converted into an oracle of promise; this was possibly a later redaction in light of the sudden lifting of the siege of the Assyrian army against Jerusalem in 701 BC, or possibly simply represents a more salvific strand of the Zion tradition which the prophet felt should supplement the invective-threat.[25]

None of this form-criticism need be known by the reader of the text in its present shape. The point is that a reader or hearer might take away from it the impression either of judgment *against* Ariel (vv. 1–4), or Ariel as a minister *of* divine judgment (vv. 5–10). I suggest that the graphic account of the thunder, wind, tempest, and fire inflicted on the enemies of Ariel might well lead to the latter being the predominant effect of the whole passage. This is fostered by the Genevan text beginning simply, "Ah altar (Ariel)," rather than, "Wo unto thee O Ariel," as in the Bishops' Bible, and God's call, "Ah Ariel," is certainly closer to Prospero's call, "Approach, my Ariel." The Vaughans urge in their Arden edition of the play that, "whether [Shakespeare] turned directly to the Bible or drew on subconscious recollections while he wrote, the image of Ariel as the 'lyon of God' speaking through flood and fire reverberates in *The Tempest*."[26]

I have already drawn attention to the presence of fire in Shakespeare's tempest, as in Isaiah's, and perhaps most remarkably there is the vocabulary of sleep and dreaming which is applied to the experience of both the enemies of Jerusalem in Isaiah 29 and Prospero's enemies in the play. In Isaiah 29, their experience is "as a dream or vision by night" (v. 7). Further, "And it shall be like as an hungry man dreameth, and behold, he eateth and when he awaketh his soul is empty: or like as a thirsty man dreameth, and lo, he is drinking, and when he awaketh, behold he is faint. . . . For the Lord hath covered you with a spirit of slumber, and hath shut up your eyes" (vv. 8, 10).[27] As the Vaughans also point out, a "strange drowsiness" possesses the Neapolitans (2.1.98), and in 3.3 the banquet apparently laid before them vanishes. The mariners are "asleep under the hatches" (5.1.88). Sleep is an instrument of Prospero's judgment, as it is of God's judgment in Isaiah 29. Perhaps there is also a resonance in sense, if not in language, between God's question, "shall the work say of him that made it, He made me not, or the thing formed, say of him that fashioned it, He had none understanding?" (v. 16) and Prospero's impatient question to Miranda, "[is] my foot my tutor?" (1.2.470).

Such allusions to the language of Isaiah 29 make no large theological point. They simply support the general sense that Prospero has the judgment of the whole island in his hands, and that Prospero and Ariel together are bringing judgment on their enemies. Of course, with Ariel's name Shakespeare is also punning on "aerial," pertaining to the "air," as Shaheen maintains;[28] Ariel is described as "an ayrie spirit" in the cast list, and in 5.1.21 Prospero addresses Ariel as one "which art but air." But if Ariel simply is another spelling of "aerial" then there is no pun at all; a pun only works if there is a play of words on the name "Ariel" gathered from a *different* context from that of "air." Scriptural expressions in Ariel's speech underline the picture of Prospero as judge and Ariel as his agent. He declares to the "three men of sin" that "I and my fellows / Are ministers of fate" (3.3.60–61), and that this means "ministers of Prospero" is clear when shortly afterward Prospero refers to "my meaner ministers" (87); thus we have yet another resonance with the notion of "God's ministers" in Romans 13,[29] and the warning that those who resist "powers that be" shall "receive to them selves judgement" (Rom. 13:2). Ariel also warns that the wicked behavior of the three "falls / Upon your heads" (3.3.80–81), a common expression for self-incurred judgment in scripture,[30] and recalling Shylock's invocation of judgment, "My deeds upon my head."[31]

A series of scriptural allusions thus conveys to the audience the sense that Prospero is in control of events. Like Christ, he has power over the elements of nature, at least on the island. He is also, like Christ, a judge in the decisive "hour," just as the God of Israel is judge on "the day of the Lord" to which Isaiah makes reference in the context to chapter 29 (e.g., "in that day," 28:5). At the time of the eighth- and seventh-century prophets there was a popular anticipation of the "Day of the Lord" as a day of victory and glory for Israel, which the prophets shockingly reversed into a moment of defeat and judgment for a people practising injustice. Prospero wears this mantle of judgment, which Christ inherits from the God of Israel. Prospero is not, however, like Christ in opening himself to vulnerability, at least not yet; in the Christ-story, there is the paradox that authority comes from assuming powerlessness, and that this is the heart of being truly human.

Vulnerability is the theme of the scene where Ferdinand turns up at Prospero's cell, but it is not yet admitted by Prospero of himself. On first seeing Ferdinand, Miranda exclaims, "What is't, a spirit? . . . 'tis a spirit" (1.2.410), which recalls the reaction of the disciples to seeing Jesus walking on the sea, "It is a spirit" (Matt. 14:26).[32] This sea episode includes mention of a strong wind, and is a matching piece to the Gospel story of Jesus's calming the storm. However, in the Gospel story the evangelist intends to show that the disciples are wrong; Jesus is not a disembodied spirit but is as fully present in human life as they are. This is in fact what Prospero declares about Ferdinand: "A spirit. No . . . it eats . . . and hath such senses / As we have"; we recall that in the story of Jesus meeting the disciples after the resurrection, he assures them that "it is I myself: handle me, and see: for a spirit hath not flesh and bones as ye see I have" (Luke 24:35), and the account goes on that "he did eat before them" (Luke 24:37–43). Prospero is to echo these same words of the resurrected Christ once again toward the end of the play, this time referring to *himself* at the moment of self-revelation to the treacherous nobles with all disguise removed: Prospero says, "for more assurance that a living prince / Does now speak to thee, I embrace thy body" (5.1.109), and Alonso confesses "Thy pulse / Beats as of flesh and blood." Knapp suggests that this is a "kenotic" revelation, a willingness to "stoop low" in humble embodiment in both the cases of Prospero and Christ.[33] It is only when Prospero has laid aside his garment of power, renouncing his arts of control, that he can become simply the same flesh and blood as his enemies. At that stage in the play Prospero realizes a vulnerability of which earlier on he had no sense for himself, though he was willing enough to bestow it on Ferdinand.

Miranda follows up her first impression of Ferdinand with the acclamation, "I might call him / A thing divine," but her estimate becomes more realistic when she settles on what the audience would regard as a more humble Christian concept of the body as a "temple" of the Spirit: with the declaration, "There's nothing ill can dwell in such a temple" (1.2.458–59), we might compare 1 Corinthians 3:16, "Know ye not that ye are the Temple of God, and that the Spirit of God dwelleth in you?"[34] The Neoplatonic idea that physical beauty reflects a noble nature is also present, but the word "temple" indicates the scriptural allusion. Ewan Fernie celebrates the "everyday" nature of spirituality as revealed in this scene, the transfiguration of the ordinary with an "excess," as well as noting Prospero's lack of awareness of his ultimate vulnerability: "Prospero is not really directing the scene, though no doubt he'd like to be. He is pushed aside by the spiritual conjunction of Ferdinand and Miranda. . . . The distance between the spirituality that Miranda and Ferdinand perceive and normal life is nil, nothing like the magical superiority Prospero enjoys."[35]

This "magical superiority," laying claim to the dispensing of divine judgment, ensures that Prospero is more in control of the situation than any character Shakespeare ever created. He is the supreme magician, the dramatist, and virtually the god of the island. He has what we usually call "power" in abundance, and scriptural texts are referenced to make us feel this. But in solving one problem—how to integrate myth and tragicomedy—Shakespeare has set himself another problem—how to keep us as the audience *interested* when there seems to be no threat in this play, no obvious conflict. This is not a play about how Prospero defeats his enemies against overwhelming odds; the odds are all on *his* side; he holds the winning hand from the beginning because of his magical arts and his magic servants. But the problem is also an opportunity; Shakespeare has the opportunity to portray the *real* tempest—the threat and opposition that are more subtle than the crude power games being played out by the visitors to Prospero's world, and by inhabitants of our world as well. Shakespeare gives us a man who has, on his island, immeasurably more power than we in the audience have, and yet is still in some sense vulnerable, although he does not realize it until near the end of the play. He also does not seem to realize until then where the truly life-giving energies are as well, though we catch a hint of these in the growing love of Miranda and Ferdinand.

The Principalities and Powers

In tension with the seemingly all-controlling power of Prospero, Shakespeare is sketching out the threat of other powers, which lie deep within the patterns of myth. He is drawing on images of realities which appear in the New Testament writers as the "principalities and powers" (Rom. 8:38), associated with "Thrones and Dominions" (Col. 1:16), or the "worldly governors, the princes of the darkness of this world . . . spiritual wickednesses" (Eph. 6:12), or "the rudiments of the world" to which Paul's correspondents were "once in bondage" (Gal. 4:3). This last phrase is aptly translated in modern versions as "the elemental spirits of the world" (NRSV).

> For I am persuaded that neither death, nor life, nor Angels, nor principalities, nor powers, nor things present, nor things to come . . . shall be able to separate us from the love of God. (Rom. 8:38)

> By him were all things created, which are in heaven, and which are in earth, things visible and invisible: whether they be Thrones, or Dominions, or Principalities, or Powers. (Col. 1:16)

> For we wrestle not against flesh and blood, but against principalities, against powers, and against the worldly governors, the princes of the darkness of this world, against spiritual wickednesses, which are in the high places. (Eph. 6:12)

> Even so, we when we were children, were in bondage under the rudiments of the world. (Gal. 4:3)

Commenting on what he calls the "Shakespearian Renaissance" exhibited in Prospero's learning, G. Wilson Knight comments that "It has much to do with nature, with elemental forces" and, denying that this is an inversion of theology, he goes on that it "returns to the source of God's creation."[36] In this play, while Prospero is able to cope with the "principalities and powers" while he is on his island, we gain the impression that the story was different *before* he achieved his little kingdom (in "the dark backward and abysm of time"), and will be again after he has left it.

These "powers" and "rudiments" are *not* what have often been envisioned as demons, or shock-troops of a personalized devil. There are, to be sure, references to biblical texts in this play which imply *that* kind of view of spiritual powers: Antonio refers to a "spirit of persuasion" that gives false hope to the king that his son is still alive (2.1.225);[37] Sebastian determines to fight whatever fiends are on the island, though they be "legion" (3.3.103–4);[38] Ferdinand vows to resist his "worser genius," or his bad angel;[39] and we have seen that Sebastian accuses Prospero with the words, "The devil speaks in him." But we cannot read *The Tempest* as any kind of discourse on evil spirits and demons, despite interest in these entities at the time, not least by King James I himself. These allusions just form the background to something both more mysterious and all-embracing shadowed forth in the play and indicated by the biblical phrase "principalities and powers."

According to the Bible, there are cosmic powers that are in essence neither simply bad nor good; created by God to administer the cosmos, they have been seduced by worship offered to them by human beings and their aims have become distorted.[40] These powers also take visible form in something more down-to-earth—in the authorities of the state that ought to be administering God's justice but that have demanded absolute allegiance and have become corrupt, self-serving, and oppressive. As the theologian Paul Tillich has put it, powers that should be nurturing life have become "demonic."[41] Another theologian, Walter Wink, notes that the Apostle Paul has already taken key steps toward demythologizing these powers by categorizing them as the forces of "law, sin, and death," and that we should follow his lead by understanding "the Powers" as the inner aspect of material manifestations of power in the world.[42] Such powers are often many-sided and ambiguous. Shakespeare, I suggest, is echoing this scriptural ethos of "principalities and powers" without using the precise term or holding the exact theology. They find their face, not in a general "great Nature," but in more specific figures that inhabit this mythical landscape.

As early as the second scene of the play Shakespeare gives us a hint of the ambiguities and subtleties of power with the figure of Ariel. This airy sprite is completely under Prospero's control, his "minister," and yet there is a resistance to Prospero's art, some mysterious danger there in Ariel, who represents a cosmic element, a force of nature that is not completely tamed by human skills. Prospero has saved and released Ariel from his painful prison,

twisted in the knots of the pine tree; but he is still "moody," resentful at doing
Prospero's bidding. Prospero cries in amazement, "Dost thou forget / From
what torment I did free thee?" and in exasperation calls him "thou malignant
thing" (1.2.244–57). A near-rebellion by Ariel comes to nothing. He cannot
help but carry out Prospero's commands until Prospero has achieved all his
plans, and then Prospero will finally free him "to the elements" (5.1.318) according to his promise. Ariel is never out of Prospero's control, and we feel
comfortable about this; but there is still something disturbing about this
spirit, this neutral force that is neither good nor evil, that feels no apparent
affection for Prospero. When he asks, "Do you love me, master?" and follows
it up with the expected "No?" (4.1.48), we feel the detachment of the question. We sense that things may be very different when Prospero is no longer
the magician-king of the island. There is just a hint here of an alien tempest
in which human beings can be caught.

But if a hint is given with Ariel about potential conflict, this becomes
much more obvious with the figure of Caliban, whom we also meet in
scene 2 and who represents lack of European civilization. Again, we have
no doubt that Prospero has control over Caliban, at least outwardly. He
can force Caliban to fetch wood, to carry burdens, to make their fire; at
the least sign of resistance he can afflict Caliban with "cramps / side-stitches
that shall pen thy breath up." But there is something deep in Caliban that
Prospero cannot control. What this "something" is remains ambiguous in
Shakespeare's portrayal of the one who appears in the cast-list as "a savage and deformed slave." In Prospero's view, the something is simply evil.
Prospero speaks on behalf of all European colonial conquerors when he
judges that there are savages—whether in the Americas, Africa, or Ireland
(and all have been claimed as settings for *The Tempest*)—where the grafting
of "nurture" onto "nature"[43] will never succeed, even with the imparting of
a smattering of education: "Thy vile race / (Though thou didst learn) had
that in't which good natures / Could not abide to be with." In Prospero's
view, there is an inherent evil in Caliban that cannot be controlled by all
the human arts there are. Here he appears to voice the arguments of the
humanist scholar Juan Ginés de Sepúlveda, who maintained the view that
Amerindians were "natural slaves" whose vicious practices justified war
and enslavement, over against the defense of the conquered races by the
Dominican Friar Bartolomé de las Casas in the well-known Valladolid debates of 1550–51. Las Casas argued that Aristotle's definition of "barbarian"
and "natural slave" did not apply to the Indians, all of whom were fully
capable of reason.[44] According to his own report, Prospero had taken this
kind of approach to start with, attempting not enslavement but education,
and had welcomed Caliban to live with them in his own dwelling; he had
changed his mind when Caliban had tried to rape Miranda (1.2.352), and

Caliban himself does not deny the facts of this account. We cannot know which side of the Valladolid debates, which resounded throughout Europe long beyond the 1550s, Shakespeare himself would have espoused. Caliban certainly stands for what the Elizabethans imagined to be humanity in the state of nature, the exotic savage, or the "wild man" of European folklore.[45] We *can* say that Shakespeare seems to be throwing doubt on any mere romanticizing of the primitive such as we find in the philosopher Montaigne, whose essay "Of the Caniballes" in John Florio's translation Shakespeare drew upon for Gonzalo's utopian speech on the ideal commonwealth (2.1.148–65).[46] Montaigne, comparing the Brazilians with European civilization, had offered the optimistic view that "In those are the most true and profitable vertues, and naturall properties most livelie and vigorous, which in these we have bastardized, applying them to the pleasure of our corrupted taste,"[47] and had pointed out that Europeans also consume each other, through inflicting torture and painful death: "I think there is more barbarisme in eating men alive, than to feed upon them being dead."[48] Perhaps Shakespeare is showing some sympathy for Montaigne's objection to the imposing of European culture, denoted by the striking word "bastardized," since he donates the term to Perdita in her debate with Polixenes about the grafting of flowers in The Winter's Tale (4.4.83), although she is allowed to get bested in argument by Polixenes.[49]

Shakespeare's view of Caliban, whose name may be an anagram of "Caniball" (in the general sense), thus shows—typically—a variety of perspectives, which may be best summed up in the biblical language of "the powers." The something that Prospero cannot control includes inherent evil, but also consists of a deep passion which might issue in either sexual violence or a sensitivity to beauty. He is the "other" to European culture, and like all "others" (including Ariel), he cannot be easily categorized. Coleridge judged that Caliban was "a noble being . . . a man in the sense of the *imagination*."[50] He speaks some of the best poetry in the play, and the sleep that befalls others as a judgment has no terrors for him:

> Be not afeard; the isle is full of noises,
> Sounds and sweet airs, that give delight, and hurt not.
> Sometimes a thousand twangling instruments
> Will hum about mine ears; and sometimes voices,
> That, if I then had wak'd after long sleep,
> Will make me sleep again; and then, in dreaming,
> The clouds methought would open, and show riches
> Ready to drop upon me; that, when I wak'd,
> I cried to dream again. (3.2.148–56)

Caliban speaks on behalf of all subjugated peoples in turning the language of the colonial power against itself: "You taught me language and my profit on't / Is I know how to curse" (1.2.364–65). But the situation is more complex than this: he uses language to articulate the dream of art, knowing its beauty, while speaking in almost the very next line about destroying Prospero so that he and his conspirators can have their music free of charge. The audience is encouraged to be positive about Caliban's intuitive passions for nature, music—and perhaps love—by his reference, in an appreciative tone, to learning how "To name the bigger light and how the less / That burn by day and night" (1.2.336–37), in which they would have noticed a resonance with Genesis 1:16: "God then made two great lights: the greater light to rule the day, and the less light to rule the night."

Since the nineteenth century, Caliban's violent behavior has been pushed into the background of his just grievances; after all, his hereditary land has been taken from him by the European invader, and he suffers the horrendous evil of slavery.[51] But Shakespeare is evoking some force in Caliban which is more ambiguous. In him we feel the depth of a passion which can turn either toward the good and the beautiful or toward the dark mystery of evil, so that passion itself has something morally neutral about it. Coleridge's comment on Ariel, that he is "neither born of heaven, nor of earth, but as it were, between both,"[52] might also apply to Caliban. Prospero is, by contrast, portrayed as being uncomfortable with any expressions of passion, and exhibits an obsession about preserving Miranda's virginity during her period of betrothal to Ferdinand.[53] The masque he presents to celebrate their engagement explicitly excludes Venus and Cupid, in favor of general songs about fertility offered by Ceres and Juno.

The imprecise location of the island, somewhere between Naples and Tunis, further encourages commentators and producers to adopt a highly flexible interpretation of Ariel and Caliban, and I suggest that the ambiguity and mystery of the forces they both represent leaves us with a sense of vulnerability to "principalities and powers." Insofar as Shakespeare is critical of the absolute human power that dominates others, and is sympathetic to Caliban's protest that "I am all the subjects that you have / Which was first mine own king," we can observe as we have often done Shakespeare's evenhandedness to different institutions of religion. Though resonances of the Valladolid debate tend to give the play a Catholic coloring, yet through the deliberate vagueness of the geographical setting we cannot tell whether we are seeing the results of Catholic imperialism in South America, or Protestant colonization in Virginia, or Protestant subjugation of Ireland, or both Catholic and Protestant exploitation of African peoples.[54] It seems likely, as Shell suggests, that Prospero's speech beginning, "our revels now are ended," envisaging the end of the theater, has borrowed from Protestant-Puritan antitheatricalists' rhetoric,[55] and Asquith makes the further interesting (if speculative) claim that the pinning of Ariel within the sinews of a pine tree by the witch Sycorax symbolizes the censorship of the theater by the Elizabethan state. But this does not make *The Tempest* a partisan play, committed to Catholicism and identifying Elizabeth—as Asquith does—with the wicked queen Sycorax.[56] Knapp proposes that Prospero's reference to having the same flesh and blood as his opponents, built on the resurrection appearance of Jesus, is "the religion that Shakespeare believed himself to have espoused in tying his art, as Prospero ultimately does, to bodies instead of books." This is a "sociable," or "fellowly," Christian belief, disavowing sectarianism, in which "players can forge a . . . congregational fellowship in the theater by encouraging the imaginative participation of their audiences."[57]

If we feel an untameable evil within Caliban, this is even more true of the noble lords of Naples and Milan. They have had all the benefits of civilization and education, but there is still a deep corruption, and—as Montaigne puts it—a desire to "eat" each other. In this they typify the principalities and powers of the state ("in high places") that have become demonic. Antonio (Prospero's wicked brother) incites Sebastian to kill Alonso while he is asleep. Just as Antonio conspired with Alonso to overthrow Prospero to gain Milan, so he now conspires with Sebastian (Alonso's brother) to overthrow Alonso, and to free Milan from the overlordship of Naples. Sebastian and Antonio are a most unpleasant couple, though we are assured that while they are all on the island they cannot succeed in their plots. Ariel hovers nearby, to plunge them into sleep, to freeze their weapons in their hands, to wake up those in danger. But the more we are assured that Prospero is in control on the island, the more we are caused to think, what happens when this island interlude is over? For no art of Prospero can destroy the evil itself in the human heart, the darkness at the heart of the human personality that makes earthly powers and authorities hostile to the flourishing of life.

THE POWERS OF TIME AND DEATH

Despite all Prospero's power, Caliban and the nobles witness that evil is still present and may break out in new forms. Ariel and Caliban testify that there are more ambiguous forces that are still dangerous and potentially harmful. We are made even more strongly aware of this as we are brought to face two allied powers, time and death. In act 4, toward the end of the play, Prospero becomes the dramatist and stage manager once again, and produces a charming pageant about the goddess of fertility, Ceres. By now Ferdinand and Miranda have fallen in love with each other, and are pledged to be married—as

Prospero had hoped and planned from the beginning. Prospero has promised them an entertainment to celebrate their engagement, and puts on a show of music, singing, and dancing much like a court masque of the time. The actors and dancers are, naturally, some of the spirits of the air that Prospero uses as his servants on the island. Suddenly, in the middle of the little play within a play, Prospero becomes highly disturbed. He recalls, in an aside, a plot against his life by the absurd trio of Caliban, Trinculo, and Stephano (the monster, the fool, and the drunkard), who mirror, at the lower end of the social scale, the earlier coalition of three who deprived him of his dukedom. He determines to deal with the plot, stopping the performance, and breaking up the dance and music. "This is strange," exclaims Ferdinand, "Your father's in some passion / That works him strongly," and Miranda responds, "Never till this day / Saw I him touched with anger so distempered!" At this point Prospero explains:

> You do look, my son, in a moved sort,
>   As if you were dismayed. Be cheerful, sir.
>   Our revels now are ended. These our actors,
>   As I foretold you, were all spirits and
>   Are melted into air, into thin air:
>   And—like the baseless fabric of this vision–
>   The cloud-capped towers, the gorgeous palaces,
>   The solemn temples, the great globe itself,
>   Yea, all which it inherit, shall dissolve,
>   And like this insubstantial pageant faded,
>   Leave not a rack behind. We are such stuff
>   As dreams are made on, and our little life
>   Is rounded with a sleep. (4.1.146–58)

There is a multilayered reality about this speech: "our revels now are ended." What revels have ended, or as he warns, will end? There are at least five answers to this, all of which interweave in our consciousness as we watch the scene. First, they are the pageant-play which has just been acted out by the spirits, and which Prospero has produced for the lovers. Second, they are the events on the island, which Prospero has also stage-managed to bring about the reconciliation he wants; they are the music and the visions with which he has amazed and bewildered the castaways, and which Caliban calls a dream. Third, the revels are the play *The Tempest* itself. The play is about to end, and here the play-writer speaks with Prospero. Fourth, the end of the revels is the end of a person's life, which will surely come to all of us: "We are such stuff / As dreams are made on, and our little life / Is rounded with a sleep." At the end of the play, Prospero declares, "Every third thought shall be my grave." Finally, the revels are the whole world, "the great globe itself / Yea all which it inherit" which will dissolve on the day of judgment. Once again, as in King Lear, images of "end" and "judgement" are being taken from the biblical tradition to make poetry. The term "dissolve" seems to come from a text in 2 Peter 3:10 about the Day of the Lord: "The heavens shall pass away with a noise, and the elements shall melt with heat. . . . Seeing therefore that all these things must be dissolved, and the earth . . . [at] the day of God, by which the heavens, being on fire, shall be dissolved."[58]

Shakespeare has already employed the word "resolve" with the meaning "dissolve" in Hamlet for the end of human life, probably in reference to the same text.[59] Roland Frye has suggested that the vocabulary of the speech also draws on a long tradition in Christian writing of conceiving of life as a passing vision and an evanescent vapor, quoting as an example from Calvin's commentary on Job, which, in translation by Golding, we have already seen was available to Shakespeare.[60] Calvin writes, "the shape of this world passeth away and all the things therein do glide and vanish away."[61] We may also compare "leave not a rack [mist] behind" with Psalm 102:3, "For my days pass away like smoke." In commenting elsewhere on 1 Corinthians 7:31, "the fashion of this world goeth away," Calvin detects the image of "pauillions or halles, in the which . . . the tapestrie and hangings are pulled downe, and wrapped up in a moment."[62] The possible influence on this speech of a passage from The Tragedie of Darius by William Alexander ("Those golden Pallaces, those gorgeous halles / . . . Evanishe all like vapours in the aire")[63] does not exclude resonances of scripture in a rich intertextuality.

The powers of time and death are not in themselves enemies to life. According to Christian theology they are good creations of God; they are not the consequence of human sinfulness, but are part of a life which flourishes and is fulfilled in historical process and a natural boundary to existence. It is not death itself which is portrayed as the result of Adam's disobedience in the myth of Genesis 3, but what death becomes in light of this slipping from the Good; the death human beings actually know is a distorted power which threatens life,[64] as the Apostle Paul makes clear in his insight that death is "the last enemy because 'the sting of death is sin'" (1 Cor. 15:56). Similarly, Augustine portrays God as creating time as something beneficial along with creation, but confesses that as he actually experiences time it is a power that fragments his existence, as he cannot bring future, present, and past into harmony.[65]

We realize now why Prospero is so disturbed by remembering the plot of Caliban against his life. On the face of it, this is as perplexing to the audience as to Ferdinand and Miranda. We have been assured that Prospero has

everything under his control, and that there can be no real threat from the rebellion of Caliban; Prospero knows all about it and can thwart it with a quick
word to Ariel. But at this point the audience is made to feel a considerable
sense of suspense, as if something actually does hang in the balance. There
is anxiety indeed, but not about what is happening at this precise moment.
It is about what *will* happen in the future when Prospero has abandoned his
magic arts, drowned his magic book, broken his magic staff, and has returned
to Milan as he intends to do; it is about what will happen after the interlude
of the island, when he will be truly exposed to such hazards as the plots of
a Caliban. Shakespeare's point is that conflict awaits in the future, that the
enemies of time and death make the inherent evil in human life even harder
to bear and deal with. Prospero abruptly terminates the pageant of the spirits
as a sign that he must bring his magic to an end.

In Prospero's great speech on time and death we have a reflection on the
end of a piece of *art* (the pageant, the whole play) and the end of *life* (an individual's life, the whole of history), while the events on the island are a kind
of symbolic link between them. The levels of meaning intersect, for instance,
in the dissolving of the "great globe," which refers both to the earth and the
Globe Playhouse for which Shakespeare wrote plays from 1599. Prospero's
magic arts with which he stage-manages events and visions are a mythical way
of talking about the human arts such as drama, music, and poetry. As Harold
Bloom perceives, this is why, despite his renunciation of his magic within
the framework of the play, Prospero is not a Faust-figure, and indeed may
have been drawn in deliberate contrast to Marlowe's character.[66] The magic
circle he draws and into which he draws the enchanted nobles from Naples
and Milan might well be the "wooden O" of the Globe Playhouse.[67] The central image here that holds the levels of meaning together is that of the island,
set in the midst of the sea—an island full of dreams and strange sounds. The
characters come out of the sea onto the island, and then at the end leave
the island to enter the sea again. In that future, Prospero, too, faces the judgment of sleep he has inflicted on his enemies on the island; like Hamlet,
he must wonder "in that sleep . . . what dreams may come" (3.1.65). So, in the
same way, a person's life is an island set in a sea, a dream surrounded by a sea
of sleep; we come from sleep in the womb, we move into the dream of life as
shaped by the human arts and then move back into the sleep of death. So it
is also with the theater; from life outside the theater, into the dream of the
drama and then back outside to life again. Coming for an evening performance in an indoor theater like Blackfriars, the audience comes in from dark
streets to the lighted stage, and then back outside to the night once more.[68]

The result of this multiple vision is that the boundaries are blurred
between the play and real life, between the actors and the audience. It brings

them all (us all) into one reality, into one story, and all are exposed to the threat of hostile forces. In Shakespeare's earlier plays we have several examples of presenting a play before the audience on the stage; the nobles at the end of *A Midsummer Night's Dream*, we recall, watch the hilarious tragedy of Pyramus and Thisbe, and as we watch it with them, we learn what it is to see more clearly. The royal court in *Hamlet* watches a performance of a play called "The Mousetrap," with which Hamlet plans to "catch the conscience of the king," and we become viewers with them.[69] But in these examples we know quite clearly from the start that we are watching a play-within-the-play; we see the audience on the stage settling down to observe the play, and we join them in our own seats. In *The Tempest*, however, as Ann Righter points out,[70] the play begins with what we assume to be a real storm, as real as those reported by the colonists who had gone out to the New World in 1609 to settle in Virginia. It is only when the scene shifts and we find Prospero and Miranda watching the storm like a kind of audience, that we discover that the storm has been an illusion of Prospero's art, stage-managed by him. The sailors and the travelers in the ship have been unknowing and unwilling actors in the piece, while the ship is in fact safe in the harbor of the island, and we have been unaware witnesses of a play-within-the play.

Continually, as the play progresses, we do not know whether the sights we are seeing belong to the framework of reality as set up by the play, or whether they are illusions created by the director and stage manager, Prospero, *within* that primary suspension of disbelief. He is producing plays-*within*-the-play to amaze his audience, which in the first place is the party of nobles cast ashore on the island. This blurring of art and reality within the play itself is increased by another factor, which Ann Righter again points out.[71] In the earlier comedies we know who the actors within the play-within-a-play are in the "real life" of the outer play; we know, for example, that the part of Pyramus is being played, hilariously badly, by Bottom the Weaver. But here we cannot see the actors unless they are playing their parts, because they are spirits of the air; they are only visible in their roles, and so we cannot compare the actor with the role. Shakespeare is going to loose another surprise upon us at the end of the play, further to confuse the audience, but let us leave that for the moment.

As we are drawn into the reality of the play, we feel the limits of its art. We are aware that it is bound to end, and so by extension we feel the limits of all human creativity; we are brought to face the reality that *this* play will end, and because we have become a part of it, *we* are not allowed to escape from the reality of the end of our own life, confronted by the enemies of time and death. The *dramatist's* dream, his play, will come to an end; it will cease to be performed, the script will be lost. And *our* dream too, our art, our life, faces the limit of our life's span and history itself. In each of these dreams, the mysterious threat of evil and the ambiguous threat of the "principalities and powers" is made more sinister and more powerful by the limits to existence constituted by time and death. This sense of human limits is prompted by all plays where the dramatist has the skill to enable the audience to participate; it is certainly true of all Shakespeare's plays, not just these last Romances. But not knowing the truth about Hermione's survival in *The Winter's Tale* means that our sense of vulnerability in face of forces of life and death expressed in myth is amplified as we witness the moving statue and her "return" to life. In *The Tempest*, not knowing the truth about the various levels of the drama presented to us means that this sense is increased virtually from moment to moment. Perhaps Asquith is right to judge that "More than any of his other works, this play about the theatre draws the audience into the action."[72] Certainly, in this play, the growing awareness of vulnerability is given explicit and even shocking expression in the speech beginning, "Our revels now are ended."

When Prospero is back in Milan, after the island interlude, he will be vulnerable to all the plots and plotters he has overcome on the island. An intertextuality with passages and images of scripture builds up the impression that on the island Prospero can cope with all threats as controller of nature and judge of the wicked while—meeting the technical challenge of the drama—holding the action together. But it also builds the sense that there are dangerous and hostile forces that wait at the margins for their opportunity. Shakespeare takes away conflict on the island in order to push the tempest into the future, in Milan and Naples and all the cities where we as the audience live.[73] As in other plays, we doubt that the story of art is enough finally to overcome death, though it will "hold its swift foot back"[74] for a while. As in *The Winter's Tale*, this resonance with scriptural texts is preparing to commend a spirituality, not a dogma. Part of that spirituality is the need to live life in awareness of the boundary of death and the pressure of time that "Goes upright with his carriage,"[75] but along with this there is, centrally, the element of forgiveness. This is a repetition of the theme which Shakespeare offers in many of his plays, and which he very recently emphasized in *The Winter's Tale*, but—as in a musical theme—it returns with variation which I suggest will be significant for the impact of *The Tempest* on theology "in front of the text."

THE SPIRITUALITY OF FORGIVENESS

Shakespeare does not *leave* us with the speech on death and judgment at the end of act 4. In act 5 he opens up the possibility that something can be said and done in the face of death, opening up hope. Art and education are weak in the face of death, but there is another power which the world calls weakness—that is the power of forgiveness. In *The Merchant of Venice*, Portia had reminded the courtroom audience of the plea in the Lord's Prayer to be forgiven as we also forgive others:

> we do pray for mercy,
> And that same prayer, doth teach us all the render
> The deeds of mercy. (4.1.194–98)

This phrase is to be virtually repeated in the final words of *The Tempest*: "As *you* from crimes would pardoned be." Prospero begins act 5 with a declaration of forgiveness as he is to end by requesting it:

> Though with their high wrongs I am struck to th' quick,
> Yet with my nobler reason 'gainst my fury
> Do I take part; the rarer action is
> In virtue than in vengeance. They being penitent,
> The sole drift of my purpose doth extend
> Not a frown further. Go, release them Ariel:
> My charms I'll break; their senses I'll restore;
> And they shall be themselves. (5.1.25–32)

"Virtue" here, as the Vaughans point out, is used "to stand for forgiveness and mercy,"[76] and shortly Prospero is to say clearly, "I do forgive thee, / Unnatural though thou art" (78–79). The highlighting of reason as a motivation for forgiveness perhaps stems from an essay by Montaigne,[77] but Prospero has also just appealed to "a feeling / Of their afflictions" and the state of being "moved." The insight of *The Winter's Tale* that forgiveness requires a journey of empathy is not being denied. Another note is, however, being sounded in this spirituality of forgiveness. Prospero's total control over external matters like imposing sleep and paralysis on his enemies only throws into greater relief the nature of his helplessness about the one key matter, expressed in the words "they being penitent." Forgiveness can be offered, but cannot be effective without penitence; without penitence forgiveness is incomplete, and Prospero cannot compel this. He appears to assume it here, but as the final moments of the play unfold he is proved to be overconfident; here is both the power and the risks of forgiveness. In the four hours' space of the play Prospero uses the dramatic skills of his spirits, music, singing, sleep, and enchantment in order to give his enemies space and opportunity to learn repentance. He can also arrange a day of judgment, when at the end of act 3 Ariel appears to accuse them of their crimes (3.3.53–56), but finally Prospero has no power over the tempest of evil in their minds and hearts. He cannot make them repent and accept his forgiveness. Forgiveness is weak and vulnerable, opening itself to being freely accepted or rejected. A whole act intervenes while judgment is allowed to have its effect, and at the end, faced by Prospero, Alonso does repent his part in the plot against him. He restores Prospero's dukedom; he receives Ferdinand back from the dead, and gains a daughter in Miranda, from whom he asks forgiveness:

> I am hers:
> But, O, how oddly will it sound that I
> Must ask my child forgiveness! (5.1.197–99)

But repentance and acceptance of forgiveness cannot be compelled. Nor can Ferdinand's falling in love with Miranda be forced, which Prospero desires but for which he can only arrange the external circumstances. Love and forgiveness are miracles of grace. Through the intertextuality of the play with scripture, Prospero has been laying claim to the power of Christ over nature and to the judgment of God; now, through the prospect of confronting the "principalities and powers" without the aid of magic, and experiencing the weakness of forgiveness, he finds the human vulnerability to which scripture also bears witness.

The vulnerability of forgiveness is shown by the reaction of Antonio and Sebastian. Antonio remains silent, making no response to the forgiving words of Prospero, and it seems clear that he is not won over, not reconciled. Sebastian is more ambiguous, but we are not greatly encouraged by him either, since his only response to Prospero is, "The devil speaks in him." The fact that probably two out of the four nobles whom Miranda meets are unrepentant lends a sharp irony to her words as she sees them for the first time:

> O, wonder!
> How many goodly creatures are there here!
> How beauteous mankind is! O brave new world,
> That has such people in't! (5.1.181–84)

Prospero replies with realism, "'Tis new to *thee*." This is the twist in the tail: Shakespeare offers forgiveness as the only effective way of living in the vulnerability human persons feel when faced by the remorseless patterns of life and death and the mysterious threat of the "principalities and powers"; and yet the one who forgives is vulnerable to being rejected and exploited. The irony is brought to our attention by the fact that it is the finally uncontrollable spirit, Ariel, who rebukes Prospero and urges him to forgive. It is as if forgiveness belongs in the same free sphere of life as the liberated Ariel will live, who now appeals to Prospero that "if you now beheld them, your affections / Would become tender" (5.1.18–19). In Greenaway's film, Ariel recovers his own voice at this point, and he also writes this appeal to Prospero in Prospero's Book of Dialogues (i.e., the script for *The Tempest*) for himself, the first time that anyone except Prospero has written in it. Responding and pledging himself to forgive, Prospero breaks his quill in two. Henceforth all the characters will speak in their own voices, will write their own lines, and will be released from Prospero's control; as Prospero promises, "they shall be themselves" (5.1.32).[78]

But if they *are* themselves, or—as Gonzalo puts it—have "found" themselves where before "no man was his own" (5.1.12–13), they cannot be manipulated into forgiveness and reconciliation. This is the flip-side of "finding" a self which was once lost, which seems to be a reference to Matthew 16:25, "whosoever will lose their life for my sake, will find it."[79] Gonzalo's words conclude what is yet another invocation in a Shakespearean text of the parable of the prodigal son.[80] Summing up, if a little sententiously, the events that have unfolded, he says:

> In one voyage
> Did Claribel her husband find at Tunis,
> And Ferdinand, *her brother, found a wife*
> *Where he himself was lost;* Prospero his dukedom
> In a poor isle; and all of us ourselves,
> When no man was his own. (5.1.209–13; my italics)

We hear an echo here of Luke 15:51, "This thy brother . . . was lost, but he is found." Ferdinand has returned to his father after being apparently dead, and—more to the point—has reconciled with his new father, Prospero, whom he had offended at least by association with his family who had aligned with the usurper. Antonio himself, who cannot be reconciled, is cast for the role of the elder brother who excludes himself from the feast of forgiveness. The reference to the parable relates the romance theme of loss and finding to the "finding" of one another in the act of forgiveness. The only power of forgiveness is in the empathy which can win response from the other; this is the dynamic that lies within the journey of forgiveness, but it is not as fully portrayed in *The Winter's Tale*, where nobody rejects the forgiveness offered, painful though the process is.

The Theologian in the Play: Forgiveness
and Reconciliation

As with the preceding seven plays, I now want to ask what happens when the theologian inhabits the play, to inquire what excess of meaning emerges and how theology can be shaped by it. Dwelling in the drama leads the theologian, I suggest, to take a particular view on a disputed question: is forgiveness unconditional? Prospero offers forgiveness, but it is unclear whether this depends on repentance, leaving us with a question. Though his declaration of forgiveness contains what appears to be either an explanatory or a conditional clause, "they being penitent," nevertheless Antonio and Sebastian, two out of the three "men of sin," appear to remain obstinately *unrepentant*. Yet Prospero still assures them, addressing his words to Antonio in particular, "I do forgive you." Though "Holy Gonzalo" rejoices that they have all "found" themselves, what Antonio and Sebastian have found is a self which is resistant to conversion. Now, within the Christian tradition, the view has often been taken that forgiveness is conditional on repentance. Richard Swinburne, for example, as a philosopher of religion, insists that it is a logical sequence for forgiveness to follow repentance.[81] Indeed, it is also in his view "morally appropriate" that it should follow reparation as well (an effort to repair the damage done).[82] In our relation with God, he argues that reparation is not "logically necessary" for God to forgive us, but that because it is appropriate God has provided it vicariously in the death of Jesus. Through repentance, then, we enter the moral realm of forgiveness.

On the other hand, the philosopher Jacques Derrida has put up a strong case for forgiveness to be totally unconditional, limitless, and noninstrumental.[83] For Derrida the whole point of forgiveness is that it rises above all mechanisms of reciprocation and an economic marketplace. Forgiveness is not about calculation, or balancing the accounts: "There is in forgiveness a force, a desire, an impetus, a movement . . . that demands that forgiveness be granted even to someone who does not ask for it, who does not repent or confess or improve or redeem himself."[84] Forgiveness is given only to the unforgivable.[85] It is the "impossible possibility." We might say that it resists the economy of exchange that King Lear espoused so disastrously in his maxim, "Nothing will come of nothing." The Jesus of the Gospel story in fact seems to announce forgiveness *before* the evidence of repentance. Jesus takes the initiative, entering sympathetically into the lives of tax collectors (extortioners and quislings as they were), prostitutes, and those who were too ignorant to keep the religious laws properly, in order to entice them to an obedient response to God's purpose. By sharing table-fellowship with them he is sharing their life, and offering them a place at the Messianic feast, the festival of joy that would be ushered in by God's new creation of all things at the end of the age. Though Jesus hopes the sinners will repent, he offers forgiveness on God's behalf without prior conditions.

The theologian may make sense of this by understanding forgiveness as a creative act. As we have seen in reflecting on *The Winter's Tale*, forgiveness is no mere legal declaration of pardon, but a journey of empathy undertaken by the forgiver, entering into the experience of another to draw out a response. Forgiveness *enables* penitence, drawing out a reaction which will be manifest in acts of sorrow. Now, inhabiting the island-world of *The Tempest*, the theologian discovers in imagination the difference between forgiveness and reconciliation, the unconditional and the conditional. Prospero speaks unconditional forgiveness, and the whole movement of the plot requires this climax; he could hardly withdraw forgiveness after the lifting of punishment, disclosure of Ferdinand and Miranda, announcement of their marriage and his preparations for return to Milan. We want forgiveness to be given, for the lost to be found, but we also realize that it needs to be *completed* in a response that will mean reconciled relationships. To achieve its work, forgiveness must be received, and reception means a whole change of being; reconciliation is clearly conditional on the offender's penitence and his own sympathetic entry into the feelings of the victim. This is what Antonio and Sebastian resist, and Prospero has no power to compel them. With Prospero, the audience is anxious about what the future beyond the island may hold, exposed to a tempest of forces that can no longer be controlled, and yet the movement of the play leads the audience toward the *hope* of reconciliation. This is grounded largely in the love of Miranda and Ferdinand for each other, reaffirming Shakespeare's continual affirmation of the indestructability of love. Their falling in love with each other is in, indeed, another inner reality that Prospero cannot control, although he can arrange the circumstances.

Taking a clue from the words of Portia in *The Merchant of Venice*, that "in the course of justice none of us / Should see *salvation*," the theologian roots the human journey of empathy in a divine voyage of entry into human life and into the depths of human estrangement in the cross of Jesus Christ. This is God's great offer of forgiveness, not a legal transaction but a creative movement, enabling human response. An attitude of forgiveness does not lack moral seriousness, but the nature of empathy and the theological dynamic of atonement as a transforming act prevents us from keeping back the word "forgiveness" for reconciliation and restoration at the end of the journey. However untidy it appears, we find that the initiating act of identification and empathy with a wrongdoer *is* forgiveness. We cannot hold back the generous utterance, "I forgive you," until the end of the road. In this untidy, extravagant quality of forgiveness lies its transformative power. The ethicist

Nigel Biggar in his work on war and peace similarly identifies an unconditional "compassion-forgiveness" and a conditional "absolution-forgiveness."[86] The first is "inaugural" and the second "conclusive."[87] However, in my view he does not sufficiently allow for the moving boundary between these moments in the process of forgiveness-reconciliation. For him the first movement is an entirely internal work of compassion within the mind of the forgiver, without initiating any relations with the other; it is only in the second moment that the forgiver goes to the offender and speaks the words, "I forgive you." Sometimes, however, as with Prospero, words of forgiveness need to be spoken in relation with the other which are unconditional and creative, although not as yet achieving reconciliation. At other times, admittedly, the first movement must be only internal, and I consider this further below.

The experience of the play and the complementary theological perspective of atonement as transformative will thus lead us to approve Derrida's insistence on unconditionality, but also to take issue with him. In Derrida's view, forgiveness in its purity must be offered without any hope, *expectation*, or intention that the offender will in due time face up to his or her crime, be repentant, seek reconciliation, offer reparation, and be transformed. Even holding hope for the offender is, in Derrida's view, entering an economy of exchange. This view seems to arise from associating forgiveness radically with *forgetting*. In a paper beginning, "Pardon, yes, pardon," Derrida sets out the affinity between forgiveness (*pardon*) and the *don*, or donation (gift).[88] Forgiveness is a gift, not a deal; as a gift, it must resist becoming a reciprocal system or calculation. In true giving, both the act of giving and the gift must be forgotten. Derrida writes, "forgetting would be in the condition of the gift and the gift in the condition of forgetting."[89] So also with forgiving: "forgiveness and gift have perhaps this in common, that they never *present themselves* as such to what is commonly called an experience, a presentation to consciousness or to existence."[90] I have already argued, in the previous chapter, that forgiveness cannot mean forgetting. Derrida's vision of unconditionality excludes from forgiveness the hope of any reconciliation or restoration. If this were *demanded* or required from either victim or offender, then of course this would be a system of exchange and calculation that Derrida rightly thinks destroys the gift. But empathy in the journey of forgiveness, by contrast, relies on remembering. Prospero's whole initiating action on the island arises from memory, looking into the "dark backward and abysm of time." It is from remembering and not forgetting, as Paul Ricoeur tells us, that there arises forgiveness and hope for the future.[91]

If we understand forgiveness as mutuality of relations and reciprocal empathy, the objection may be raised that where relations do not exist, the very notion of forgiveness becomes problematic. This could be the case, as with

Antonio, when someone refuses to be reconciled, and also applies where people are not present to be reconciled because they have died, or when it is not safe for someone who has been abused to make any contact with the abuser. However, in such cases, the one who forgives can still set out in spirit and imagination on the path of empathy toward the other, so becoming the kind of person who is freed from the chains of the past. The forgiver can still benefit himself or herself from the attitude of forgiveness, "moving on" from the prison of bitterness and resentment, even where this does not reach destination and closure in reconciliation. The philosopher Charles Griswold considers this case too, and concludes that forgiveness is possible when we can construct an "imaginative and credible narrative" about an offender, finding reasons to think that conditions for forgiveness such as remorse might have been or *might be* fulfilled in a different situation.[92] He himself argues, against my approach, that forgiveness must be conditional even at the beginning of the process,[93] but he is willing to think that such a beginning could be based on confidence in the basic humanity of the offender, *imagining* him or her to be capable of fulfilling the conditions in repentance.

A theological paradigm, which understands forgiveness to have an initiating effect because it is based in divine empathy, has several advantages over this particular exercise of the imagination. First, forgivers are making their journey of imagination "in God," and because all things are held together in the triune God, existing in the midst of interweaving relations of love and justice, it can have incalculable effects in the lives of others. The journey of human forgiveness becomes part of God's own journey, and so has persuasive power in creating reconciliation in the world as created love is added to the uncreated love of God. Those who forgive cannot know what this will achieve, either in the one with whom they desire to be reconciled, or in others who need to be reconciled and of whom they are quite unaware. Second, the person who truly sets out on the road of forgiveness in God may still hope that the offender may come to a restorative response in the end. The symbol of the Last Judgment in Christian eschatology is an assurance that where truth has not been exposed in this life, it will nevertheless finally be made plain in another context. Judgment, then, is not an image of exclusion but of healing, brought about through the painful act of admitting what is true about ourselves and others. As I have emphasized before, however, such eschatological hopes can only be held in metaphors, not literally.

The story of Prospero raises another question about forgiveness. His behavior toward his enemies does not appear, by his own admission, to be motivated by forgiveness since he admits a change of mind when rebuked by Ariel. He *does* intend to bring them to repentance and to bring Ferdinand and Miranda into love. Living through the drama of the island, we are thus bound to ask whether it is legitimate for even a first movement of compassion toward the offender to be withheld, as seems to be the case with Prospero. This is the position of feminist writers such as Pamela Sue Anderson, who believe this may necessary, especially in extreme cases of harm such as abuse, to preserve the integrity, well-being, and freedom of the victim as well as to make clear to the abuser the terrible depths of the harm inflicted.[94] Moving from the myth of Prospero to the human experiences we know, we may agree that the initiation of forgiveness may have to be delayed. Yet we might suppose that persons who cannot forgive at a particular moment, and yet who do not have a fixed unforgiving attitude, might begin the journey of forgiveness and so escape being trapped in resentment by imagining conditions in which they *might* take a first unconditional movement of forgiveness. They might envisage a situation in which they themselves were in a better position to take this move, or in which the offender were in a different frame of mind or attitude. The very willingness to imagine that forgiveness might be possible, though it is impossible at present, is taking a place in the empathetic journey of God which can in proper time enable further steps to be taken. The advantage of a theological dynamic here is the belief that such a movement of love and justice is actually there, ahead of us, and can be participated in.

Shakespeare's Spiritual Vision

The Tempest is a play about a man totally in control of outward events on his little island; Prospero is the supreme magician, artist, dramatist, stage-manager. But this only emphasizes what escapes his control—the elemental forces of nature, the mystery of evil, the graces of love and repentance. And he must leave the island behind, the brief lighted stage, and go out into the world where the tempest must be faced.

> But this rough magic
> I here abjure; and, when I have required
> Some heavenly music (which even now I do)
> . . . I'll break my staff,
> Bury it certain fathoms in the earth,
> And deeper than did ever plummet sound
> I'll drown my book. (5.1.50–57)

He has played for a while at being God on the island, but he cannot arrange repentance and love. When he resigns the role of being God (or Christ), he is only making clear what has been true all along; he never did have control at the deepest level of human life. It is a lesson that the playwright also needs to learn as the play comes to an end; finally, people must take responsibility for themselves—even art cannot do this for them.

In Shakespeare's spiritual outlook as we have surveyed it in this book, what really matters in life is human relationships, and these must take priority over structures of power in the state. He encourages us to live with constant awareness of death that brings an end, to cherish love that outlasts the ravages of time, and to remember that forgiveness is essential in a world of human frailty.[95] In all this we are in quest of a story for our lives that is both tragedy and comedy. Shakespeare's intertextuality with the Bible and other ecclesial and theological texts of his time is employed not to promote any particular doctrines, but to progress plot, build characters, and spin a web of words and images in which this spirituality can be held. The situation of his time, with a general blurring between the sharp edges of religious confessions, gives him the space in which to use scripture in this flexible way. I have been maintaining that the resulting work has a continuous impact "in front of the text," creating new intertextualities, and that a theologian must take advantage of this. It is not necessary to think that Shakespeare himself expected his plays to have such an effect, but that he might have done is shown by one final surprise that he springs on us in *The Tempest*.

When act 5 is over, when all has been restored, when Ariel has been set free, Prospero steps to the front of the stage for an epilogue.

> But release me from my bands
> With the help of your good hands:
> Gentle breath of yours my sails
> Must fill, or else my project fails,
> Which was to please. Now I want
> Spirits to enforce, Art to enchant;
> And my ending is despair,
> Unless I be relieved by prayer,
> Which pierces so, that it assaults
> Mercy itself, and frees all faults.
>> As you from crimes would pardoned be,
>> Let your indulgence set me free.

This speech is a shock to the audience. It was conventional in plays of Shakespeare's time for the actor to step forward, doff the apparel he had been wearing for his character, and to ask for applause. The appeal would have been along the lines, "the play is now over; I was a king, but now I am just a beggar; we ask you to express your approval with a good hand-clap." But not with Prospero. He remains Prospero. He asks for our applause and our prayers to help him get back to Naples and Milan, and he asks for our breath to fill his sails as he has lost all his magic arts. Making two final references to religious texts, he quotes the Lord's Prayer, asking for us to forgive as we hope to be forgiven, and echoes the phrase in a homily that "the prayer of them that humble themselves, shall pearce through the clouds."[96] Both allusions have already appeared in the courtroom scene of *The Merchant of Venice*.[97] Shell suggests that the request for prayers reflects the competition of theater and church for the same audience,[98] and yet the very last line leaves us typically uncertain about Shakespeare's own confessional allegiance: the word "indulgence" might be a nod and a wink to Catholics that the church practice of giving relief from purgatory by indulgences and prayers was valid ("set me free"),[99] or a similar hint to Protestants that he was making an "irreverent pun"[100] and really only valued payments into the actors' coffers.

The whole plea is unprecedented. Even more than the device of "plays within a play," we as the audience are being drawn into a play that still appears to be going on. Here, we who view or read the play are specifically being asked to be forgiving. Conventionally the actor asks for forgiveness for the inadequacies of the play, and that is no doubt included here, but the appeal "as you from crimes would pardoned be" reaches into the future. We are being asked to face the dark unknown with forgiveness in our own hearts, and the barrier is truly down between art and life. One set of revels is over, but we are all still part of a larger drama, in which we are fellow-actors with Prospero. When the theologian allows a text of a Shakespearean play to have influence upon the text she or he is writing, and so to shape its thought, the theologian is acknowledging that she or he is participating in the same drama as Prospero and—behind him—Shakespeare. This has been my own aim in this book, for which, with Prospero at the last, I now beg my readers' indulgence.

In this epilogue to *The Tempest* actor and author anticipate the world "in front of the text" and expect that, with Hamlet, there will be "more things in heaven and earth" to come from it. Many other authors have had this expectation, and not least one whose text Shakespeare has drawn upon throughout his work. The writer of the Fourth Gospel ends his account by anticipating other texts to be written which will extend his own narrative of the words and works of Christ, "the which if they should be written every one, I suppose the world could not contain the books that should be written."[101]

NOTES

1. Shakespeare's "More Things" and Religion

1. So Thompson and Taylor, eds., *Hamlet*, 225; see also Jenkins, ed., *Hamlet*, 226.
2. See 1623 Folio in Thompson and Taylor, eds., *Hamlet: The Texts of 1603 and 1623*, 218. Q1 and Q2 read "your."
3. Greenblatt, *Renaissance Self-Fashioning*, 7–8.
4. So Shaheen, *Biblical References in Shakespeare's Plays*, 545.
5. Shakespeare, *Anthony and Cleopatra*, 1.1.17. Cf. 2 Pet. 3:13, "We look for new heavens, and a new earth"; and Isa. 65:17, "I will create new heavens and a new earth."
6. Brady, "Confessionalization—The Career of a Concept," 2.
7. Walsh, *Unsettled Toleration*, 2n2; see also A. Milton, *Catholic and Reformed*, 7.
8. Hooker, *Laws of Ecclesiastical Polity*, VIII.i.2, in *Works*, 2:485.
9. Hodgetts, "A Certificate of Warwickshire Recusants, 1592," 20–31.
10. Richard Wilson, *Secret Shakespeare*, 50–52.
11. Richard Wilson, *Secret Shakespeare*, 48–49, following and expanding Ernst Honigmann, *Shakespeare: The "Lost Years"* (Manchester, UK: Manchester University Press, 1985), 15–30.
12. Bearman, "John Shakespeare: A Papist or Just Penniless?," 411–33. Admittedly, crypto-Catholics could offer "fear of process for debt" as an excuse for nonattendance (see Richard Wilson, *Secret Shakespeare*, 49).
13. Kastan, *Will to Believe*, 22–25.
14. Kastan, *Will to Believe*, 27.
15. Richard Wilson, *Secret Shakespeare*; see also Asquith, *Shadowplay*.
16. For example, in Robert Greene's *The Spanish Masquerado*.
17. Shell, *Shakespeare and Religion*, 61.
18. So Kastan, *Will to Believe*, 69–71. Stevenson, *Shakespeare's Religious Frontier*, 45–46, stresses the Puritan nature of Vincentio's behavior.
19. *Pericles*, 3.1.58–64.
20. See Walsh, *Unsettled Toleration*, 177–85.
21. Walsh, *Unsettled Toleration*, 172.
22. Richard Wilson, *Secret Shakespeare*, 298.
23. Greenblatt, *Shakespearean Negotiations*, 126.
24. Dawson, "Shakespeare and Secular Performance," 84–87.
25. Cummings, *Mortal Thoughts*, 15–18.
26. So Cummings, *Mortal Thoughts*, 176–77.
27. Cummings, *Mortal Thoughts*, 182.
28. Cummings, *Mortal Thoughts*, 183.

29. Jeffrey Knapp, *Shakespeare's Tribe*, 27–29.
30. Walsh, *Unsettled Toleration*, 10.
31. For diversity in Puritanism, see Hill, *Society and Puritanism*, 20–24.
32. This latter group was considerably weakened during the 1590s under persecution by Archbishops John Whitgift and Richard Bancroft (see Hill, *Society and Puritanism*, 28).
33. See Fiddes, "Covenant and the Inheritance of Separatism," 63–92.
34. *Twelfth Night*, 2.3.140–41; 3.2.30. Keir Elam, editor of *Twelfth Night*, 23, proposes that Sir Andrew is associating Brownists with politicians as both being occupied with Machiavellian policy.
35. So Powers, "What He Wills," 222–23.
36. *Twelfth Night*, 5.1.371–72.
37. *Measure for Measure*, 1.3.50, possibly also at 3.1.95 (for "prenzie").
38. So Walsh, *Unsettled Toleration*, 114.
39. Lake, *Antichrist's Lewd Hat*, 622n79.
40. For example, Phillip Stubbes, "The horryble vice of whordome," in Stubbes, *Anatomie of Abuses*, 50–59. In 1650, the Puritan government of the Commonwealth actually put the death penalty for adultery and fornication on the statute books, but it was never actualized (*Acts and Ordinances of the Interregnum*, 387–89). See Shuger, *Political Theologies in Shakespeare's England*, 10–11, 118–19.
41. See Groves, *Texts and Traditions*, 159–61.
42. Walsh, *Unsettled Toleration*, 115.
43. Walsh, *Unsettled Toleration*, 124.
44. So Kastan, ed., *King Henry IV Part 1*, 52–53.
45. J. Milton, *Reason of Church-government*, 24 (wrongly printed as 32).
46. Shaheen, *Biblical References in Shakespeare's Plays*, 137.
47. Poole, *Radical Religion*, 37; Kastan, ed., *King Henry IV Part 1*, 61.
48. Hamilton, "Mocking Oldcastle," 146–48.
49. *Henry IV Part II*, 5.5.46.
50. C. Williams, *English Poetic Mind*, 40.
51. So Lever, ed., *Measure for Measure*, 10.
52. Kastan, *Will to Believe*, 75; he appeals for support to Marsh, *Popular Religion in Sixteenth-Century England*.
53. Mullaney, "Affective Technologies," 71.
54. This is Mullaney's term, in his "Affective Technologies," 71, apparently adopted by Walsh in *Unsettled Toleration*.
55. See Scarisbrick, *The Reformation and the English People*; Haigh, "The Continuity of Catholicism in the English Reformation," 176–208; and Duffy, *Stripping of the Altars*.
56. So Kastan, *Will to Believe*, 29.
57. Everett, "Saint Shakespeare," 32–34. She is quoting from T. S. Eliot, "the draughty church at smokefall," in "Burnt Norton," in *The Complete Poems and Plays of T. S. Eliot* (London: Faber and Faber, 1969), 173. See also Daniell, "Shakespeare and the Protestant Mind," 1–12.
58. These were John Greenwood and Henry Barrow (see Watts, *Dissenters*, 34–38).

59. See B. R. White, *English Separatist Tradition*, 44–66.

60. Kastan, *Will to Believe*, 76.

61. Shuger, "A Protesting Catholic Puritan in Elizabethan England," 624.

62. P. White, "The *via media* in the Early Stuart Church," 211–30.

63. I define "spiritual" later; see chapter 2 below.

64. Miles Coverdale's translation of the Bible was the first complete version to be printed in English (1535). Later he prepared a separate translation of the Psalms for the Great Bible, which became the basis of the Psalter in the Book of Common Prayer.

65. Shaheen, *Biblical References in Shakespeare's Plays*, 54–55.

66. See Shaheen, *Biblical References in Shakespeare's Plays*, 44–48. The Geneva Bible was first published in Geneva in 1560, and was first published in complete form in England in 1576 (following the New Testament only in 1575). In 1587 a version was published which bound Laurence Tomson's revision of the Geneva NT (including notes by Beza) with the Geneva Old Testament.

67. The First Book of Homilies, *Certayne Sermons, or Homilies*, was issued in 1547 under Edward V, mainly written by Thomas Cranmer; henceforth in notes = *Homilies I*. The Second Book of Homilies was issued under Elizabeth I in 1563, and in a further edition of 1571, a homily "Against Disobedience and Wilful Rebellion" was added on account of the Northern Rebellion of November 1569, in *The Second Tome of Homilees of such matters as were promised . . .* ; henceforth in notes = *Homilies II*. The two books were not issued in one volume until 1632.

68. Allen, *Intertextuality*, 2.

69. I am using this term according to the first definition in the *Oxford English Dictionary*: "A text considered in the light of its relation (esp. in terms of allusion) to other texts." The intertext may then be either a text quoted in another text, or that other text itself.

70. Bakhtin, *Problems of Dostoevsky's Poetics*, 6.

71. See Bakhtin, "Discourse in the Novel," in Bakhtin, *Dialogic Imagination*, 259–422.

72. Bakhtin, *Dialogic Imagination*, 276.

73. Claassens, "Biblical Theology as Dialogue," 130.

74. Bakhtin, *Dialogic Imagination*, 284.

75. Bakhtin, *Dialogic Imagination*, 291.

76. Julia Kristeva, "The Bounded Text," in Kristeva, *Desire in Language*, 36.

77. Kristeva, "Semiotics: A Critical Science and/or a Critique of Science," 80–85. Mary Orr, *Intertextuality: Debates and Contexts*, 24–32, complains that Kristeva's key role in developing the theory of intertextuality has been overlooked.

78. Jacques Derrida, "Afterword," in Derrida, *Limited Inc*, 148.

79. Derrida, *Limited Inc*, 136.

80. Allen, *Intertextuality*, 35.

81. Barthes, "Theory of the Text," 39; Barthes, *Pleasure of the Text*, 157.

82. Sonnets are quoted from *Shakespeare's Sonnets*, edited by Katherine Duncan-Jones.

83. Burnet, "Shakespeare and the Marginalia of the Geneva Bible," 113–14.

84. Groves, "Shakespeare's Sonnets and the Genevan Marginalia," 121.
85. See Black, *Edified by the Margent,* 8.
86. Barthes, *Image-Music-Text,* 160.
87. Kristeva, *Desire in Language,* 36–37.
88. Barthes, *Image-Music-Text,* 146.
89. *Macbeth,* 5.3.6.
90. Holinshed, *Historie of Scotland,* 174, 175, 176.
91. Shaheen, *Biblical References in Shakespeare's Plays,* 639.
92. Shaheen, *Biblical References in Shakespeare's Plays,* 9.
93. *Timon of Athens,* 5.2.100–101.
94. Shaheen, *Biblical References in Shakespeare's Plays,* 44.
95. The other example is *Othello,* 3.3.206–7: "Their best conscience / Is not to leave't undone."
96. Clark and Mason, eds., *Macbeth,* 274.
97. Another instance is *Julius Caesar,* 4.2.8–9: "Hath given me some worthy cause to wish / Things done, undone."
98. Allen, *Intertextuality,* 71.

2. Shakespeare's "More Things" and Spirituality

1. This was classically expressed by Matthew Arnold in the nineteenth century in, for example, *Culture and Anarchy,* 56–58.
2. Knight, *Shakespeare and Religion,* 2, 36, 301.
3. Haigh, *English Reformations,* 291.
4. Kastan, *Will to Believe,* 37.
5. Derrida, *Positions,* 19–20; cf. Derrida, *Of Grammatology,* 49–50.
6. Marion, *Being Given,* 196–99.
7. Fernie, "Introduction: Shakespeare, Spirituality and Contemporary Criticism," 8–11.
8. Derrida, *Specters of Marx,* 44.
9. Fernie, "The Last Act," 195–97.
10. Fernie, "The Last Act," 197–99.
11. *Hamlet,* 5.2.7. Fernie, "Last Act," 199, compares Kierkegaard's notion of the act of faith, exceeding morality, in his *Fear and Trembling,* but wrongly claims that Kierkegaard actually uses the word "rashness."
12. Fernie, "Last Act," 199, 209.
13. Fernie, "Last Act," 207, citing Bradley, *Shakespearean Tragedy,* 139.
14. So Shaheen, *Biblical References in Shakespeare's Plays,* 644–45, who also tentatively suggests Ecclesiastes 3:18–20 for "feeds beast as man" and Ecclesiastes 3:12, 13, 22 for "The nobleness of life / Is to do thus."
15. So Wilders, ed., *Anthony and Cleopatra,* 92; cf. 2 Pet. 3:13 and Isa. 65:17.
16. *Romeo and Juliet,* 3.1.69.
17. See below in this chapter, sec. "The Shape of the Story."
18. Schwartz, *Loving Justice, Living Shakespeare,* 51, 53.

19. *Love's Labour's Lost*, 4.3.137–39 (see main text) and *Titus Andronicus*, 4.2.43, the sarcastic comment, "a charitable wish and full of love."

20. For the "last syllable," see Dan. 7:10; and Rev. 20:12. For "dusty death," see Ps. 22:15 ("the dust of death"); Gen. 3:19; and the Burial Service: "Ashes to ashes, dust to dust." For "out, brief candle," see Job 18:6 ("his candle shall be put out"); and Job 21:17. For "walking shadow," see Ps. 39:7 (v. 6 Geneva): "Man walketh in a vain shadow"; and the Burial Service: "he fleeth as it were a shadow." The Burial Service is in the *Booke of Common Prayer* (1559), U.i–iv.

21. Cummings, *Mortal Thoughts*, 205–6.

22. Cf. *Timon*, 5.3.3: "Timon is dead, who hath out-stretch'd his span"; *Othello*, 2.3.71–72: "A soldier's a man; / O, man's life's but a span." So also *King Henry VIII*, 1.1.223: "My life is spanned already." In Psalm 35, both Geneva and Bishops' Bible have "handsbreadth."

23. *Hamlet*, 3.1.65, 82.

24. Calvin, *Institutes*, 3.19.15; 4.10.3. See Bradbury, "Non-Conformist Conscience?," 32–35.

25. *Anthony and Cleopatra*, 5.2.279–80, 294–95.

26. *Romeo and Juliet*, 5.3.115.

27. *Anthony and Cleopatra*, 4.14.52; 5.2.227–28.

28. *Shakespeare's Sonnets*, Sonnet 65.

29. "Gossips" are godparents, invited, among other relatives and friends, to the feast celebrating birth and baptism.

30. So, tentatively, Cartwright, ed., *Comedy of Errors*, 300.

31. Kinney, "Shakespeare's *Comedy of Errors* and the Nature of Kinds," 50.

32. *Comedy of Errors*, 1.2.99; cf. Acts 19:19. See *Comedy of Errors*, 50–55. Shakespeare has changed the classical Epidamnum of Plautus's *Menaechmi*, the Old Comedy of separated twins, into the Christian Ephesus.

33. *Comedy of Errors*, 2.1.7–25; 2.2.116–52: see Cartwright, ed., *Comedy of Errors*, 166, 186, 187; Kinney, "Shakespeare's *Comedy of Errors*," 36, 39, 50–52. Modern scholars doubt that the church in Ephesus was the sole recipient of Ephesians, and think it unlikely that Paul himself wrote Ephesians, which does nevertheless seem to quote extensively from his writings (see Houlden, *Paul's Letters from Prison*, 233–55). Pauline authorship would have been undisputed in Shakespeare's time.

34. Charlton, *Shakespearian Comedy*, 52; Muir, *Sources of Shakespeare's Plays*, 16.

35. Eph. 5:31, referring to Gen. 2:24.

36. Eph. 5:2, 15, 28.

37. According to the 1559 Act of the Uniformity of Common Prayer. So Shaheen, *Biblical References in Shakespeare's Plays*, 587, on the use of the petition in *Othello*, 2.3.107–8 ("God forgive us our sins!"); see also Swift, *Shakespeare's Common Prayers*, 48–51.

38. Examples are *The Merry Wives of Windsor*, 3.3.209–12; 5.5.31; *The Tempest*, 3.2.130; and *Henry VIII*, 3.2.135.

39. *Hamlet*, 5.2.313; *King Lear*, 5.3.164.

40. *Henry VIII*, 2.1.82–83. See McMullan, ed., *King Henry VIII*, 266n.

41. *Ecclesiasticus* (The Wisdom of Jesus Ben Sirach) is a favorite source of quotation and reference for Shakespeare.
42. *Henry V*, 2.2.79–80. The scene is based on the anonymous *The Famous Victories of Henry V* (1594, published 1598), but the incident related is Shakespeare's own addition.
43. *King Richard II*, 5.3.130.
44. *King Lear*, 5.3.8–11.
45. So Coleridge, "some little faulty admixture of pride and sullenness in Cordelia's 'Nothing'" (Coleridge, *Select Poetry and Prose*, 394).
46. See the dictum of Sir Henry Coke, in dispute with James I, that the king is "not under man, but under God and the Law" (*non sub homine, sed sub deo et lege*) (Holdsworth, *History of English Law*, 430 and nn. 2–3).
47. Erasmus, *Education of a Christian Prince* (1540), 189.
48. See, for example, the speeches of the Lord Chief Justice in 2 *Henry IV*, 5.2.35–44, 65–118. Cf. Eure, "Shakespeare and the Legal Process," 410–11.
49. Lake, *Antichrist's Lewd Hat*, 660–61.
50. So Berman, "Shakespeare and the Law," 142–43, 145–46.
51. Schanzer, *Problem Plays of Shakespeare*, 100. Muir, *Shakespeare's Comic Sequence*, 136–37, suggests the audience is uncertain whether to sympathize with her. But Schafer, *Theatre and Christianity*, 19, insists that "within [a] layered religious context, Isabella embarks on a staggering spiritual journey."
52. See Elyot, *The Boke named the Gouernour*, 2:80–81.
53. William Perkins's *Hepieíkeia: or, a treatise of Christian Equitie and Moderation*, is an extended meditation on Philippians 4:5, "Let your moderation be known to all men. The Lord is at hand"; Perkins urges that the nearness of divine justice demands a humble conduct in our justice; echoing Ps. 85:10 (often appealed to in Christian exposition of the atonement), justice must shake hands with her sister mercy in human judgment (see O'Donovan, *Desire of the Nations*, 261).
54. Substitutions run throughout the play, bringing life to various characters (even Barnadine), but these are not related to atonement. Nor can the whole play be seen as an allegory of atonement, as proposed by Neville Coghill in "Comic Form in *Measure for Measure*," 8, 14–27. Nuttall, in *Shakespeare the Thinker*, 262–76, finds an allegory of substitutionary atonement, but a "gnostic" version in which the appeased Father (the Duke) is an evil creator.
55. Knight, *Wheel of Fire*, 82–96. But Shuger, *Political Theologies in Shakespeare's England*, 54, points out that language of divinity (5.1.364–68) refers to the Duke's status as a sacral ruler; and Groves, *Texts and Traditions*, 155–57, finds deliberate reference to James I.
56. For example, Norbrook, "Rhetoric, Ideology and the Elizabethan World Picture," 154–56; and Elton, "Shakespeare's Ulysses and the Problem of Value," 98–101.
57. Bevington, ed., *Troilus and Cressida*, 17.
58. See Shaheen, *Biblical References in Shakespeare's Plays*, 567.

59. *Homilies I*, R.iii/3.
60. *Homilies I*, R.iii/4: "Take awaye Kynges, Princes, Rulers, Magistrates, Iudges, and suche states of Gods ordre."
61. *Homilies II*, 580.
62. Shaheen, *Biblical References in Shakespeare's Plays*, 531.
63. Heidegger, *Being and Time*, 236–37, 279–80.
64. Shaheen, *Biblical References in Shakespeare's Plays*, 641, cites three proverbial sayings.
65. *The Winter's Tale*, 5.3.116–17.
66. So Leontes in *The Winter's Tale*, 5.3.153–55. See Richard Wilson, *Secret Shakespeare*, 93, for the "truth after the play."
67. In this section I use ideas, and some text, from my chapter "Comedy and Tragedy: The Shakesperean Boundary," in Fiddes, *Freedom and Limit*, 65–82.
68. Bethell uses this phrase in *Shakespeare and the Popular Dramatic Tradition*, 108, in his assessment of Elizabethen audiences.
69. This is Shakespeare's own kind of tragicomedy, not the sort commended by his contemporary Giambattista Guarini, author of *Il Pastor Fido*, who advocated some miraculous intervention in the denouement.
70. On the place of confusion, see below, chap. 4, sec. "The Confusions of Comedy and the Healing of Disorder."
71. *The Comedy of Errors*, 5.1.397. Cartwright (299) finds "sympathized" to mean not only being "correspondingly affected" but to indicate a kind of sympathetic magic in which feelings are shared between characters.
72. *As You Like It*, 1.1.35–37: "Shall I keep your hogs and eat husks with them? What prodigal portion have I spent, that I should come to such penury?"; cf. Luke 15:15–16. The Geneva version is the first English translation to have "husks," and whereas the Gospel passage does not contain the word "prodigal," the Geneva and Bishops' Bibles head it "The Prodigal Son" (see Shaheen, *Biblical References in Shakespeare's Plays*, 216).
73. *Twelfth Night*, 5.1.371; *As You Like It*, 5.4.193; *Merchant of Venice*, 4.1.391.
74. *Much Ado about Nothing*, 1.3.25; 5.4.126.
75. *Measure for Measure*, 5.1.492, 535–38.
76. The Royal Shakespeare Company production of the play in 1970, directed by John Barton, first explored the possibility that Isabella might not marry the Duke (see Schafer, *Theatre and Christianity*, 26–27).
77. *Much Ado about Nothing*, 5.4.120.
78. *The Tempest*, 4.1.153–54.
79. So Honigmann, ed., *Othello*, 120, referring both to Exodus 4:14 and 1 Corinthians 15:10.
80. Brooke, *Shakespeare's Early Tragedies*, 83–84, judges that this is the pivotal point where the play moves from comedy to tragedy.
81. Knight, *Imperial Theme*, 265.
82. *Anthony and Cleopatra*, 1.4.47: the phrase is used here of the common body of the people.

83. Henn, *Harvest of Tragedy*, 288–90 (cf. 162, 251–56), also finds the center of tragedy to lie in the tension between human freedom and the limits of environment, but locates the failure of the tragic hero simply in his proud disregard of creaturely limits; from a Christian perspective he identifies this as sin, and finds its typical Shakespearean form in the failure to observe the due time for things ("unripeness").

84. So Bradley, *Shakespearean Tragedy*, 324–25: "though in one sense and outwardly [the hero] has failed ... [he] is, in some way which we do not seek to define, untouched by the doom that overtakes him." Cf. Courtney, *Shakespeare's World of Death*, 22–23.

85. Gardner, "The Noble Moor," 203.

86. Shaheen, "Like the Base Judean," 93–95. He argues that the location of Judas in the tribe of Judah may be evidence that Shakespeare owned a Geneva-Tomson edition of the Bible as only Tomson makes this identification, in a gloss on Matthew 10:4. Hamlin, *Bible in Shakespeare*, 113, also prefers the reading "Judean."

87. *Anthony and Cleopatra*, 4.14.107–8.

88. *Anthony and Cleopatra*, 5.2.78–87.

89. *Anthony and Cleopatra*, 5.2.93–94. All these quotations from the book of Revelation have been identified by Shaheen, *Biblical References in Shakespeare's Plays*, 653, 655–56.

90. Groves, *Texts and Traditions*, 77–80, 83–84.

91. Groves, *Texts and Traditions*, 85.

92. Groves, *Texts and Traditions*, 86–87.

93. Marion, *Being Given*, 199–212.

3. Shakespeare's "More Things" and Theology

1. Hawkes, *Shakespeare in the Present*, 22.

2. Maguire, *Where There's a Will There's a Way*, 2.

3. Greenblatt, *Hamlet in Purgatory*, 5–7.

4. Ricoeur, *Interpretation Theory*, 87.

5. Ricoeur, "The Function of Fiction in Shaping Reality," 127.

6. Fernie, "Shakespeare and the Prospect of Presentism," 58, 175.

7. For the infinite "deferral" of meaning in a text, see Derrida, "Différance," 6–15; Derrida, *Of Grammatology*, 7; and Roland Barthes, "From Work to Text," in Barthes, *Image, Music, Text*, 155–64.

8. Kristeva, *Revolution in Poetic Language*, 59–60.

9. Kristeva, *Revolution in Poetic Language*, 25–30.

10. Kristeva, *Revolution in Poetic Language*, 63–67, 86–89.

11. Kristeva, *Revolution in Poetic Language*, 17.

12. Barthes, *Pleasure of the Text*, 78–80.

13. Barthes, *Image-Music-Text*, 148.

14. Barthes, *Image-Music-Text*, 126–27.

15. Barthes, *Image-Music-Text*, 148.

16. Bloom, *Map of Misreading*, 19.

17. Bloom, *Anxiety of Influence*, 70.

18. Bloom, *Poetics of Influence*, 405–24.

19. Bloom, *Shakespeare: The Invention of the Human*, xxvii–xxviii.

20. The famous essay by W. K. Wimsatt and Monroe Beardsley "The Intentional Fallacy" (1942) does not foreclose considering authorial intention altogether but warns against making it decisive in establishing meaning or "success" (see reprint in Wimsatt, *Studies in the Meaning of Poetry*, 3–18).

21. Lothe, "Authority, Reliability and the Challenge of Reading," 104–9.

22. Barthes, *Image-Music-Text*, 159; Derrida, *Dissemination*, 224–26.

23. See Lindbeck, *Nature of Doctrine*, 79–84; cf. Hauerwas, *Approaching the End*, 22–24.

24. Fiddes, *Freedom and Limit*, 15, 33–35; Fiddes, *Promised End*, 5–8.

25. Gombrich, *Art and Illusion*, 271.

26. In the following paragraphs I repeat ideas and some text from my article "Concept, Image and Story in Systematic Theology," 3–23.

27. Ricoeur, *Time and Narrative*, 2: 21–28.

28. Murdoch, "Sublime and the Beautiful Revisited," 261, 285.

29. Murdoch, "Sublime and the Beautiful Revisited," 275, 283.

30. On the method of correlation, see Tillich, *Systematic Theology*, 2:67–73. Tracy, *Analogical Imagination*, 64, stresses that the correlation must be two-way.

31. Coleridge, *Biographia Literaria*, 1:102.

32. For Karl Barth, for example, dogmatics (theology) tests the proclamation of the church (the preached word) against revelation as the incarnate word (Christ), which is known through the written word (the Bible) (see Barth, *Church Dogmatics*, I/1, 273–87).

33. Derrida, "Of an Apocalyptic Tone Newly Adopted in Philosophy," 63–66.

34. Tillich, *Systematic Theology*, 1:88–93, 181–84; 2:203–4; 3:235–37.

35. Tillich, *Theology of Culture*, 54, 72–73.

36. Rahner, *Foundations of Christian Faith*, 32.

37. Rahner, *Foundations of Christian Faith*, 127.

38. Rahner, *Foundations of Christian Faith*, 153–62.

39. So Macquarrie, *In Search of Humanity*, 25–37.

40. In the following paragraphs I repeat ideas and some text from chapter 10 of my book *Seeing the World and Knowing God*.

41. What he was opposing was shortly to appear in print in the approaches of Frei, *Eclipse of Biblical Narrative*, 29–36; and Lindbeck, *Nature of Doctrine*, 118–24.

42. Certeau, "How is Christianity Thinkable Today?," 148.

43. Certeau, *Practice of Everyday Life*, 172.

44. Certeau, *Practice of Everyday Life*, 186.

45. Ricoeur, *Oneself as Another*, 4.

46. Ricoeur, *Conflict of Interpretations*, 17.

47. Ricoeur, *Oneself as Another*, 355.

48. Barth recognizes this in *Church Dogmatics* I/1, 55, although he stresses that it is not the task of the Christian theologian to build a religion on these other "texts" in the world.

49. Ricoeur, "Philosophical Hermeneutics and Biblical Hermeneutics," 97. Here Ricoeur regards scripture as a regional case of general hermeneutics.

50. See Levinas, *Otherwise Than Being*, 114–26.

51. See above, chap. 2, sec. "A Spirituality of Love and Death."

52. Certeau, "How Is Christianity Thinkable Today?," 149.

53. On "lack," see Lacan, *Ecrits*, 287–88, 316–17.

54. Derrida, *Dissemination*, 202–3. In this context the text of the body is the face of the silent Pierrot.

55. See Frye, *The Great Code*, xii–xvi.

56. D. Ford, *Christian Wisdom*, 57.

57. So Lindbeck, *Nature of Doctrine*, 16–20.

58. Macquarrie, *Principles of Christian Theology*, 90–96.

59. Barth, *Church Dogmatics* I/1, 145–49.

60. Augustine, *Contra Faustum Manichaeum*, 32.20.

61. Augustine, *Confessions*, XIII.15.16–17 (282–83), citing Isa. 34:4; Ps. 103:28; and Ps. 8:3–4.

62. See Southgate, *Groaning of Creation*, 67–75.

63. Ricoeur, *Hermeneutics and the Human Sciences*, 201–2.

64. Derrida, *Writing and Difference*, 102.

65. So Balthasar, *Glory of the Lord*, vol. 1: *Seeing the Form*, 443–44.

66. Cf. Barth, *Church Dogmatics* I/1, 168–76.

67. Balthasar, *Theo-Logic*, vol. 1: *The Truth of the World*, 235–38.

68. In the next two sections, I repeat ideas and some text from my *Seeing the World and Knowing God*, 149–57; see also Fiddes, *Participating in God*, 34–46.

69. Heidegger, "The Onto-theo-logical Constitution of Metaphysics," 58.

70. Athanasius, *Contra Arianos*, 3.4–6; cf. 1.9, 39, 58.

71. See, for example, Gregory Nazianzen, *Orationes* 29.16; and Augustine, *De Trinitate*, 5.6–13.

72. A similar case for taking subsistent relations seriously is made by Cunningham, *These Three Are One*, 59–71; cf. 168–69. But Cunningham still refers to "addressing" or "speaking to" the relations (72) rather than "speaking in" the flow of relations.

73. A translation of *perichōrēsis* used by G. L. Prestige in his *God in Patristic Thought*, 282–300, and made popular by the poet and literary critic Charles Williams (see Williams, *Descent of the Dove*, 52: "The Godhead itself was in Co-inherence").

74. Augustine, *De Trinitate* 5.6.

75. Aquinas, *Summa theologiae*, 1a.29.4.

76. Barth, *Church Dogmatics*, II/1, 263.

77. Kant, *Critique of Pure Reason*, 87, 149.

78. 2 Cor. 1:19–21; cf. Heb. 5:7–10.

79. Moltmann, *Crucified God*, 247.

80. See, for example, Matt. 6:6; John 14:16; Heb. 7:25; and Eph. 6:18.

81. See Jacobs, *Living Illusions*, 68–71.

82. Prov. 3:17, 8:20–22, 9:6; Ecclus. 24:1–7; Ws. 6:16, 7:29–8:1, 9:9; cf. John 1:1; and Col. 1:17. Later, see Hildegard of Bingen, "O Virtus Sapientiae," in Hildegard, *Symphonia,* 100–101; and Julian of Norwich, *Revelations of Divine Love,* 58 (137).

83. Jüngel, *God's Being Is in Becoming,* 29.

84. Murdoch, *Metaphysics as a Guide to Morals,* 511–12, commends "a theology which can continue without God," which "treats of those matters of 'ultimate concern,' our experience of the unconditioned and our continued sense of what is holy." The expression "ultimate concern" derives from Tillich, *Systematic Theology,* 1:15–16.

85. Derrida, *Of Grammatology,* 13–15.

86. See above, chap. 1, sec. "Intertextuality in Shakespeare's Own Practice."

87. Derrida, *Writing and Difference,* 67

88. See below, chap. 5, sec. "Making Theology: Inclusivism and the Covenant."

89. Davies, *Creativity of God,* 140; italics original.

90. Balthasar, *Theo-Drama,* vol. 1: *Prolegomena,* 20.

91. Cavell, *Disowning Knowledge,* 200–201, 220–21.

92. Cavell, *Disowning Knowledge,* 218. See also Hawkes, "Shakespeare and New Critical Approaches," 294–95.

93. This gives a relational content to the impersonal "force" discerned by Ewan Fernie in *Hamlet* (Fernie, ed., *Spiritual Shakespeares,* 199).

94. Summary by Murphy, "Hans Urs von Balthasar," 12.

95. Balthasar, *Theo-Logic,* vol. 1: *The Truth of the World,* 142.

96. Balthasar, *Glory of the Lord,* vol. 1: *Seeing the Form,* 125; Balthasar, *Glory of the Lord,* vol. 7: *Theology: The New Covenant,* 391–98.

97. Balthasar, *Theo-Drama,* vol. 4: *The Action,* 329–30.

98. Balthasar, *Theo-Drama,* vol. 4: *The Action,* 329–30, 333–34.

99. So Barth, *Church Dogmatics,* II/1, 281; II/2, 6.

100. Barth, *Church Dogmatics,* II/1, 271, 273–74; cf. I/1, 434.

101. Saussure, *Course in General Linguistics,* 116.

102. Derrida, "Différance," 6–15.

103. Aquinas, *Summa theologiae,* 1a.30.4.

104. Rahner, *The Trinity,* 104–6.

105. Mühlen, *Die Veränderlichkeit Gottes,* 26. See also Jüngel, *God as the Mystery of the World,* 317–20, 374–75.

106. Balthasar, *Mysterium Paschale,* ix.

107. Derrida, *Dissemination,* 352.

108. Magliola, *Derrida on the Mend,* 134.

109. Magliola, *Derrida on the Mend,* 149. However, we also have to abandon any notion of persons as "subjects" in God, to which Magliola at least is still attached in his adherence to the teaching of the Catholic Magisterium.

110. Merleau-Ponty, *Visible and Invisible,* 248–49.

111. See Bowie, *The Anthropology of Religion,* 55–61.

4. A MIDSUMMER NIGHT'S DREAM AND SEEING WITH THE EYES OF LOVE

1. Pepys, 29 September 1662, in *Diary of Samuel Pepys*, 3:208; Halliday, *Shakespeare and His Critics*, 169.
2. See Wind, *Pagan Mysteries in the Renaissance*, 53, 80.
3. See Marshall, "Exchanging Visions," 543–75; and, earlier, Kermode, "The Mature Comedies," 211–27.
4. See, for example, 1 *Henry VI*, 4.2.37 (2 Chron. 9:6), 2.5.8–9 (Job 17:7); 2 *Henry VI*, 3.2.395 (Gen. 46:4); 3 *Henry VI*, 1.1.24; and *Henry V*, 3.2.115–16 (Ps. 132:4), 3 *Henry VI*, 1.4.37 (Ps. 123:2), 5.4.74–75 (Ps. 80:5); *Richard II* 3.2.36–46 (Job 24:13–17); *Merchant of Venice* 2.2.158 (Luke 4:5, "twinkling"); *Hamlet* 1.1.111 (Luke 6:42); and *Macbeth*, 4.1.109 (1 Sam. 2:33).
5. Shaheen, *Biblical References in Shakespeare's Plays*, 150. Shakespeare also uses the phrase "apple of her eye" in *Love's Labour's Lost*, 5.2.475.
6. Possibly that of Elizabeth Carey, granddaughter of the Lord Chamberlain, to Thomas Berkeley at Blackfriars on 19 February 1595 (see *A Midsummer Night's Dream*, ed. Brooks, lv–lvii).
7. *Romeo and Juliet*, 1.1.6.
8. So Shaheen, *Biblical References in Shakespeare's Plays*, 146, but Shaheen quotes the parallel text in Matthew 16:24, so missing the significance of the word "daily" in Luke 9:23.
9. So Knapp, *Image Ethics in Shakespeare and Spenser*, 103, maintaining that the fusion of love with the cross is "the critical synthesizing gesture of Platonism and Christianity" (102).
10. See Panofsky, *Studies in Iconology*, 122–24.
11. See Daniell, "Shakespeare and the Traditions of Comedy," 108–9.
12. 1.2.230; on "doting," see 1.2.225 (Lysander); 4.1.44 (Titania); 4.1.167 (Demetrius); cf. Kermode, *Shakespeare's Language*, 60–61.
13. See Tillyard, *Elizabethan World Picture*, 7–15, 77–95.
14. Probably there is a topical allusion here to the foul weather and disturbed seasons that people had experienced from 1594 to 1595, when the play was written (see Brooks, ed., *A Midsummer Night's Dream*, xxxvii).
15. See above, chap. 2, sec. "A Spirituality of Authority."
16. *Homilies I*, R.iii/3.
17. Interview by Brian Magee, 1978, printed in Magee, ed., *Men of Ideas*, 230.
18. On the implications of the Rosalind/Ganymede identity, see Orgel, "Shakespeare, Sexuality and Gender," 18–19, 44, 56–57.
19. In Shakespeare's source for the Pyramus-Thisbe story in Ovid's *Metamorphoses*, book 4, the fruit of the mulberry tree marking their death for love changes color from white to dark red, but this is not associated with the power of a love-charm.
20. Barkan, "Diana and Actaeon," 358. See also Bate, *Soul of the Age*, 111.
21. Joughin, "Bottom's Secret," 133–38. Cf. Daniell, "Shakespeare and the Traditions of Comedy," 109: "the play brushes the numinous."

22. However, the words that follow appear nowhere exactly in scripture—the closest is Isa. 64:3 (LXX): see Barrett, *Epistle to the Romans*, 73.

23. For a discussion of the possible echo of "bottom," see Stroup, "Bottom's Name and His Epiphany," 79–82; this is disputed by Robert F. Wilson, "God's Secrets and Bottom's Name: A Reply," 407–8. Hamlin, *Bible in Shakespeare*, 109, cites theologians of the period who write of the "bottom" of "God's secrets."

24. Joughin, "Bottom's Secret," 139, quoting Brooks, ed., *A Midsummer Night's Dream*, cxvii.

25. Kermode, *Shakespeare, Spenser, Donne*, 200–218.

26. See above, chap. 2, sec. "A Spirituality of Love and Death."

27. Joughin, "Bottom's Secret," 154–55.

28. 5.1.12ff. See Fernie, *Spiritual Shakespeares*, 4.

29. Hamlin, *Bible in Shakespeare*, 109.

30. Erasmus, *Praise of Folie*, T.iii/1.

31. Erasmus, *Praise of Folie*, T.ii/1.

32. Erasmus, *Praise of Folie*, T.iii/2.

33. Montrose, *Purpose of Playing*, 190–98; cf. Bate, *Soul of the Age*, 55–57.

34. Joughin, "Bottom's Secret," 134, 138.

35. See D. Ford, *Christian Wisdom*, 380–82.

36. Nussbaum, *Upheavals of Thought*, 3–4, 27; cf. Nussbaum, *Love's Knowledge*, 262–63, 280–84.

37. Nussbaum, *Upheavals of Thought*, 465, 474, 64.

38. For example, Levinas, *Totality and Infinity*, 188–91, 295–97; Derrida *Writing and Difference*, 91–92; and Derrida, "The Principle of Reason," 10, 20.

39. Kant, *Critique of Practical Reason*, 137–39, 142–46.

40. Barth, *Church Dogmatics*, II/1, 16–17.

41. Barth, *Church Dogmatics*, II/1, 21–23.

42. Barth, *Church Dogmatics*, III/1, 36.

43. Barth, *Church Dogmatics*, II/1, 59–62.

44. Barth, *Church Dogmatics*, I/I, 165–69.

45. See above, chap. 3, sec. "Text and Trinity."

46. Barth, *Church Dogmatics*, II/1, 264.

47. Barth, *Church Dogmatics*, II/1, 274–75. Barth asserts that God is "act" or "a distinct happening" in the event of revelation, but because revelation is God's self-revelation, there is a correspondence with "what God is in Himself and in His eternal essence" (274; cf. I/1, 371).

48. Shaheen, *Biblical References in Shakespeare's Plays*, 150, compares Dan 5:27; Job 6:2; Job 31:6; and Ps. 62:9.

49. Notably, Augustine, *De civitate Dei*, 14:11–17

50. Gandolfo, "Encountering God and Being Human 'Where the Wild Things Are,'" 303–8.

51. Sollereder, *God, Evolution, and Animal Suffering*, 92–104; Southgate, *Theology in a Suffering World*, 114–20.

52. Dostoyevsky, *Brothers Karamazov*, 287.

53. Hick, *Evil and the God of Love*, 265–66; Swinburne, *Providence and the Problem of Evil*, 126–31.

54. See Fiddes, *Creative Suffering of God*, 221–29; Fiddes, *Participating in God*, 144–48; Southgate, *Groaning of Creation*, 61–64.

55. Hick, *Evil and the God of Love*, 260–61, 277–83, 374–77.

56. See Fiddes, *Participating in God*, 164–70; Southgate, *Groaning of Creation*, 50–54; Page, *God and the Web of Creation*, 40–43.

57. In process theology, God is bound to create by the principle of creativity (see Hartshorne, *Divine Relativity*, 74). By contrast, I argue that God needs our love, because he has freely desired to be a loving creator (so Fiddes, *Creative Suffering of God*, 66–68; and Brümmer, *Model of Love*, 237).

58. *Twelfth Night*, 1.5.28–29.

59. Few modern New Testament scholars think that Paul is the author of Ephesians, but as with the use of the Letter to the Ephesians in *The Comedy of Errors* (see above, chap. 2, sec. "A Spirituality of Love and Death"), no question would have been raised about his authorship in Shakespeare's time.

60. Elsewhere it simply means "separation" (see *A Midsummer Night's Dream*, 3.2.210; *2 Henry IV*, 4.1.194; and *Cymbeline* 1.6.37).

61. Groves, *Texts and Traditions*, 60–61; see also Groves, "The Wittiest Partition," 277–82; cf. Chaudhuri, *A Midsummer Night's Dream*, 271.

62. Snodgrass, *In Radical Pursuit*, 218.

63. Chaudhuri, ed., *A Midsummer Night's Dream*, 84, 106.

64. May Day, Midsummer, St. Valentine's Day: as in title, 1.1.167; 4.1.132; 4.1.147.

65. Bakhtin, *Rabelais and His World*, 203–12; on carnival in Bakhtin, see also above, chap. 3, sec. "Intertextuality and the Afterlife of a Text."

66. Chaudhuri, ed., *Midsummer Night's Dream*, 99.

67. Oberon, 2.1.78–80, names four women who were victims of Theseus's rapacious behavior; according to Plutarch, *Lives*, 28:1–2, he finally abandoned Hippolyta (under the name of Antiope) (see Chaudhuri, ed., *A Midsummer Night's Dream*, 66–68).

68. See Laroque, "Popular Festivity," 65–66.

69. So Orgel, *Imagining Shakespeare*, 85–86.

70. Chaudhuri, *A Midsummer Night's Dream*, 97.

71. King James I, *Daemonologie*, K.3/4–L.1/1 (section 3.5), refers to witches' acquaintance with the king and queen of the fairies. Reginald Scot, though skeptical himself about both witches and fairies, provides considerable evidence for belief in the connection between them: so Scot, *Discouerie of Witchcraft*, 15.9–10, referring to invocations of "sisters of fairies" and a powerful fairy, Sibylia.

72. Burton, *The Anatomy of Melancholy* (1621), 1:192.

73. Agrippa, *Three books of Occult Philosophy*, 3:32 (450): "A certain kind of spirits, not so noxious, but most neer to men, so that they are even affected with humane passions, and many of these delight in mans society . . . So the Fairies."

74. Rom. 8:38; cf. Col. 1:16; Eph. 6:12. See below, chap. 10, sec. "The Principalities and Powers."

75. Anselm, *Cur Deus homo* 1.10–14; Calvin, *Institutes,* 2.16.2–5; cf. 2.12.3.

76. Rom. 6:3–6.

77. Calvin, *Institutes,* 3.11.10.

78. Peter Abelard, Commentary on the Epistle to the Romans, 2.3.26, in Fairweather, ed., *Scholastic Miscellany,* 28.

79. See the critique of Abelard in Bernard, *Letters,* 190, trans. L. W. Grensted, *A Short History of the Doctrine of the Atonement,* 106.

80. Abelard, Commentary on the Epistle to the Romans, 2.3.26, in Faithweather, *Scholastic Miscellany,* 283.

81. See, e.g., Bulgakov, *Bride of the Lamb,* 297–99, 300–306; and Lossky, *Mystical Theology of the Eastern Church,* 98–113.

82. See Oberon's comment: "all this derision / Shall seem a dream," 3.2.370–71. Norman Holland, "Hermia's Dream," 75, conceives the play as "a dream of a dream of a dream."

83. On Italian pastoral, see Clubb, "Italian Stories on the Stage," 37–38.

84. Jensen, *Religion and Revelry in Shakespeare's Festive World,* 113–14.

85. Greenblatt, *Shakespearean Negotiations,* 11.

86. See Richard Wilson, *Secret Shakespeare,* 144–47.

87. Jensen, *Religion and Revelry in Shakespeare's Festive World,* 106.

88. Schwartz, "Othello and the Horizon of Justice," 42–44, notes that the Body of Christ was already central to the action and meaning of medieval Corpus Christi plays and so gave them a kind of "sacramental reality."

89. Fiddes and Taylor, "Seeing with the Eyes of Love," 83–108.

90. Fiddes, "Shakespeare in Church," 199–217.

91. See Bria, *The Liturgy after the Liturgy.* Cf. the Catholic appeal to "eucharistic life" in, for example, Benedict XVI, Apostolic Exhortation, *Sacramentum Caritatis* (2007), 71.

92. Girard, *A Theatre of Envy,* 36–39.

93. Girard, *Violence and the Sacred,* 77–103.

94. Girard, *Things Hidden since the Foundation of the World,* 219; cf. 182, 430.

5. The Merchant of Venice and the Covenant of Love

1. Shapiro, *Shakespeare and the Jews,* 84–85.

2. Danson, *Harmonies of "The Merchant of Venice,"* 149.

3. *The Merchant of Venice,* ed. Drakakis, 8–17, 98–102.

4. Luther, *Trade and Usury,* in *Luther's Works,* 45:298–310.

5. By, for example, T. Wilson, *Discourse uppon Vsurye,* 4–5.

6. "Give to everyone who begs from you; and if anyone takes away your goods, do not ask for them again . . . lend, expecting nothing in return."

7. This restored an act of 1545 which had been repealed in 1552.

8. Gross, *Shylock: A Legend and Its Legacy,* nevertheless shows that Shakespeare did not capitulate to the simple stereotype of the usurer, unlike later reception of Shylock on the stage (50, 285–90, 317).

9. So Shaheen, *Biblical References in Shakespeare's Plays,* 160.

10. So Brown, ed., *The Merchant of Venice*, 8.

11. Brown, *Shakespeare and His Comedies*, 65.

12. For example, Eagleton, *Sweet Violence*, 165–66; Danson, *Harmonies of "The Merchant of Venice*," 60–62; and Nuttall, *A New Mimesis*, 123–24.

13. "Oracles" in Romans 3:2 includes the sense both of inspired utterance and promise (see Käsemann, *Commentary on Romans*, 79): "the reference is to the promise of the gospel."

14. So Lewalski, "Biblical Allusion and Allegory in *The Merchant of Venice*," 327–43.

15. See above, chap. 2, sec. "A Spirituality of Forgiveness and Mercy."

16. Similarly, the version of the flesh-bond story in book 3 of Anthony Munday's *Zelauto* (1580) contains a speech by the judge which associates the judgment and mercy of God, and the atonement in Christ, with the legal case in front of him—though the moneylender in this case is a fellow-Christian and the penalty demanded is loss of the right eye; for *Zelauto*, see Brown, ed., *Merchant of Venice*, 164–65.

17. "Lord of Sabaoth (hosts or armies)" is a frequent ascription of God in the Old Testament. However, Q2 corrects to "Sabbath," and both Drakakis and Brown accept this as Shakespeare's intention.

18. "When thou has vowed a vow unto God, defer not to pay it." However, Kerrigan, *Shakespeare's Binding Language*, 185–87, argues that since Shylock has also sworn "by my soul" his "oath in heaven" is of the kind that—according to the *Kol Nidrei* declaration—could be expunged by God's mercy on the Day of Atonement. This would make Shylock unnecessarily legalistic, according to his own religious culture.

19. For Luther's view of the alliance between reason and law, see Gerrish, *Grace and Reason*, 84–99.

20. Luther, *Galatervorlesung* (*Lectures on Galatians*), WA 40 (1): 36.2, 268.13, 389.21, 603.27, 666.28.

21. Drakakis, ed., *Merchant of Venice*, 21.

22. Greenblatt, *Learning to Curse*, 43.

23. But *contra*, Shapiro maintains that Shakespeare fails to embed a perception of difference into his structure of romantic comedy, so that he capitulates to a Marlovian "exclusion" of the alien (Shapiro, "Which Is *the Merchant* Here, and Which *the Jew?*," 269–70, 272, 274).

24. Hamlin, *Bible in Shakespeare*, 107; similarly, Klause, "Catholic and Protestant, Jesuit and Jew," 182.

25. Hamlin, *Bible in Shakespeare*, 107n71.

26. There is a crossover between the commerce of Venice and the love-world of Belmont, as Bassanio himself is always in danger of commercializing love (see Nuttall, *New Mimesis*, 121–23).

27. Brown, ed., *Merchant of Venice*, 173.

28. See Fiddes and Bader, "Whatever Happened to a Pauline Text?," 3–7.

29. Shaheen, *Biblical References in Shakespeare's Plays*, 176.

30. The first Quarto has "wood," defended by Drakakis, ed., *Merchant of Venice*, 267; but Brown, ed., *Merchant of Venice*, 60, follows Samuel Johnson's conjecture, emending to "tombs."

31. For text, see Brown, ed., *Merchant of Venice*, 174.

32. For text, see Brown, ed., *Merchant of Venice*, 172.

33. For text, see Brown, ed., *Merchant of Venice*, 142.

34. Brown, ed., *Merchant of Venice*, xxix–xxx, dismisses the theory that a lost play, called *The Jew* (ca. 1579), had already combined the caskets story with the plot of *Il Pecorone*.

35. See the first story of the fourth day in Giovanni Fiorentino, *Il Pecorone* (Milan, 1558), text in Brown, ed., *Merchant of Venice*, 140–53.

36. Klause, "Catholic and Protestant, Jesuit and Jew," 193–97.

37. For example, Milward, *Shakespeare's Religious Background*, 54–59.

38. Klause, "Catholic and Protestant, Jesuit and Jew," cites, for example, Southwell, *Epistle of Comfort*, 17; *Humble Supplication*, 12, 35; *Marie Magdalens Funeral Teares*, 42.

39. Southwell, *Epistle of Comfort*, 34r; cited in Klause, "Catholic and Protestant, Jesuit and Jew," 195.

40. Klause, "Catholic and Protestant, Jesuit and Jew," 194–95.

41. Shaheen, *Biblical References in Shakespeare's Plays*, 180; Drakakis, ed., *Merchant of Venice*, 347. See also Gross, *Shylock: A Legend and Its Legacy*, 96.

42. Luke 11.4; cf. Matt. 6:12, 14–15.

43. Shaheen, *Biblical References in Shakespeare's Plays*, 180–82, makes an attempt.

44. Drakakis, ed., *Merchant of Venice*, 339.

45. Matt. 27:25. See also 3.1.85–86, "The curse on our nation."

46. Gross, *Shylock: A Legend and Its Legacy*, 96–97, pointing out that there were stereotypes of both Jew and Gentile current.

47. Text in Brown, ed., *Merchant of Venice*, 164–65.

48. Kastan, *Will to Believe*, 99–100.

49. See Girard, *Theatre of Envy*, 250–51: "The Christians use the word 'mercy' with such perversity that they can justify their own revenge with it."

50. Quoted by Drakakis, ed., *Merchant of Venice*, 104, from an unpublished MS.

51. For example, Augustine in *De spiritu et littera*, 4.6, 5.7–8; and Luther in his *Psalmenvorlesung*, WA 55 (1): 4.25. For discussion, see Fiddes and Bader, "Whatever Happened to a Pauline Text?," 4–5.

52. Gen. 29:15–30.

53. However, we should note that there were very few Jews actually resident in London at this period; the play records a prejudice against exotic foreigners rather than a civil conflict actually going on.

54. Eagleton, *William Shakespeare*, 37; see also Miller, "Matters of State," 203.

55. Coghill, "The Governing Idea," 9–16. Another defense of Portia's quibble is mounted by J. D. Wilson, *Shakespeare's Happy Comedies*, 106.

56. See St. Paul in Gal. 3:10; Rom 2:12; Rom. 7:9–11; and 2 Cor. 3:6–9.

57. Kastan, *Will to Believe*, 100.

58. Kastan, *Will to Believe*, 102. He cites, for example, William Perkins, *A Reformed Catholike*, A.8 (=14–16)

59. Kastan, *Will to Believe*, 102.

60. Luther, *Galatervorlesung*, WA 40 (1), 473.7–9. Translated by Gerrish, in *Grace and Reason*, 89.

61. *Homilies I*, J.iii/2.

62. Danson, *Harmonies of "The Merchant of Venice,"* 78–80; Cohen, "The Merchant of Venice and the Possibilities of Historical Criticism," 769.

63. Klause, "Catholic and Protestant, Jesuit and Jew," 186, 204, 206.

64. Richard Wilson, *Secret Shakespeare*, 255–56; Klause, "Catholic and Protestant, Jesuit and Jew," 216–17.

65. Klause, "Catholic and Protestant, Jesuit and Jew," 206–7.

66. Richard Wilson, *Secret Shakespeare*, 162.

67. See *Council of Trent* (1545–69), Sixth Session on Justification, Canon 1: "If any one saith, that man may be justified before God by his own works, whether done through the teaching of human nature, or that of the law, without the grace of God through Jesus Christ; let him be anathema." Canon 9: "If any one saith, that by faith alone the impious is justified; in such wise as to mean, that nothing else is required to co-operate in order to the obtaining the grace of Justification, and that it is not in any way necessary, that he be prepared and disposed by the movement of his own will; let him be anathema" (from *Papal Encyclicals Online*, https://www.papalencyclicals.net/councils/trent.htm).

68. For example, Luther, *Psalmenvorlesung*, WA 4:262 (on Psalm 115:1): see Lillback, *Binding of God*, 60–62.

69. Luther, *Galatervorlesung*, WA 40(1) 485 = *Lectures on Galatians*, in *Luther's Works*, 26:312–13.

70. Luther, *Galatervorlesung*, WA 40(1) 249–53 = *Lectures on Galatians*, in *Luther's Works*, 26:143–45.

71. Ursinus, *The Svmme of Christian Religion*, 261.

72. See Kendall, *Calvin and English Calvinism*, 26–41; Bruggink, "Calvin and Federal Theology," 16–20; and Barth, CD 4/1, 58.

73. Calvin, *Institutes*, 2.10.1.

74. Calvin, *Institutes*, 2.11.7–8.

75. See Melanchthon, *Loci communes theologici*, 105–7.

76. For instance, Lillback, *Binding of God*, 287–311.

77. Perkins, *Workes*, 1:32–70.

78. A Puritan Shylock is proposed by Milward, *Shakespeare's Religious Background*, 159; Kirschbaum, *Character and Characterization in Shakespeare*, 9–10; and Seigel, *Shakespeare in His Time and Ours*, 242–43.

79. See Girard, *Theatre of Envy*, 248–50, identifying Shylock as a scapegoat. Drakakis, ed., *Merchant of Venice*, 33, quotes from the play *Three Ladies of London* by Robert Wilson, containing the judgment, "Jewes seek to excell in Christianity, and Christians in Jewishness."

80. Drakakis, ed., *Merchant of Venice*, 205.

81. Milward, *Shakespeare's Religious Background*, 160.

82. Kastan, *Will to Believe*, 93.

83. Adelman, *Blood Relations*, 67–96. She proposes that this insistence reflects Christian anxiety and guilt about its simultaneous dependence on and disavowal of Judaism; like Jessica, Christianity has left its father's house and is uneasy about a Judaism it can neither own nor disown.

84. Drakakis, ed., *Merchant of Venice*, 40–41, 62–67, spells the name "Lancelet Giobbe," finding a pun with "Job" and scriptural resonances in Lancelet's father's name (Iobbe); in my view this would undermine the parallel between the Old Gobbo–Launcelot and Isaac-Jacob relations, and I retain the traditional spelling.

85. So Shaheen, *Biblical References in Shakespeare's Plays*, 178.

86. Adelman, *Blood Relations*, 82.

87. For example, Isa. 40:5–6, 40:26, 66:23; Jer. 25:31, 32:37; Ezek. 20:48, 21:5; Joel 2:28; Matt. 16.17; 1 Cor. 15.50; Eph 6.12; Gal. 1.16; and Heb. 2.14.

88. Here I disagree with Shaheen, *Biblical References in Shakespeare's Plays*, 170.

89. Eagleton, *William Shakespeare*, 43.

90. Eagleton, *William Shakespeare*, 42–48.

91. Eagleton, *William Shakespeare*, 43; see also Kerrigan, *Shakespeare's Binding Language*, 175: "Antonio and Shylock are joined by the carnality of their legal bond."

92. So also Greenblatt, *Learning to Curse*, 43: a "sameness . . . that runs like a dark current through the play."

93. See above, chap. 4, sec. "Love's Knowledge."

94. Murdoch, "Against Dryness," in Murdoch, *Existentialists and Mystics*, 293–95; Murdoch, *Metaphysics as a Guide to Morals*, 52–53.

95. Drakakis, ed., *Merchant of Venice*, 110, makes this point.

96. Cf. Kerrigan, *Shakespeare's Binding Language*, 201, pointing to the parallel between the flesh-bond and the rings: "Oaths and vows in themselves do not secure trust, but rather point to where the trust should be."

97. See G. Williams, *Glossary of Shakespeare's Sexual Language*, 219; Partridge, *Shakespeare's Bawdy*, 157; cf. *All's Well That Ends Well*, 4.2.40–51.

98. Newman, "Reprise: Gender, Sexuality and Theories of Exchange," 111; cf. Novy, *Shakespeare and Feminist Theory*, 108.

99. Isaac thinks he recognizes Esau's hairiness on Jacob, but is tricked by a goatskin (Gen. 27: 22–23); Gobbo mistakes the hair on Launcelot's head for a beard (2.2.88).

100. Gallagher, "Waiting for Gobbo," 86.

101. Derrida, *Gift of Death*, 105–8; Gallagher, "Waiting for Gobbo," 87.

102. Gallagher, "Waiting for Gobbo," 84.

103. Hamlin, *Bible in Shakespeare*, 69–71.

104. Gallagher, "Waiting for Gobbo," 90.

105. The Jewish scholar David Novak distinguishes between "hard supersessionism" and a "soft supersessionism" in which the new covenant is seen as extending

or adding to the old without canceling it (Novak, "The Covenant in Rabbinic Thought," 66).

106. Hick, "Whatever Path Men Choose Is Mine," 182; Hick, *God and the Universe of Faiths*, 130–32.

107. Hick, "Whatever Path Men Choose Is Mine," 189.

108. Klause, "Catholic and Protestant, Jesuit and Jew," 183.

109. Cited by Küng, ed., *Christianity and the World's Religions*, 23.

110. *Lumen Gentium*, 16, in Flannery, ed., *Vatican II*, 367.

111. Küng, ed., *Christianity and the World's Religions*, 24; Küng, *On Being a Christian*, 89–114.

112. Speech by Hans Küng cited in Neuner, *Christian Revelation and World Religions*, 55–56.

113. Hick, *God and the Universe of Faiths*, 129

114. Rahner, *Theological Investigations*, 5:131.

115. Raymond Panikkar, "Unknown Christ of Hinduism," 138.

116. Panikkar, *Unknown Christ of Hinduism*, 49.

117. Panikkar, "Unknown Christ of Hinduism," 140.

118. Panikkar, "Unknown Christ of Hinduism," 148; cf. 146. See also Panikkar, *Unknown Christ of Hinduism*, 75–83.

119. Panikkar, *Unknown Christ of Hinduism*, 168.

120. Panikkar, *Experience of God*, 74.

121. Panikkar, "Unknown Christ of Hinduism," 139.

122. Michael O'Siadhail, "Shylock," written for the (unpublished) liturgy "Living by the Risks of Love," created by Paul S. Fiddes. This is the second in a series of intertextual liturgies drawing on plays of Shakespeare; the first, *Seeing with the Eyes of Love*, is noted above, chap. 4, sec. "Art, Life, and Ritual." *Living by the Risks of Love*, based on *The Merchant of Venice*, was first presented at the Church of St. Minver, Cornwall, on 3 November 2018.

123. Panikkar, "Unknown Christ of Hinduism," 139.

124. Panikkar, *Experience of God*, 68–75.

125. See above, chap. 3, sec. "Text and Trinity."

126. Panikkar, "Unknown Christ of Hinduism," 138.

127. The New Testament affirmation that Christ is a personal "mediator" in the sense of healing a broken relationship between human beings and God (1 Tim. 2:5; cf. Heb. 12:24) was turned into the cosmic mediation of Logos according to the Middle-Platonist philosophy of the time.

128. Justin Martyr, *Dialogue with Trypho*, chap. 60, in *Ante-Nicene Fathers*, 1:227; Justin Martyr, *First Apology*, chap. 60, in *Ante-Nicene Fathers*, 1:183.

129. Panikkar, *Experience of God*, 77.

130. For Wolfhart Pannenberg, the human son is the "same" as the divine son (see Pannenberg, *Jesus—God and Man*, 334–38).

131. See the idea of several covenant-makings in Jenson, "What Kind of God Can Make a Covenant," 16–18.

132. Gen. 9:9–10, 15.

133. Brett, "Permutations of Sovereignty in the Priestly Tradition," 383–92. See also Brett, *Political Trauma and Healing*, 91–109.
134. Moltmann, *Open Church*, 90, 105.
135. Rothenberg, "Three Forms of Otherness," 94–95. Hans Küng sees the same potential in the Noachide commandments, in Küng, *Judaism*, 32–35.
136. Rothenberg, "Three Forms of Otherness," 98.
137. Rothenberg, "Three Forms of Otherness," 95.
138. Qur'an 5:12–13.
139. Qur'an 5:14.
140. For example, Qur'an 9:17, 33:23–24.
141. See Weiss, "Covenant and Law in Islam," 66.
142. Weiss, "Covenant and Law in Islam," 66.
143. Qur'an 33:7, 3:81.
144. Yaffe, *Shakespeare and the Jewish Question*, 165.
145. Weisberg, *Poethics*, 67, 96. For a nuanced critique of Weisberg's contrast between verbal mediation and law in this play, see Hartman, "The Tricksy Word," 72–74.
146. Novak, *Covenantal Rights*, 118–25, 154–56, 187–95.

6. *King Lear* and a Journey to Nothingness

1. For example, Lucretius, *De rerum natura*, 1.149–50. Hass, *Auden's O*, xi, cites classical and medieval precedents for the dictum.
2. See Foakes, ed., *King Lear*, 164.
3. For example, Augustine, *Confessions*, 12.7; Aquinas *Summa contra Gentiles* 2.c.16. *Creatio ex nihilo* was formally defined as a dogma by the fourth Lateran Council in 1215.
4. Aquinas, *Summa contra Gentiles*, 2.c.34.
5. Shaheen, *Biblical References in Shakespeare's Plays*, 605.
6. Kermode, *Sense of an Ending*, 5–17.
7. Eagleton, *William Shakespeare*, 81–82.
8. *Anthony and Cleopatra*, 1.1.14–15.
9. Hamlin, *Bible in Shakespeare*, 312.
10. Calvin, *Sermons*, 33.
11. Schwartz, *Loving Justice, Living Shakespeare*, 15.
12. See Foakes, ed., *King Lear*, 278; and Montaigne, *Essayes*, 2:280: "Truely, when I consider man all naked . . . We may be excused for borrowing those which nature had therein favored more than vs, with their beauties to adorne vs, and vnder their spoiles of wooll, of haire, of fethers, and of silke to shroude vs."
13. Parsons, *Booke of Christian Exercise*, 295.
14. Parsons, *Booke of Christian Exercise*, 293.
15. Hamlin, *Bible in Shakespeare*, 309.
16. Parsons, *Booke of Christian Exercise*, 295–96. Spelling of the text as in Parsons.
17. Only the Geneva version has "consider" here.

18. Montaigne, *Essayes*, 2:274. So Foakes, ed., *King Lear*, 278; cf. Elton, *King Lear and the Gods*, 194.

19. The author's positive point is that nevertheless we do "see Jesus, crowned with glory and honour" (Heb. 2:9). See below, chap. 7, sec. "The Mental State of Hamlet."

20. So Shaheen, *Biblical References in Shakespeare's Plays*, 620.

21. Harsnett, *Declaration of Egregious Popish Impostures*, 281: "the spirit of Enuie in the similitude of a Dog: the spirit of Gluttony in the forme of a Wolfe." A demonic fox also appears, 220.

22. Harsnett, *Declaration of Egregious Popish Impostures*, 147–48, where "Modu" and "Mahu" (*Lear*, 3.4.139–40) are also mentioned.

23. Foakes, ed., *King Lear*, 312.

24. Shaheen, *Biblical References in Shakespeare's Plays*, 615, notes a similar image in *King Leir* (1242–46), but judges that "Shakespeare is considerably closer in meaning to the pasage in John 15."

25. So Snyder, "King Lear and the Prodigal Son," 361–64.

26. Colin Burrow, "What Is a Shakespearean Tragedy?," in McEachern, ed., *Cambridge Companion to Shakespearean Tragedy*, 14–16, finds Shakespeare giving a "twist of novelty" to a Senecan tragic hero in this speech.

27. So Bishop Bilson in his coronation sermon before James I (1603), *A Sermon preached at Westminster*, A.6.

28. See above, chap. 2, sec. "A Spirituality of Forgiveness and Mercy."

29. Using the arrangement of syntax by Muir, ed., *King Lear*, 175.

30. Heidegger, *Being and Time*, 236–37, 279–80.

31. Bradley, *Shakespearean Tragedy*, 284–85, refers to "the redemption of King Lear."

32. So Muir, *Shakespeare's Tragic Sequence*, 139.

33. So Mason, *Shakespeare's Tragedies of Love*, 202.

34. See above, chap. 4, sec. "Looking with the Eyes of Love and the Limits of Reason."

35. Following the Folio reading; Q assigns the words to Lear, but F makes more sense of the dialogue. On the "allowed fool," see Welsford, *Fool*, 158–61.

36. For the wide range of meaning of this term, see A. R. Johnson, *Vitality of the Individual*, 3–22.

37. Cf. Psalm 6:5; and Ecclesiastes 9:5–6. See Martin-Achard, *From Death to Life*, 17–18, 36–46.

38. So Elton, *King Lear and the Gods*, 213–25; cf. 178–83, 198–202.

39. Snyder, "King Lear and the Psychology of Dying," 456–57.

40. Shell, *Shakespeare and Religion*, 186–87.

41. Shell, *Shakespeare and Religion*, 194–96. Similarly, Keefer, "Accommodation and Synecdoche," 147–68.

42. Hamlin, *Bible in Shakespeare*, 318–19, citing *Sermons of M. Iohn Caluin*, A.2.

43. Calvin, *Sermons*, 451; sermon 88 on Job 23:1–7.

44. Calvin, *Sermons*, A.2; Hamlin, *Bible in Shakespeare*, 319.

45. He repents (40:6) because he realizes he has been insisting that God should act in a certain way, namely to vindicate him (see Fiddes, *Seeing the World and Knowing God*, 237).

46. Hamlin, *Bible in Shakespeare*, 323.

47. Luther, *Heidelberg Disputation* (1518), Thesis 21; see also Theses 19 and 20, in Atkinson, ed. and trans., *Luther: Early Theological Works*, 290–92. The following paragraphs expand ideas from my book *The Promised End*, 72–73.

48. See Fiddes, *Seeing the World and Knowing God*, 233–38.

49. Luther, *Bondage of the Will*, in *Luther's Works*, 33:291.

50. For example, Moltmann, *Crucified God*, 202–13, based on Luther's theology of the cross.

51. Calvin, *Institutes*, 1.15.4. What remains of God's image in human beings is "confused, mutilated and disease-ridden" (Calvin, *Institutes of the Christian Religion*, 1:190).

52. Luther, *Die zweite Disputationen gegen die Antinomer*, WA 39 (1), 470; cf. Jüngel, "The World as Possibility and Actuality," 107.

53. Luther, *Psalmenvorlesung* (1519–21), WA 5, 167 (on Psalm 5).

54. Luther, *Psalmenvorlesung*, WA 5, 216 (on Psalm 6). For "driving back to nothing," see also comments on Psalm 72:22; and Luther, *Heidelberg*, 24.

55. Luther, *Lectures on Romans*, in *Luther's Works*, 25:365.

56. Calvin, *Epistles of Paul the Apostle to the Romans and to the Thessalonians*, 96.

57. Cf. Muir, *Shakespeare's Tragic Sequence*, 139: "the Christian virtues prove to be necessities."

58. Shaheen, *Biblical References in Shakespeare's Plays*, 615–16. See Homilies I, C.i/1.

59. Butler, "Lear's Crown of Weeds," 395–406, fails to make any reference to Hebrews 2 or Psalm 8.

60. Shaheen, *Biblical References in Shakespeare's Plays*, 616–17.

61. Shaheen, *Biblical References in Shakespeare's Plays*, 606, finds a possible source in Sidney's *The Countesse of Pembrokes Arcadia*, 3:10, where Cecropia says that to suppose the gods are concerned about men is as reasonable "as if flies should thinke, that men take great care which of them hums sweetest."

62. See Shaheen, *Biblical References in Shakespeare's Plays*, 614.

63. So Knight, *Wheel of Fire*, 201: "he falls back on the simplicity of love."

64. Cf. Cox, *Seeming Knowledge*, 94–96, on "the transformative power of love." McEachern, *Believing in Shakespeare*, 273, maintains that Lear has sustained his love for Cordelia throughout the play, a "love . . . above and beyond the call of duty, in excess of his political function."

65. Gardner, *King Lear*, 27–28. See also Mack, *"King Lear" in Our Time*, 116.

66. Cf. Knight, *Wheel of Fire*, 176: "what smiling destiny is this he sees at the last instant of racked mortality?," comparing 4.3.19–20: "Those happy smilets / That played on her ripe lip."

67. So Dowden, *Shakespeare: A Critical Study*, 59. Danby envisages Cordelia as a kind of goddess, or "idea" of nature, "the redemptive principle itself" (Danby, *Shakespeare's Doctrine of Nature*, 124–26).

68. Foakes, ed., *King Lear*, 323.

69. Foakes, ed., *King Lear*, 22, 34–35.

70. So Danby, *Shakespeare's Doctrine of Nature*, 125; Hamlin, *Bible in Shakespeare*, 324.

71. MacKinnon, *Borderlands of Theology*, 102; MacKinnon, *Explorations in Theology*, 185, 187.

72. MacKinnon, *Problem of Metaphysics*, 136.

73. MacKinnon, *Problem of Metaphysics*, 145; cf. Janz, *God, the Mind's Desire*, 171–72.

74. Following Luther's expression *theologia crucis*, this is often called "theology of the cross" (*Kreuzestheologie*). See, on the historical development, McGrath, *Luther's Theology of the Cross*, 161–81; in modern theology, Link, "Zur Kreuzes-theologie," 337–45; and Moltmann, *Crucified God*, 207–27.

75. Cullmann, *Immortality of the Soul*, 23–27.

76. Steiner, *Death of Tragedy*, 331. See Ward, "Tragedy as Subclause," 274–87.

77. Steiner, *Death of Tragedy*, 332.

78. Hebblethwaite, "MacKinnon and the Problem of Evil," 140.

79. Hebblethwaite, "MacKinnon and the Problem of Evil," 141.

80. Hebblethwaite, "MacKinnon and the Problem of Evil," 142. Reinhold Niebuhr took a similar view much earlier in "Christianity and Tragedy," in Niebuhr, *Beyond Tragedy*, 153–69.

81. Küng, *On Being a Christian*, 433: "This senseless death acquires a meaning"; cf. 432.

82. Fiddes, *Creative Suffering of God*, 104–6; Fiddes, *Participating in God*, 244; cf. 176.

83. Jüngel, "Vom Tod des lebendigen Gottes," 105–8.

84. Pannenberg, *Jesus—God and Man*, 74.

85. Richard Wilson, *Secret Shakespeare*, 284n67.

86. Richard Wilson, *Secret Shakespeare*, 284, citing Southwell, *Epistle of Comfort* 17. See above, chap. 5, sec. "In Belmont: Love and the Caskets."

87. Richard Wilson, *Secret Shakespeare*, 271–74.

88. Geninges, *Life and Death of Mr Edmund Geninges Priest*, 3–4. Its place of publication at St. Omer in the Spanish Netherlands was a center for English Catholic exiles.

89. Shell, *Shakespeare and Religion*, 94–96.

90. Foakes, ed., *King Lear*, 1.

91. Richard Wilson, *Secret Shakespeare*, 286.

92. It evokes not only the classical reference to Ixion but medieval popular theology about the pains of hell, which Lear clearly considers to be befalling him in this life.

93. Küng, *On Being a Christian*, 432.

94. On tragicomedy in Shakeseare, see above, chap. 2, sec. "The Shape of the Story."

95. Whitehead, *Adventures of Ideas*, 356, 380–81.

96. See Augustine, *Enchiridion*, 11; Augustine, *De civitate Dei*, 11.9.

97. Hartshorne, *Man's Vision of God*, 294; cf. Fiddes, *Creative Suffering of God*, 105–6.

98. Aquinas, *Summa theologiae*, 1a.2.3; 3.1; 9.1.

99. I develop this distinction in Fiddes, *Creative Suffering of God*, 65–67. Cf. Barth, *Church Dogmatics*, II/2, 10: God "ordains that He should not be entirely self-sufficient, as He might be."

100. Balthasar, *Theo-Drama*, 4:324–28.

101. This expression is from Robinson, *Cross in the Old Testament*, 185.

102. The following paragraphs draw on ideas from my book *The Promised End*, 40–49.

103. Jüngel, "The World as Possibility and Actuality," 107–16.

104. The proverbial tag, *ex nihilo nihil fit*, is not found in Aristotle himself, but cf. "everything that is produced is something produced from something and by something" (Aristotle, *Metaphysics*, 1049b.24–29).

105. Jüngel, "The World as Possibility and Actuality," 115–17.

106. Moltmann, *Future of Creation*, 29–31; cf. Moltmann, *Way of Jesus Christ*, 317–18; and Moltmann, *Coming of God*, 25–26.

107. Ricoeur, "Freedom in the Light of Hope," 409–12.

108. Ricoeur, *Time and Narrative*, 3, 233–35; cf. 75–96.

109. Ricoeur, *Interpretation Theory*, 87; Ricoeur, "Freedom in the Light of Hope," 405–7, 410–11; so, earlier, Ricoeur, *History and Truth*, 126–27.

110. Ricoeur, *Freedom and Nature*, 48, 54.

111. Foakes, ed., *King Lear*, 332; Duthie and J. D. Wilson, eds., *King Lear*, 245; Shaheen, *Biblical References in Shakespeare's Play*, 616.

112. See above, chap. 6, sec. "A Journey to Nothingness: Images of Disintegration."

113. Marion, *Being Given*, 196–206.

7. Hamlet, Hesitation, and Remembrance

1. Jenkins, ed., *Hamlet*, 136, thinks it is legitimate to identify delay in the plot. So James, *Dream of Learning*, 47. Others impatient with the idea include Philip Brockbank, "Hamlet the Bonesetter," 30, 109.

2. Kastan, *Will to Believe*, 118.

3. Two main sources are the fifth volume of the *Histoires tragiques* by François Belleforest (1570), which expands the narrative of the twelfth-century *Historiae Danicae* by Saxo Grammaticus, and a lost play called *Hamlet* (the "Ur-Hamlet") by Thomas Kyd, which was owned by Shakespeare's company in the 1590s. John Marston's play *Antonio's Revenge* was probably similarly influenced by Kyd's *Hamlet*, rather than being another source for Shakespeare's play.

4. Shaheen, *Biblical References in Shakespeare's Plays*, 535.

5. S. T. Coleridge, from *Lectures 1818*, in Jump, ed., *Hamlet: A Casebook*, 30–31.

6. J. D. Wilson, *What Happens in "Hamlet,"* 217.

7. Samuel Johnson, from his edition of Shakespeare's plays, 1765, in Jump, ed., *Hamlet: A Casebook*, 24.

8. See Burton, *Anatomy*, 1.3.2.4 (vol. 1, 418–19).

9. So Jenkins, ed., *Hamlet*, 187.

10. *Homilies I*, Q.iii/3.

11. *Homilies II*, 491; so Shaheen, *Biblical References in Shakespeare's Plays*, 540.

12. Shaheen, *Biblical References in Shakespeare's Plays*, 545, cites the Psalm but does not make this judgment.

13. For a similar use of Hebrews in *King Lear*, see above, chap. 6, sec. "The Reformation Context: Being Brought to Nothing."

14. So Shaheen, *Biblical References in Shakespeare's Plays*, 556.

15. *Homilies I*, M.iii/4.

16. Greenblatt, *Hamlet in Purgatory*, 241–42, suggests there is a Protestant joke concealed here about the Eucharist, where—according to transubstantiaton—the host does not eat but is eaten.

17. So Shaheen, *Biblical References in Shakespeare's Plays*, 556.

18. See Shakespeare's use of the notion of "one flesh" in *Comedy of Errors* and *Merchant of Venice*: above, chap. 2, "A Spirituality of Love and Death," and chap. 5, sec. "The Body, Flesh, and Blood."

19. So Noble, *Shakespeare's Biblical Knowledge*, 205.

20. One Dane who had studied at Wittenberg was quite well known in England: an exposition of the Gospels by the Danish Lutheran theologian Niels Hemmingsen (studied at Wittenberg 1537–42 under Melanchthon) had been translated by Arthur Golding, was widely used in parishes, and had gone through at least four editions from 1569 to 1585.

21. Kastan, *Will to Believe*, 136, proposes that the sentence is presented as if the topic for a disputation.

22. For election, see, for example, Isa. 45:4; Rom. 9:5–7; 1 Thess. 1:4; 2 Pet. 1:10; and Col. 3:11; for the metaphorical use of sealed, see Job 14:17; Isa. 8:16; Song 4:12; Rom. 4:11; 1 Cor. 9:2; and Rev. 22:10.

23. See above, chap. 2, sec. "The Shape of the Story."

24. So J. D. Wilson, ed., *Hamlet*, lvi–lviii; Knight, *Wheel of Fire*, 25–26; Muir, *Shakespeare's Tragic Sequence*, 82–83.

25. Jenkins, ed., *Hamlet*, 150.

26. 1 Cor. 7:8: "It is good for them if they abide even as I do" (Geneva Bible).

27. See Jenkins, "Hamlet and Ophelia," 146; Muir, *Shakespeare's Tragic Sequence*, 83.

28. On the ambiguities of revenge, see Watson, "Tragedies of Revenge and Ambition," 184–87.

29. *Homilies I*, R.iii/4.

30. *Homilies I*, S.i/2.

31. Kastan, *Will to Believe*, 133.

32. See Shaheen, *Biblical References in Shakespeare's Plays*, 555.

33. So the Homily *Concerning Prayer*: "the soule of man, passing out of his body, goeth straightwayes eyther to heaven, or els to hell" (*Homilies II*, 255).

34. See Donne, *Devotions*, 137–38; Donne, *Sermons*, 7:167–68. Cf. *Concerning Prayer*, *Homilies II*, 255: "The only Purgatorie . . . is the death and blood of Christ, which . . . purgeth and cleanseth vs from all our sinnes." Thompson

and Taylor, eds., *Hamlet*, 332, oddly note that "purging implies a connection between prayer in this world and the possibility of purgatory to come," failing to see Hamlet's point.

35. Greenblatt, *Hamlet in Purgatory*, 231.

36. Greenblatt, *Hamlet in Purgatory*, 233.

37. In the Supplement to his *Summa theologiae*, compiled by his disciples (see Le Goff, *Birth of Purgatory*, 276).

38. For example, More, *Supplycacyon of Soulys*, throughout.

39. For example, Cranmer, *Confutatio[n] of vnwritte[n] Verities*, chap. 5.

40. See *The Ghast of Gy*, an account of haunting that took place in 1323 or 1324 in southern France—originally a report by Dominican Prior Jean Gobi presented to Pope John XXII, circulating in numerous prose and rhymed versions throughout the fourteenth century; extensively cited by Greenblatt, *Hamlet in Purgatory*, 103–20.

41. Greenblatt, *Hamlet in Purgatory*, 240.

42. This is a kind of "double purgatory"—on the earth and in the place of fire (see Greenblatt, *Hamlet in Purgatory*, 115–16).

43. See Shaheen, *Biblical References in Shakespeare's Plays*, 538.

44. So Greenblatt, *Hamlet in Purgatory*, 234–35; he gives reference to the prayer in 307n38.

45. Shaheen, *Biblical References in Shakespeare's Plays*, 547–48.

46. For example, Perkins, *Salve for a Sicke Man*, 48. Kastan, *Will to Believe*, 138, draws attention to Perkins's assurance that a man may rest "nothing at all troubled with dreames or fantasies." See also Jewel, *An Expositio[n] upon the two Epistles*, 162–63, on 1 Thess. 4:13–14 ("them which sleep in Iesus.").

47. For example, also Deut. 31:16; 2 Sam. 2:12; and 1 Cor. 15:51.

48. So Kastan, *Will to Believe*, 137.

49. Kastan, *Will to Believe*, 139–40.

50. More, *Supplycacyon of Soulys*, xliiii/2.

51. Foxe, *Acts and Monuments*, 8:1011–14.

52. Foxe, *Acts and Monuments*, 8:1014.

53. Greenblatt, *Hamlet in Purgatory*, 208.

54. Greenblatt, *Hamlet in Purgatory*, 253.

55. Greenblatt, *Hamlet in Purgatory*, 257–58.

56. Greenblatt, *Hamlet in Purgatory*, 40.

57. So Thompson and Taylor, eds., *Hamlet*, 430.

58. However, here Paul finds the "old stock" (Israel) to be "holy." For another use of the image of grafting, see Polixenes's speech in *The Winter's Tale*, below, chap. 9, sec. "Reconciliation."

59. Gardner, "The Historical Approach to Hamlet," 142–44.

60. Gardner, "The Historical Approach to Hamlet," 148–49.

61. So Shaheen, *Biblical References in Shakespeare's Plays*, 563. The Psalm verse is, however, echoed more closely in *Titus Andronicus* 3.1.270–74: "all these mischiefs be *returned* again" (so Beatrice Groves, personally).

62. Gardner, "The Historical Approach to Hamlet," 147.

63. Gardner, "The Historical Approach to Hamlet," 148.

64. Calvin, *Institution of Christian Religion*, trans. Norton, fol. 59.

65. Calvin, *Institutes*, 1.16.1: "cherishing & caring for, with singular providence every one of those things that he hath created even to the least sparow," in *Institution*, trans. Norton, fol. 52.

66. See, for example, Perkins, "Exposition of the Symbol or Creed of the Apostles," in Perkins, *Workes*, 1:160.

67. Shaheen, *Biblical References in Shakespeare's Plays*, 562, also compares 1 Tim. 6:7, though this is only a parallel in meaning if we follow the Folio text: "no man ha's ought of what he leaves." Thompson and Taylor, eds., *Hamlet*, follow the Second Quarto here.

68. Whitmore, *Culture of Accidents*, 109.

69. Geneva Bible, marginal note f. to 1 Sam. 6:8–9; cited by Cummings, *Mortal Thoughts*, 222.

70. Calvin, *Institution*, trans. Norton, fol. 56 (*Institutes*, 1.16.9).

71. Calvin, *Institutes*, ed. McNeill, trans. Battles, 208.

72. Cummings, *Mortal Thoughts*, 235.

73. See above, chap. 2, sec. "The Shape of the Story."

74. So Swift, *Shakespeare's Common Prayers*, 159–60.

75. Swift, *Shakespeare's Common Prayers*, 159, calls it a "jumbled translation," but Shakespeare is working with purpose.

76. So Shaheen, *Biblical References in Shakespeare's Plays*, 563.

77. Sowerby, *Angels in Early Medieval England*, 112–17; Thompson and Taylor, eds., *Hamlet*, 460. Any mention of administering angels is removed from the Burial Service of the reformed English Prayer Book, perhaps to avoid misunderstanding, but the prayers of praise of the angels are retained in the Communion Service, as Swift points out in *Shakespeare's Common Prayers*, 160.

78. Unfortunately, Shakespeare's intention here was completely undermined by the Stratford RSC production of 2013 (directed David Farr), which cut the final forty lines of the play, entirely omitting the arrival of Fortinbras, and oddly ending abruptly at the line "Why does the drum come hither?" In place of Fortinbras's drum, the director substituted the ringing of the theater fire alarm and the setting off of one somewhat forlorn water sprinkler onto the stage.

79. See Prospero's speech on the ending of revels, in *The Tempest*, 4.1.146–58; see also below, chap. 10, sec. "The Powers of Time and Death."

80. So Shaheen, *Biblical References in Shakespeare's Plays*, 561.

81. See Jenkins, ed., *Hamlet*, 143–47, on the pairing of Hamlet and Laertes.

82. Lewis, "Hamlet: The Prince or the Poem?," 66.

83. Lewis, "Hamlet: The Prince or the Poem?," 64.

84. Lewis, "Hamlet: The Prince or the Poem?," 70.

85. See, for example, Cummings, *Mortal Thoughts*, 213–14.

86. Raleigh, *Johnson on Shakespeare*, 191; my italics.

87. Greenblatt, *Hamlet in Purgatory*, 40.

88. Duffy, *Stripping of the Altars*, 475.
89. Greenblatt, *Hamlet in Purgatory*, 253.
90. See Levinas, *Otherwise Than Being*, 181.
91. See above, chap. 6, sec. "A General Spirituality: A Journey to Look on Death."
92. Forster, *A Passage to India*, 157: "Religion appeared, poor little, talkative Christianity."
93. The following discussion reuses some content from my book *The Promised End*, chapter 4, but in a new structure of argument.
94. Hick, *Death and Eternal Life*, 280, 283.
95. Davis, "The Resurrection of the Dead," 119–44; see also Davis, "Is Personal Identity Retained in the Resurrection?," 329–40.
96. Badham and Badham, *Immortality or Extinction?*, chap. 6.
97. Unlike the others cited, Richard Swinburne leaves open the possibility that an omnipotent God *might* find another way to "light up" the soul than by "plugging it" into a new body and brain after a period of inert activity (see Swinburne, *Evolution of the Soul*, 307–11).
98. Hick, "A Possible Conception of Life after Death," 195.
99. Swinburne, *Evolution of the Soul*, 305–8; cf. 191–97.
100. This is stressed by Geach, *God and the Soul*, 25–28.
101. Penelhulm, *Survival and Disembodied Existence*, 55–62.
102. Nielsen, "The Faces of Immortality," 1–28.
103. See, for example, the cry of Lear over the dead Cordelia: "Thou'lt come no more, / Never, never, never, never, never!" (*King Lear*, 5.3.307–8).
104. See above, chap. 3, sec. "Text and Trinity."
105. Rom. 8:29; cf. Phil. 3:21, and 2 Cor. 3:18.
106. Paul Tillich and Charles Hartshorne maintain a view of survival in the divine memory, but without the further stage of bodily resurrection (Tillich, *Systematic Theology*, 3:424–27; Hartshorne, *Logic of Perfection*, 245–62).
107. See Soelle, *Christ the Representative*, 51–56, 137–42, with regard to Christ's representing of God.
108. See E. A. Johnson, *Friends of God*, esp. 131–37, on praying with the saints; McCarthy, *Sharing God's Good Company*, esp. 37–42; and Fiddes, Haymes, and Kidd, *Baptists and the Communion of Saints*, esp. 73–102.
109. See Hartshorne, *Divine Relativity*, 72–74, 134–38; L. S. Ford, *Lure of God*, 82–85; Fiddes, *Participating in God*, 131–44; Southgate, *Groaning of Creation*, 60–71; and Oord, *Uncontrolling Love of God*, 178–86.
110. Polkinghorne, *Belief in God in an Age of Science*, 90: "A credible eschatology, which takes account of the eventual death of the universe and looks beyond it to God's new creation, is surely an indispensable component in realistic Christian thinking."
111. Parfit, *Reasons and Persons*, 251, 281–82.
112. Macquarrie, *Principles of Christian Theology*, 367–68.

8. King Richard II, King John, and the Ambiguities of Power

1. Robyn Bolam observes that this is a drama about language, its power and weakness (Bolam, "*Richard II*: Shakespeare and the Languages of the Stage," 141–43). Earlier, Mahood, *Shakespeare's Wordplay*, 73–88.
2. W. B. Yeats, "At Stratford-on-Avon," in Yeats, *Essays and Introductions*, 106.
3. Brooke, *Shakespeare's Early Tragedies*, 5–6.
4. Shaheen, *Biblical References in Shakespeare's Plays*, 382–83.
5. Shaheen, *Biblical References in Shakespeare's Plays*, 381.
6. In the mystery play *The Agony and the Betrayal*, 1.248; so Forker, ed., *Richard II*, 394.
7. Kantorowicz, "The King's Two Bodies," in Brooke, ed., *Richard II*, 172–75.
8. Hooker, *Laws of Ecclesiastical Polity*, in *Works*, 2:6.1.3–4 (237); 7.6.7 (354); 7.15.6 (410); 8.1.1 (483).
9. Henry VIII used this term with regard to the church, but Elizabeth later changed it to "Supreme Governor."
10. *Homilies I*, T.i/1.
11. *Homilies I*, S.ii/1.
12. Forker, ed., *Richard II*, 321.
13. Hamlin, *Bible in Shakespeare*, 139.
14. As Forker, ed., *Richard II*, 317, suggests, there may be also an allusion here to the fable of Cadmus, who sowed dragons' teeth which then sprang up as soldiers, but the reference to stones is more biblical.
15. Shaheen, *Biblical References in Shakespeare's Plays*, 384, suggests these references as "analogies."
16. Caird, *Revelation of St John the Divine*, 245.
17. *King Lear*, 4.6.98–102. See above, chap. 6, sec. "A Journey to Judgment: A Biblical Perspective."
18. See Forker, ed., *Richard II*, 410.
19. McEachern, *Believing in Shakespeare*, 215–19, draws a parallel between Richard's final soliloquy and the soliloquy of Christ in Gethsemane, the latter a contemporary subject of theological debate over the authenticity of Christ's suffering.
20. Cummings, *Mortal Thoughts*, 190–91.
21. Shell, *Shakespeare and Religion*, 134.
22. Cummings, *Mortal Thoughts*, 188.
23. See Edgerton, "Shakespeare and the Needle's Eye," 549–50.
24. Cummings, *Mortal Thoughts*, 195.
25. Luke 11.4; cf. Matt. 6:12, 14–15.
26. *The Merchant of Venice*, 4.1.197–98.
27. Shell, *Shakespeare and Religion*, 129.
28. Shell, *Shakespeare and Religion*, 137.
29. See Forker, ed., *Richard II*, 75–76; Bryant, "The Linked Analogies of Richard II," 189–97.
30. Hamlin, *Bible in Shakespeare*, 141.

31. Hamlin, *Bible in Shakespeare*, 143.
32. Nashe, *Cristes Teares over Jerusalem*, 38r, 92v, 70r. See Groves, *Destruction of Jerusalem*, 171–81.
33. Matt. 23:38. "Behold, your habitation will be left to you desolate."
34. *Homilies II*, 614.
35. Rom. 5:12–21; 1 Cor. 15:20–22, 45. See VanMaaren, "The Adam-Christ Typology in Paul and Its Development in the Early Church Fathers," 275–97.
36. Forker, ed., *Richard II*, 77; Bryant, "Linked Analogies of *Richard II*," 194–95.
37. *Woodstock*, 5.3.106. On *Woodstock* as a source for *Richard II*, see Forker, ed., *Richard II*, 144–52.
38. *Homilies I*, T.i/1.
39. Calvin, *Institutes*, ed. McNeill, trans. Battles, 2:4.20.34.
40. Henri de Bracton's famous sentence that the king is "sub Deo et sub lege, quia lex facit regem" is quoted by Hooker, *Laws*, 8.2.3 (*Works*, 2:495).
41. See Talbert, *Problem of Order*, 59–64, 68–70, 77–79; and Hattaway, "Tragedy and Political Authority," 118–19.
42. Hooker, *Laws of Ecclesiastical Piety*, 8.2.12, in *Works*, 502.
43. Hooker, *Laws of Ecclesiastical Piety*, 1.10.8, in *Works*, 190–91; 8.2.13–18 (*Works*, 503–8), 8.6.12–14 (*Works*, 550–52).
44. Hooker, *Laws of Ecclesiastical Piety* 1.16.5, in *Works*, 225–26.
45. Supposedly, in August 1601. Quoted by Bolam, "*Richard II*: Shakespeare and the Languages of the Stage," 145, relying on Nichols, *Progression and Public Processions*, 3:552.
46. *Declaration*, probably by Richard Verstegan, 60, lists "exactions, lones, impostes, forfaictures, confiscations, forced beneuolences, subsidies." Attention was drawn to this pamphlet by Simpson, "Richard II and Elizabethan Politics," 242.
47. See the cautiously worded confession before his judges of John Penry, who played an important part in the printing of the Tracts, became a member of the London Separatist congregation previously pastored by Barrow and Greenwood, and shared their fate in 1593: "the Lord requireth that hir eclesiasticall [laws] be warented by his writtē word wich expressely conteyneth whatsoever belongeth to his worship: & her ciuill [laws] to be gronded vpon the rules of common iustice and equitie" (John Penry, document of 1593).
48. Elton, "Shakespeare and the Thought of His Age," 29–30.
49. See above, chap. 2, sec. "A Spirituality of Authority."
50. Forker, ed., *Richard II*, 77.
51. See Ure, ed., *Richard II*, 151.
52. Church of England, *Articles*, C.iii.
53. *Homilies I*, T.ii/1.
54. Foxe, *Acts and Monuments*, 4:283.
55. *Homilies II*, 608–9.
56. Bate, *Soul of the Age*, 23–42, notes his significant place in the issue of "who speaks for England?" Traversi, *Approach to Shakespeare*, 1:181–86, finds that he typifies the problem of relating morality to politics.

57. The bull of Pope Pius V, *Regnans in Excelsis*, issued on 25 February 1570, declared Elizabeth to be a heretic and released her Catholic subjects from their duty to be loyal to her. In 1588 Sixtus V issued a further bull against Elizabeth, upholding her excommunication and supporting the Catholic Armada.

58. Groves, *Texts and Contexts*, 110–15. Roy Battenhouse and Sandra Billington had already compared this scene to the sacrifice of Isaac in the mystery plays (see Battenhouse, "Religion in *King John*: Shakespeare's View," 146–47; and Billington, "A Response to Roy Battenhouse," 290–92).

59. For example, Mather, *Figures or Types of the Old Testament*, 107; cited by Groves, *Texts and Contexts*, 113.

60. Groves, *Texts and Contexts*, 116–18.

61. Shaheen, *Biblical References in Shakespeare's Plays*, 403.

62. *The Troublesome Raigne of King John*, 15.98–101; cited by Groves, *Texts and Contexts*, 95.

63. Groves, *Texts and Contexts*, 96.

64. *Hamlet*, 5.2.322.

65. Shaheen, *Biblical References in Shakespeare's Plays*, 404.

66. Piesse, "King John: Changing Perspectives," 137, suggests that Arthur shows "the potential process of history."

67. Richard Wilson, *Secret Shakespeare*, 62, notes that Shakespeare "toned down his anti-Catholic source."

68. Groves, *Texts and Contexts*, 120.

69. Groves, *Texts and Contexts*, 114. Here she sees again the influence of medieval dramatizations of Isaac, which show a similar response to Abraham as Arthur makes to Hubert.

70. See above, chap. 6, sec. "The Theologian in the Play: Christianity as a Tragic Faith."

71. *Short Confession of Faith* (Amsterdam, 1610), para. 14, in Lumpkin, *Baptist Confessions of Faith*, 106.

72. Hooker, *Laws of Ecclesiastical Polity*, 7.6.7, in *Works*, 2:354.

73. Helwys, *Short Declaration*, "The principal matters handled in the Booke," recto; and p. 49.

74. In the "Prayer for the whole state of Christs church," in the Communion Service, *Prayer Book*, 1559.

75. Helwys, *Short Declaration*, 69.

76. Asquith, *Shadowplay*, 205.

77. My italics.

78. Asquith, *Shadowplay*, 237–38. Anabaptists (including Mennonites) refused to swear oaths at all, but this was not the situation with English Separatists and later Baptists and Independents.

79. Asquith, *Shadowplay*, 206–8.

80. Asquith, *Shadowplay*, 296.

81. For example, the Baptist minister Robert Hall insists on the "rights of man" in "An Apology for the Freedom of the Press and for General Liberty" (1793), 3:122.

82. For example, Baptist minister Caleb Evans, *Political Sophistry Detected*, 14, 35.

83. For early Baptist appeals to conscience, see Smyth et al., *Propositions and Conclusions concerning True Christian Religion* (1612), para 84, in Lumpkin, *Baptist Confessions*, 140; and Busher, *Religions Peace: Or a Plea for Liberty of Conscience*, claiming to be a reprint of a first edition printed in 1614.

84. Calvin, *Institutes*, 1.15.2; see Bradbury, "Non-Conformist Conscience?," 34–35.

85. Craig A. Evans, *Mark 8:27–16:20*, 247–48. Cf. Myers, *Binding the Strong Man*, 312, suggesting that what belongs to God is the land of Israel, and that this is therefore a highly revolutionary statement.

86. Barth, *Epistle to the Romans*, 492–93.

87. Craig A. Evans, *Mark 8:27–16:20*, 247.

88. Tillich, *Systematic Theology*, 3:108–13.

89. Lehmann, *Transfiguration of Politics*, 64.

90. Barth, *Epistle to the Romans*, 493.

91. Lehmann, *Transfiguration of Politics*, 270, 68.

92. Boff, *Passion of Christ, Passion of the World*, 123.

93. See Segundo, *Faith and Ideologies*, 277–82; and Gutierrez, *Theology of Liberation*, 91–92.

94. Bonino, *Towards a Christian Political Ethics*, 95–115.

95. See Wink, *Engaging the Powers*, 139–55.

96. See Gutierrez, *Theology of Liberation*, 126n41. See also the discussion of Ramsey and Hauerwas, *Speak up for Just War or Pacifism*, 70–75.

97. Bonhoeffer, *Letters and Papers from Prison*, 219.

98. See above, chap. 6, sec. "The Theologian in the Play: Hope and Human Suffering."

99. Hart, *Beauty of the Infinite*, 383–86.

100. Girard, *Violence and the Sacred*, 77–103; Girard, *Things Hidden since the Foundation of the World*, 326–51.

101. Hart, *Beauty of the Infinite*, 383–84.

102. Schopenhauer, *World as Will and Representation*, 1:242–54 (para. 51).

103. Girard, *Things Hidden since the Foundation of the World*, 180–87, 219; Girard, *Scapegoat*, 100–124. See also Wink, *Engaging the Powers*, 13–31.

104. Hart, *Beauty of the Infinite*, 385.

105. See Dunn, *Christology in the Making*, 22–33.

106. Hart, *Beauty of the Infinite*, 385.

107. See Faber, *God as Poet of the World*, 227–28.

108. See above, chap. 3, sec. "Text and Trinity."

9. The Winter's Tale and the Renewal of Life

1. Strachey, "Shakespeare's Final Period," in Strachey, *Books and Characters: French and English*, 64.

2. On reality in the Romances, see Daniell, "Shakespeare and the Traditions of Comedy," 118–19.

3. First released 21 July 1989, dir. Rob Reiner, screenplay by Nora Ephron.

4. See above, chap. 2, sec. "The Shape of the Story."

5. Thus O'Connell, "The Experiment of Romance," 224–26, identifies "experiments" in *Winter's Tale*.

6. Wells, *Shakespeare, Sex and Love*, 193–96.

7. So Felperin, "Tongue-tied Our Queen?," 10–12.

8. Traversi, *Approach to Shakespeare*, 2:286, relates "nothing" here to a sense of chaos.

9. Tolkien, *Tree and Leaf*, 46.

10. See note 13 below.

11. Pafford, ed., *The Winter's Tale*, 9, supposes it means that they would have been guilty of no sins other than original sin, and this interpretation seems to be followed by Pitcher, ed., *The Winter's Tale*, 155; and Shaheen, *Biblical References in Shakespeare's Plays*, 722 (alternative explanation). But this does not explain the claim that they would be cleared of having something "hereditary."

12. So Hamlin, *Bible in Shakespeare*, 172.

13. A key text for Augustine was Romans 5:12, where Paul had actually stated that, after Adam, death spread to all people "*inasmuch as/because (eph ho)* all have sinned." Paul thus insists, paradoxically, upon every person's own responsibility for a fallenness in which all are nevertheless entangled. Augustine reduced this paradox by reading in his Latin text *in whom* (*in quo*, reflecting a corrupt Greek text *en ho*), that is, "in Adam, all sinned," and were thus guilty (Augustine *De peccatorum mentis et remissione*, 3.14).

14. Anselm, *De conceptu virginali et de originali peccato*, chaps. 7, 22; Abelard, *Commentala in epistolam Pauli ad Romanos*, 2.5.19.

15. For Anabaptists, see Hillerbrand, "Anabaptism and the Reformation," 408–10. Among Baptists, Grantham, *Christianismus Primitivus*, 2.2.1 (3–4), argues that all young children, having no personal guilt of their own, may "by the grace of God" be heirs of the salvation achieved by Christ.

16. This would be consistent with my exegesis of 1.2.66–74: they have inherited original sin, but guilt comes with the first sin they commit themselves, and for which they are responsible.

17. So Pitcher, ed., *The Winter's Tale*, 156.

18. The Geneva Bible has: "mine heart shall rejoice."

19. Hamlin, *Bible in Shakespeare*, 173.

20. Augustine, *De nuptiis et concupiscentia*, 1:20, 2:25, 2:36.

21. Pitcher, ed., *The Winter's Tale*, 166, referring to the *Oxford English Dictionary*, offers this as the second meaning of "forked"; it also carries the undertone, "she has been fucked" (Pitcher's meaning, 5).

22. So Pitcher, ed., *The Winter's Tale*, 49.

23. In the series of biblical references to sin, "Affection?—thy intention stabs the centre" (2.1.138) is perhaps an echo of Romans 7:5, "the affections of sin wrought in us": so Kermode, *Shakespeare's Language*, 276.

24. Shakespeare probably borrowed details of the "isle" from Virgil's *Aeneid*, 3:73–92, but there are still undertones of Eden here.

25. Cf. Hamlin, *Bible in Shakespeare*, 175.

26. See above, chap. 8, sec. "The Two Adams."

27. Shaheen, *Biblical References in Shakespeare's Plays*, 725.

28. See above, chap. 7, sec. "Hamlet Waits Faithfully."

29. Shell, *Shakespeare and Religion*, 202.

30. Shell, *Shakespeare and Religion*, 206.

31. Shell, *Shakespeare and Religion*, 214.

32. Shell, *Shakespeare and Religion*, 215. Hartwig, *Shakespeare's Tragicomic Vision*, 19–20, stresses that divine control is a signal characteristic of Shakespeare's tragicomedies.

33. Shell, *Shakespeare and Religion*, 201–2.

34. Shell, *Shakespeare and Religion*, 215.

35. Dillon, "Shakespeare's Tragicomedies," 170, sees this as "the classic tragicomic move from death to life."

36. John 3:1–16; 2 Pet. 1:23; cf. being "born of God" in 1 John 2:9; 3:9; 4:7; 5:1, 4, 18.

37. Pitcher, ed., *The Winter's Tale*, 328

38. Shaheen, *Biblical References in Shakespeare's Plays*, 721.

39. McCoy, *Faith in Shakespeare*, 137.

40. Robert Greene, *Pandosto: The Triumph of Time*, 3.2.132–36, in Pafford, ed., *The Winter's Tale*, 196. Pafford prints the edition of 1595, collated with the editions of 1588 and 1592 in his *Winter's Tale*, 182–225.

41. See above, chap. 4, sec. "The Mechanism of Healing: Exposing the Truth."

42. Pitcher, ed., *The Winter's Tale*, 49.

43. Bushnell, *Green Desire*, 101; cit. Hamlin, *Bible in Shakespeare*, 177.

44. Hamlin, *Bible in Shakespeare*, 177; my italics.

45. See Shaheen, *Biblical References in Shakespeare's Plays*, 728–29.

46. So Battenhouse, "Theme and Structure in *The Winter's Tale*," 135.

47. On the "wonder" in the dialectic between art and nature, see Bishop, *Shakespeare and the Theatre of Wonder*, 164–67.

48. Luke 19:39–40; see Shaheen, *Biblical References in Shakespeare's Plays*, 733

49. See above, chap. 8, sec. "The Word of 'King.'"

50. So also Muir, *Shakespeare's Comic Sequence*, 167–68; and Bethell, *Winter's Tale*, 103.

51. See above, chap. 6, secs. "A General Spirituality: A Journey to Look on Death," and "The Theologian in the Play: Hope and Human Suffering." Boitani, *Gospel According to Shakespeare*, 84–85, finds an echo not with the resurrection of Jesus but the revival of Lazarus (John 11:1–44): "Paulina's commands—'descend,' 'approach'—have the force of 'Lazarus, come forth!'" (85)

52. So Bate, *Shakespeare and Ovid*, 234–38; and Barkan, *The God Made Flesh*, 283–87. Shakespeare may have merged this scene with the restoration of Almeda's dead wife, Alcestis, to him as a veiled figure, supposedly a substitute, in Euripedes's *Alcestis*. *Much Ado about Nothing* certainly uses this story, from the Latin translation of George Buchanan, for the restoration of Hero to Claudio.

53. McCoy, *Faith in Shakespeare*, 115, 141–45.

54. See Jeffrey Knapp, *Shakespeare's Tribe*, 182; and Bishop, *Shakespeare and the Theatre of Wonder*, 169, "surprise at a pertinence beyond the moment."

55. Matt. 9:22; Mark 5:34; 10:52; Luke 8:48, 17:18; cf. Luke 7:50, 18:42. Given Paulina's name, Paul's words in Romans 1:17 are also apt (see Orgel, ed., *The Winter's Tale*, 59–60).

56. Hamlin, *Bible in Shakespeare*, 175.

57. Beckwith, *Shakespeare and the Grammar of Forgiveness*, 130.

58. Shaheen, *Biblical References in Shakespeare's Plays*, 732.

59. Maslen, *Shakespeare and Comedy*, 35–36, compares *Winter's Tale* and *Pandosto* as tragicomedies.

60. So Pitcher, ed., *The Winter's Tale*, 30.

61. So Knight, *Crown of Life*, 90.

62. Cf. *Cymbeline*, 5.5.142.

63. See above in this chapter, sec. "Loss."

64. Creaser, "Forms of Confusion," 95–96, writes of "episodes that put us at a unique disadvantage."

65. It has been suggested that the story of the ghost of Hermione is the trace of an earlier version of the play, as produced at the Globe in 1611, in which Hermione actually dies and that the statue scene was added for the transfer to the Blackfriars Theatre in 1613 (see Spens, *Elizabethan Drama*, 92; Richard Wilson, *Secret Shakespeare*, 258; and Muir, *Shakespeare's Sources*, 1:245, 251). But the only evidence is a report of seeing the play at the Globe by the physician Simon Forman, who does not mention the statue scene; Muir comments that "it was possible that his memory was inaccurate" (Muir, ed., *Shakespeare: The Winter's Tale*, 12, 23).

66. See Shaheen, *Biblical References in Shakespeare's Plays*, 731–32; cf. *Lear*, 5.1.77: "forget and forgive."

67. Shaheen, *Biblical References in Shakespeare's Plays*, 732.

68. Shakespeare personally owned the upper part of the Gatehouse from 1613, and his company, the King's Men, leased the theater from 1608 (Richard Wilson, *Secret Shakespeare*, 259; cf. Greenblatt, *Will in the World*, 379).

69. Richard Wilson, *Secret Shakespeare*, 262. Milward, *Jacobean Shakespeare*, 77–79, finds a Catholic allegory, identifying Leontes as Henry III, Hermione as Katherine, and Camillo as Thomas More, but this seems arbitrary.

70. Richard Wilson, *Secret Shakespeare*, 264.

71. Lupton, *Afterlives of the Saints*, 177, 206–7, 210–18.

72. So Pitcher, ed., *The Winter's Tale*, 46–47.

73. Foxe, *Acts and Monuments*, 3:405–579.

74. Jeffrey Knapp, *Shakespeare's Tribe*, 181.

75. See above in this chapter, sec. "Loss."

76. McCoy, *Faith in Shakespeare*, 138.

77. McCoy, *Faith in Shakespeare*, 119.

78. Joughin, "Bottom's Secret," 141. Joughin cites Derrida, *Gift of Death*, 63, 95, 108, but does not make clear that the "secret" for Derrida is the ineffable self which cannot become part of an exchange mechanism.

79. Joughin, "Bottom's Secret," 144–45.
80. For instance, in the dance of the Satyrs in this play (see Pitcher, ed., *The Winter's Tale*, 70).
81. See above, chap. 4, sec. "The Mechanism of Healing: Exposing the Truth."
82. Ewbank, "The Triumph of Time," 104–6.
83. Shaheen, *Biblical References in Shakespeare's Plays*, 729, points out that the First Prayer Book of Edward VI (1549) has the rubric that the priest himself would cast earth on the corpse.
84. Cf. "the seeds of time" in *Macbeth*, 1.3.58.
85. Shaheen, *Biblical References in Shakespeare's Plays*, 729.
86. *Twelfth Night*, 2.4.38–39; cf. Shakespeare, *The Passionate Pilgrim*, 10, in Shakespeare, *Shakespeare's Poems*, ed. Duncan-Jones and Woudhuysen, 397–98.
87. Beckwith, *Shakespeare and the Grammar of Forgiveness*, 133–35, stresses that Leontes's repentance and forgiveness involves the painful "recognition of the reality" of another person through memory, and compares liturgical remembrance in "performing the body of Christ."
88. Mackintosh, *Christian Experience of Forgiveness*, 191. The following paragraphs reuse and adapt material from my account of forgiveness in Fiddes, *Past Event and Present Salvation*, 173–83.
89. Mackintosh, *Christian Experience of Forgiveness*, 191.
90. Tillich, *Courage to Be*, 159–71.
91. Lee, *Freud and Christianity*, 141–54.
92. Pitcher, ed., *The Winter's Tale*, 37.
93. See Tatspaugh, *Winter's Tale*, 33–39.
94. Coate, *Sin, Guilt and Forgiveness*, 91.
95. Mackintosh, *Christian Experience of Forgiveness*, 211.
96. Cavell, *Disowning Knowledge*, 218.
97. For these moments in *Measure for Measure* and *Merchant of Venice*, see above, chap. 2, sec. "A Spirituality of Forgiveness and Mercy," and chap. 5, sec. "The Law, the Bond, and the Judgment."
98. Anselm, *Cur Deus homo* 1.7–8, 11; Calvin, *Institutes*, 2.16.5.
99. See Fiddes, *Past Event and Present Salvation*, 98–101.
100. See above, chap. 8, sec. "A Theology of Resistance and Tragedy."
101. For example, Mark 2:1–12; and Luke 7:36–50. Jeremias, *New Testament Theology* 1:114, refers also to pictures of forgiveness: debt remitted, the stray brought home, the lost found, the child accepted into the father's house.
102. Compare Mark 15:34/Matt. 27:46 with Luke 23:34.
103. Tillich, *Systematic Theology*, 2:40.
104. Hegel, *Christian Religion*, 3:212, 217.
105. I deal with implications for the so-called "timelessness" of God in Fiddes, *Creative Suffering of God*, 98–104.
106. Barth, *Church Dogmatics*, II/1, 303; my italics.
107. Farley, *Divine Empathy*, 282.
108. Grey, *Redeeming the Dream*, 61–63, 95–97.
109. Metz, "The Future in the Memory of Suffering," 9–25.

110. Beckwith, *Shakespeare's Grammar of Forgiveness*, 128, proposes that Shakespeare is producing a "theatre of recollection."

111. See above, chap. 7, sec. "Theological Doubts about the Ghost."

112. Volf, *End of Memory*, 67. In what follows, I draw on some material from Fiddes, "Memory, Forgetting and the Problem of Forgiveness," 118–23, 127–30.

113. 1 Pet. 4:8

114. Isa. 43:25, 44:2; cf. Ps. 53:1, 9.

115. Kierkegaard, *Works of Love*, 239–40.

116. Volf, *End of Memory*, 169.

117. Volf, *End of Memory*, 203.

118. Volf, *Exclusion and Embrace*, 134–38.

119. Volf, *End of Memory*, 184

120. Barth, *Church Dogmatics*, III/3, 352.

121. Volf, *End of Memory*, 214.

122. For advocacy of a temporal or quasi-temporal eternity, see Pike, *God and Timelessness*, 184; Swinburne, *The Christian God*, 138–44; and Fiddes, *The Promised End*, 123–25.

123. Hauerwas, "Why Time Cannot and Should Not Heal the Wounds of History but Time Has Been and Can Be Redeemed," 42–43.

124. Barth, *Church Dogmatics*, II/1, 608–12; Barth is ambiguous about whether this is strictly nontemporal.

125. Volf, *End of Memory*, 185–86.

126. See Epstein, *Melting the Venusberg*, 160–73.

127. See above, chap. 6, sec. "The Theologian in the Play: Hope and Human Suffering."

128. Jer. 31:34; Isa. 65:1; Isa 43:18, cited in Volf, *Exclusion and Embrace*, 136.

129. Ricoeur, *Memory, History and Forgetting*, 412.

130. Ricoeur, *Memory, History and Forgetting*, 494–505.

131. Ricoeur, *Memory, History and Forgetting*, 414–16.

132. Ricoeur, *Memory, History and Forgetting*, 448; Ricoeur, "Memory and Forgetting," 9. Volf cites Ricoeur with approval on this point in *End of Memory*, 195.

133. Ricoeur, "Memory and Forgetting," 6–7; Ricoeur, *Memory, History and Forgetting*, 444–47.

10. THE TEMPEST AND THE RISKS OF FORGIVENESS

1. Dir. Peter Greenaway; screenplay by John Greenaway and William Shakespeare; starring John Gielgud as Prospero, released 30 August 1991.

2. Greenaway, *Prospero's Books*, 9.

3. Greenaway, *Prospero's Books*, 9.

4. See Derrida, *Grammatology*, 18.

5. Tillyard, *Shakespeare's Last Plays*, 67–68, refers similarly to "many planes of reality" and a "complexity of possible worlds" in the final Romances.

6. Defended by Sir Philip Sidney, in Sidney, *Defence of Poesy*, 243–44.

7. See Kermode, ed., *The Tempest*, xxvi–xxx.
8. Most influential seems to have been a long letter written to an "excellent Lady" in England in July 1610, by William Strachey, secretary to the governor, which circulated in manuscript form under the title "A True Reportory of the Wracke, and Redemption of Sir Thomas Gates, Knight." Relevant excerpts are printed in Vaughan and Vaughan, eds., *The Tempest*, 310–24, from which quotations come throughout. Shakespeare seems to have taken the name Setebos for Sycorax's devil from the account of another voyage, Magellan's circumnavigation of the world (1521–22), translated into English by Richard Eden in 1557.
9. Nuttall, *Shakespeare the Thinker*, 366–70, describes Caliban as "sexually mature, but emotionally a child."
10. Shaheen, *Biblical References in Shakespeare's Plays*, 740–71, notes some of them, but misses the Christological link between them.
11. Noble, *Shakespeare's Biblical Knowledge*, 249.
12. Strachey, "True Reportory," in Vaughan and Vaughan, eds., *The Tempest*, 314.
13. The Geneva margin rightly notes that the expression in Hebrew refers to an angel. Calvin also explains the title this way, but adds that Nebuchadnezzar "could not recognize the only-begotten Son of God" (Calvin, *Commentaries on the Prophet Daniel*, 231).
14. Shaheen, *Biblical References in Shakespeare's Plays*, 740. See *Julius Caesar*, 2.2.58; and *Richard II*, 4.1.169–70, as above, chap. 8, sec. "The Word of 'King.'"
15. Luke 11:18; John 7:20, 8:48, 8:52, 10:20.
16. See, for example, Vaughan and Vaughan, eds., *The Tempest*, 288; and Bate, *Shakespeare and Ovid*, 252.
17. *Hamlet*, 1.1.114–16; *Julius Caesar*, 2.2.18; Shaheen, *Biblical References in Shakespeare's Plays*, 749.
18. Luke 7:14–15 (widow of Nain's son); Luke 8:52–53 / Mark 5:41–42 (Jairus's daughter).
19. John 2:4, 4:23, 5:25, 7:30, 8:20, 12:23, 12:27, 13:1, 17:1.
20. The phrase is C. H. Dodd's, in his *Parables of the Kingdom*, 41.
21. Bate, *Shakespeare and Ovid*, 252–54; Vaughan and Vaughan, eds., *The Tempest*, 62–66.
22. See James I's view of magic, in his *Daemonologie*, 10.
23. Slater, "Variations within a Source," 125–35. Similarly, Esolen, "The Isles Shall Wait for His Law," 221–47.
24. Kaiser, *Isaiah 13–39*, 266–67.
25. Childs, *Isaiah and the Assyrian Crisis*, 13–17; Kaiser, *Isaiah 13–39*, 268.
26. Vaughan and Vaughan, eds., *The Tempest*, 28.
27. The last phrase appears, in the text of Isaiah, to be addressed to the inhabitants of Jerusalem (see Kaiser, *Isaiah 13–39*, 269–71).
28. Shaheen, *Biblical References in Shakespeare's Plays*, 738.
29. See above, chap. 8, sec. "The Word of 'King.'"
30. For example, Ezek. 9:10; Josh. 2:19; and 1 Sam. 25:39.
31. *The Merchant of Venice*, 202; cf. *Henry VIII*, 2.1.137.

32. Shaheen, *Biblical References in Shakespeare's Plays*, 742.

33. Jeffrey Knapp, *Shakespeare's Tribe*, 54, but he makes too literal an identification when he writes, "he reveals himself to his enemies . . . in the guise of the resurrected Christ"; see also 204n111.

34. So Shaheen, *Biblical References in Shakespeare's Plays*, 742.

35. Fernie, ed., *Spiritual Shakespeares*, 23.

36. Knight, *Crown of Life*, 242. Harold Bloom's assertion, in *Shakespeare: The Invention of the Human*, 668, that "Shakespeare took considerable care to exclude Christian references" from this play shows lack of familiarity with biblical resonances. Bate, *Soul of the Age*, 127–30, proposes that the play shows a critique of humanism from the viewpoint of Christian virtues of kindness and grace.

37. Cf. 1 Kings 22:21.

38. Cf. Mark 5:9.

39. The medieval belief that each person has a good and a bad angel assigned to them from birth arises from the text of Jesus in Matthew 18:10 about the angels of the "little ones" that behold the face of God; see also Sowerby, *Angels*, 81–86.

40. See Caird, *Principalities and Powers*, 2–8.

41. Tillich, *Systematic Theology*, 1:55, 126, 149–50, 239–40; 3:108–13, 184–94.

42. Wink, *Naming the Powers*, 104.

43. On *The Winter's Tale*, see above, chap. 9, sec. "Reconciliation."

44. See Brunstetter and Zartner, "Just War against Barbarians," 739–43.

45. Harris, "Shakespeare and Race," 202–4.

46. Montaigne, *Essayes*, 101–3. For reference to Montaigne in *King Lear*, see above, chap. 6, sec. "A Journey to Nothingness: Images of Disintegration"; cf. Elton, "Shakespeare and the Thought of His Time," 27–28.

47. Montaigne, *Essayes*, 102.

48. Montaigne, *Essayes*, 104.

49. Murray, "Shakespeare's Dream," 115–18, finds a "subtle change of Montaigne" here.

50. Coleridge, *Shakespearean Criticism*, 2:138, despite Coleridge's view earlier that Caliban is "all earth, all condensed and gross in feelings and images" (1:34).

51. For this change in assessment of Caliban, see Vaughan and Vaughan, *Shakespeare's Caliban*; see also Vaughan and Vaughan, eds., *The Tempest*, 89–110. Buchanan, *Shakespeare on Film*, 157–58, finds that in the unmade film "Magic Island" (Michael Powell, 1969–79), the projected scene of Caliban's capering on the island after Prospero's departure, "rewards the voice of the colonially dispossessed."

52. Coleridge, *Shakespearean Criticism*, 2:136–37.

53. However, Tillyard, *Shakespeare's Last Plays*, 56, thinks the audience would have sympathized.

54. Buccola, "Shakespeare's Fairy Dance with Religio-Political Controversy," 162–63, suggests the indeterminate position of the island sufficiently detaches it from the "Protestant confines" of the British Isles to allow Shakespeare to make religio-political criticisms. Kott, "Prospero's Staff," 250–52, finds that the island represents the world, and its story world-history.

55. Shell, *Shakespeare and Religion*, 37.

56. Asquith, *Shadowplay*, 237–38.

57. Jeffrey Knapp, *Shakespeare's Tribe*, 53–55.

58. Some readers have suggested a sixth meaning, that this is a farewell to Shakespeare's career as a playwright. It is thus Shakespeare as Prospero who breaks his staff and drowns his book. An early suggestion along these lines was Dowden, *Shakespeare: A Critical Study*, 370–74. A more recent proposal is by Asquith, *Shadowplay*, 265–66, and Greenblatt seriously entertains the idea in his *Will in the World*, 372–87. However, I tend to discount this as a piece of romantic biography in hindsight.

59. *Hamlet*, 1.2.130, "resolve into a dew": see above, chap. 7, sec. "The Mental State of Hamlet." Cf. Cleopatra's cry, "dissolve my life" (*Anthony and Cleopatra*, 3.13.167), on which see Traversi, *Shakespeare: The Roman Plays*, 152–53.

60. Frye, *Shakespeare and Christian Doctrine*, 148–49.

61. Calvin, *Sermons*, f. 31/2.

62. Calvin, *Commentarie vpon S. Paules epistles to the Corinthians*, f. 87/1.

63. Cit. Shaheen, *Biblical References in Shakespeare's Plays*, 748.

64. So Rahner, *Theology of Death*, 45.

65. It brings *distentio* into the mind: Augustine, *Confessions*, 11.26. For discussion of *distentio*, see Ricoeur, *Time and Narrative*, 1:5–30.

66. Bloom, *Shakespeare: The Invention of the Human*, 666–68. Much earlier, Knight, *Crown of Life*, 241–43, 253, describes Prospero's "art" as "symbolizing the Renaissance," and judges the play to be "an expression of the Renaissance imagination under pressure from British puritanism."

67. Cf. *Henry V*, Prologue 13.

68. The second Blackfriars Theatre (materials from the first being used to construct the Globe Theatre in 1599), erected like the first on the site of the Blackfriars Monastery, was used as winter quarters by Shakespeare's company, the King's Men, from 1608 onward (see Ackroyd, *Shakespeare*, 439–41).

69. Cf. Berry, *The Shakespeare Inset*, 129–38.

70. Righter, ed., *The Tempest*, 44–46.

71. Righter, ed., *The Tempest*, 47–48.

72. Asquith, *Shadowplay*, 272.

73. The dark uncertainty at the end of the play is underlined by Nuttall, *Shakespeare the Thinker*, 370–73.

74. Shakespeare, Sonnet 65.

75. *The Tempest*, 5.1.2—that is, swiftly and without stooping because the burden is not heavy.

76. Vaughan and Vaughan, eds., *The Tempest*, 286.

77. Montaigne, "Of Crueltie," in *Essayes*, 243.

78. In late-modern context, in which Greenaway is deliberately writing, they are released from the domination of a transcendent word (see Derrida, *Grammatology*, 34; and Derrida, *Positions*, 31).

79. So Shaheen, *Biblical References in Shakespeare's Plays*, 749, who suggests that the text is also cited in *Love's Labour's Lost*, 4.3.358–59, "Let us once lose our

oaths to find ourselves," and in *All's Well That Ends Well*, 1.1.130–32, "Virginity, by being once lost, may be ten times found."

80. See *Richard II*, 3.4.31; *As You Like It*, 1.1.35–37; *King Lear* 4.7.39–40; and *The Winter's Tale*, 4.3.97. All these instances are discussed elsewhere in this book.

81. Swinburne, *Responsibility and Atonement*, 83–85.

82. Swinburne, *Responsibility and Atonement*, 148–52, 160–62.

83. Derrida, "To Forgive: The Unforgivable and the Imprescriptible," 25–30.

84. Derrida, "To Forgive: The Unforgivable and the Imprescriptible," 28; cf. 8.

85. "Forgiveness demands impossibility, the unforgivable" (Derrida, *On Cosmopolitanism and Forgiveness*, 32).

86. Biggar, *In Defence of War*, 62.

87. Biggar, *In Defence of War*, 66.

88. Derrida, "To Forgive: The Unforgivable and the Imprescriptible," 21–23.

89. Derrida, *Given Time*, 18.

90. Derrida, "To Forgive: The Unforgivable and the Imprescriptible," 22.

91. Ricoeur, *Memory, History, Forgetting*, 494–96; see above, chap. 9, sec. "A Theology of Forgiveness and Memory."

92. Griswold, *Forgiveness*, 124.

93. Griswold, *Forgiveness*, 49–52.

94. See Anderson, "Unselfing in Love: A Contradiction in Terms," 257–61; Anderson, "When Justice and Forgiveness Come Apart," 115–17. I engage with Anderson in Fiddes, "Forgiveness, Empathy and Vulnerability," 109–25.

95. For the significance of the theme of forgiveness in Shakespeare, see Maguire, *Where There's a Will There's a Way*, 149–60.

96. The homily "On Common Prayer and Sacraments," *Homilies II*, 293; cited by Shaheen, *Biblical References in Shakespeare's Plays*, 749.

97. *The Merchant of Venice*, 4.1.125, 196–98.

98. Shell, *Shakespeare and Religion*, 76–78.

99. So Asquith, *Shadowplay*, 272–73.

100. So Vaughan and Vaughan, eds., *The Tempest*, 308.

101. John 21:25. The evangelist also expects there to be many future readers of his own work, as is clear from his putting into the mouth of Jesus a blessing for those who "do not see" the earthly Christ, but believe (John 20:29).

BIBLIOGRAPHY

All quotations from the works of Shakespeare in the main text and the notes, except where otherwise indicated, are from the Third Series of the Arden Shakespeare, as referenced below.

LITERATURE FROM THE PERIOD 1500–1700

Acts and Ordinances of the Interregnum, 1642–1660. Edited by C. H. Firth and R. S. Rait. London: His Majesty's Stationery Office, 1911.

Agrippa von Nettesheim, Heinrich Cornelius. *Three books of Occult Philosophy [. . .] translated out of the Latin into the English tongue by J. F.* London: R.W., 1651.

Bilson, Thomas. *A Sermon preached at Westminster before the King and Queenes Maiesties at their Coronations [. . .] by the Lord Bishop of Winchester.* London: Clement Knight, 1603.

The Booke of Common Prayer, and Administracion of the Sacramentes, and other Rites and Ceremonies in the Churche of England. London: Richard Iugge and Iohannis Cawood, 1559.

Burton, Robert. *The Anatomy of Melancholy.* 1621. Edited by Holbrook Jackson. 3 vols. London: Dent, 1932.

Busher, Leonard. *Religions Peace: Or a Plea for Liberty of Conscience.* London: John Sweeting, 1646.

Calvin, John. *A Commentarie vpon S. Paules epistles to the Corinthians. Written by M. Iohn Caluin: and translated out of Latine into Englishe by Thomas Timme minister.* London: Thomas Dawson, 1577.

———. *Commentaries on the Prophet Daniel.* Translated by Thomas Myers. Edinburgh: Calvin Translation Society, 1852.

———. *Epistles of Paul the Apostle to the Romans and to the Thessalonians.* Translated by Ross Mackenzie. Edinburgh: St Andrew Press, 1972.

———. *Institutes of the Christian Religion.* Edited by John T. McNeill; translated by Ford Lewis Battles. Library of Christian Classics. 2 vols. London: SCM, 1961.

———. *The Institution of Christian Religion written in Latine by M. John Caluine, and translated into Englishe according to the authors last edition, by Thomas Norton.* London: Thomas Vautrollier, 1574.

———. *Sermons of Master Iohn Caluin, vpon the Booke of Iob. Translated out of French by Arthur Golding.* London: Henry Bynneman for Lucas Harison and George Byshop, 1574.

Church of England. *Articles whereupon it was agreed by the archbishops and byshops [. . .] for the avoyding of diuersities of opinions, and for the stablishing of consent touching true religion.* London: Christopher Barker, 1593.

Cranmer, Thomas. *A Confutatio[n] of vnwritte[n] Verities both by the Holye Scriptures and moste Auncient Autors [. . .] translated and set forth by E. P. Wesel.* J. Lambrecht, 1556.

Donne, John. *Devotions upon Emergent Occasions.* Ann Arbor: University of Michigan, 1959.

———. *Sermons.* Edited by George Potter and Evelyn Simpson. 10 vols. Berkeley: University of California Press, 1953–62.

Elyot, Thomas. *The Boke named the Gouernour.* Edited by Stephen Croft. 2 vols. London: Kegan Paul, 1883.

Erasmus, Desiderius. *The Education of a Christian Prince.* 1540. Translated by L. K. Born. New York: Columbia University Press, 1936.

———. *The Praise of Folie. Moriæ encomium a booke made in latine by that great clerke Erasmus Roterodame. Englisshed by sir Thomas Chaloner knight.* London: Thomas Berthelet, 1549.

Foxe, John. *The Unabridged Acts and Monuments Online* (1576 edition) or *TAMO.* The Digital Humanities Institute, Sheffield, 2011. Available from: http://www .dhi.ac.uk/foxe.

Geneva Bible. *The Bible and Holy Scriptures conteyned in the olde and newe testament. translated according to the ebrue and greke, and conferred with the best translations in diuers languges. with moste profitable annotations vpon all the hard places, and other things of great importance as may appeare in the epistle to the reader.* Geneva: printed by Rouland Hall, 1560.

Geninges, John. *The Life and Death of Mr Edmund Geninges Priest, crowned with martyrdome at London [. . .].* St Omer: Charles Boscard, 1614.

Grantham, Thomas. *Christianismus Primitivus: or, The Ancient Christian Religion.* London: Francis Smith, 1678.

Greene, Robert. *The Spanish Masquerado.* London: Roger Ward, 1589.

Harsnett, Samuel. *A Declaration of Egregious Popish Impostures to with-draw the Harts of Her Maiesties Subiects from their allegeance, and from the Truth of Christian Religion professed in England [. . .].* London: James Roberts, 1603.

Helwys, Thomas. *A Short Declaration of the Mistery of Iniquity.* N.p., 1612.

Holinshed, Raphael. *The Historie of Scotland.* In Holinshed, *Chronicles of England, Scotlande, and Irelande,* vol. 2. London: Henry Denham, 1587.

Homilies I = Certayne Sermons, or Homilies, appoynted by the Kynges Maiestie to be declared and redde, by all persones, vycares, or curates, euery Sonday in their churches, where they haue cure. London: Edward Whitchurche: 1547.

Homilies II = The Second Tome of Homilees of such matters as were promised, and intituled in the former part of homilees. Set out by the aucthoritie of the Queenes Majestie: and to be read in euery parishe church agreeably. London: Richard Iugge and Iohn Cawood, 1571.

Hooker, Richard. *Of the Laws of Ecclesiastical Polity.* In *The Works of [. . .] Mr Richard Hooker. With an Account of his Life and Death by Isaac Walton.* 2 vols. Oxford: Clarendon, 1885.

James I, King. *Daemonologie. In Forme of a Dialogve.* London: William Cotton, 1603.

Jewel, John. *An expositio[n] upon the two Epistles of the Apostle S. Paul to the Thessalonians.* London: Raife Newberie, 1584.

Lumpkin, William L. *Baptist Confessions of Faith.* Chicago: Judson, 1959.

Luther, Martin. *The Bondage of the Will.* In *Luther's Works*, vol. 33: *The Career of the Reformer III*, translated by Philip Watson. Philadelphia: Fortress, 1957.

———. *D. Martin Luthers Werke: Kritische Gesamtausgabe* = WA (Weimarer Ausgabe). Weimar: H. Bohlaus Nachfolger, 1883–1929.

———. *Galatervorlesung (Lectures on Galatians).* In *D. Martin Luthers Werke,* 40 (1).

———. *Heidelberg Disputation* (1518). In *Luther: Early Theological Works,* edited and translated by J. Atkinson. Library of Christian Classics. London: SCM, 1962.

———. *Lectures on Galatians.* In *Luther's Works*, vol. 26, edited by Jaroslav Pelikan. Philadelphia: Fortress, 2007.

———. *Lectures on Romans.* In *Luther's Works*, vol. 25, edited by Hilton C. Oswald. St. Louis, MO: Concordia, 1972.

———. *Psalmenvorlesung (Lectures on the Psalms, 1513–15).* In *D. Martin Luthers Werke,* 4, and 55 (1) *(Glossen).*

———. *Psalmenvorlesung (Lectures on the Psalms, 1519–21).* In *D. Martin Luthers Werke,* 5.

———. *Trade and Usury.* In *The Christian in Society,* vol. 45 of *Luther's Works,* edited by C. M. Jacobs, 298–310. Philadelphia: Fortress, 1962.

———. *Die zweite Disputationen gegen die Antinomer.* In *Disputationen 1535–38, D. Martin Luthers Werke* 39 (1).

Mather, Samuel. *The Figures or Types of the Old Testament by which Christ and the heavenly things of the gospel were preached and shadowed to the people of God of old.* Dublin, sold at London: H. Sawbridge . . . and A. Churchill, 1685.

Melanchthon, *Loci Communes theologici.* In *Melanchthon and Bucer,* edited by Wilhelm Pauck. Library of Christian Classics. London: SCM, 1969.

Milton, John. *Reason of Church-government urg'd against Prelaty.* London: E. G., 1642.

Montaigne, Michel de. *The Essayes or Morall, Politike and Millitarie Discourses of lo: Michaell de Montaigne, knight of the noble order of St. Michaell, and one of the gentlemen in ordinary of the French King [. . .] now done into English by [. . .] Iohn Florio.* London: Val. Sims for Edward Blount, 1603.

More, Thomas. *The Supplycacyon of Soulys made by Syr Thomas More knyght [. . .] Agaynst the Supplycacyon of Beggars.* London: William Rastell, 1529.

Nashe, Thomas. *Cristes Teares over Jerusalem.* London: James Roberts, 1593.

Parsons, Robert. *A Booke of Christian Exercise [. . .] by R.P., Perused and accompanied now with a Treatise tending to Pacification: by Edm. Bunny.* London: N. Newton and A. Hatfield, 1584.

Penry, John. *I Iohn Penry, doo heare as I shall answere before the Lord my God in that great day of iudgement set downe sumarily the Whole truth and nothing but the truth which I hold and professe [. . .].* Document 1593, retrieved from https://ezproxy -prd.bodleian.ox.ac.uk:2082/docview/2240950498?accountid=13042.

Pepys, Samuel. *The Diary of Samuel Pepys: A New and Complete Transcription.* Edited by Robert Latham and William Matthews. 11 vols. Berkeley: University of California Press.

Perkins, William. *Hepieíkeia: or, a treatise of Christian Equitie and Moderation.* Cambridge: John Legat, 1604.

———. *A Reformed Catholike, or, A Declaration shewing how neere we may come to the present Church of Rome in sundrie points of Religion.* London: John Legat, 1597.

———. *A Salve for a Sicke Man: or, A treatise containing the nature, differences, and kindes of death; as also the right manner of dying well.* Cambridge: John Legatt, 1600.

———. *The Workes of that famous and vvorthie Minister of Christ, in the Vniuersitie of Cambridge, M. W. Perkins.* 3 vols. Cambridge: John Legate, 1608–9.

Scot, Reginald. *The Discouerie of Witchcraft.* 2nd ed. London: Henry Durham, 1584.

Shakespeare, William. *Anthony and Cleopatra.* Edited by John Wilders. Arden Shakespeare Third Series. London: Bloomsbury, 1995.

———. *As You Like It.* Edited by Juliet Dussinberre. Arden Shakespeare Third Series. London: Thomson Learning, 2006.

———. *The Comedy of Errors.* Edited by Kent Cartwright. Arden Shakespeare Third Series. London: Bloomsbury, 2017.

———. *Cymbeline.* Edited by Valerie Wayne. Arden Shakespeare Third Series. London: Bloomsbury, 2017.

———. *Hamlet.* Edited by Harold Jenkins. Arden Shakespeare Second Series. London: Methuen, 1982.

———. *Hamlet.* Edited by Ann Thompson and Neil Taylor. Arden Shakespeare Third Series. London: Bloomsbury, 2006.

———. *Hamlet. The Texts of 1603 and 1623.* Edited by Ann Thompson and Neil Taylor. Arden Shakespeare Third Series. London: Bloomsbury, 2006.

———. *Hamlet.* Edited by John Dover Wilson. Cambridge New Shakespeare. Cambridge: Cambridge University Press, 1936.

———. *Julius Caesar.* Edited by David Daniell. Arden Shakespeare Third Series. London: Bloomsbury, 2011.

———. *King Henry IV Part 1.* Edited by David Scott Kastan. Arden Shakespeare Third Series. London: Bloomsbury, 2002.

———. *King Henry IV Part 2.* Edited by James C. Bulman. Arden Shakespeare Third Series. London: Bloomsbury, 2016.

———. *King Henry V.* Edited by T. W. Craik. Arden Shakespeare Third Series. London: Routledge: 1995.

———. *King Henry VI Part 1.* Edited by Edward Burns. Arden Shakespeare Third Series. London: Thomson Learning, 2000.

———. *King Henry VI Part 2.* Edited by Ronald Knowles. Arden Shakespeare Third Series. London: Bloomsbury 2009.

———. *King Henry VI Part 3.* Edited by John D. Cox and Eric Rasmussen. Arden Shakespeare Third Series. London: Bloomsbury 2010.

———. *King Henry VIII.* Edited by Gordon McMullan. Arden Shakespeare Third Series. London: Bloomsbury, 2009.

———. *King John.* Edited by Jesse Lander and J. J. M. Tobin. Arden Shakespeare Third Series. London: Bloomsbury, 2018.

———. *King Lear.* Edited by George Ian Duthie and John Dover Wilson. Cambridge New Shakespeare. Cambridge: Cambridge University Press, 1969.

———. *King Lear.* Edited by R. A. Foakes. Arden Shakespeare Third Series. London: Methuen, 1997.

———. *King Lear.* Edited by Kenneth Muir. Arden Shakespeare Second Series. London: Methuen, 1964.

———. *King Richard II.* Edited by Charles R. Forker. Arden Shakespeare Third Series. London: Bloomsbury, 2009.

———. *King Richard II.* Edited by Peter Ure. Arden Shakespeare Second Series. London: Methuen, 1961.

———. *King Richard III.* Edited by James R. Siemon. Arden Shakespeare Third Series. London: Bloomsbury, 2009.

———. *Love's Labour's Lost.* Edited by H. R. Woudhuysen. Arden Shakespeare Third Series. London: Methuen, 1988.

———. *Macbeth.* Edited by Sandra Clark and Pamela Mason. Arden Shakespeare Third Series. London: Bloomsbury: 2015.

———. *Measure for Measure.* Edited by A. R. Braunmuller and Robert N. Watson. Arden Shakespeare Third Series. London: Bloomsbury, 2020.

———. *Measure for Measure.* Edited by J. W. Lever. Arden Shakespeare Second Series. London: Methuen, 1965.

———. *The Merchant of Venice.* Edited by John Russell Brown. Arden Shakespeare Second Series. London: Methuen, 1955.

———. *The Merchant of Venice.* Edited by John Drakakis. Arden Shakespeare Third Series. London: Bloomsbury, 2011.

———. *The Merry Wives of Windsor.* Edited by Giorgio Melchiori. Arden Shakespeare Third Series. London: Bloomsbury, 2009.

———. *A Midsummer Night's Dream.* Edited by Harold F. Brooks. Arden Shakespeare Second Series. London: Methuen, 1979.

———. *A Midsummer Night's Dream.* Edited by Sukanta Chaudhuri. Arden Shakespeare Third Series. London: Bloomsbury, 2017.

———. *Much Ado about Nothing.* Edited by Claire McEachern. Arden Shakespeare Third Series. London: Methuen, 2006.

———. *Othello.* Edited by E. A. J. Honigmann. Arden Shakespeare Third Series. London: Bloomsbury, 1997.

———. *Pericles.* Edited by Suzanne Gossett. Arden Shakespeare Third Series. London: Bloomsbury, 2014.

———. *Romeo and Juliet.* Edited by René Weis. Arden Shakespeare Third Series. London: Bloomsbury, 2012.

———. *The Tempest.* Edited by Frank Kermode. Arden Shakespeare Second Series. London: Methuen, 1954.

———. *The Tempest.* Edited by Ann Righter. Penguin Shakespeare. Harmondsworth: Penguin, 1974.

———. *The Tempest*. Edited by Virginia Mason Vaughan and Alden T. Vaughan. Arden Shakespeare Third Series. London: Bloomsbury, 2011.

———. *Timon of Athens*. Edited by Anthony B. Dawson and Gretchen E. Minton. Arden Shakespeare Third Series. London: Bloomsbury, 2008.

———. *Titus Andronicus*. Edited by John Dover Wilson. Cambridge New Shakespeare. Cambridge: Cambridge University Press, 1968.

———. *Troilus and Cressida*. Edited by David Bevington. Arden Shakespeare Third Series. London: Arden Shakespeare, 2001.

———. *Twelfth Night*. Edited by Keir Elam. Arden Shakespeare Third Series. London: Bloomsbury, 2008.

———. *The Winter's Tale*. Edited by Stephen Orgel. Oxford Shakespeare. Oxford: Oxford University Press, 1996.

———. *The Winter's Tale*. Edited by J. H. P. Pafford. Arden Shakespeare Second Series. London: Methuen, 1963.

———. *The Winter's Tale*. Edited by John Pitcher. Arden Shakespeare Third Series. London: Blomsbury, 2010.

———. *Shakespeare's Poems*. Edited by Katherine Duncan-Jones and H. R. Woudhuysen. Arden Shakespeare Third Series. London: Arden Shakespeare, 2007.

———. *Shakespeare's Sonnets*. Edited by Katherine Duncan-Jones. Arden Shakespeare Third Series. London: Arden Shakespeare, 2005.

A Short Confession of Faith. Amsterdam, 1610. In Lumpkin, *Baptist Confessions of Faith*, 102–13.

Sidney, Philip. *The Countesse of Pembrokes Arcadia [. . .] now since the first edition augmented and ended*. London: John Windet for William Ponsonbie, 1593.

———. *Defence of Poesy*. In *Sir Philip Sidney: The Major Works*, edited by Katherine Duncan-Jones. Rev. ed. Oxford: Oxford University Press, 2002.

Smyth, John et al. *Propositions and Conclusions concerning True Christian Religion, containing a Confession of Faith of certain English people, living at Amsterdam* (1612). In Lumpkin, *Baptist Confessions*, 124–42.

Southwell, Robert. *An Epistle of Comfort*. English Recusant Literature, vol. 211. Ilkley, UK: Scolar Press, 1974.

———. *An Humble Supplication to Her Maiestie*. Edited by R. C. Bald. Cambridge: Cambridge University Press, 1953.

———. *Marie Magdalens Funeral Teares*. Edited by Vincent B. Leitch. Delmar, NY: Scholars' Facsimilies and Reprints, 1974.

Stubbes, Phillip. *The Anatomie of Abuses containing, a discouerie, or briefe summarie of such notable vices and imperfections, as now raigne in many countreyes of the world [. . .]*. London: John Kingston for Richard Jones 1583.

The Troublesome Raigne of King John, King of England. Edited by J. W. Sider. New York: Garland, 1979.

Ursinus, Zacharius. *The Svmme of Christian Religion: Deliuered by Zacharias Vrsinus in his lectures vpon the catechism autorised by the noble Prince Frederick, throughout his dominions [. . .]. Translated into English by Henrie Parrie, out of the last & best Latin editions [. . .]*. Oxford: Ioseph Barnes, 1587.

Wilson, Thomas. *A Discourse uppon Vsurye, by way of Dialogues and Oracions*. London: Rychard Tottell, 1572.

Woodstock. A Moral History. Edited by Arthur P. Rossiter. London: Chatto and Windus, 1946.

OTHER LITERATURE

Ackroyd, Peter. *Shakespeare: The Biography*. London: Chatto and Windus, 2005.

Adelman, Janet. *Blood Relations: Christian and Jew in "The Merchant of Venice."* Chicago: University of Chicago Press, 2008.

The Agony and the Betrayal. In *The York Plays*, edited by Richard Beadle. York Medieval Texts. London: Edward Arnold, 1982.

Allen, Graham. *Intertextuality*. 2nd ed. London: Routledge, 2011.

Anderson, Pamela Sue. "Unselfing in Love: A Contradiction in Terms." In *Faith in the Enlightenment? The Critique of the Enlightenment Revisited*, edited by Lieven Boeve, Joeri Schrijvers, Wessel Stoker, and Hendrik M. Vroom, 244–68. Amsterdam: Rodopi, 2006.

———. "When Justice and Forgiveness Come Apart: A Feminist Perspective on Restorative Justice and Intimate Violence." *Oxford Journal of Law and Religion* 5, no. 1 (2016): 113–34.

Arnold, Matthew. *Culture and Anarchy*. Edited by J. Dover Wilson. Cambridge: Cambridge University Press, 1960.

Asquith, Clare. *Shadowplay. The Hidden Beliefs and Coded Politics of William Shakespeare*. New York: Public Affairs, 2005.

Augustine. *Confessions*. Translated by Henry Chadwick. Oxford: Oxford University Press, 1992.

Badham, Paul, and Linda Badham. *Immortality or Extinction?* 2nd ed. London: SPCK, 1984.

Bakhtin, Mikhail M. *The Dialogic Imagination: Four Essays*. Edited and translated by C. Emerson and M. Holquist. Austin: University of Texas Press, 1981.

———. *Problems of Dostoevsky's Poetics*. Edited and translated by C. Emerson. Minneapolis: University of Minnesota Press, 1984.

———. *Rabelais and His World*. Translated by Hélène Iswolsky. Bloomington: University of Indiana Press, 1984.

Balthasar, Hans Urs von. *The Glory of the Lord*. Vol. 1: *Seeing the Form*. Translated by Erasmo Leiva-Merikakis. Edinburgh: T. & T. Clark; and San Francisco: Ignatius, 1982.

———. *The Glory of the Lord*. Vol. 7: *Theology: The New Covenant*. Translated by Brian McNeil, C.R.V. Edinburgh: T. & T. Clark; and San Francisco: Ignatius, 1989.

———. *Mysterium Paschale*. Translated by Aidan Nichols. Edinburgh: T. & T. Clark, 1990.

———. *Theo-Drama: Theological Dramatic Theory*. Vol. 1: *Prolegomena*. Translated by Graham Harrison. San Francisco: Ignatius, 1988.

————. *Theo-Drama: Theological Dramatic Theory.* Vol. 4: *The Action.* Translated by Graham Harrison. San Francisco: Ignatius, 1994.

————. *Theo-Logic: Theological Logical Theory.* Vol. 1: *The Truth of the World.* Translated by Adrian J. Walker. San Francisco: Ignatius, 2000.

Barkan, Leonard. "Diana and Actaeon: The Myth as Synthesis." *English Literary Renaissance* 10 (1980): 317–59.

————. *The God Made Flesh: Metamorphosis and the Pursuit of Paganism.* New Haven, CT: Yale University Press, 1990.

Barrett, C. K. *The Epistle to the Romans.* London: A. & C. Black, 1962.

Barth, Karl. *Church Dogmatics.* Translated and edited by G. W. Bromiley and T. F. Torrance. 13 vols. Edinburgh: T. & T. Clark, 1936–77.

————. *The Epistle to the Romans.* Translated from the 6th edition by Edwyn C. Hoskins. Oxford: Oxford University Press, 1933.

Barthes, Roland. *Image-Music-Text.* Essays selected and translated by Stephen Heath. London: Fontana, 1977.

————. *The Pleasure of the Text.* Translated by Richard Miller. New York: Hill and Wang, 1975.

————. "Theory of the Text." In *Untying the Text: A Post-structuralist Reader,* edited by Robert Young, 31–47. London: Routledge and Kegan Paul, 1981.

Bate, Jonathan. *Shakespeare and Ovid.* Oxford: Clarendon, 2001.

————. *Soul of the Age: A Biography of the Mind of William Shakespeare.* New York: Random, 2009.

Battenhouse, Roy. "Religion in *King John:* Shakespeare's View." *Connotations* 1, no. 2 (1991): 146–47.

————. "Theme and Structure in 'The Winter's Tale.'" In *Shakespeare Survey* 33, edited by Kenneth Muir, 123–38. Cambridge: Cambridge Univerity Press, 1980.

Bearman, Robert. "John Shakespeare: A Papist or Just Penniless?" *Shakespeare Quarterly* 56, no. 4 (2005): 411–33.

Beckwith, Sarah. *Shakespeare and the Grammar of Forgiveness.* Ithaca, NY: Cornell University Press, 2011.

Berman, Ronald. "Shakespeare and the Law." *Shakespeare Quarterly* 18, no. 2 (1967): 141–50.

Berry, Francis. *The Shakespeare Inset: Word and Picture.* Carbondale and Edwardville: Southern Illinois University Press, 1965.

Bethell, S. L. *Shakespeare and the Popular Dramatic Tradition.* London: King and Staples, 1944.

————. *The Winter's Tale.* Oxford: Clarendon, 1956.

Biggar, Nigel. *In Defence of War.* Oxford: Oxford University Press, 2013.

Billington, Sandra. "A Response to Roy Battenhouse." *Connotations* 1, no. 3 (1991): 290–92.

Bishop, Tom. *Shakespeare and the Theatre of Wonder.* Cambridge: Cambridge University Press, 1996.

Black, James. *Edified by the Margent: Shakespeare and the Bible: An Inaugural Professorial Lecture.* Calgary: University of Calgary, 1979.

Bloom, Harold. *The Anxiety of Influence: A Theory of Poetry*. Oxford: Oxford University Press, 1973.

———. *A Map of Misreading*. Oxford: Oxford University Press, 1975.

———. *Poetics of Influence: New and Selected Criticism*. New Haven, CT: Henry Schwab, 1988.

———. *Shakespeare: The Invention of the Human*. London: Fourth Estate, 1997.

Boff, Leonardo. *Passion of Christ, Passion of the World*. Maryknoll, NY: Orbis, 1987.

Boitani, Piero. *The Gospel According to Shakespeare*. Translated by Vittorio Montemaggi and Rachel Jacoff. Notre Dame, IN: Notre Dame University Press, 2014.

Bolam, Robyn. "*Richard II*: Shakespeare and the Languages of the Stage." In Hattaway, ed., *Shakespeare's History Plays*, 141–57.

Bonhoeffer, Dietrich. *Letters and Papers from Prison*. Enlarged ed. Edited by Eberhard Bethge. London: SCM, 1971.

Bonino, Miguel. *Towards a Christian Political Ethics*. London: SCM, 1983.

Bowie, Fiona. *The Anthropology of Religion*. Oxford: Blackwell, 2000.

Bradbury, John P. "Non-Conformist Conscience? Individual Conscience and the Authority of the Church from John Calvin to the Present." *Ecclesiology* 10, no. 1 (2014): 32–52.

Bradley, A. C. *Shakespearean Tragedy: Lectures on Hamlet, Othello, King Lear, Macbeth*. 2nd ed. London: Macmillan, 1971.

Brady, Thomas A. "Confessionalization—The Career of a Concept." In *Confessionalization in Europe, 1555–1700*, edited by John M. Headley, Hans J. Hillerbrand, and Anthony J. Papalas, 1–20. Burlington, VT: Ashgate, 2004.

Brett, Mark. "Permutations of Sovereignty in the Priestly Tradition." *Vetus Testamentum* 63, no. 3 (2013): 383–92.

———. *Political Trauma and Healing: Biblical Ethics for a Post-Colonial World*. Grand Rapids, MI: Eerdmans, 2016.

Bria, Ion. *The Liturgy after the Liturgy; Mission and Life in an Orthodox Perspective*. Geneva: World Council of Churches, 1996.

Brockbank, Philip. "Hamlet the Bonesetter." In *Shakespeare Survey 30*, edited by Kenneth Muir, 103–15. Cambridge: Cambridge University Press, 1977.

Brooke, Nicholas, ed. *Shakespeare: Richard II: A Casebook*. London: Macmillan, 1973.

———. *Shakespeare's Early Tragedies*. London, 1968.

Brown, John Russell. *Shakespeare and His Comedies*. London: Methuen, 1967.

Bruggink, Donald J. "Calvin and Federal Theology." *Reformed Review* 13, no. 1 (1959–60): 15–22.

Brümmer, Vincent. *The Model of Love*. Cambridge: Cambridge University Press, 1993.

Brunstetter, Daniel R., and Dana Zartner. "Just War against Barbarians: Revisiting the Valladolid Debates between Sepúlveda and Las Casas." *Political Studies* 59, no. 3 (2011): 733–52.

Bryant, J. A., Jr. "The Linked Analogies of *Richard II*." In Brooke, ed., *Richard II*, 186–97.

Buccola, Regina. "Shakespeare's Fairy Dance with Religio-Political Controversy in *The Merry Wives of Windsor*." In Taylor and Beauregard, *Shakespeare and the Culture of Christianity*, 159–79.

Buchanan, Judith. *Shakespeare on Film*. Harlow, UK: Pearson Longman, 2005.

Bulgakov, Sergius. *The Bride of the Lamb*. Translated by Boris Jakim. Grand Rapids, MI: Eerdmans, 2002.

Burnet, R. A. L. "Shakespeare and the Marginalia of the Geneva Bible." *Notes and Queries* 26 (1979): 113–14.

Burrow, Colin. "What Is a Shakespearean Tragedy?" In McEachern, ed., *Cambridge Companion to Shakespearean Tragedy*, 1–22.

Bushnell, Rebecca. *Green Desire: Imagining Early Modern English Gardens*. Ithaca, NY: Cornell University Press, 2003.

Butler, F. G. "Lear's Crown of Weeds." *English Studies* 70 (1989): 395–406.

Caird, George B. *Principalities and Powers. A Study in Pauline Theology*. Oxford: Clarendon, 1956.

———. *The Revelation of St John the Divine*. London: Adam and Charles Black, 1966.

Cavell, Stanley. *Disowning Knowledge: In Seven Plays of Shakespeare*. Updated ed. Cambridge: Cambridge University Press, 2003.

Certeau, Michel de. "How Is Christianity Thinkable Today?" Translated by F. C. Bauerschmidt and C. Hanley. In *The Postmodern God: A Theological Reader*, edited by Graham Ward, 142–55. Oxford: Blackwell, 1997.

———. *The Practice of Everyday Life*. Translated by S. Rendall. Berkeley: University of California Press, 1988.

Charlton, H. B. *Shakespearian Comedy*. London: Methuen, 1966.

Childs, Brevard S. *Isaiah and the Assyrian Crisis*. London: SCM, 1967.

Claassens, Juliana M. "Biblical Theology as Dialogue: Continuing the Conversation on Mikhail Bakhtin and Biblical Theology." *Journal of Biblical Literature* 122 (2003): 127–44.

Clubb, Louise George. "Italian Stories on the Stage." In Leggatt, ed., *Cambridge Companion to Shakespearean Comedy*, 32–46.

Coate, Mary Ann. *Sin, Guilt and Forgiveness: The Hidden Dimensions of a Pastoral Process*, London: SPCK, 1994.

Coghill, Neville. "Comic Form in *Measure for Measure*." In *Shakespeare Survey* 8, edited by Allardyce Nicoll, 14–27. Cambridge: Cambridge University Press, 1955.

———. "The Governing Idea." *Shakespeare Quarterly* 1, no. 1 (1948): 9–16.

Cohen, Walter. "The Merchant of Venice and the Possibilities of Historical Criticism." *English Literary History* 49, no. 4 (1982): 765–89.

Coleridge, S. T. *Biographia Literaria*. Edited by J. Shawcross. 2 vols. London: Oxford University Press, 1907.

———. *Select Poetry and Prose*. Edited by Stephen Potter. London: Nonesuch, 1962.

———. *Shakespearean Criticism*. Edited by Thomas Middleton Raysor. 2 vols. London: Dent, 1960.

Courtney, Richard. *Shakespeare's World of Death: The Early Tragedies*. Toronto: Simon and Pierre, 1995.

Cox, John D. *Seeming Knowledge. Shakespeare and Sceptical Faith*. Waco, TX: Baylor University Press, 2007.

Creaser, John. "Forms of Confusion." In Leggatt, ed., *Cambridge Companion to Shakespearean Comedy*, 81–101.

Cullmann, Oscar. *Immortality of the Soul or Resurrection of the Dead?* London: Epworth, 1958.

Cummings, Brian. *Mortal Thoughts: Religion, Secularity and Identity in Shakespeare and Early Modern Culture*. Oxford: Oxford University Press, 2013.

Cunningham, David. *These Three Are One: The Practice of Trinitarian Theology*. Oxford: Blackwell, 1998.

Danby, John F. *Shakespeare's Doctrine of Nature: A Study of King Lear*. London: Faber and Faber, 1961.

Daniell, David. "Shakespeare and the Protestant Mind." In *Shakespeare Survey 54*, edited by Peter Holland, 1–12. Cambridge: Cambridge University Press, 2001.

———. "Shakespeare and the Traditions of Comedy." In Wells, *The Cambridge Companion to Shakespeare Studies*, 101–22.

Danson, Lawrence. *The Harmonies of "The Merchant of Venice."* New Haven, CT: Yale University Press, 1978.

Davies, Oliver. *The Creativity of God: World, Eucharist, Reason*. Cambridge: Cambridge University Press, 2004.

Davis, Stephen T., ed. *Death and Afterlife*. Basingstoke, UK: Macmillan, 1989.

———. "Is Personal Identity Retained in the Resurrection?" *Modern Theology* 2, no. 4 (1986): 329–40.

———. "The Resurrection of the Dead." In Davis, ed., *Death and Afterlife*, 119–44.

Dawson, Anthony. "Shakespeare and Secular Performance." In *Shakespeare and the Cultures of Performance*, edited by Paul Yachnin and Patricia Badir, 83–97. Aldershot, UK: Ashgate, 2008.

Derrida, Jacques. "Différance." In Derrida, *Margins of Philosophy*, translated by Alan Bass, 1–27. New York: Harvester Wheatsheaf, 1982.

———. *Dissemination*. Translated by B. Johnson. Chicago: University of Chicago, 1981.

———. *The Gift of Death*. Translated by D. Wills. Chicago: University of Chicago Press, 1995.

———. *Given Time: I. Counterfeit Money*. Translated by Peggy Kamuf. Chicago: Chicago University Press, 1992.

———. *Limited Inc*. Translated by Samel Weber. Evanston, IL: Northwestern University Press, 1988.

———. "Of an Apocalyptic Tone Newly Adopted in Philosophy." Translated by J. Leavey. In *Derrida and Negative Theology*, edited by Harold Coward and Toby Foshay, 25–72. Albany: State University of New York Press, 1992.

———. *Of Grammatology*. Translated by G. C. Spivak. Baltimore and London: Johns Hopkins University Press, 1976.

———. *On Cosmopolitanism and Forgiveness*. New York: Columbia University Press, 2001.

————. *Positions*. Translated by A. Bass. Chicago: University of Chicago Press, 1981.

————. "The Principle of Reason: The University in the Eyes of Its Pupils." *Diacritics* 13 (1983): 3–20.

————. *Specters of Marx: The State of the Debt, the Work of Mourning, and the New International*. Translated by Peggy Kamuf. London: Routledge, 1994.

————. "To Forgive: The Unforgivable and the Imprescriptible." In *Questioning God*, edited by J. D. Caputo, M. Dooley, and M. J. Scanlon, 21–51. Bloomington: Indiana University Press, 2001.

————. *Writing and Difference*. Translated by Alan Bass. London: Routledge and Kegan Paul, 1978.

Dillon, Janette. "Shakespeare's Tragicomedies." In de Grazia and Wells, eds., *New Cambridge Companion to Shakespeare*, 169–84.

Dodd, C. H. *The Parables of the Kingdom*. London: Collins/Fontana, 1961.

Dostoyevsky, Fyodor. *The Brothers Karamazov*. Translated by D. Magarshack. Harmondsworth: Penguin, 1982.

Dowden, Edward, *Shakespeare: A Critical Study of His Mind and Art*. 3rd ed. London: Kegan Paul, 1877.

Duffy, Eamon. *Stripping of the Altars: Traditional Religion in England c.1400–c.1580*. New Haven, CT: Yale University Press, 1992.

Dunn, James D. G. *Christology in the Making: An Enquiry into the Origins of the Doctrine of the Incarnation*. London: SCM, 1982.

Eagleton, Terry. *Sweet Violence. The Idea of the Tragic*. Oxford: Oxford University Press, 2003.

————. *William Shakespeare: Re-Reading Literature*. Oxford: Blackwell, 1986.

Edgerton, William J. "Shakespeare and the Needle's Eye." *Modern Language Notes* 66 (1951): 549–50.

Elton, William R. *King Lear and the Gods*. Lexington: University of Kentucky Press, 1988.

————. "Shakespeare and the Thought of his Age." In Wells, ed., *Cambridge Companion to Shakespeare Studies*, 17–34.

————. "Shakespeare's Ulysses and the Problem of Value." *Shakespeare Studies* 2 (1966): 95–111.

Epstein, Heidi. *Melting the Venusberg: A Feminist Theology of Music*. New York: Continuum, 2004.

Esolen, Anthony M. "'The Isles Shall Wait for His Law': Isaiah and *The Tempest*." *Studies in Philology* 94, no. 2 (1997): 221–47.

Eure, John D. "Shakespeare and the Legal Process: Four Essays." *Virginia Law Review* 61, no. 2 (1975): 390–433.

Evans, Caleb. *Political Sophistry Detected; or, Reflections on the Rev. Mr. Fletcher's Late Tract Entitled "American Patriotism."* Bristol, UK: William Pine, 1776.

Evans, Craig A. *Mark 8:27–16:20*. Word Biblical Commentaries. Nashville, TN: Thomas Nelson, 2001.

Everett, Barbara. "Saint Shakespeare." *London Review of Books* 32, no. 16 (2010): 32–34.

Ewbank, Inga-Stina. "The Triumph of Time." In Muir, ed., *The Winter's Tale: A Casebook*, 98–115.

Faber, Roland. *God as Poet of the World: Exploring Process Theologies*. Translated by Douglas Stott. Louisville, KY: Westminster John Knox, 2008.

Fairweather, E. R., ed. *A Scholastic Miscellany: Anselm to Ockam*. Library of Christian Classics vol. 10. London: SCM, 1956.

Farley, Edward. *Divine Empathy: A Theology of God*. Minneapolis, MN: Fortress, 1996.

Felperin, Howard. "'Tongue-tied Our Queen?' The Deconstruction of Presence in *The Winter's Tale*." In *Shakespeare and the Question of Theory*, edited by Patricia Parker and Geoffrey Hartman, 3–18. London: Methuen, 1985.

Fernie, Ewan. "Introduction: Shakespeare, Spirituality and Contemporary Criticism." In Fernie, ed., *Spiritual Shakespeares*, 1–27.

———. "The Last Act: Presentism, Spirituality and the Politics of Hamlet." In Fernie, ed., *Spiritual Shakespeares*, 186–211.

———. "Shakespeare and the Prospect of Presentism." In *Shakespeare Survey* 58, edited by Peter Holland, 169–84. Cambridge: Cambridge University Press, 2005.

———, ed. *Spiritual Shakespeares*. London: Routledge, 2005.

Fiddes, Paul S. "Concept, Image and Story in Systematic Theology." *International Journal of Systematic Theology* 11, no. 1 (2009): 3–23.

———. "Covenant and the Inheritance of Separatism." In *The Fourth Strand of the Reformation: The Covenant Ecclesiology of Anabaptists, English Separatists, and Early General Baptists*, edited by Fiddes, 63–92. Oxford: Centre for Baptist History and Heritage, 2018.

———. *The Creative Suffering of God*. Oxford: Oxford University Press, 1988.

———. "Forgiveness, Empathy and Vulnerability: An Unfinished Conversation with Pamela Sue Anderson." In *Love and Vulnerability: Thinking with Pamela Sue Anderson*, edited by Pelagia Goulimari. *Angelaki* 25, nos. 1–2 (2020): 109–25.

———. *Freedom and Limit: A Dialogue between Literature and Christian Doctrine*. Basingstoke, UK: Macmillan, 1991.

———. "Memory, Forgetting and the Problem of Forgiveness. Reflecting on Volf, Derrida and Ricoeur." In *Forgiving and Forgetting. Theology and the Margins of Soteriology*, edited by Hartmut von Sass and Johannes Zachhuber. Tübingen: Mohr Siebeck, 2015.

———. *Participating in God: A Pastoral Doctrine of the Trinity*. London: Darton Longman and Todd, 2000.

———. *Past Event and Present Salvation: The Christian Idea of Atonement*. London: Darton Longman and Todd, 1989.

———. *The Promised End: Eschatology in Theology and Literature*. Oxford: Blackwell, 2000.

———. *Seeing the World and Knowing God: Hebrew Wisdom and Christian Doctrine in a Late-Modern Context*. Oxford: Oxford University Press, 2015.

———. "Shakespeare in Church: Reflection on an Intertextual Liturgy Based on *A Midsummer Night's Dream*." *Ecclesial Practices* 4, no. 2 (2017): 199–217.

Fiddes, Paul S., and Günter Bader. "Whatever Happened to a Pauline Text? 2 Cor. 3.6 and Its Afterlife." In *The Spirit and Letter: A Tradition and a Reversal*, edited by Fiddes and Bader, 3–27. London: T. & T. Clark, 2013.

Fiddes, Paul S., Brian Haymes, and Richard L. Kidd. *Baptists and the Communion of Saints: A Theology of Covenanted Disciples*. Waco, TX: Baylor University Press, 2014.

Fiddes, Paul S., and Andrew Taylor. "'Seeing with the Eyes of Love': A New Liturgy Based on Shakespeare's *Midsummer Night's Dream*." In *New Places: Shakespeare and Civic Creativity*, edited by Paul Edmonson and Ewan Fernie, 83–108. London: Arden Shakespeare, 2018.

Flannery, Austin, O.P., ed. *Vatican II. The Conciliar and Post Conciliar Documents*. Dublin: Dominican Publications, 1977.

Ford, David. *Christian Wisdom: Desiring God and Learning in Love*. Cambridge: Cambridge University Press, 2007.

Ford, Lewis S. *The Lure of God: A Biblical Background for Process Theism*. Philadelphia: Fortress, 1978.

Forster, E. M. *A Passage to India*. London: Edward Arnold, 1947.

Frei, Hans. *The Eclipse of Biblical Narrative: A Study of Eighteenth and Nineteenth Century Hermeneutics*. New Haven, CT: Yale University Press, 1974.

Frye, Northrop. *The Great Code: The Bible and Literature*. London: Ark, 1983.

Frye, Roland M. *Shakespeare and Christian Doctrine*. Princeton, NJ: Princeton University Press, 1963.

Gallagher, Lowell. "Waiting for Gobbo." In Fernie, ed., *Spiritual Shakespeares*, 73–93.

Gandolfo, Elizabeth O'Donnell. "Encountering God and Being Human 'Where the Wild Things Are': Maternal Experiences as an Eco-Feminist Source for Theological Anthropology." *Louvain Studies* 41 (2018): 298–316.

Gardner, Helen. "The Historical Approach to Hamlet." In Jump, ed., *Hamlet: A Casebook*, 137–50.

———. *King Lear: The John Coffin Memorial Lecture 1966*. London: Athlone, 1967.

———. "The Noble Moor." *Proceedings of the British Academy* 41 (1955): 189–205.

Geach, Peter. *God and the Soul*. London: Routledge and Kegan Paul, 1969.

Gerrish, B. A. *Grace and Reason: A Study in the Theology of Luther*. Oxford: Clarendon, 1962.

Girard, René. *The Scapegoat*. Translated by Yvonne Freccero. London: Athlone, 1986.

———. *A Theatre of Envy: William Shakespeare*. Leominster, UK: Gracewing, 2000.

———. *Things Hidden since the Foundation of the World*. Research undertaken in collaboration with J.-M. Oughourlian and G. Lefort. Translated by S. Bann and Michael Metteer. 1978. London: Athone, 1987.

———. *Violence and the Sacred*. Translated by Patrick Gregory. 1977. London: Athlone, 1995.

Gombrich, E. H. *Art and Illusion: Studies in the Psychology of Pictorial Representation*. 5th ed. Oxford: Oxford University Press, 1983.

Grazia, Margreta de, and Stanley Wells, eds. *The New Cambridge Companion to Shakespeare*. Cambridge: Cambridge University Press, 2010.

Greenaway, Peter. *Prospero's Books: A Film of Shakespeare's "The Tempest."* New York: Four Walls Eight Windows, 1991.

Greenblatt, Stephen. *Hamlet in Purgatory*. Princeton, NJ: Princeton University Press, 2013.

———. *Learning to Curse: Essays in Early Modern Culture*. London: Routledge, 2016.

———. *Renaissance Self-Fashioning: From More to Shakespeare*. Chicago: University of Chicago Press, 1984.

———. *Shakespearean Negotiations: The Circulation of Social Energy in Renaissance England*. Berkeley: University of California Press, 1988.

———. *Will in the World: How Shakespeare Became Shakespeare*. London: Jonathan Cape, 2004.

Grensted, L. W. *A Short History of the Doctrine of the Atonement*. Manchester: Manchester University Press, 1962.

Grey, Mary. *Redeeming the Dream, Feminism, Redemption and the Christian Tradition*. London: SPCK, 1989.

Griswold, Charles. *Forgiveness: A Philosophical Exploration*. Cambridge: Cambridge University Press, 2007.

Gross, John. *Shylock: A Legend and Its Legacy*. New York: Simon and Schuster, 1992.

Groves, Beatrice. *The Destruction of Jerusalem in Early Modern English Literature*. Cambridge: Cambridge University Press, 2015.

———. "Shakespeare's Sonnets and the Genevan Marginalia." *Essays in Criticism* 57, no. 2 (2007): 114–28.

———. *Texts and Traditions: Religion in Shakespeare 1592–1604*. Oxford: Oxford University Press, 2007.

———. "'The Wittiest Partition': Bottom, Paul and Comedic Resurrection." *Notes and Queries* 252, no. 3 (2007): 277–82.

Gutierrez, Gustavo. *A Theology of Liberation*. Translated and edited by Caridad Inda and John Eagleson. London: SCM, 1981.

Haigh, Christopher, "The Continuity of Catholicism in the English Reformation." In *The English Reformation Revised*, edited by Haigh, 176–208. Cambridge: Cambridge University Press, 1987.

———. *English Reformations: Religion, Politics, and Society under the Tudors*. Oxford: Oxford University Press, 1993.

Hall, Robert. "An Apology for the Freedom of the Press and for General Liberty." 1793. In vol. 3 of *The Works of Robert Hall*, edited by Olinthus Gregory. 6 vols. London: Holdsworth and Ball, 1832.

Halliday, F. E. *Shakespeare and His Critics*. London: Duckworth, 1963.

Hamilton, Gary D. "Mocking Oldcastle: Notes toward Exploring a Possible Catholic Presence in Shakespeare's Henriad." In Taylor and Beauregard, eds., *Shakespeare and the Culture of Christianity*, 141–58.

Hamlin, Hannibal. *The Bible in Shakespeare*. Oxford: Oxford University Press, 2013.

Harris, Jonathan Gil. "Shakespeare and Race." In de Grazia and Wells, eds., *New Cambridge Companion to Shakespeare*, 201–16.

Hart, David Bentley. *The Beauty of the Infinite: The Aesthetics of Christian Truth.* Grand Rapids, MI: Eerdmans, 2003.

Hartman, Geoffrey. "The Tricksy Word: Richard Weisberg on *The Merchant of Venice.*" *Law and Literature* 23, no. 1 (2011): 71–79.

Hartshorne, Charles. *The Divine Relativity: A Social Conception of God.* New Haven, CT: Yale University Press, 1948.

———. *The Logic of Perfection.* Lasalle, IL: Open Court, 1973.

———. *Man's Vision of God and the Logic of Theism.* Hamden, CT: Archon, 1964.

Hartwig, Joan. *Shakespeare's Tragicomic Vision.* Baton Rouge: Louisiana State University Press, 1972.

Hass, Andrew W. *Auden's O: The Loss of One's Sovereignty in the Making of Nothing.* Albany: State University of New York Press, 2015.

Hattaway, Michael, ed. *The Cambridge Companion to Shakespeare's History Plays.* Cambridge: Cambridge University Press, 2002.

———. "Tragedy and Political Authority." In McEachern, ed., *Cambridge Companion to Shakespearean Tragedy,* 110–31.

Hauerwas, Stanley. *Approaching the End: Eschatological Reflections on Church, Politics and Life.* London: SCM, 2014.

———. "Why Time Cannot and Should Not Heal the Wounds of History but Time Has Been and Can Be Redeemed." *Scottish Journal of Theology* 53, no. 1 (2000): 33–49.

Hawkes, Terence. "Shakespeare and New Critical Approaches." In Wells, ed., *Cambridge Companion to Shakespeare Studies,* 287–302.

———. *Shakespeare in the Present.* London: Routledge, 2002.

Hebblethwaite, Brian. "MacKinnon and the Problem of Evil." In *Christ, Ethics and Tragedy,* edited by Kenneth Surin, 131–45. Cambridge: Cambridge University Press, 1989.

Hegel, G. W. F. *The Christian Religion: Lectures on the Philosophy of Religion.* Part 3: *The Revelatory, Consummate, Absolute Religion.* Edited and translated by P. Hodgson. Missoula, MT: Scholars Press, 1979.

Heidegger, Martin. *Being and Time.* Translated by J. Macquarrie and E. Robinson. Oxford: Basil Blackwell, 1973.

———. "The Onto-theo-logical Constitution of Metaphysics." In Heidegger, *Identity and Difference,* translated by Joan Stambaugh, 42–74. Chicago: University of Chicago Press, 2002.

Henn, T. R. *The Harvest of Tragedy.* 2nd ed. London: Methuen, 1966.

Hick, John. *Death and Eternal Life.* London: Collins, 1976.

———. *Evil and the God of Love.* New ed. Basingstoke: Palgrave Macmillan, 2010.

———. *God and the Universe of Faiths.* London: Collins/Fount, 1977.

———. "A Possible Conception of Life after Death." In Davis, ed., *Death and Afterlife,* 183–96.

———. "Whatever Path Men Choose Is Mine." In Hick and Hebblethwaite, eds., *Christianity and Other Religions,* 171–90.

Hick, John, and Brian Hebblethwaite, eds. *Christianity and Other Religions: Selected Readings.* Glasgow: Collins/Fount, 1980.

Hildegard of Bingen. *Symphonia.* Edited and translated Barbara Newman. 2nd ed. Ithaca, NY: Cornell University Press, 1998.

Hill, Christopher. *Society and Puritanism in Pre-Revolutionary England.* London: Mercury, 1966.

Hillerbrand, Hans J. "Anabaptism and the Reformation." *Church History* 29, no. 4 (1960): 404–23.

Hodgetts, Michael. "A Certificate of Warwickshire Recusants, 1592." *Worcestershire Recusant* 5 (1965): 20–31.

Holdsworth, William S. *A History of English Law.* 4th ed. London: Methuen, 1927.

Holland, Norman. "Hermia's Dream." In *Shakespeare's Comedies*, edited by Gary F. Waller, 75–92. London: Longman, 1991.

Houlden, J. L. *Paul's Letters from Prison.* Harmondsworth, UK: Penguin, 1970.

Jacobs, Michael. *Living Illusions: A Psychology of Belief.* London: SPCK, 1993.

James, D. G. *The Dream of Learning: An Essay on the Advancement of Learning, "Hamlet" and "King Lear."* Oxford: Clarendon, 1951.

Janz, Paul D. *God, the Mind's Desire: Reference, Reason and Christian Thinking.* Cambridge: Cambridge University Press, 2004.

Jenkins. Harold. "Hamlet and Ophelia." *Proceedings of the British Academy* 49 (1964): 135–51.

Jensen, Phebe. *Religion and Revelry in Shakespeare's Festive World.* Cambridge: Cambridge University Press, 2008.

Jenson, Robert W. "What Kind of God Can Make a Covenant?" In *Covenant and Hope: Christian and Jewish Responses*, edited by Jenson and Eugene B. Korn, 3–18. Grand Rapids, MI: Eerdmans, 2012.

Jenson, Robert W., and Eugene B. Korn, eds. *Covenant and Hope: Christian and Jewish Responses.* Grand Rapids, MI: Eerdmans, 2012.

Jeremias, Joachim. *New Testament Theology.* Vol. 1: *The Proclamation of Jesus.* Translated by John Bowden. London: SCM, 1971.

Johnson, Aubrey R. *The Vitality of the Individual in the Thought of Ancient Israel.* Cardiff: University of Wales Press, 1964.

Johnson, Elizabeth A. *Friends of God and Prophets: A Feminist Theological Reading of the Communion of Saints.* London: SCM, 1998.

Joughin, John J. "Bottom's Secret. . . ." In Fernie, ed., *Spiritual Shakespeares*, 130–56.

Julian of Norwich. *Revelations of Divine Love.* Translated by E. Spearing. London: Penguin, 1998.

Jump, John, ed. *Shakespeare: Hamlet: A Casebook.* London: Macmillan, 1968.

Jüngel, Eberhard. *God as the Mystery of the World: On the Foundation of the Theology of the Crucified One in the Dispute between Theism and Atheism.* Translated by Daniel L. Guder. Edinburgh: T. & T. Clark, 1983.

———. *God's Being Is in Becoming: The Trinitarian Being of God in the Theology of Karl Barth.* Translated by John Webster. Edinburgh: T. & T. Clark, 2001.

———. "Vom Tod des lebendigen Gottes: Ein Plakat." In Jüngel, *Untwerwegs zur Sache: Theologische Bermerkungen*, 105–25. Munich: Chr. Kaiser, 1972.

———. "The World as Possibility and Actuality: The Ontology of the Doctrine of Justification." In *Eberhard Jüngel: Theological Essays*, translated and edited by John Webster, 95–123. Edinburgh: T. & T. Clark, 1989.

Justin Martyr. *Dialogue with Trypho*. In *The Ante-Nicene Fathers*, vol. 1, edited by Alexander Roberts and James Donaldson. Grand Rapids, MI: Eerdmans, 1975.

———. *First Apology*. In *The Ante-Nicene Fathers*, vol. 1, edited by Alexander Roberts and James Donaldson. Grand Rapids, MI: Eerdmans, 1975.

Kaiser, Otto. *Isaiah 13–39: A Commentary*. Translated by R. A. Wilson. London: SCM, 1974.

Kant, Immanuel. *Critique of Pure Reason*. Translated by N. Kemp Smith. London: Macmillan, 1933.

Kantorowicz, E. H. "The King's Two Bodies." In Brooke, ed., *Richard II: A Casebook*, 169–85.

Käsemann, Ernst. *Commentary on Romans*. Translated by Geoffrey Bromiley. London: SCM, 1980.

Kastan, David Scott. *A Will to Believe: Shakespeare and Religion*. Oxford: Oxford University Press, 2014.

Keefer, Michael H. "Accommodation and Synecdoche: Calvin's God in *King Lear*." *Shakespeare Studies* 20 (1988): 147–68.

Kendall, R. T. *Calvin and English Calvinism to 1649*. Oxford: Oxford University Press, 1979.

Kermode, Frank. "The Mature Comedies." In *Early Shakespeare*, edited by John Russell Brown and Bernard Harris, Stratford-upon-Avon Studies 3, 211–27. London: Edwards Arnold, 1961.

———. *The Sense of an Ending: Studies in the Theory of Fiction*. Oxford: Oxford University Press, 1968.

———. *Shakespeare, Spenser, Donne: Renaissance Essays*. Abingdon, UK: Routledge, 2005.

———. *Shakespeare's Language*. London: Penguin, 2000.

Kerrigan, John. *Shakespeare's Binding Language*. Oxford: Oxford University Press, 2016.

Kierkegaard, Søren. *Works of Love*. Translated by David F. Swenson and Lillian M. Swenson. London: Oxford University Press, 1946.

Kinney, Arthur F. "Shakespeare's *Comedy of Errors* and the Nature of Kinds." *Studies in Philology* 85, no. 1 (1988): 29–52.

Kirschbaum, Leo. *Character and Characterization in Shakespeare*. Detroit, MI: Wayne State University Press, 1962.

Klause, John. "Catholic and Protestant, Jesuit and Jew: Historical Religion in *The Merchant of Venice*." In Taylor and Beauregard, eds., *Shakespeare and the Culture of Christianity*, 180–221.

Knapp, James A. *Image Ethics in Shakespeare and Spenser*. London: Palgrave Macmillan 2011.

Knapp, Jeffrey. *Shakespeare's Tribe: Church, Nation, and Theater in Renaissance England*. Chicago: University of Chicago Press, 2002.

Knight, G. Wilson. *The Crown of Life: Essays in Interpretation of Shakespeare's Final Plays*. London: Methuen, 1965.

———. *The Imperial Theme. Further Interpretations of Shakespeare's Tragedies, Including the Roman Plays*. 3rd ed. London: Methuen, 1951.

———. *Shakespeare and Religion*. New York: Simon and Shuster, 1968.

———. *The Wheel of Fire: Interpretations of Shakespearian Tragedy*. Rev. ed. London: Methuen, 1965.

Kott, Jan. "Prospero's Staff." In Palmer, ed., *The Tempest: A Casebook*, 244–58.

Kristeva, Julia. *Desire in Language: A Semiotic Approach to Literature and Art*. Edited by Leon S. Roudiez; translated by Thomas Gora, Alice Jardine, and Leon S. Roudiez. Oxford: Basil Blackwell, 1980.

———. *Revolution in Poetic Language*. Translated by Margaret Waller. New York: Columbia University Press, 1984.

———. "Semiotics: A Critical Science and/or a Critique of Science." In *The Kristeva Reader*, edited by Toril Moi, 80–85. Oxford: Basil Blackwell, 1986.

Küng, Hans, ed. *Christianity and the World's Religions: Paths of Dialogue with Islam, Hinduism and Buddhism*. Translated by Peter Heinegg. London: Collins/Fount, 1987.

———. *Judaism: The Religious Situation of Our Time*. Translated by John Bowden. London: SCM, 1992.

———. *On Being a Christian*. Translated by Edward Quinn. London: Collins, 1977.

Lacan, Jacques. *Ecrits: A Selection*. Translated by Alan Sheridan. New York: Norton, 1977.

Lake, Peter. *The Antichrist's Lewd Hat: Protestants, Papists and Players in Post-Reformation England*. New Haven, CT: Yale University Press, 2002.

Laroque, François. "Popular Festivity." In Leggatt, ed., *Cambridge Companion to Shakespearean Comedy*, 64–80.

Le Goff, Jacques. *The Birth of Purgatory*. Translated by Arthur Goldhammer. Chicago: University of Chicago Press, 1984.

Lee, R. S. *Freud and Christianity*. Harmondsworth, UK: Penguin, 1967.

Leggatt, Alexander, ed. *The Cambridge Companion to Shakespearean Comedy*. Cambridge: Cambridge University Press, 2002.

Lehmann, Paul. *The Transfiguration of Politics*. London: SCM, 1975.

Levinas, Emmanuel. *Otherwise Than Being: Or Beyond Essence*. Translated by A. Lingis. Pittsburgh, PA: Duquesne University Press, 1998.

———. *Totality and Infinity: An Essay on Interiority*. Translated by A. Lingis. Pittsburgh, PA: Duquesne University Press, 1965.

Lewalski, Barbara K. "Biblical Allusion and Allegory in *The Merchant of Venice*." *Shakespeare Quarterly* 13, no. 3 (1962): 327–43.

Lewis, C. S. "Hamlet: The Prince or the Poem?" In *They Asked for a Paper*, by Lewis, 51–71. London: Bles, 1962.

Lillback, Peter A. *The Binding of God: Calvin's Role in the Development of Covenant Theology*. Grand Rapids, MI: Baker, 2001.

Lindbeck, George. *The Nature of Doctrine: Religion and Theology in a Postliberal Age.* London: SPCK, 1984.

Link, H. G. "Zur Kreuzestheologie." *Evangelisches Theologie* 33 (1973): 337–45.

Lossky, Vladimir. *The Mystical Theology of the Eastern Church.* Cambridge: James Clarke, 1957.

Lothe, Jakob. "Authority, Reliability and the Challenge of Reading." In *Narrative Ethics,* edited by Lothe and Jeremy Hawthorn, 103–18. Amsterdam: Rodopi, 2013.

Lupton, Julia Reinhard. *Afterlives of the Saints: Hagiography, Typology and Renaissance Literature.* Stanford, CA: Stanford University Press, 1996.

Mack, Maynard. *"King Lear" in Our Time.* Berkeley: University of California Press, 1965.

MacKinnon, Donald. *Borderlands of Theology and Other Essays.* London: Lutterworth, 1968.

———. *Explorations in Theology.* London: SCM, 1979.

———. *The Problem of Metaphysics.* Cambridge: Cambridge University Press, 2009.

Mackintosh, H. R. *The Christian Experience of Forgiveness.* London: Nisbet, 1934.

Macquarrie, John. *In Search of Humanity: A Theological and Philosophical Approach.* London: SCM, 1982.

———. *Principles of Christian Theology.* Rev. ed. London: SCM, 1966.

Magee, Brian, ed. *Men of Ideas, Some Creators of Contemporary Philosophy.* Oxford: Oxford University Press, 1982.

Magliola, Robert. *Derrida on the Mend.* West Lafayette, IN: Purdue University Press, 1984.

Maguire, Laurie. *Where There's a Will There's a Way: Or, All I Really Need to Know I Learned from Shakespeare.* London: Nicholas Brealey, 2007.

Mahood, M. M. *Shakespeare's Wordplay.* London: Methuen, 1957.

Marion, Jean-Luc. *Being Given: Towards a Phenomenology of Givenness.* Translated by Jeffrey L. Kossky. Stanford, CA: Stanford University Press, 2002.

Marsh, Christopher. *Popular Religion in Sixteenth-Century England: Holding Their Peace.* Basingstoke, UK: Macmillan, 1993.

Marshall, David. "Exchanging Visions: Reading *A Midsummer Night's Dream.*" *English Literary History* 49, no. 3 (1982): 543–75.

Martin-Achard, Robert. *From Death to Life: A Study of the Development of the Doctrine of the Resurrection in the Old Testament.* Translated by J. Penney-Smith. Edinburgh and London: Oliver and Boyd, 1960.

Maslen, Robert W. *Shakespeare and Comedy.* Arden Critical Companions. London: Arden Shakespeare, 2006.

Mason, H. A. *Shakespeare's Tragedies of Love: An Examination of the Possibility of Common Readings of "Romeo and Juliet," "Othello," "King Lear" & "Anthony and Cleopatra."* London: Chatto and Windus, 1970.

McCarthy, David Matzk. *Sharing God's Good Company: A Theology of the Communion of Saints.* Grand Rapids, MI: Eerdmans, 2012.

McCoy, Richard C. *Faith in Shakespeare.* Oxford: Oxford University Press, 2015.

McEachern, Claire. *Believing in Shakespeare: Studies in Longing.* Cambridge: Cambridge University Press, 2018.

———, ed. *The Cambridge Companion to Shakespearean Tragedy.* 2nd ed. Cambridge: Cambridge University Press, 2013.

McGrath, Alister E. *Luther's Theology of the Cross: Martin Luther's Theological Breakthrough.* Oxford: Blackwell, 1985.

Merleau-Ponty, Maurice. *Visible and Invisible.* Translated by A. Lingis. Evanston, IL: Northwestern University Press, 1969.

Metz, J. B. "The Future in the Memory of Suffering." *Concilium* 8, no. 6 (1972): 9–25.

Miller, Anthony. "Matters of State." In Leggatt, ed., *Cambridge Companion to Shakespearean Comedy,* 198–214.

Milton, Anthony. *Catholic and Reformed: The Roman and Protestant Churches in English Protestant Thought, 1600–1640.* Cambridge: Cambridge University Press.

Milward, Peter, S.J. *Jacobean Shakespeare.* Naples, Italy: Sapientia, 2007.

———. *Shakespeare's Religious Background.* Bloomington: Indiana University Press, 1973.

Moltmann, Jürgen. *The Coming of God: Christian Eschatology.* Translated by M. Kohl. London: SCM, 1996.

———. *The Crucified God: The Cross of Christ as the Foundation and Criticism of Christian Theology.* Translated by R. A. Wilson and J. Bowden. London: SCM, 1974.

———. *The Future of Creation.* Translated by M. Kohl. London: SCM, 1979.

———. *The Open Church: Invitation to a Messianic Life Style.* Translated by Douglas Meeks. London: SCM, 1978.

———. *The Way of Jesus Christ: Christology in Messianic Dimensions.* Translated by M. Kohl. London: SCM, 1990.

Montrose, Louis. *The Purpose of Playing: Shakespeare and the Cultural Politics of the Elizabethan Theatre.* Chicago: Chicago University Press, 1996.

Mühlen, Heribert. *Die Veränderlichkeit Gottes als Horizont einer zukünftigen Christologie.* Münster: Aschendorf, 1969.

Muir, Kenneth, ed. *Shakespeare: The Winter's Tale: A Casebook.* Asheville, NC: Aurora, 1970.

———. *Shakespeare's Comic Sequence.* Liverpool: Liverpool University Press, 1979.

———. *Shakespeare's Sources.* Vol. 1: *Comedies and Tragedies.* London: Methuen, 1957.

———. *Shakespeare's Tragic Sequence.* Liverpool: Liverpool University Press, 1979.

———. *The Sources of Shakespeare's Plays.* London: Methuen, 1977.

Mullaney, Stephen. "Affective Technologies: Towards an Emotional Logic of the Elizabethan Stage." In *Environment and Embodiment in Early Modern England,* edited by Mary Floyd Wilson and Garrett A. Sullivan Jr., 71–89. New York: Palgrave, 2007.

Murdoch, Iris. "Against Dryness." In Murdoch, *Existentialists and Mystics,* 287–96.

———. *Existentialists and Mystics: Writings on Philosophy and Literature,* edited by Peter Conradi. London: Chatto and Windus, 1997.

———. *Metaphysics as a Guide to Morals.* London: Chatto and Windus, 1992.

———. "The Sublime and the Beautiful Revisited." In Murdoch, *Existentialists and Mystics*, 261–86.

Murphy, Francesca Ann. "Hans Urs von Balthasar: Beauty as a Gateway to Love." In *Theological Aesthetics after von Balthasar*, edited by Oleg V. Bychkov and James Fodor, 5–18. Aldershot, UK: Ashgate, 2008.

Murray, J. Middleton. "Shakespeare's Dream." In Palmer, ed., *The Tempest: A Casebook*, 109–21.

Myers, Ched. *Binding the Strong Man: A Political Reading of Mark's Story of Jesus*. Maryknoll, NY: Orbis, 1988.

Neuner, Joseph, S.J., ed. *Christian Revelation and World Religions*. London: Burns and Oates, 1967.

Newman, Karen. "Reprise: Gender, Sexuality and Theories of Exchange." In *The Merchant of Venice: Theory in Practice*, edited by Nigel Wood, 102–18. Buckingham, UK: Open University Press, 1996.

Nichols, John. *The Progression and Public Processions of Queen Elizabeth*. 3 vols. London: Society of Antiquaries, 1823.

Niebuhr, Reinhold. *Beyond Tragedy: Essays on the Christian Interpretation of History*. London: Nisbet, 1938.

Nielsen, Kai. "The Faces of Immortality." In Davis, ed., *Death and Afterlife*, 1–28.

Noble, Richmond. *Shakespeare's Biblical Knowledge and Use of the Book of Common Prayer*. London: SPCK, 1935.

Norbrook, David. "Rhetoric, Ideology and the Elizabethan World Picture." In *Renaissance Rhetoric*, edited by Peter Mack, 104–64. London: Palgrave, 1994.

Novak, David. "The Covenant in Rabbinic Thought." In *Two Faiths, One Covenant? Jewish and Christian Identity in the Presence of the Other*, edited by Eugene B. Korn, 65–80. Lanham, MD: Rowman and Littlefield, 2004.

———. *Covenantal Rights: A Study in Jewish Political Theory*. Princeton, NJ: Princeton University Press, 2009.

Novy, Marianne. *Shakespeare and Feminist Theory*. London: Bloomsbury, 2017.

Nussbaum, Martha C. *Love's Knowledge: Essays on Philosophy and Literature*. Oxford: Oxford University Press, 1990.

———. *Upheavals of Thought: The Intelligence of Emotions*. Cambridge: Cambridge University Press, 2001.

Nuttall, A. D. *A New Mimesis: Shakespeare and the Representation of Reality*. London: Methuen, 1983.

———. *Shakespeare the Thinker*. New Haven, CT: Yale University Press, 2007.

O'Connell, Michael. "The Experiment of Romance." In Leggatt, ed., *Cambridge Companion to Shakespearean Comedy*, 215–29.

O'Donovan, Oliver. *The Desire of the Nations: Rediscovering the Roots of Political Theology*. Cambridge: Cambridge University Press, 1996.

Oord, Thomas Jay. *The Uncontrolling Love of God: An Open and Relational Account of Providence*. Downers Grove, IL: IVP Academic, 2015.

Orgel, Stephen. *Imagining Shakespeare: A History of Texts and Visions*. Basingstoke, UK: Macmillan, 2003.

———. "Shakespeare, Sexuality and Gender." In de Grazia and Wells, eds., *New Cambridge Companion to Shakespeare*, 217–32.

Orr, Mary. *Intertextuality: Debates and Contexts*. Cambridge: Polity, 2003.

Page, Ruth. *God and the Web of Creation*. London: SCM, 2006.

Palmer, D. J., ed. *Shakespeare: The Tempest: A Casebook*. London: Macmillan, 1975.

Panikkar, Raimundo (Raymond, Raimon). *The Experience of God: Icons of the Mystery*. Minneapolis, MN: Fortress, 2006.

———. *The Unknown Christ of Hinduism*. Revised and enlarged ed. London: Darton, Longman and Todd, 1981.

———. "The Unknown Christ of Hinduism." In Hick and Hebblethwaite, eds., *Christianity and Other Religions*, 122–50.

Pannenberg, Wolfhart. *Jesus—God and Man*. Translated by Lewis L. Wilkins and Duane A. Priebe. London: SCM, 1968.

Panofsky, Erwin. *Studies in Iconology: Humanistic Themes in the Art of the Renaissance*. New York: Routledge, 1962.

Parfit, Derek. *Reasons and Persons*. Oxford: Clarendon, 1984.

Partridge, Eric. *Shakespeare's Bawdy*. London: Routledge and Kegan Paul, 1968.

Penelhulm, Terence. *Survival and Disembodied Existence*. London: Routledge and Kegan Paul, 1970.

Piesse, A. J. "King John: Changing Perspectives." In Hattaway, ed., *Cambridge Companion to Shakespeare's History Plays*, 126–40.

Pike, Nelson. *God and Timelessness*. London: Routledge and Kegan Paul, 1970.

Polkinghorne, John. *Belief in God in an Age of Science*. New Haven, CT: Yale University Press, 1998.

Poole, Kristin. *Radical Religion from Shakespeare to Milton*. Cambridge: Cambridge University Press, 2000.

Powers, Alan. "'What He Wills': Early Modern Rings and Vows in *Twelfth Night*." In *Twelfth Night: New Critical Essays*, edited by James Schiffer, 217–28. New York: Routledge, 2011.

Prestige, G. L. *God in Patristic Thought*. London: Heinemann, 1936.

Rahner, Karl. *Foundations of Christian Faith: An Introduction to the Idea of Christianity*. Translated by W. V. Dych. London: Darton, Longman and Todd, 1978.

———. *On the Theology of Death*. Translated by C. Henkey. London: Burns and Oates; Freiburg: Herder, 1961.

———. *Theological Investigations*. Vol. 5: *Later Writings*. Translated by Karl-H. Kruger. London: Darton, Longman and Todd, 1975.

———. *The Trinity*. Translated by J. Donceel. London: Burns & Oates, 1975.

Raleigh, Walter. *Johnson on Shakespeare: Essays and Notes Selected and Set Forth with an Introduction*. London: Henry Frowde, 1908.

Ramsey, Paul, and Stanley Hauerwas. *Speak up for Just War or Pacifism*. Eugene, OR: Wipf and Stock, 2016.

Ricoeur, Paul. *The Conflict of Interpretations: Essays in Hermeneutics*. Edited by Don Ihde. Evanston, IL: Northwestern University Press, 1974.

————. *Freedom and Nature: The Voluntary and the Involuntary.* Translated by E. V. Kohak. Evanston, IL: Northwestern University Press, 1966.

————. "Freedom in the Light of Hope." Translated by R. Sweeney. In *Conflict of Interpretations,* by Ricoeur, 402–24.

————. "The Function of Fiction in Shaping Reality." *Man and World* 12, no. 2 (1979): 123–41.

————. *Hermeneutics and the Human Sciences: Essays on Language, Action and Interpretation.* Edited and translated by John B. Thompson. Cambridge: Cambridge University Press, 2016.

————. *History and Truth.* Translated by C. Kelbley. Evanston, IL: Northwestern University Press, 1965.

————. *Interpretation Theory: Discourse and the Surplus of Meaning.* Fort Worth: Texas Christian University Press, 1976.

————. "Memory and Forgetting." In *Questioning Ethics: Contempary Debates in Philosophy,* edited by Richard Kearney and Mark Dooley, 5–11. London: Routledge, 1999.

————. *Memory, History and Forgetting.* Translated by Katherine Blamey and David Pellauer. Chicago: University of Chicago Press, 2004.

————. *Oneself as Another.* Translated by Kathleen Blamey. Chicago: University of Chicago Press, 1992.

————. "Philosophical Hermeneutics and Biblical Hermeneutics." In Ricoeur, *From Text to Action: Essays in Hermeneutics* II, edited and translated by K. Blamey and J. B. Thompson, 89–101. Evanston, IL: Northwestern University Press, 1991.

————. *Time and Narrative.* Translated by K. McLaughlin and D. Pellauer. 3 vols. Chicago and London: University of Chicago Press, 1985.

Robinson, H. Wheeler. *The Cross in the Old Testament.* London: SCM, 1955.

Rothenberg, Naftali. "Three Forms of Otherness: Covenant, Mission, and Relation to the Other in Rabbinic Perspective." In Jenson and Korn, eds., *Covenant and Hope: Christian and Jewish Responses,* 80–98.

Saussure, Ferdinand de. *Course in General Linguistics.* Translated by R. Harris. London: Duckworth, 1983.

Scarisbrick, J. J. *The Reformation and the English People.* Oxford: Oxford University Press, 1984.

Schafer, Elizabeth. *Theatre and Christianity.* London: Red Globe, 2019.

Schanzer, Ernest. *The Problem Plays of Shakespeare.* London: Routledge, 1963.

Schopenhauer, Arthur. *The World as Will and Representation.* Translated by E. F. J. Payne. 2 vols. New York: Dover, 1969.

Schwartz, Regina. *Loving Justice, Living Shakespeare.* Oxford: Oxford Univesity Press, 2016.

————. "Othello and the Horizon of Justice." In *Transcendence: Philosophy, Literature, and Theology Approach the Beyond,* edited by Schwartz, 81–104. London: Routledge, 2004.

Segundo, Juan Luis. *Faith and Ideologies.* Translated by John Drury. Maryknoll, NY: Orbis, 1984.

Seigel, Paul N. *Shakespeare in His Time and Ours.* Notre Dame, IN: University of Notre Dame Press, 1968.

Shaheen, Naseeb. *Biblical References in Shakespeare's Plays.* Newark: University of Delaware Press, 2011.

———. "Like the Base Judean." *Shakespeare Quarterly* 31, no.1 (1980): 93–95.

Shapiro, James. *Shakespeare and the Jews.* Twentieth Anniversary Edition. New York: Columbia University Press, 1996.

———. "'Which Is *the Merchant* Here, and Which *the Jew?*' Shakespeare and the Economics of Influence." *Shakespeare Studies* 20 (1988): 269–79.

Shell, Alison. *Shakespeare and Religion.* London: Arden Shakespeare, 2010.

Shuger, Debora K. *Political Theologies in Shakespeare's England: The Sacred and the State in "Measure for Measure."* New York: Palgrave, 2001.

———. "A Protesting Catholic Puritan in Elizabethan England." *Journal of British Studies* 48 (2009): 587–630.

Simpson, Richard. "Richard II and Elizabethan Politics." In *Shakespeare: The Critical Tradition: Richard II*, edited by Charles R. Forker, 240–46. London: Athlone, 1998.

Slater, Ann Pasternak. "Variations within a Source: From Isaiah XXIX to *The Tempest.*" In *Shakespeare Survey* 25, edited by Kenneth Muir, 125–35. Cambridge: Cambridge University Press, 1972.

Snodgrass, W. D. *In Radical Pursuit: Critical Essays and Lectures.* New York: Harper and Row, 1975.

Snyder, Susan. "King Lear and the Prodigal Son." *Shakespeare Quarterly* 17, no. 4 (1966): 361–69.

———. "King Lear and the Psychology of Dying." *Shakespeare Quarterly* 33, no. 4 (1982): 449–60.

Soelle, Dorothee. *Christ the Representative.* Translated by D. Lewis. London: SCM, 1967.

Sollereder, Bethany N. *God, Evolution, and Animal Suffering: Theodicy without a Fall.* London: Routledge, 2019.

Southgate, Christopher. *The Groaning of Creation: God, Evolution and the Problem of Evil.* Louisville, KY: Westminster John Knox, 2008.

———. *Theology in a Suffering World: Glory and Longing.* Cambridge: Cambridge University Press, 2018.

Sowerby, Richard. *Angels in Early Medieval England.* Oxford: Oxford University Press, 2016.

Spens, Janet. *Elizabethan Drama.* London: Methuen, 1922.

Steiner, George. *The Death of Tragedy.* London: Faber and Faber, 1961.

Stevenson, Robert. *Shakespeare's Religious Frontier.* The Hague: Martinus Nijhoff, 1958.

Strachey, Lytton. *Books and Characters: French and English.* New York: Harcourt, Brace, 1922.

Stroup, Thomas B. "Bottom's Name and His Epiphany." *Shakespeare Quarterly* 29, no. 1 (1978): 79–82.

Swift, Daniel. *Shakespeare's Common Prayers: The Book of Common Prayer and the Elizabethan Age*. Oxford: Oxford University Press, 2013.

Swinburne, Richard. *The Christian God*. Oxford: Clarendon, 1994.

———. *The Evolution of the Soul*. Oxford: Clarendon, 1986.

———. *Providence and the Problem of Evil*. Oxford: Oxford University Press, 1998.

———. *Responsibility and Atonement*. Oxford: Clarendon, 1989.

Talbert, Ernest William. *The Problem of Order: Elizabethan Political Commonplaces and an Example of Shakespeare's Art*. Chapel Hill: University of North Carolina Press, 1962.

Tatspaugh, Patricia. *The Winter's Tale*. Shakespeare at Stratford. London: Arden Shakespeare, 2002.

Taylor, Dennis, and David Beauregard, eds. *Shakespeare and the Culture of Christianity in Early Modern England*. New York: Fordham University Press, 2003.

Tillich, Paul. *The Courage to Be*. London: Collins/Fontana, 1962.

———. *Systematic Theology*. Combined volume. Welwyn: James Nisbet, 1968.

———. *Theology of Culture*. Edited by R. C. Kimball. New York: Oxford University Press, 1959.

Tillyard, E. M. W. *The Elizabethan World Picture*. London: Chatto and Windus, 1942.

———. *Shakespeare's Last Plays*. 1938. London: Athlone, 1990.

Tolkien, J. R. R. *Tree and Leaf*. London: Unwin, 1964.

Tracy, David. *The Analogical Imagination*. London: SCM, 1981.

Traversi, Derek. *An Approach to Shakespeare*. Vol. 1: "Henry VI" to "Twelfth Night." 3rd ed. London: Hollis and Carter, 1968.

———. *Shakespeare: The Roman Plays*. London: Hollis and Carter, 1963.

VanMaaren, John. "The Adam-Christ Typology in Paul and Its Development in the Early Church Fathers." *Tyndale Bulletin* 64, no. 2 (2013): 275–97.

Vaughan, Alden T., and Virginia Mason Vaughan. *Shakespeare's Caliban: A Cultural History*. Cambridge: Cambridge University Press, 1991.

Verstegan, Richard (prob.). *A Declaration of the True Causes of the Great Troubles, presupposed to be intended against the realme of England*. Antwerp: J. Trognesius, 1752.

Volf, Miroslav. *The End of Memory: Remembering Rightly in a Violent World*. Grand Rapids, MI: Eerdmans, 2006.

———. *Exclusion and Embrace: A Theological Exploration of Identity, Otherness and Reconciliation*. Nashville, TN: Abingdon, 1996.

Walsh, Brian. *Unsettled Toleration: Religious Difference on the Shakespearean Stage*. Oxford: Oxford University Press, 2016.

Ward, Graham. "Tragedy as Subclause: Steiner and MacKinnon." *Heythrop Journal* 34 (1993): 274–87.

Watson, Robert N. "Tragedies of Revenge and Ambition." In McEachern, ed., *Cambridge Companion to Shakespearean Tragedy*, 171–94.

Watts, Michael R. *The Dissenters: From the Reformation to the French Revolution*. Oxford: Oxford University Press, 1978.

Weisberg, Richard. *Poethics and Other Strategies of Law and Literature.* New York: Columbia University Press, 1992.

Weiss, Bernard. "Covenant and Law in Islam." In *Religion and Law: Biblical-Judaic and Islamic Perspectives,* edited by E. Firmage, Weiss, and J. Welch. Winona Lake, IN: Eisenbrauns, 1990.

Wells, Stanley, ed. *The Cambridge Companion to Shakespeare Studies.* Cambridge: Cambridge University Press, 1996.

———. *Shakespeare, Sex and Love.* Oxford: Oxford University Press, 2010.

Welsford, Enid. *The Fool: His Social and Literary History.* London: Faber and Faber, 1968.

White, B. R. *The English Separatist Tradition: From the Marian Martyrs to the Pilgrim Fathers.* Oxford: Oxford University Press, 1971.

White, Peter. "The *via media* in the Early Stuart Church." In *The Early Stuart Church, 1603–1642,* edited by Kenneth Fincham, 211–30. Stanford: Stanford University Press, 1993.

Whitehead, A. N. *Adventures of Ideas.* London: Cambridge University Press, 1933.

Whitmore, Michael. *Culture of Accidents: Unexpected Knowledge in Early Modern England.* Stanford, CA: Stanford University Press, 2001.

Williams, Charles. *The Descent of the Dove: A Short History of the Holy Spirit in the Church.* London: Longmans, 1939.

———. *The English Poetic Mind.* Oxford: Oxford University Press, 1932.

Williams, Gordon. *A Glossary of Shakespeare's Sexual Language.* London: Athlone, 1997.

Wilson, John Dover. *Shakespeare's Happy Comedies.* London: Faber and Faber, 1962.

———. *What Happens in "Hamlet."* Cambridge: Cambridge University Press, 1962.

Wilson, Richard. *Secret Shakespeare: Studies in Theatre, Religion and Resistance.* Manchester: Manchester University Press, 2004.

Wilson, Robert F. "God's Secrets and Bottom's Name: A Reply." *Shakespeare Quarterly* 30, no. 3 (1979): 407–8.

Wimsatt, W. K. *Studies in the Meaning of Poetry.* London: Methuen, 1970.

Wind, Edgar. *Pagan Mysteries in the Renaissance.* Rev. ed. Harmondsworth, UK: Penguin, 1967.

Wink, Walter. *Engaging the Powers. Discernment and Resistance in a World of Domination.* Minneapolis: Fortress, 1992.

———. *Naming the Powers: The Language of Power in the New Testament.* Basingstoke, UK: Marshall, Morgan and Scott, 1988.

Yaffe, Martin. *Shakespeare and the Jewish Question.* Baltimore: John Hopkins University Press, 1997.

Yeats, W. B. *Essays and Introductions.* London: Macmillan, 1961.

INDEX

Abelard, Peter, 86, 232

Ackroyd, Peter, 337n68

Adelman, Janet, 110, 315n83

Agony and the Betrayal, The, 326n6

Agrippa, Heinrich Cornelius, 84, 310n73

Allen, Graham, 14, 17

Anderson, Pamela Sue, 293, 338n94

Anselm, of Canterbury, 85, 232, 257

Aquinas, Thomas, 53, 59, 122, 149, 164–65, 181, 196

Arnold, Matthew, 300n1

Asquith, Clare, 218, 280, 285, 297n15, 337n58

Augustine, of Hippo, 51, 53, 99, 181, 232, 282, 306n71, 330n13

Badham, Paul, 181

Bakhtin, Mikhail M., 12, 13, 40, 41, 82–83

Balthasar, Hans Urs von, 52, 56, 57–58, 60, 149

Barkan, Leonard, 69, 331n52

Barrett, C. K., 309n22

Barrow, Henry, 203, 217, 298n58, 327n47

Barth, Karl, 51, 59, 74, 75, 219, 220, 258, 305n32, 305n48, 306n66, 309n47, 314n72, 321n99, 334n124

Barthes, Roland, 12, 14, 15, 17, 41–43, 52, 304n7

Bate, Jonathan, 308n20, 309n33, 327n56, 331n52, 335n16, 335n21, 336n36

Battenhouse, Roy, 328n58, 331n46

Bearman, Robert, 297n12

Beckwith, Sarah, 243, 333n87, 334n110

Belleforest, François, 321n3

Berman, Ronald, 302n50

Berry, Francis, 337n69

Bethell, S. L., 303n68, 331n50

Bevington, David, 302n57

Bible, the, 11–12, 14–15, 16; Genesis, 11, 92, 93, 94, 113, 129, 157, 158, 159, 198, 200, 213, 214, 231, 233, 234, 279, 282, 301n20, 301n35, 308n4, 313n52, 315n99, 316n132; Exodus, 35, 110, 125, 216, 303n79; Leviticus, 132, 234; Deuteronomy, 64, 94, 132, 323n47; Joshua, 235n30; Ruth, 207; 1 Samuel, 168, 308n4, 324n69, 335n30; 2 Samuel, 136, 323n47; 1 Kings, 235, 336n37; 2 Chronicles, 308n4; Job, 16, 65, 123, 127–28, 136, 137–39, 141, 148, 159, 168, 282, 301n20, 308n4, 309n48, 315n84, 318n43, 322n22; Psalms, 11, 14, 15, 20, 22, 30, 31, 64, 95, 128, 129, 130, 132, 136, 140, 141, 144, 157, 173, 177, 191, 192, 199, 212, 224, 232, 237, 282, 299n64, 301n20, 301n22, 302n53, 306n61, 308n4, 309n48, 314n68, 318n37, 319nn53–54, 319n59, 334n114; Proverbs, 64, 307n82; Ecclesiastes, 96, 156, 157, 300n14, 318n37; Song of Songs, 322n22; Isaiah, 11, 55, 136, 139, 162, 204, 214, 270–73, 297n5, 300n15, 306n61, 309n22, 315n87, 322n22, 334n114, 334n128, 335n24, 335n27; Jeremiah, 248, 253, 315n87, 334n128; Lamentations, 64, 199; Ezekiel, 248, 315n87, 335n30; Daniel, 20, 168, 202, 268, 301n20, 309n48, 335n13; Hosea, 119; Joel, 215n87; Zechariah, 64; Malachi, 192; Ecclesiasticus, 11–12, 25, 31, 101, 241, 307n82; Wisdom of Solomon, 127, 168; Matthew, 17, 25, 36, 55, 95, 99, 101, 102, 109, 111, 130, 133, 135, 151, 159, 167, 172, 174–75, 179, 188, 189, 190, 191, 192, 193, 194, 200, 212, 215, 220, 235, 241, 268, 269, 273, 288, 304n86, 306n80, 308n8, 313n42, 313n45, 315n87, 326n25, 327n33, 332n55, 333n102, 336n39; Mark, 131, 159, 189, 190, 195, 214, 219, 224, 237, 267–69, 329n85, 329n87, 332n55, 333nn101–2, 335n18, 336n38; Luke, 25, 65, 94, 95, 99, 126, 131, 142, 151, 159, 167, 177, 189, 190, 191, 214, 216, 238, 243, 248, 267–68, 274, 288, 303n72, 308n4, 308n8, 313n42, 326n25, 331n48, 332n55, 333nn101–2, 335n15, 335n18; John, 16, 64, 131, 132, 135, 144, 189, 190, 212,

367

Richard E. Myers Lectures

*Making the World Over: Confronting Racism,
Misogyny, and Xenophobia in U.S. History*
R. Marie Griffith